International Financial Reporting Standards

*Including Abbreviated Versions
of IAS 1 to IAS 41*

International Financial Reporting Standards

Including Abbreviated Versions of IAS 1 to IAS 41

The text of this publication is based on the International Accounting Standards Bound Volume 2003.

International Accounting Standards Board®
30 Cannon Street
London EC4M 6XH
United Kingdom

Telephone: +44 (0)20 7246 6410
Fax: +44 (0)20 7246 6411
E–mail: iasb@iasb.org.uk
Web: www.iasb.org.uk

IASCF Publications Department
30 Cannon Street
London EC4M 6XH
United Kingdom

Publications Telephone: +44 (0)20 7246 6410
Publications Fax: +44 (0)20 7332 2749
E–mail: publications@iasb.org.uk
Web: www.iasb.org.uk

Contents

Contents

Introduction

This edition of International Financial Reporting Standards (IFRSs) has been prepared specially as an introduction for students and others. It is based on the authoritative complete text of standards and interpretations that is published annually by the International Accounting Standards Board (IASB). This edition contains an abridged text of the standards adopted by the IASB as at 1 January 2003. It omits certain material and abbreviates some of the text. A description of these textual alterations is given below.

We are indebted to Dr Rudolf Federmann of the Universität der Bundeswehr Hamburg who edited the first version of this book, which was published in Germany for students as *IAS-STUD* by Erich Schmidt Verlag.

Features of this edition

This edition includes a table of contents, the IASB *Framework*, an abridged text of all extant IASs and a list of the titles of extant SIC Interpretations, as at 1 January 2003.

The main abridgements in the standards are as follows. The *Introduction* (where applicable) and the *Objective* section have been omitted. The text of each standard therefore begins with its *Scope* section. In general the texts do not include:

- sections on effective dates and transitional provisions
- examples
- footnotes
- appendices (including the basis for conclusions, where applicable)

and for brevity:

- tables of contents have been summarised
- references to "International Accounting Standard(s)" have been shortened to "IAS(s)"
- references to standards as "IAS X, Title in Words" have been shortened to "IAS X".

Where entire paragraphs or examples are omitted, the text is marked "[Not printed]". Where sentences, or parts of sentences, are omitted, the omission is denoted by "..." or "(...)".

Lastly, this edition omits the IAS 39 Implementation Guidance, Glossary of Terms, and History of International Financial Reporting Standards and Exposure Drafts that are included in the full edition of *International Financial Reporting Standards*.

Readers of this edition are advised that for a fuller understanding of international standards and interpretations they should consult the complete text of those pronouncements and their accompanying material.

In recent years the demand of global financial markets for a common financial reporting architecture has grown. Indeed, it was in response to this demand that the IASB was created in 2001 as a vehicle for the development of accounting standards that can be used globally. Further evidence of the desire for a truly international approach to financial reporting became clear in June 2002 when the Council of Ministers of the European Union approved the adoption of a Regulation proposed by the European Commission and supported by the European Parliament, requiring that by 1 January 2005 the consolidated accounts of all listed companies in the European Union should conform to the IASB's standards after a formal endorsement process. A month later the Financial Reporting Council of Australia formally agreed that the 2005 deadline for compliance with IASB standards should also apply to Australian companies, and subsequently New Zealand announced a similar change by 2007 with the option to change in 2005. Later in July 2002 the Russian Prime Minister announced that all companies and banks in Russia would be required to prepare their financial statements in accordance with IASB standards starting in January 2004. Thus the momentum for change has gathered pace.

By February 2003 some 37 countries were reported to require the use of international standards for some or all domestic listed companies, and some others based their standards very closely on them, modifying them only when absolutely necessary to meet local legal requirements or other conditions. The decisions announced in 2002 open the prospect of another 21 countries adopting international standards between 2003 and 2007, with the possibility of eight more when the EU is enlarged in 2004. Also in 2002, an agreement reached between the IASB and the United States standard-setter, the Financial Accounting Standards Board (FASB), to work towards eliminating the differences between the IASB's and US standards marked a big step towards the goal that transactions taking place throughout the world will be accounted for in exactly the same way, with consequential benefits for the cost of capital, and hence for investment, growth and employment.

It is the context of this growing support for international standards that the IASB commends this special edition.

About the IASB

The IASB is the standard-setting body of the International Accounting Standards Committee Foundation (IASC Foundation). Based in London, the IASB began operations in 2001. The 14 IASB members (12 of whom are full-time) reside in nine countries and have a variety of professional backgrounds. The IASB is committed to developing, in the public interest, a single set of high quality, global accounting standards that require transparent and comparable information in general purpose financial statements. In pursuit of this objective, the IASB cooperates with national accounting standard-setters to achieve convergence in accounting standards around the world.

The Trustees

Nineteen Trustees are responsible for general oversight of the IASC Foundation, including the IASB and its related committees. Under the IASC Foundation's constitution, the Trustees appoint the members of the IASB, the Standards Advisory

Council and International Financial Reporting Interpretations Committee. The Trustees also monitor the IASB's effectiveness, raise funds for the IASB, approve its budget and have responsibility for constitutional changes. The organisation is funded by contributions collected by its Trustees from the major accounting firms, private financial institutions and industrial companies throughout the world, central and development banks, and other international and professional organisations.

The IASB

The IASB has sole responsibility for setting accounting standards. The foremost qualification for IASB membership is technical expertise and the Trustees exercise their best judgement to ensure that any particular constituency or regional interest does not dominate the Board. At 1 January 2003, the IASB members were:

Sir David Tweedie, *Chairman*	Thomas E Jones, *Vice-Chairman*
Professor Mary E Barth *(part-time)*	Hans-Georg Bruns *(Liaison with the German standard-setter)*
Anthony T Cope	Robert P Garnett
Gilbert Gélard *(Liaison with the French standard-setter)*	James J Leisenring *(Liaison with the US standard-setter)*
Warren McGregor *(Liaison for the Australian and New Zealand standard-setters)*	Patricia O'Malley *(Liaison with the Canadian standard-setter)*
Harry K Schmid	John T Smith *(part-time)*
Geoffrey Whittington *(Liaison with the UK standard-setter)*	Tatsumi Yamada *(Liaison with the Japanese standard-setter)*

In April 2001 the IASB adopted the body of International Accounting Standards (IASs) issued by its predecessor, the International Accounting Standards Committee (IASC). The accounting standards approved and developed by the Board will be known as *International Financial Reporting Standards* (IFRSs). As a general term, 'IFRSs' includes standards and interpretations approved by the IASB as well as IASs and interpretations issued by IASC.

Standards Advisory Council

The Standards Advisory Council (SAC) provides a forum for participation by organisations and individuals, with an interest in international financial reporting, to give advice to the IASB and, as requested, to advise the Trustees. The SAC is appointed by the Trustees and comprises about fifty members, having a diversity of geographical and functional backgrounds. It has the objective of (a) giving advice to the IASB on priorities in the IASB's work, (b) informing the IASB of the implications of proposed standards for users and preparers of financial statements and (c) giving other advice to the IASB or the Trustees. The SAC normally meets at least three times a year. It is to be consulted by the IASB on all major projects and its meetings are open to the public.

International Financial Reporting Interpretations Committee

The International Financial Reporting Interpretations Committee (IFRIC) replaced the former Standing Interpretations Committee (SIC) and began work in March 2002. The IFRIC's mandate is to review, on a timely basis, newly identified financial reporting issues not specifically addressed in the IASB's standards or issues where unsatisfactory or conflicting interpretations have developed, or seem likely to develop in the absence of authoritative guidance, with a view to reaching a consensus on the appropriate treatment. It thus promotes the rigorous and uniform application of IFRSs.

The IFRIC has twelve voting members, appointed by the Trustees for a renewable term of three years. The International Organization of Securities Commissions (IOSCO) and the European Commission are non-voting observers. The Trustees have appointed the IASB's Director of Technical Activities to chair the IFRIC, with the right to speak to the technical issues being considered but not to vote.

The IASB publishes a report on IFRIC decisions immediately after each IFRIC meeting. This report is made available (in electronic format) as soon as possible to subscribers and, subsequently, posted to the IASB Website (www.iasb.co.uk).

IASB staff

A staff based in London, headed by the chairman of the IASB, supports the Board. At 1 January 2003 the project managers and other technical staff included people from Australia, Austria, Bermuda, China, Denmark, France, Japan, New Zealand, Russia, Sweden, the United Kingdom and the United States.

The IASB's operating procedures do not generally allow IASB staff to give advice on the meaning or detailed application of IFRSs.

IASB due process

The IASB published its due process in the *Preface to International Financial Reporting Standards* in May 2002. IFRSs are developed through an international due process that involves accountants, financial analysts and other users of financial statements, the business community, stock exchanges, regulatory and legal authorities, academics and other interested individuals and organisations from around the world. The IASB consults, in public meetings, the SAC on major projects, agenda decisions and work priorities, and discusses technical matters in meetings that are open to public observation.

IFRIC due process

Interpretations of IASs and IFRSs are developed through an international due process that involves accountants, financial analysts and other users of financial statements, the business community, stock exchanges, regulatory and legal authorities, academics and other interested individuals and organisations from around the world. The IFRIC discusses technical matters in meetings that are open to public observation.

Voting

Each IASB member has one vote on technical and other matters. The publication of an exposure draft, standard, or final IFRIC interpretation requires approval by eight of the 14 IASB members. Other decisions, including the publication of a draft statement of principles, or discussion paper, require a simple majority of the members of the IASB present at a meeting that is attended by at least 60 per cent of the members.

Each member of the IFRIC has one vote on an interpretation. Nine voting IFRIC members constitute a quorum. Approval of draft or final interpretations requires that no more than three of the voting members vote against.

Openness of meetings

IASB and IFRIC meetings are open to public observation. However, at the IASB's discretion, certain IASB discussions (normally about selection, appointment and other personnel issues) are held in private. Portions of the Trustees' meetings are also open to the public, at the discretion of the Trustees.

The IASB publishes in advance on its Website the agenda for each meeting of the Trustees, the IASB, the SAC and the IFRIC and publishes promptly a summary of the technical decisions made at IASB and IFRIC meetings and, where appropriate, decisions of the Trustees.

Comment periods

The IASB publishes each exposure draft of a standard and discussion documents for public comment, with a normal comment period of 90 days. In certain circumstances, it may expose proposals for a longer or shorter period. Draft IFRIC Interpretations are normally exposed for a 60-day period, although a shorter period of not less than 30 days may be used in certain circumstances.

IASB *Framework*

The IASB has a *Framework for the Preparation and Presentation of Financial Statements*. IFRSs are based on the *Framework*, which addresses the concepts underlying the information presented in general purpose financial statements. The objective of the *Framework* is to facilitate the consistent and logical formulation of IFRSs. The *Framework* also provides a basis for the use of judgement in resolving accounting issues.

The IASB's technical activities

Details of the IASB's current expectations about the timing of projects on its active agenda, and of the progress of the Board's deliberations, are given on the IASB Website. The timing of individual projects is subject to change as the IASB's deliberations proceed.

The IASB also reports on its technical projects in its quarterly newsletter, IASB *Insight* and on its Website. It publishes a report on IASB decisions immediately after each Board meeting in its newsletter IASB *Update*.

IASB publications and translations

The IASC Foundation holds the copyright of the IASB's accounting standards, exposure drafts, and other IASB publications in all countries and all languages. The approved text of IFRSs (including IASs) is that published in the English language by the IASC Foundation. All rights are reserved. No part of those publications may be translated, reprinted or reproduced or utilised in any form either in whole or in part or by any electronic, mechanical or other means, now known or hereafter invented, including photocopying and recording, or in any information storage and retrieval system, without the prior express permission of the IASC Foundation in writing.

From 2003, approved translations of the IASB's standards are available in the languages of all Member States of the European Union. In addition, approved translations are available in Brazilian Portuguese, Chinese, Czech, Japanese, Latvian, Lithuanian, Polish, Romanian, Russian, Slovak, Slovenian, and Ukrainian. The IASC Foundation will consider making approved translations available in other languages.

The IASB's standards have been translated unofficially into more than 30 languages. Further details are available from IASCF Publications Department.

More information

More information about the IASB, copies of its publications and details of subscription services may be obtained from:

IASCF Publications Department
30 Cannon Street, London EC4M 6XH, United Kingdom
Telephone: +44 (0)20 7246 6410
Facsimile: +44 (0)20 7332 2749
E-mail: publications@iasb.org.uk
Web: www.iasb.org.uk

A. Basis for Financial Reporting

Objective FW 12–21, IAS 1.5	Users FW 9–11	Responsibility IAS 1.6	Components of Financial Statements IAS 1.7–9	Scope FW 5–8, IAS 1.1–4
Financial Position/Presentation/Compliance — FW 15–20/46, IAS 1.10–13				

B. Basic Accounting Principles

Accounting Policies	Going Concern	Accrual Basis	Consistency of Presentation	Materiality, Aggregation	Offsetting	Comparability	Changes in Accounting Estimates, Errors and Accounting Policies	Events After the Balance Sheet Date	Qualitative Characteristics of Financial Statements
IAS 1.20–22	FW 23, IAS 1.23–24, IAS 10.13–15	FW 22, IAS 1.25–26	IAS 1.27	FW 29–30, IAS 1.29–32	IAS 1.33–37	FW 39–42, IAS 1.38–41	IAS 8.23–57	IAS 10	FW 24–45

C. Structure and Content of Financial Statements

Identification of Financial Statements IAS 1.44–48	Balance Sheet	Income Statement	Changes in Equity	Cash Flow Statement	Notes
Reporting Period IAS 1.49–51; Timeliness IAS 1.52	Recognition of Elements FW 82–98; Information on the Balance Sheet IAS 1.66–71; Information on the Balance Sheet or in the Notes IAS 1.72–74; Elements FW 47–52, FW 53–68, Example: IAS 1 Appendix; Measurement FW 99–101, Capital Maintenance FW 81, 102–110	FW 69–80 Income; FW 92–93 Expenses FW 94–98; Information on the Income Statement IAS 1.75–76; Information on the Income Statement or in the Notes IAS 1.77–85; Example: IAS 1 Appendix	IAS 1.86–89 Example: IAS 1 Appendix	IAS 1.90	IAS 1.91–102

D. Structure and Content of Financial Statements (Continued)

Balance Sheet		Income Statement		Other			Consolidation
Assets	Liabilities	Expenses	Revenue				
Intangible Assets IAS 38 Property, Plant and Equipment IAS 16 Investments IAS 27.29–30 IAS 28.12–15 IAS 31.42 Inventories IAS 2	Provisions IAS 37	Borrowing Costs IAS 23 Impairment of Assets IAS 36 Income Taxes IAS 12	Revenue IAS 18	Cash Flow Statements IAS 7 Example: IAS 7 Appendix	Segment Reporting IAS 14 Example: IAS 14 Appendix	Interim Financial Reporting IAS 34 Example: IAS 34 Appendix	Financial Statements IAS 27 Investments in Associates IAS 28 Joint Ventures IAS 31
Financial Instruments IAS 32, 39 Deferred Taxes IAS 12 Contingent Assets/Contingent Liabilities IAS 37		Annual Earnings: Net Profit or Loss for the Period IAS 8 Earnings per Share IAS 33					

E. Specific Items

Structural Processes	Finance-Related	Employee-Related	Manufacturing-Related
Business Combinations IAS 22 Discontinuing Operations IAS 35 Related Parties IAS 24	Changing Prices IAS 15 Hyperinflation IAS 29 Changes in Exchange Rates IAS 21 Government Grants IAS 20 Leases IAS 17	Employee Benefits IAS 19 Retirement Benefit Plans IAS 26	Construction Contracts IAS 11

F. Accounting in Certain Industries

Financial Institutions IAS 30	Agriculture IAS 41

Framework for the Preparation and Presentation of Financial Statements

IASB Framework for the Preparation and Presentation of Financial Statements (FW)		
Purpose and Status FW 1–4	Scope FW 5–8	Users and Their Information Needs FW 9–11

The Objective of Financial Statements FW 12–21
Financial Position, Performance and Changes in Financial Position FW 15–21
Notes and Supplementary Schedules FW 21

Underlying Assumptions FW 22–23	
Accrual Basis FW 22	Going Concern FW 23

Qualitative Characteristics of Financial Statements FW 24–46								
Under-stand-ability FW 25	Rele-vance (Includ-ing Materi-ality) FW 26–30	Reliability FW 31–38					Compa-rability FW 39–42	True and Fair View/ Fair Presen-tation FW 46
		Faithful Repre-senta-tion FW 33–34	Sub-stance Over Form FW 35	Neutral-ity FW 36	Pru-dence FW 37	Com-plete-ness FW 38		
		Constraints on Relevant and Reliable Information FW 43–45						
Timeliness FW 43		Balance between Benefit and Cost FW 44		Balance between Qualitative Characteristics FW 45				

Introduction

Purpose and Status

This Framework sets out the concepts that underlie the preparation and presentation of financial statements for external users. The purpose of the Framework is to: **1**

(a) assist the Board of IASC in the development of future IASs and in its review of existing IASs;

IASB Framework (FW) (Continued)							
The Elements of Financial Statements FW 47–81							
Balance Sheet FW 49–68				Income Statement FW 69–80			Capital Mainte-
Financial Position FW 49–52	Assets FW 53–59	Liabilities FW 60–64	Equity FW 65–68	Perform-ance FW 69–73	Income FW 74–77	Expenses FW 78–80	nance Adjust-ments FW 81

Recognition of the Elements of Financial Statements FW 82–98					
General FW 85–88		Balance Sheet FW 89–91		Income Statement FW 92–98	
The Probability of Future Economic Benefit FW 85	Reliability of Measurement FW 86–88	Recognition of Assets FW 89–90	Recognition of Liabilities FW 91	Recognition of Income FW 92–93	Recognition of Expenses FW 94–98

Measurement of the Elements of Financial Statements FW 99–101		
General FW 99	Measurement Bases FW 100	Adopted Measurement Bases FW 101

Concepts of Capital and Capital Maintenance FW 102–110	
Concepts of Capital FW 102–103	Concepts of Capital Maintenance and the Determination of Profit FW 104–110

(b) assist the Board of IASC in promoting harmonisation of regulations, accounting standards and procedures relating to the presentation of financial statements by providing a basis for reducing the number of alternative accounting treatments permitted by IASs;

(c) assist national standard–setting bodies in developing national standards;

(d) assist preparers of financial statements in applying IASs and in dealing with topics that have yet to form the subject of an IAS;

(e) assist auditors in forming an opinion as to whether financial statements conform with IASs;

(f) assist users of financial statements in interpreting the information contained in financial statements prepared in conformity with IASs; and

(g) provide those who are interested in the work of IASC with information about its approach to the formulation of IASs.

2   This Framework is not an IAS and hence does not define standards for any particular measurement or disclosure issue. Nothing in this Framework overrides any specific IAS.

The Board of IASC recognises that in a limited number of cases there may be a conflict **3** between the Framework and an IAS. In those cases where there is a conflict, the requirements of the IAS prevail over those of the Framework. As, however, the Board of IASC will be guided by the Framework in the development of future Standards and in its review of existing Standards, the number of cases of conflict between the Framework and IASs will diminish through time.

The Framework will be revised from time to time on the basis of the Board's experience **4** of working with it.

Scope

The Framework deals with: **5**
(a) the objective of financial statements;
(b) the qualitative characteristics that determine the usefulness of information in financial statements;
(c) the definition, recognition and measurement of the elements from which financial statements are constructed; and
(d) concepts of capital and capital maintenance.

The Framework is concerned with general purpose financial statements (hereafter **6** referred to as "financial statements") including consolidated financial statements. Such financial statements are prepared and presented at least annually and are directed toward the common information needs of a wide range of users. Some of these users may require, and have the power to obtain, information in addition to that contained in the financial statements. Many users, however, have to rely on the financial statements as their major source of financial information and such financial statements should, therefore, be prepared and presented with their needs in view. Special purpose financial reports, for example, prospectuses and computations prepared for taxation purposes, are outside the scope of this Framework. Nevertheless, the Framework may be applied in the preparation of such special purpose reports where their requirements permit.

Financial statements form part of the process of financial reporting. A complete set of **7** financial statements normally includes a balance sheet, an income statement, a statement of changes in financial position (...), and those notes and other statements and explanatory material that are an integral part of the financial statements. They may also include supplementary schedules and information based on or derived from, and expected to be read with, such statements. Such schedules and supplementary information may deal, for example, with financial information about industrial and geographical segments and disclosures about the effects of changing prices. Financial statements do not, however, include such items as reports by directors, statements by the chairman, discussion and analysis by management and similar items that may be included in a financial or annual report.

The Framework applies to the financial statements of all commercial, industrial and **8** business reporting enterprises, whether in the public or the private sectors. A reporting enterprise is an enterprise for which there are users who rely on the financial statements as their major source of financial information about the enterprise.

Users and Their Information Needs

9   The users of financial statements include present and potential investors, employees, lenders, suppliers and other trade creditors, customers, governments and their agencies and the public. They use financial statements in order to satisfy some of their different needs for information. These needs include the following:

(a) *Investors*. The providers of risk capital and their advisers are concerned with the risk inherent in, and return provided by, their investments. They need information to help them determine whether they should buy, hold or sell. Shareholders are also interested in information which enables them to assess the ability of the enterprise to pay dividends.

(b) *Employees*. Employees and their representative groups are interested in information about the stability and profitability of their employers. They are also interested in information which enables them to assess the ability of the enterprise to provide remuneration, retirement benefits and employment opportunities.

(c) *Lenders*. Lenders are interested in information that enables them to determine whether their loans, and the interest attaching to them, will be paid when due.

(d) *Suppliers and other trade creditors*. Suppliers and other creditors are interested in information that enables them to determine whether amounts owing to them will be paid when due. Trade creditors are likely to be interested in an enterprise over a shorter period than lenders unless they are dependent upon the continuation of the enterprise as a major customer.

(e) *Customers*. Customers have an interest in information about the continuance of an enterprise, especially when they have a long–term involvement with, or are dependent on, the enterprise.

(f) *Governments and their agencies*. Governments and their agencies are interested in the allocation of resources and, therefore, the activities of enterprises. They also require information in order to regulate the activities of enterprises, determine taxation policies and as the basis for national income and similar statistics.

(g) *Public*. Enterprises affect members of the public in a variety of ways. For example, enterprises may make a substantial contribution to the local economy in many ways including the number of people they employ and their patronage of local suppliers. Financial statements may assist the public by providing information about the trends and recent developments in the prosperity of the enterprise and the range of its activities.

10 While all of the information needs of these users cannot be met by financial statements, there are needs which are common to all users. As investors are providers of risk capital to the enterprise, the provision of financial statements that meet their needs will also meet most of the needs of other users that financial statements can satisfy.

11 The management of an enterprise has the primary responsibility for the preparation and presentation of the financial statements of the enterprise. Management is also interested in the information contained in the financial statements even though it has access to additional management and financial information that helps it carry out its planning, decision–making and control responsibilities. Management has the ability to determine the form and content of such additional information in order to meet its own needs. The reporting of such information, however, is beyond the scope of this Framework. Nevertheless, published financial statements are based on the information used by management about the financial position, performance and changes in financial position of the enterprise.

The Objective of Financial Statements

The objective of financial statements is to provide information about the financial **12** position, performance and changes in financial position of an enterprise that is useful to a wide range of users in making economic decisions.

Financial statements prepared for this purpose meet the common needs of most users. **13** However, financial statements do not provide all the information that users may need to make economic decisions since they largely portray the financial effects of past events and do not necessarily provide non–financial information.

Financial statements also show the results of the stewardship of management, or the **14** accountability of management for the resources entrusted to it. Those users who wish to assess the stewardship or accountability of management do so in order that they may make economic decisions; these decisions may include, for example, whether to hold or sell their investment in the enterprise or whether to reappoint or replace the management.

Financial Position, Performance and Changes in Financial Position

The economic decisions that are taken by users of financial statements require an **15** evaluation of the ability of an enterprise to generate cash and cash equivalents and of the timing and certainty of their generation. This ability ultimately determines, for example, the capacity of an enterprise to pay its employees and suppliers, meet interest payments, repay loans and make distributions to its owners. Users are better able to evaluate this ability to generate cash and cash equivalents if they are provided with information that focuses on the financial position, performance and changes in financial position of an enterprise.

The financial position of an enterprise is affected by the economic resources it controls, **16** its financial structure, its liquidity and solvency, and its capacity to adapt to changes in the environment in which it operates. Information about the economic resources controlled by the enterprise and its capacity in the past to modify these resources is useful in predicting the ability of the enterprise to generate cash and cash equivalents in the future. Information about financial structure is useful in predicting future borrowing needs and how future profits and cash flows will be distributed among those with an interest in the enterprise; it is also useful in predicting how successful the enterprise is likely to be in raising further finance. Information about liquidity and solvency is useful in predicting the ability of the enterprise to meet its financial commitments as they fall due. Liquidity refers to the availability of cash in the near future after taking account of financial commitments over this period. Solvency refers to the availability of cash over the longer term to meet financial commitments as they fall due.

Information about the performance of an enterprise, in particular its profitability, is **17** required in order to assess potential changes in the economic resources that it is likely to control in the future. Information about variability of performance is important in this respect. Information about performance is useful in predicting the capacity of the enterprise to generate cash flows from its existing resource base. It is also useful in forming judgements about the effectiveness with which the enterprise might employ additional resources.

18   Information concerning changes in the financial position of an enterprise is useful in order to assess its investing, financing and operating activities during the reporting period. This information is useful in providing the user with a basis to assess the ability of the enterprise to generate cash and cash equivalents and the needs of the enterprise to utilise those cash flows. ...

19   Information about financial position is primarily provided in a balance sheet. Information about performance is primarily provided in an income statement. Information about changes in financial position is provided in the financial statements by means of a separate statement.

20   The component parts of the financial statements interrelate because they reflect different aspects of the same transactions or other events. Although each statement provides information that is different from the others, none is likely to serve only a single purpose or provide all the information necessary for particular needs of users. For example, an income statement provides an incomplete picture of performance unless it is used in conjunction with the balance sheet and the statement of changes in financial position.

Notes and Supplementary Schedules

21   The financial statements also contain notes and supplementary schedules and other information. For example, they may contain additional information that is relevant to the needs of users about the items in the balance sheet and income statement. They may include disclosures about the risks and uncertainties affecting the enterprise and any resources and obligations not recognised in the balance sheet (...). Information about geographical and industry segments and the effect on the enterprise of changing prices may also be provided in the form of supplementary information.

Underlying Assumptions

Accrual Basis

22   In order to meet their objectives, financial statements are prepared on the accrual basis of accounting. Under this basis, the effects of transactions and other events are recognised when they occur (and not as cash or its equivalent is received or paid) and they are recorded in the accounting records and reported in the financial statements of the periods to which they relate. Financial statements prepared on the accrual basis inform users not only of past transactions involving the payment and receipt of cash but also of obligations to pay cash in the future and of resources that represent cash to be received in the future. Hence, they provide the type of information about past transactions and other events that is most useful to users in making economic decisions.

Going Concern

23   The financial statements are normally prepared on the assumption that an enterprise is a going concern and will continue in operation for the foreseeable future. Hence, it is assumed that the enterprise has neither the intention nor the need to liquidate or curtail materially the scale of its operations; if such an intention or need exists, the financial statements may have to be prepared on a different basis and, if so, the basis used is disclosed.

Qualitative Characteristics of Financial Statements

Qualitative characteristics are the attributes that make the information provided in **24** financial statements useful to users. The four principal qualitative characteristics are understandability, relevance, reliability and comparability.

Understandability

An essential quality of the information provided in financial statements is that it is **25** readily understandable by users. For this purpose, users are assumed to have a reasonable knowledge of business and economic activities and accounting and a willingness to study the information with reasonable diligence. However, information about complex matters that should be included in the financial statements because of its relevance to the economic decision–making needs of users should not be excluded merely on the grounds that it may be too difficult for certain users to understand.

Relevance

To be useful, information must be relevant to the decision–making needs of users. **26** Information has the quality of relevance when it influences the economic decisions of users by helping them evaluate past, present or future events or confirming, or correcting, their past evaluations.

The predictive and confirmatory roles of information are interrelated. For example, **27** information about the current level and structure of asset holdings has value to users when they endeavour to predict the ability of the enterprise to take advantage of opportunities and its ability to react to adverse situations. The same information plays a confirmatory role in respect of past predictions about, for example, the way in which the enterprise would be structured or the outcome of planned operations.

Information about financial position and past performance is frequently used as the **28** basis for predicting future financial position and performance and other matters in which users are directly interested, such as dividend and wage payments, security price movements and the ability of the enterprise to meet its commitments as they fall due. To have predictive value, information need not be in the form of an explicit forecast. The ability to make predictions from financial statements is enhanced, however, by the manner in which information on past transactions and events is displayed. For example, the predictive value of the income statement is enhanced if unusual, abnormal and infrequent items of income or expense are separately disclosed.

Materiality

The relevance of information is affected by its nature and materiality. In some cases, **29** the nature of information alone is sufficient to determine its relevance. For example, the reporting of a new segment may affect the assessment of the risks and opportunities facing the enterprise irrespective of the materiality of the results achieved by the new segment in the reporting period. In other cases, both the nature and materiality are important, for example, the amounts of inventories held in each of the main categories that are appropriate to the business.

Information is material if its omission or misstatement could influence the economic **30** decisions of users taken on the basis of the financial statements. Materiality depends on the size of the item or error judged in the particular circumstances of its omission or misstatement. Thus, materiality provides a threshold or cut–off point rather than being a primary qualitative characteristic which information must have if it is to be useful.

Reliability

31 To be useful, information must also be reliable. Information has the quality of reliability when it is free from material error and bias and can be depended upon by users to represent faithfully that which it either purports to represent or could reasonably be expected to represent.

32 Information may be relevant but so unreliable in nature or representation that its recognition may be potentially misleading. For example, if the validity and amount of a claim for damages under a legal action are disputed, it may be inappropriate for the enterprise to recognise the full amount of the claim in the balance sheet, although it may be appropriate to disclose the amount and circumstances of the claim.

Faithful Representation

33 To be reliable, information must represent faithfully the transactions and other events it either purports to represent or could reasonably be expected to represent. Thus, for example, a balance sheet should represent faithfully the transactions and other events that result in assets, liabilities and equity of the enterprise at the reporting date which meet the recognition criteria.

34 Most financial information is subject to some risk of being less than a faithful representation of that which it purports to portray. This is not due to bias, but rather to inherent difficulties either in identifying the transactions and other events to be measured or in devising and applying measurement and presentation techniques that can convey messages that correspond with those transactions and events. In certain cases, the measurement of the financial effects of items could be so uncertain that enterprises generally would not recognise them in the financial statements; for example, although most enterprises generate goodwill internally over time, it is usually difficult to identify or measure that goodwill reliably. In other cases, however, it may be relevant to recognise items and to disclose the risk of error surrounding their recognition and measurement.

Substance Over Form

35 If information is to represent faithfully the transactions and other events that it purports to represent, it is necessary that they are accounted for and presented in accordance with their substance and economic reality and not merely their legal form. The substance of transactions or other events is not always consistent with that which is apparent from their legal or contrived form. For example, an enterprise may dispose of an asset to another party in such a way that the documentation purports to pass legal ownership to that party; nevertheless, agreements may exist that ensure that the enterprise continues to enjoy the future economic benefits embodied in the asset. In such circumstances, the reporting of a sale would not represent faithfully the transaction entered into (if indeed there was a transaction).

Neutrality

36 To be reliable, the information contained in financial statements must be neutral, that is, free from bias. Financial statements are not neutral if, by the selection or presentation of information, they influence the making of a decision or judgement in order to achieve a predetermined result or outcome.

Prudence

The preparers of financial statements do, however, have to contend with the **37** uncertainties that inevitably surround many events and circumstances, such as the collectability of doubtful receivables, the probable useful life of plant and equipment and the number of warranty claims that may occur. Such uncertainties are recognised by the disclosure of their nature and extent and by the exercise of prudence in the preparation of the financial statements. Prudence is the inclusion of a degree of caution in the exercise of the judgements needed in making the estimates required under conditions of uncertainty, such that assets or income are not overstated and liabilities or expenses are not understated. However, the exercise of prudence does not allow, for example, the creation of hidden reserves or excessive provisions, the deliberate understatement of assets or income, or the deliberate overstatement of liabilities or expenses, because the financial statements would not be neutral and, therefore, not have the quality of reliability.

Completeness

To be reliable, the information in financial statements must be complete within the **38** bounds of materiality and cost. An omission can cause information to be false or misleading and thus unreliable and deficient in terms of its relevance.

Comparability

Users must be able to compare the financial statements of an enterprise through time **39** in order to identify trends in its financial position and performance. Users must also be able to compare the financial statements of different enterprises in order to evaluate their relative financial position, performance and changes in financial position. Hence, the measurement and display of the financial effect of like transactions and other events must be carried out in a consistent way throughout an enterprise and over time for that enterprise and in a consistent way for different enterprises.

An important implication of the qualitative characteristic of comparability is that users **40** be informed of the accounting policies employed in the preparation of the financial statements, any changes in those policies and the effects of such changes. Users need to be able to identify differences between the accounting policies for like transactions and other events used by the same enterprise from period to period and by different enterprises. Compliance with IASs, including the disclosure of the accounting policies used by the enterprise, helps to achieve comparability.

The need for comparability should not be confused with mere uniformity and should **41** not be allowed to become an impediment to the introduction of improved accounting standards. It is not appropriate for an enterprise to continue accounting in the same manner for a transaction or other event if the policy adopted is not in keeping with the qualitative characteristics of relevance and reliability. It is also inappropriate for an enterprise to leave its accounting policies unchanged when more relevant and reliable alternatives exist.

Because users wish to compare the financial position, performance and changes in **42** financial position of an enterprise over time, it is important that the financial statements show corresponding information for the preceding periods.

Constraints on Relevant and Reliable Information

Timeliness

43 If there is undue delay in the reporting of information it may lose its relevance. Management may need to balance the relative merits of timely reporting and the provision of reliable information. To provide information on a timely basis it may often be necessary to report before all aspects of a transaction or other event are known, thus impairing reliability. Conversely, if reporting is delayed until all aspects are known, the information may be highly reliable but of little use to users who have had to make decisions in the interim. In achieving a balance between relevance and reliability, the overriding consideration is how best to satisfy the economic decision-making needs of users.

Balance between Benefit and Cost

44 The balance between benefit and cost is a pervasive constraint rather than a qualitative characteristic. The benefits derived from information should exceed the cost of providing it. The evaluation of benefits and costs is, however, substantially a judgmental process. Furthermore, the costs do not necessarily fall on those users who enjoy the benefits. Benefits may also be enjoyed by users other than those for whom the information is prepared; for example, the provision of further information to lenders may reduce the borrowing costs of an enterprise. For these reasons, it is difficult to apply a cost–benefit test in any particular case. Nevertheless, standard-setters in particular, as well as the preparers and users of financial statements, should be aware of this constraint.

Balance between Qualitative Characteristics

45 In practice a balancing, or trade–off, between qualitative characteristics is often necessary. Generally the aim is to achieve an appropriate balance among the characteristics in order to meet the objective of financial statements. The relative importance of the characteristics in different cases is a matter of professional judgment.

True and Fair View/Fair Presentation

46 Financial statements are frequently described as showing a true and fair view of, or as presenting fairly, the financial position, performance and changes in financial position of an enterprise. Although this Framework does not deal directly with such concepts, the application of the principal qualitative characteristics and of appropriate accounting standards normally results in financial statements that convey what is generally understood as a true and fair view of, or as presenting fairly such information.

The Elements of Financial Statements

47 Financial statements portray the financial effects of transactions and other events by grouping them into broad classes according to their economic characteristics. These broad classes are termed the elements of financial statements. The elements directly related to the measurement of financial position in the balance sheet are assets, liabilities and equity. The elements directly related to the measurement of performance in the income statement are income and expenses. The statement of changes in financial position usually reflects income statement elements and changes in balance sheet elements; accordingly, this Framework identifies no elements that are unique to this statement.

The presentation of these elements in the balance sheet and the income statement **48** involves a process of sub–classification. For example, assets and liabilities may be classified by their nature or function in the business of the enterprise in order to display information in the manner most useful to users for purposes of making economic decisions.

Financial Position

The elements directly related to the measurement of financial position are assets, **49** liabilities and equity. These are defined as follows:
(a) An asset is a resource controlled by the enterprise as a result of past events and from which future economic benefits are expected to flow to the enterprise.
(b) A liability is a present obligation of the enterprise arising from past events, the settlement of which is expected to result in an outflow from the enterprise of resources embodying economic benefits.
(c) Equity is the residual interest in the assets of the enterprise after deducting all its liabilities.

The definitions of an asset and a liability identify their essential features but do not **50** attempt to specify the criteria that need to be met before they are recognised in the balance sheet. Thus, the definitions embrace items that are not recognised as assets or liabilities in the balance sheet because they do not satisfy the criteria for recognition discussed in paragraphs 82 to 98. In particular, the expectation that future economic benefits will flow to or from an enterprise must be sufficiently certain to meet the probability criterion in paragraph 83 before an asset or liability is recognised.

In assessing whether an item meets the definition of an asset, liability or equity, **51** attention needs to be given to its underlying substance and economic reality and not merely its legal form. ...

Balance sheets drawn up in accordance with current IASs may include items that do not **52** satisfy the definitions of an asset or liability and are not shown as part of equity. The definitions set out in paragraph 49 will, however, underlie future reviews of existing IASs and the formulation of further Standards.

Assets

The future economic benefit embodied in an asset is the potential to contribute, directly **53** or indirectly, to the flow of cash and cash equivalents to the enterprise. The potential may be a productive one that is part of the operating activities of the enterprise. It may also take the form of convertibility into cash or cash equivalents or a capability to reduce cash outflows, such as when an alternative manufacturing process lowers the costs of production.

An enterprise usually employs its assets to produce goods or services capable of **54** satisfying the wants or needs of customers; because these goods or services can satisfy these wants or needs, customers are prepared to pay for them and hence contribute to the cash flow of the enterprise. Cash itself renders a service to the enterprise because of its command over other resources.

55 The future economic benefits embodied in an asset may flow to the enterprise in a number of ways. For example, an asset may be:
  (a) used singly or in combination with other assets in the production of goods or services to be sold by the enterprise;
  (b) exchanged for other assets;
  (c) used to settle a liability; or
  (d) distributed to the owners of the enterprise.

56 Many assets, for example, property, plant and equipment, have a physical form. However, physical form is not essential to the existence of an asset; hence patents and copyrights, for example, are assets if future economic benefits are expected to flow from them to the enterprise and if they are controlled by the enterprise.

57 Many assets, for example, receivables and property, are associated with legal rights, including the right of ownership. In determining the existence of an asset, the right of ownership is not essential; thus, for example, property held on a lease is an asset if the enterprise controls the benefits which are expected to flow from the property. Although the capacity of an enterprise to control benefits is usually the result of legal rights, an item may nonetheless satisfy the definition of an asset even when there is no legal control. For example, know–how obtained from a development activity may meet the definition of an asset when, by keeping that know–how secret, an enterprise controls the benefits that are expected to flow from it.

58 The assets of an enterprise result from past transactions or other past events. Enterprises normally obtain assets by purchasing or producing them, but other transactions or events may generate assets; ... Transactions or events expected to occur in the future do not in themselves give rise to assets; hence, for example, an intention to purchase inventory does not, of itself, meet the definition of an asset.

59 There is a close association between incurring expenditure and generating assets but the two do not necessarily coincide. Hence, when an enterprise incurs expenditure, this may provide evidence that future economic benefits were sought but is not conclusive proof that an item satisfying the definition of an asset has been obtained. Similarly the absence of a related expenditure does not preclude an item from satisfying the definition of an asset and thus becoming a candidate for recognition in the balance sheet; for example, items that have been donated to the enterprise may satisfy the definition of an asset.

Liabilities

60 An essential characteristic of a liability is that the enterprise has a present obligation. An obligation is a duty or responsibility to act or perform in a certain way. Obligations may be legally enforceable as a consequence of a binding contract or statutory requirement. This is normally the case, for example, with amounts payable for goods and services received. Obligations also arise, however, from normal business practice, custom and a desire to maintain good business relations or act in an equitable manner. If, for example, an enterprise decides as a matter of policy to rectify faults in its products even when these become apparent after the warranty period has expired, the amounts that are expected to be expended in respect of goods already sold are liabilities.

61 A distinction needs to be drawn between a present obligation and a future commitment. A decision by the management of an enterprise to acquire assets in the future does not, of itself, give rise to a present obligation. An obligation normally arises only when the asset is delivered or the enterprise enters into an irrevocable agreement to acquire the asset. In the latter case, the irrevocable nature of the agreement means that the economic consequences of failing to honour the obligation, for example, because of the existence of a substantial penalty, leave the enterprise with little, if any, discretion to avoid the outflow of resources to another party.

The settlement of a present obligation usually involves the enterprise giving up **62** resources embodying economic benefits in order to satisfy the claim of the other party. Settlement of a present obligation may occur in a number of ways, for example, by:
(a) payment of cash;
(b) transfer of other assets;
(c) provision of services;
(d) replacement of that obligation with another obligation; or
(e) conversion of the obligation to equity.
An obligation may also be extinguished by other means, such as a creditor waiving or forfeiting its rights.

Liabilities result from past transactions or other past events. ... **63**

Some liabilities can be measured only by using a substantial degree of estimation. Some **64** enterprises describe these liabilities as provisions. In some countries, such provisions are not regarded as liabilities because the concept of a liability is defined narrowly so as to include only amounts that can be established without the need to make estimates. The definition of a liability in paragraph 49 follows a broader approach. Thus, when a provision involves a present obligation and satisfies the rest of the definition, it is a liability even if the amount has to be estimated. Examples include provisions for payments to be made under existing warranties and provisions to cover pension obligations.

Equity

Although equity is defined in paragraph 49 as a residual, it may be sub–classified in the **65** balance sheet. For example, in a corporate enterprise, funds contributed by shareholders, retained earnings, reserves representing appropriations of retained earnings and reserves representing capital maintenance adjustments may be shown separately. Such classifications can be relevant to the decision–making needs of the users of financial statements when they indicate legal or other restrictions on the ability of the enterprise to distribute or otherwise apply its equity. They may also reflect the fact that parties with ownership interests in an enterprise have differing rights in relation to the receipt of dividends or the repayment of capital.

The creation of reserves is sometimes required by statute or other law in order to give **66** the enterprise and its creditors an added measure of protection from the effects of losses. Other reserves may be established if national tax law grants exemptions from, or reductions in, taxation liabilities when transfers to such reserves are made. The existence and size of these legal, statutory and tax reserves is information that can be relevant to the decision–making needs of users. Transfers to such reserves are appropriations of retained earnings rather than expenses.

The amount at which equity is shown in the balance sheet is dependent on the **67** measurement of assets and liabilities. Normally, the aggregate amount of equity only by coincidence corresponds with the aggregate market value of the shares of the enterprise or the sum that could be raised by disposing of either the net assets on a piecemeal basis or the enterprise as a whole on a going concern basis.

68   Commercial, industrial and business activities are often undertaken by means of enterprises such as sole proprietorships, partnerships and trusts and various types of government business undertakings. The legal and regulatory framework for such enterprises is often different from that applying to corporate enterprises. ... Nevertheless, the definition of equity and the other aspects of this Framework that deal with equity are appropriate for such enterprises.

Performance

69   Profit is frequently used as a measure of performance or as the basis for other measures, such as return on investment or earnings per share. The elements directly related to the measurement of profit are income and expenses. The recognition and measurement of income and expenses, and hence profit, depends in part on the concepts of capital and capital maintenance used by the enterprise in preparing its financial statements. These concepts are discussed in paragraphs 102 to 110.

70   The elements of income and expenses are defined as follows:
      (a) Income is increases in economic benefits during the accounting period in the form of inflows or enhancements of assets or decreases of liabilities that result in increases in equity, other than those relating to contributions from equity participants.
      (b) Expenses are decreases in economic benefits during the accounting period in the form of outflows or depletions of assets or incurrences of liabilities that result in decreases in equity, other than those relating to distributions to equity participants.

71   The definitions of income and expenses identify their essential features but do not attempt to specify the criteria that would need to be met before they are recognised in the income statement. Criteria for the recognition of income and expenses are discussed in paragraphs 82 to 98.

72   Income and expenses may be presented in the income statement in different ways so as to provide information that is relevant for economic decision–making. For example, it is common practice to distinguish between those items of income and expenses that arise in the course of the ordinary activities of the enterprise and those that do not. This distinction is made on the basis that the source of an item is relevant in evaluating the ability of the enterprise to generate cash and cash equivalents in the future; for example, incidental activities such as the disposal of a long–term investment are unlikely to recur on a regular basis. When distinguishing between items in this way consideration needs to be given to the nature of the enterprise and its operations. Items that arise from the ordinary activities of one enterprise may be unusual in respect of another.

73   Distinguishing between items of income and expense and combining them in different ways also permits several measures of enterprise performance to be displayed. These have differing degrees of inclusiveness. For example, the income statement could display gross margin, profit from ordinary activities before taxation, profit from ordinary activities after taxation, and net profit.

Income

The definition of income encompasses both revenue and gains. Revenue arises in the **74** course of the ordinary activities of an enterprise and is referred to by a variety of different names including sales, fees, interest, dividends, royalties and rent.

Gains represent other items that meet the definition of income and may, or may not, **75** arise in the course of the ordinary activities of an enterprise. Gains represent increases in economic benefits and as such are no different in nature from revenue. Hence, they are not regarded as constituting a separate element in this Framework.

Gains include, for example, those arising on the disposal of non–current assets. The **76** definition of income also includes unrealised gains; for example, those arising on the revaluation of marketable securities and those resulting from increases in the carrying amount of long term assets. When gains are recognised in the income statement, they are usually displayed separately because knowledge of them is useful for the purpose of making economic decisions. Gains are often reported net of related expenses.

Various kinds of assets may be received or enhanced by income; examples include cash, **77** receivables and goods and services received in exchange for goods and services supplied. Income may also result from the settlement of liabilities. ...

Expenses

The definition of expenses encompasses losses as well as those expenses that arise in **78** the course of the ordinary activities of the enterprise. Expenses that arise in the course of the ordinary activities of the enterprise include, for example, cost of sales, wages and depreciation. They usually take the form of an outflow or depletion of assets such as cash and cash equivalents, inventory, property, plant and equipment.

Losses represent other items that meet the definition of expenses and may, or may not, **79** arise in the course of the ordinary activities of the enterprise. Losses represent decreases in economic benefits and as such they are no different in nature from other expenses. Hence, they are not regarded as a separate element in this Framework.

Losses include, for example, those resulting from disasters such as fire and flood, as well **80** as those arising on the disposal of non–current assets. The definition of expenses also includes unrealised losses, for example, those arising from the effects of increases in the rate of exchange for a foreign currency in respect of the borrowings of an enterprise in that currency. When losses are recognised in the income statement, they are usually displayed separately because knowledge of them is useful for the purpose of making economic decisions. Losses are often reported net of related income.

Capital Maintenance Adjustments

The revaluation or restatement of assets and liabilities gives rise to increases or decreases **81** in equity. While these increases or decreases meet the definition of income and expenses, they are not included in the income statement under certain concepts of capital maintenance. Instead these items are included in equity as capital maintenance adjustments or revaluation reserves. These concepts of capital maintenance are discussed in paragraphs 102 to 110 of this Framework.

Recognition of the Elements of Financial Statements

82 Recognition is the process of incorporating in the balance sheet or income statement an item that meets the definition of an element and satisfies the criteria for recognition set out in paragraph 83. It involves the depiction of the item in words and by a monetary amount and the inclusion of that amount in the balance sheet or income statement totals. Items that satisfy the recognition criteria should be recognised in the balance sheet or income statement. The failure to recognise such items is not rectified by disclosure of the accounting policies used nor by notes or explanatory material.

83 An item that meets the definition of an element should be recognised if:
   (a) it is probable that any future economic benefit associated with the item will flow to or from the enterprise; and
   (b) the item has a cost or value that can be measured with reliability.

84 In assessing whether an item meets these criteria and therefore qualifies for recognition in the financial statements, regard needs to be given to the materiality considerations discussed in paragraphs 29 and 30. The interrelationship between the elements means that an item that meets the definition and recognition criteria for a particular element, for example, an asset, automatically requires the recognition of another element, for example, income or a liability.

The Probability of Future Economic Benefit

85 The concept of probability is used in the recognition criteria to refer to the degree of uncertainty that the future economic benefits associated with the item will flow to or from the enterprise. The concept is in keeping with the uncertainty that characterises the environment in which an enterprise operates. Assessments of the degree of uncertainty attaching to the flow of future economic benefits are made on the basis of the evidence available when the financial statements are prepared. ...

Reliability of Measurement

86 The second criterion for the recognition of an item is that it possesses a cost or value that can be measured with reliability as discussed in paragraphs 31 to 38 of this Framework. In many cases, cost or value must be estimated; the use of reasonable estimates is an essential part of the preparation of financial statements and does not undermine their reliability. When, however, a reasonable estimate cannot be made the item is not recognised in the balance sheet or income statement. ...

87 An item that, at a particular point in time, fails to meet the recognition criteria in paragraph 83 may qualify for recognition at a later date as a result of subsequent circumstances or events.

88 An item that possesses the essential characteristics of an element but fails to meet the criteria for recognition may nonetheless warrant disclosure in the notes, explanatory material or in supplementary schedules. This is appropriate when knowledge of the item is considered to be relevant to the evaluation of the financial position, performance and changes in financial position of an enterprise by the users of financial statements.

Recognition of Assets

An asset is recognised in the balance sheet when it is probable that the future economic **89** benefits will flow to the enterprise and the asset has a cost or value that can be measured reliably.

An asset is not recognised in the balance sheet when expenditure has been incurred for **90** which it is considered improbable that economic benefits will flow to the enterprise beyond the current accounting period. Instead such a transaction results in the recognition of an expense in the income statement. This treatment does not imply either that the intention of management in incurring expenditure was other than to generate future economic benefits for the enterprise or that management was misguided. The only implication is that the degree of certainty that economic benefits will flow to the enterprise beyond the current accounting period is insufficient to warrant the recognition of an asset.

Recognition of Liabilities

A liability is recognised in the balance sheet when it is probable that an outflow of **91** resources embodying economic benefits will result from the settlement of a present obligation and the amount at which the settlement will take place can be measured reliably. In practice, obligations under contracts that are equally proportionately unperformed (for example, liabilities for inventory ordered but not yet received) are generally not recognised as liabilities in the financial statements. However, such obligations may meet the definition of liabilities and, provided the recognition criteria are met in the particular circumstances, may qualify for recognition. In such circumstances, recognition of liabilities entails recognition of related assets or expenses.

Recognition of Income

Income is recognised in the income statement when an increase in future economic **92** benefits related to an increase in an asset or a decrease of a liability has arisen that can be measured reliably. This means, in effect, that recognition of income occurs simultaneously with the recognition of increases in assets or decreases in liabilities (for example, the net increase in assets arising on a sale of goods or services or the decrease in liabilities arising from the waiver of a debt payable).

The procedures normally adopted in practice for recognising income, for example, the **93** requirement that revenue should be earned, are applications of the recognition criteria in this Framework. Such procedures are generally directed at restricting the recognition as income to those items that can be measured reliably and have a sufficient degree of certainty.

Recognition of Expenses

Expenses are recognised in the income statement when a decrease in future economic **94** benefits related to a decrease in an asset or an increase of a liability has arisen that can be measured reliably. This means, in effect, that recognition of expenses occurs simultaneously with the recognition of an increase in liabilities or a decrease in assets (...).

Expenses are recognised in the income statement on the basis of a direct association **95** between the costs incurred and the earning of specific items of income. This process, commonly referred to as the matching of costs with revenues, involves the simultaneous or combined recognition of revenues and expenses that result directly and jointly from the same transactions or other events; for example, the various components of expense making up the cost of goods sold are recognised at the same time as the income derived from the sale of the goods. However, the application of the matching concept under this Framework does not allow the recognition of items in the balance sheet which do not meet the definition of assets or liabilities.

96 When economic benefits are expected to arise over several accounting periods and the association with income can only be broadly or indirectly determined, expenses are recognised in the income statement on the basis of systematic and rational allocation procedures. This is often necessary in recognising the expenses associated with the using up of assets such as property, plant, equipment, goodwill, patents and trademarks; in such cases the expense is referred to as depreciation or amortisation. These allocation procedures are intended to recognise expenses in the accounting periods in which the economic benefits associated with these items are consumed or expire.

97 An expense is recognised immediately in the income statement when an expenditure produces no future economic benefits or when, and to the extent that, future economic benefits do not qualify, or cease to qualify, for recognition in the balance sheet as an asset.

98 An expense is also recognised in the income statement in those cases when a liability is incurred without the recognition of an asset, as when a liability under a product warranty arises.

Measurement of the Elements of Financial Statements

99 Measurement is the process of determining the monetary amounts at which the elements of the financial statements are to be recognised and carried in the balance sheet and income statement. This involves the selection of the particular basis of measurement.

100 A number of different measurement bases are employed to different degrees and in varying combinations in financial statements. They include the following:
   (a) *Historical cost.* Assets are recorded at the amount of cash or cash equivalents paid or the fair value of the consideration given to acquire them at the time of their acquisition. Liabilities are recorded at the amount of proceeds received in exchange for the obligation, or in some circumstances (for example, income taxes), at the amounts of cash or cash equivalents expected to be paid to satisfy the liability in the normal course of business.
   (b) *Current cost.* Assets are carried at the amount of cash or cash equivalents that would have to be paid if the same or an equivalent asset was acquired currently. Liabilities are carried at the undiscounted amount of cash or cash equivalents that would be required to settle the obligation currently.
   (c) *Realisable (settlement) value.* Assets are carried at the amount of cash or cash equivalents that could currently be obtained by selling the asset in an orderly disposal. Liabilities are carried at their settlement values; that is, the undiscounted amounts of cash or cash equivalents expected to be paid to satisfy the liabilities in the normal course of business.
   (d) *Present value.* Assets are carried at the present discounted value of the future net cash inflows that the item is expected to generate in the normal course of business.

Liabilities are carried at the present discounted value of the future net cash outflows that are expected to be required to settle the liabilities in the normal course of business.

The measurement basis most commonly adopted by enterprises in preparing their **101** financial statements is historical cost. This is usually combined with other measurement bases. For example, inventories are usually carried at the lower of cost and net realisable value, marketable securities may be carried at market value and pension liabilities are carried at their present value. Furthermore, some enterprises use the current cost basis as a response to the inability of the historical cost accounting model to deal with the effects of changing prices of non–monetary assets.

Concepts of Capital and Capital Maintenance

Concepts of Capital

A financial concept of capital is adopted by most enterprises in preparing their financial **102** statements. Under a financial concept of capital, such as invested money or invested purchasing power, capital is synonymous with the net assets or equity of the enterprise. Under a physical concept of capital, such as operating capability, capital is regarded as the productive capacity of the enterprise based on, for example, units of output per day.

The selection of the appropriate concept of capital by an enterprise should be based on **103** the needs of the users of its financial statements. Thus, a financial concept of capital should be adopted if the users of financial statements are primarily concerned with the maintenance of nominal invested capital or the purchasing power of invested capital. If, however, the main concern of users is with the operating capability of the enterprise, a physical concept of capital should be used. The concept chosen indicates the goal to be attained in determining profit, even though there may be some measurement difficulties in making the concept operational.

Concepts of Capital Maintenance and the Determination of Profit

The concepts of capital in paragraph 102 give rise to the following concepts of capital **104** maintenance:
(a) *Financial capital maintenance.* Under this concept a profit is earned only if the financial (or money) amount of the net assets at the end of the period exceeds the financial (or money) amount of net assets at the beginning of the period, after excluding any distributions to, and contributions from, owners during the period. Financial capital maintenance can be measured in either nominal monetary units or units of constant purchasing power.
(b) *Physical capital maintenance.* Under this concept a profit is earned only if the physical productive capacity (or operating capability) of the enterprise (or the resources or funds needed to achieve that capacity) at the end of the period exceeds the physical productive capacity at the beginning of the period, after excluding any distributions to, and contributions from, owners during the period.

The concept of capital maintenance is concerned with how an enterprise defines the **105** capital that it seeks to maintain. It provides the linkage between the concepts of capital and the concepts of profit because it provides the point of reference by which profit is measured; it is a prerequisite for distinguishing between an enterprise's return on capital and its return of capital; only inflows of assets in excess of amounts needed to maintain capital may be regarded as profit and therefore as a return on capital. Hence, profit is the residual amount that remains after expenses (including capital maintenance adjustments, where appropriate) have been deducted from income. If expenses exceed income the residual amount is a net loss.

106 The physical capital maintenance concept requires the adoption of the current cost basis of measurement. The financial capital maintenance concept, however, does not require the use of a particular basis of measurement. Selection of the basis under this concept is dependent on the type of financial capital that the enterprise is seeking to maintain.

107 The principal difference between the two concepts of capital maintenance is the treatment of the effects of changes in the prices of assets and liabilities of the enterprise. In general terms, an enterprise has maintained its capital if it has as much capital at the end of the period as it had at the beginning of the period. Any amount over and above that required to maintain the capital at the beginning of the period is profit.

108 Under the concept of financial capital maintenance where capital is defined in terms of nominal monetary units, profit represents the increase in nominal money capital over the period. Thus, increases in the prices of assets held over the period, conventionally referred to as holding gains, are, conceptually, profits. They may not be recognised as such, however, until the assets are disposed of in an exchange transaction. When the concept of financial capital maintenance is defined in terms of constant purchasing power units, profit represents the increase in invested purchasing power over the period. Thus, only that part of the increase in the prices of assets that exceeds the increase in the general level of prices is regarded as profit. The rest of the increase is treated as a capital maintenance adjustment and, hence, as part of equity.

109 Under the concept of physical capital maintenance when capital is defined in terms of the physical productive capacity, profit represents the increase in that capital over the period. All price changes affecting the assets and liabilities of the enterprise are viewed as changes in the measurement of the physical productive capacity of the enterprise; hence, they are treated as capital maintenance adjustments that are part of equity and not as profit.

110 The selection of the measurement bases and concept of capital maintenance will determine the accounting model used in the preparation of the financial statements. Different accounting models exhibit different degrees of relevance and reliability and, as in other areas, management must seek a balance between relevance and reliability. This Framework is applicable to a range of accounting models and provides guidance on preparing and presenting the financial statements constructed under the chosen model. ...

IAS 1: Presentation of Financial Statements

IAS 1: Presentation of Financial Statements					
Scope 1.1–4	Purpose of Financial Statements 1.5	Responsibility for Financial Statements 1.6	Components of Financial Statements 1.7–9	Effective Date 1.103–104	Related Interpreta– tions: SIC–8, 18, 27, 29

Overall Considerations 1.10–41							
Fair Pres- entation and Compli- ance with IASs 1.10–19	Account- ing Policies 1.20–22	Going Concern 1.23–24	Accrual Basis of Account- ing 1.25–26	Consist- ency of Presenta- tion 1.27–28	Material- ity and Aggrega- tion 1.29–32	Offsetting 1.33–37	Compara- tive Infor- mation 1.38–41

Structure and Content 1.42–102						
Introduction 1.42–52			Balance Sheet 1.53–74	Income Statement 1.75–85		Notes 1.91– 102
Identifi- cation of Finan- cial State- ments 1.44– 48	Report- ing Period 1.49–51	Time– liness 1.52	The Current/ Non–current Distinction 1.53–56			Struc- ture 1.91–96
			Current Assets 1.57– 59	Current Liabil- ities 1.60– 65	Infor- mation to be Pre- sented on the Face of the Income State- ment 1.75– 76	Infor- mation to be Present ed Either on the Face of the Income Statem ent or in the Notes 1.77– 85	Changes in Equity 1.86–89	Cash Flow State- ment 1.90	Presen- tation of Accoun ting Policies 1.97– 101
			Infor- mation to be Pre- sented on the Face of the Bal- ance Sheet 1.66– 71	Infor- mation to be Pre- sented Either on the Face of the Bal- ance Sheet or in the		Other Disclo- sures 1.102

Appendix – Illustrative Financial Statement Structure

Scope

1 *This Standard should be applied in the presentation of all general purpose financial statements prepared and presented in accordance with IASs.*

2 General purpose financial statements are those intended to meet the needs of users who are not in a position to demand reports tailored to meet their specific information needs. General purpose financial statements include those that are presented separately or within another public document such as an annual report or a prospectus. This Standard does not apply to condensed interim financial information. This Standard applies equally to the financial statements of an individual enterprise and to consolidated financial statements for a group of enterprises. However, it does not preclude the presentation of consolidated financial statements complying with IASs and financial statements of the parent company under national requirements within the same document, as long as the basis of preparation of each is clearly disclosed in the statement of accounting policies.

3 This Standard applies to all types of enterprises including banks and insurance enterprises. Additional requirements for banks and similar financial institutions, consistent with the requirements of this Standard, are set out in IAS 30.

4 This Standard uses terminology that is suitable for an enterprise with a profit objective. Public sector business enterprises may therefore apply the requirements of this Standard. Non–profit, government and other public sector enterprises seeking to apply this Standard may need to amend the descriptions used for certain line items in the financial statements and for the financial statements themselves. Such enterprises may also present additional components of the financial statements.

Purpose of Financial Statements

5 Financial statements are a structured financial representation of the financial position of and the transactions undertaken by an enterprise. The objective of general purpose financial statements is to provide information about the financial position, performance and cash flows of an enterprise that is useful to a wide range of users in making economic decisions. Financial statements also show the results of management's stewardship of the resources entrusted to it. To meet this objective, financial statements provide information about an enterprise's:
(a) assets;
(b) liabilities;
(c) equity;
(d) income and expenses, including gains and losses; and
(e) cash flows.
This information, along with other information in the notes to financial statements, assists users in predicting the enterprise's future cash flows and in particular the timing and certainty of the generation of cash and cash equivalents.

Responsibility for Financial Statements

6 The board of directors and/or other governing body of an enterprise is responsible for the preparation and presentation of its financial statements.

Components of Financial Statements

A complete set of financial statements includes the following components: 7
(a) balance sheet;
(b) income statement;
(c) a statement showing either:
  (i) all changes in equity; or
  (ii) changes in equity other than those arising from capital transactions with owners and distributions to owners;
(d) cash flow statement; and
(e) accounting policies and explanatory notes.

Enterprises are encouraged to present, outside the financial statements, a financial 8
review by management which describes and explains the main features of the
enterprise's financial performance and financial position and the principal uncertainties
it faces. Such a report may include a review of:
(a) the main factors and influences determining performance, including changes in the
  environment in which the enterprise operates, the enterprise's response to those
  changes and their effect, and the enterprise's policy for investment to maintain and
  enhance performance, including its dividend policy;
(b) the enterprise's sources of funding, the policy on gearing and its risk management
  policies; and
(c) the strengths and resources of the enterprise whose value is not reflected in the
  balance sheet under IASs.

Many enterprises present, outside the financial statements, additional statements such 9
as environmental reports and value added statements, particularly in industries where
environmental factors are significant and when employees are considered to be an
important user group. Enterprises are encouraged to present such additional statements
if management believes they will assist users in making economic decisions.

Overall Considerations

Fair Presentation and Compliance with IASs

Financial statements should present fairly the financial position, financial 10
performance and cash flows of an enterprise. The appropriate application of IASs,
with additional disclosure when necessary, results, in virtually all circumstances, in
financial statements that achieve a fair presentation.

An enterprise whose financial statements comply with IASs should disclose that fact. 11
Financial statements should not be described as complying with IASs unless they
comply with all the requirements of each applicable Standard and each applicable
Interpretation of the Standing Interpretations Committee.

Inappropriate accounting treatments are not rectified either by disclosure of the 12
accounting policies used or by notes or explanatory material.

In the extremely rare circumstances when management concludes that compliance 13
with a requirement in a Standard would be misleading, and therefore that departure
from a requirement is necessary to achieve a fair presentation, an enterprise should
disclose:

(a) that management has concluded that the financial statements fairly present the enterprise's financial position, financial performance and cash flows;

(b) that it has complied in all material respects with applicable IASs except that it has departed from a Standard in order to achieve a fair presentation;

(c) the Standard from which the enterprise has departed, the nature of the departure, including the treatment that the Standard would require, the reason why that treatment would be misleading in the circumstances and the treatment adopted; and

(d) the financial impact of the departure on the enterprise's net profit or loss, assets, liabilities, equity and cash flows for each period presented.

14   Financial statements have sometimes been described as being 'based on' or 'complying with the significant requirements of' or 'in compliance with the accounting requirements of' IASs. Often there is no further information, although it is clear that significant disclosure requirements, if not accounting requirements, are not met. Such statements are misleading because they detract from the reliability and understandability of the financial statements. In order to ensure that financial statements that state compliance with IASs will meet the standard required by users internationally, this Standard includes an overall requirement that financial statements should give a fair presentation, guidance on how the fair presentation requirement is met, and further guidance for determining the extremely rare circumstances when a departure is necessary. It also requires prominent disclosure of the circumstances surrounding a departure. The existence of conflicting national requirements is not, in itself, sufficient to justify a departure in financial statements prepared using IASs.

15   In virtually all circumstances, a fair presentation is achieved by compliance in all material respects with applicable IASs. A fair presentation requires:

(a) selecting and applying accounting policies in accordance with paragraph 20;

(b) presenting information, including accounting policies, in a manner which provides relevant, reliable, comparable and understandable information; and

(c) providing additional disclosures when the requirements in IASs are insufficient to enable users to understand the impact of particular transactions or events on the enterprise's financial position and financial performance.

16   In extremely rare circumstances, application of a specific requirement in an IAS might result in misleading financial statements. This will be the case only when the treatment required by the Standard is clearly inappropriate and thus a fair presentation cannot be achieved either by applying the Standard or through additional disclosure alone. Departure is not appropriate simply because another treatment would also give a fair presentation.

17   When assessing whether a departure from a specific requirement in IASs is necessary, consideration is given to:

(a) the objective of the requirement and why that objective is not achieved or is not relevant in the particular circumstances; and

(b) the way in which the enterprise's circumstances differ from those of other enterprises which follow the requirement.

18–19   [Not printed]

Accounting Policies

Management should select and apply an enterprise's accounting policies so that the **20**
financial statements comply with all the requirements of each applicable IAS and
Interpretation of the Standing Interpretations Committee. Where there is no specific
requirement, management should develop policies to ensure that the financial
statements provide information that is:
(a) relevant to the decision–making needs of users; and
(b) reliable in that they:
    (i) represent faithfully the results and financial position of the enterprise;
    (ii) reflect the economic substance of events and transactions and not merely the
       legal form;
    (iii)are neutral, that is free from bias;
    (iv) are prudent; and
    (v) are complete in all material respects.

Accounting policies are the specific principles, bases, conventions, rules and practices **21**
adopted by an enterprise in preparing and presenting financial statements.

In the absence of a specific IAS and an Interpretation of the Standing Interpretations **22**
Committee, management uses its judgement in developing an accounting policy that
provides the most useful information to users of the enterprise's financial statements.
In making this judgement, management considers:
(a) the requirements and guidance in IASs dealing with similar and related issues;
(b) the definitions, recognition and measurement criteria for assets, liabilities, income
    and expenses set out in the IASC Framework; and
(c) pronouncements of other standard setting bodies and accepted industry practices to
    the extent, but only to the extent, that these are consistent with (a) and (b) of this
    paragraph.

Going Concern

When preparing financial statements, management should make an assessment of an **23**
enterprise's ability to continue as a going concern. Financial statements should be
prepared on a going concern basis unless management either intends to liquidate the
enterprise or to cease trading, or has no realistic alternative but to do so. When
management is aware, in making its assessment, of material uncertainties related to
events or conditions which may cast significant doubt upon the enterprise's ability to
continue as a going concern, those uncertainties should be disclosed. When the
financial statements are not prepared on a going concern basis, that fact should be
disclosed, together with the basis on which the financial statements are prepared and
the reason why the enterprise is not considered to be a going concern.

In assessing whether the going concern assumption is appropriate, management takes **24**
into account all available information for the foreseeable future, which should be at
least, but is not limited to, twelve months from the balance sheet date. ...

Accrual Basis of Accounting

An enterprise should prepare its financial statements, except for cash flow **25**
information, under the accrual basis of accounting.

26 Under the accrual basis of accounting, transactions and events are recognised when they occur (and not as cash or its equivalent is received or paid) and they are recorded in the accounting records and reported in the financial statements of the periods to which they relate. Expenses are recognised in the income statement on the basis of a direct association between the costs incurred and the earning of specific items of income (matching). However, the application of the matching concept does not allow the recognition of items in the balance sheet which do not meet the definition of assets or liabilities.

Consistency of Presentation

27 *The presentation and classification of items in the financial statements should be retained from one period to the next unless:*
    (a) a significant change in the nature of the operations of the enterprise or a review of its financial statement presentation demonstrates that the change will result in a more appropriate presentation of events or transactions; or
    (b) a change in presentation is required by an IAS or an Interpretation of the Standing Interpretations Committee.

28 [Not printed]

Materiality and Aggregation

29 *Each material item should be presented separately in the financial statements. Immaterial amounts should be aggregated with amounts of a similar nature or function and need not be presented separately.*

30 Financial statements result from processing large quantities of transactions which are structured by being aggregated into groups according to their nature or function. The final stage in the process of aggregation and classification is the presentation of condensed and classified data which form line items either on the face of the financial statements or in the notes. If a line item is not individually material, it is aggregated with other items either on the face of the financial statements or in the notes. An item that is not sufficiently material to warrant separate presentation on the face of the financial statements may nevertheless be sufficiently material that it should be presented separately in the notes.

31 In this context, information is material if its non–disclosure could influence the economic decisions of users taken on the basis of the financial statements. Materiality depends on the size and nature of the item judged in the particular circumstances of its omission. In deciding whether an item or an aggregate of items is material, the nature and the size of the item are evaluated together. Depending on the circumstances, either the nature or the size of the item could be the determining factor. For example, individual assets with the same nature and function are aggregated even if the individual amounts are large. However, large items which differ in nature or function are presented separately.

32 Materiality provides that the specific disclosure requirements of IASs need not be met if the resulting information is not material.

Offsetting

Assets and liabilities should not be offset except when offsetting is required or **33** *permitted by another IAS.*

Items of income and expense should be offset when, and only when: **34**
(a) an IAS requires or permits it; or
(b) gains, losses and related expenses arising from the same or similar transactions and events are not material. Such amounts should be aggregated in accordance with paragraph 29.

It is important that both assets and liabilities, and income and expenses, when material, **35** are reported separately. Offsetting in either the income statement or the balance sheet, except when offsetting reflects the substance of the transaction or event, detracts from the ability of users to understand the transactions undertaken and to assess the future cash flows of the enterprise. ...

IAS 18 defines the term revenue and requires it to be measured at the fair value of **36** consideration received or receivable, taking into account the amount of any trade discounts and volume rebates allowed by the enterprise. An enterprise undertakes, in the course of its ordinary activities, other transactions which do not generate revenue but which are incidental to the main revenue generating activities. The results of such transactions are presented, when this presentation reflects the substance of the transaction or event, by netting any income with related expenses arising on the same transaction. ...

In addition, gains and losses arising from a group of similar transactions are reported **37** on a net basis, ... Such gains and losses are, however, reported separately if their size, nature or incidence is such that separate disclosure is required by IAS 8.

Comparative Information

Unless an IAS permits or requires otherwise, comparative information should be **38** *disclosed in respect of the previous period for all numerical information in the financial statements. Comparative information should be included in narrative and descriptive information when it is relevant to an understanding of the current period's financial statements.*

In some cases narrative information provided in the financial statements for the **39** previous period(s) continues to be relevant in the current period. For example, details of a legal dispute, the outcome of which was uncertain at the last balance sheet date and is yet to be resolved, are disclosed in the current period. Users benefit from information that the uncertainty existed at the last balance sheet date, and the steps that have been taken during the period to resolve the uncertainty.

When the presentation or classification of items in the financial statements is **40** *amended, comparative amounts should be reclassified, unless it is impracticable to do so, to ensure comparability with the current period, and the nature, amount of, and reason for, any reclassification should be disclosed. When it is impracticable to reclassify comparative amounts, an enterprise should disclose the reason for not reclassifying and the nature of the changes that would have been made if amounts were reclassified.*

[Not printed] **41**

Structure and Content

Introduction

42 This Standard requires certain disclosures on the face of the financial statements, requires other line items to be disclosed either on the face of the financial statements or in the notes, and sets out recommended formats as an appendix to the Standard which an enterprise may follow as appropriate in its own circumstances. IAS 7 provides a structure for the presentation of the cash flow statement.

43 [Not printed]

Identification of Financial Statements

44 *Financial statements should be clearly identified and distinguished from other information in the same published document.*

45 [Not printed]

46 *Each component of the financial statements should be clearly identified. In addition, the following information should be prominently displayed, and repeated when it is necessary for a proper understanding of the information presented:*
  (a) the name of the reporting enterprise or other means of identification;
  (b) whether the financial statements cover the individual enterprise or a group of enterprises;
  (c) the balance sheet date or the period covered by the financial statements, whichever is appropriate to the related component of the financial statements;
  (d) the reporting currency; and
  (e) the level of precision used in the presentation of figures in the financial statements.

47 [Not printed]

48 Financial statements are often made more understandable by presenting information in thousands or millions of units of the reporting currency. This is acceptable as long as the level of precision in presentation is disclosed and relevant information is not lost.

Reporting Period

49 *Financial statements should be presented at least annually. When, in exceptional circumstances, an enterprise's balance sheet date changes and annual financial statements are presented for a period longer or shorter than one year, an enterprise should disclose, in addition to the period covered by the financial statements:*
  (a) the reason for a period other than one year being used; and
  (b) the fact that comparative amounts for the income statement, changes in equity, cash flows and related notes are not comparable.

50–51 [Not printed]

Timeliness

52 The usefulness of financial statements is impaired if they are not made available to users within a reasonable period after the balance sheet date. An enterprise should be in a position to issue its financial statements within six months of the balance sheet date. ...

Balance Sheet

The Current/Non–current Distinction

Each enterprise should determine, based on the nature of its operations, whether or **53**
not to present current and non–current assets and current and non–current liabilities
as separate classifications on the face of the balance sheet. Paragraphs 57 to 65 of
this Standard apply when this distinction is made. When an enterprise chooses not
to make this classification, assets and liabilities should be presented broadly in order
of their liquidity.

Whichever method of presentation is adopted, an enterprise should disclose, for each **54**
asset and liability item that combines amounts expected to be recovered or settled
both before and after twelve months from the balance sheet date, the amount
expected to be recovered or settled after more than twelve months.

When an enterprise supplies goods or services within a clearly identifiable operating **55**
cycle, separate classification of current and non–current assets and liabilities on the face
of the balance sheet provides useful information by distinguishing the net assets that
are continuously circulating as working capital from those used in the enterprise's long–
term operations. It also highlights assets that are expected to be realised within the
current operating cycle, and liabilities that are due for settlement within the same
period.

[Not printed] **56**

Current Assets

An asset should be classified as a current asset when it: **57**
(a) is expected to be realised in, or is held for sale or consumption in, the normal
course of the enterprise's operating cycle; or
(b) is held primarily for trading purposes or for the short–term and expected to be
realised within twelve months of the balance sheet date; or
(c) is cash or a cash equivalent asset which is not restricted in its use.
All other assets should be classified as non–current assets.

This Standard uses the term 'non–current' to include tangible, intangible, operating and **58**
financial assets of a long–term nature. It does not prohibit the use of alternative
descriptions as long as the meaning is clear.

The operating cycle of an enterprise is the time between the acquisition of materials **59**
entering into a process and its realisation in cash or an instrument that is readily
convertible into cash. Current assets include inventories and trade receivables that are
sold, consumed and realised as part of the normal operating cycle even when they are
not expected to be realised within twelve months of the balance sheet date. Marketable
securities are classified as current assets if they are expected to be realised within twelve
months of the balance sheet date; otherwise they are classified as non–current assets.

Current Liabilities

A liability should be classified as a current liability when it: **60**
(a) is expected to be settled in the normal course of the enterprise's operating cycle; or
(b) is due to be settled within twelve months of the balance sheet date.
All other liabilities should be classified as non–current liabilities.

61 Current liabilities can be categorised in a similar way to current assets. Some current liabilities, such as trade payables and accruals for employee and other operating costs, form part of the working capital used in the normal operating cycle of the business. Such operating items are classified as current liabilities even if they are due to be settled after more than twelve months from the balance sheet date.

62 Other current liabilities are not settled as part of the current operating cycle, but are due for settlement within twelve months of the balance sheet date. Examples are the current portion of interest–bearing liabilities, bank overdrafts, dividends payable, income taxes and other non–trade payables. Interest–bearing liabilities that provide the financing for working capital on a long–term basis, and are not due for settlement within twelve months, are non–current liabilities.

63 *An enterprise should continue to classify its long–term interest–bearing liabilities as non–current, even when they are due to be settled within twelve months of the balance sheet date if:*
    (a) the original term was for a period of more than twelve months;
    (b) the enterprise intends to refinance the obligation on a long–term basis; and
    (c) that intention is supported by an agreement to refinance, or to reschedule payments, which is completed before the financial statements are authorised for issue.
    The amount of any liability that has been excluded from current liabilities in accordance with this paragraph, together with information in support of this presentation, should be disclosed in the notes to the balance sheet.

64 Some obligations that are due to be repaid within the next operating cycle may be expected to be refinanced or 'rolled over' at the discretion of the enterprise and, therefore, are not expected to use current working capital of the enterprise. Such obligations are considered to form part of the enterprise's long–term financing and should be classified as non–current. However, in situations in which refinancing is not at the discretion of the enterprise (as would be the case if there were no agreement to refinance), the refinancing cannot be considered automatic and the obligation is classified as current unless the completion of a refinancing agreement before authorisation of the financial statements for issue provides evidence that the substance of the liability at the balance sheet date was long–term.

65 Some borrowing agreements incorporate undertakings by the borrower (covenants) which have the effect that the liability becomes payable on demand if certain conditions related to the borrower's financial position are breached. In these circumstances, the liability is classified as non–current only when:
    (a) the lender has agreed, prior to the authorisation of the financial statements for issue, not to demand payment as a consequence of the breach; and
    (b) it is not probable that further breaches will occur within twelve months of the balance sheet date.

Information to be Presented on the Face of the Balance Sheet

66 *As a minimum, the face of the balance sheet should include line items which present the following amounts:*
    (a) property, plant and equipment;
    (b) intangible assets;
    (c) financial assets (excluding amounts shown under (d), (f) and (g));
    (d) investments accounted for using the equity method;

(e) inventories;
(f) trade and other receivables;
(g) cash and cash equivalents;
(h) trade and other payables;
(i) tax liabilities and assets as required by IAS 12;
(j) provisions;
(k) non–current interest–bearing liabilities;
(l) minority interest; and
(m) issued capital and reserves.

Additional line items, headings and sub–totals should be presented on the face of the **67** *balance sheet when an IAS requires it, or when such presentation is necessary to present fairly the enterprise's financial position.*

This Standard does not prescribe the order or format in which items are to be presented. **68** Paragraph 66 simply provides a list of items that are so different in nature or function that they deserve separate presentation on the face of the balance sheet. Illustrative formats are set out in the Appendix to this Standard. Adjustments to the line items above include the following:

(a) line items are added when another IAS requires separate presentation on the face of the balance sheet, or when the size, nature or function of an item is such that separate presentation would assist in presenting fairly the enterprise's financial position; and

(b) the descriptions used and the ordering of items may be amended according to the nature of the enterprise and its transactions, to provide information that is necessary for an overall understanding of the enterprise's financial position. ...

The line items listed in paragraph 66 are broad in nature and need not be limited to **69** items falling within the scope of other Standards. For example, the line item intangible assets includes goodwill and assets arising from development expenditure.

The judgement on whether additional items are separately presented is based on an **70** assessment of:

(a) the nature and liquidity of assets and their materiality, leading, in most cases, to the separate presentation of, goodwill and assets arising from development expenditure, monetary and non–monetary assets and current and non–current assets;

(b) their function within the enterprise, leading, for example, to the separate presentation of operating and financial assets, inventories, receivables and cash and cash equivalent assets; and

(c) the amounts, nature and timing of liabilities, leading, for example, to the separate presentation of interest–bearing and non–interest–bearing liabilities and provisions, classified as current or non–current if appropriate.

[Not printed] **71**

Information to be Presented Either on the Face of the Balance Sheet or in the Notes

An enterprise should disclose, either on the face of the balance sheet or in the notes **72** *to the balance sheet, further sub–classifications of the line items presented, classified in a manner appropriate to the enterprise's operations. Each item should be sub–classified, when appropriate, by its nature and, amounts payable to and receivable* *from the parent enterprise, fellow subsidiaries and associates and other related parties should be disclosed separately.*

73   The detail provided in sub–classifications, either on the face of the balance sheet or in the notes, depends on the requirements of IASs and the size, nature and function of the amounts involved. The factors set out in paragraph 70 are also used to decide the basis of sub–classification. The disclosures will vary for each item, for example:

(a)   tangible assets are classified by class as described in IAS 16;

(b)   receivables are analysed between amounts receivable from trade customers, other members of the group, receivables from related parties, prepayments and other amounts;

(c)   inventories are sub–classified, in accordance with IAS 2, into classifications such as merchandise, production supplies, materials, work in progress and finished goods;

(d)   provisions are analysed showing separately provisions for employee benefit costs and any other items classified in a manner appropriate to the enterprise's operations; and

(e)   equity capital and reserves are analysed showing separately the various classes of paid in capital, share premium and reserves.

74   *An enterprise should disclose the following, either on the face of the balance sheet or in the notes:*

(a) for each class of share capital:

(i)   the number of shares authorised;

(ii) the number of shares issued and fully paid, and issued but not fully paid;

(iii) par value per share, or that the shares have no par value;

(iv) a reconciliation of the number of shares outstanding at the beginning and at the end of the year;

(v) the rights, preferences and restrictions attaching to that class including restrictions on the distribution of dividends and the repayment of capital;

(vi) shares in the enterprise held by the enterprise itself or by subsidiaries or associates of the enterprise; and

(vii) shares reserved for issuance under options and sales contracts, including the terms and amounts;

(b) a description of the nature and purpose of each reserve within owners' equity;

(c) the amount of dividends that were proposed or declared after the balance sheet date but before the financial statements were authorised for issue; and

(d) the amount of any cumulative preference dividends not recognised.

An enterprise without share capital, such as a partnership, should disclose information equivalent to that required above, showing movements during the period in each category of equity interest and the rights, preferences and restrictions attaching to each category of equity interest.

Income Statement

Information to be Presented on the Face of the Income Statement

75   *As a minimum, the face of the income statement should include line items which present the following amounts:*

(a) revenue;

(b) the results of operating activities;

(c) finance costs;

(d) share of profits and losses of associates and joint ventures accounted for using the equity method;

(e) tax expense;

(f) profit or loss from ordinary activities;

(g) extraordinary items;

(h) minority interest; and

(i) net profit or loss for the period.

Additional line items, headings and sub–totals should be presented on the face of the income statement when required by an IAS, or when such presentation is necessary to present fairly the enterprise's financial performance.

[Not printed]   **76**

Information to be Presented Either on the Face of the Income Statement or in the Notes

An enterprise should present, either on the face of the income statement or in the **77** *notes to the income statement, an analysis of expenses using a classification based on either the nature of expenses or their function within the enterprise.*

Enterprises are encouraged to present the analysis in paragraph 77 on the face of the **78** income statement.

Expense items are further sub–classified in order to highlight a range of components of **79** financial performance which may differ in terms of stability, potential for gain or loss and predictability. This information is provided in one of two ways.

The first analysis is referred to as the nature of expense method. Expenses are **80** aggregated in the income statement according to their nature, (for example depreciation, purchases of materials, transport costs, wages and salaries, advertising costs), and are not reallocated amongst various functions within the enterprise. This method is simple to apply in many smaller enterprises because no allocations of operating expenses between functional classifications is necessary. An example of a classification using the nature of expense method is as follows:

Revenue	X
Other operating income	X
Changes in inventories of finished goods and work in progress	X
Raw materials and consumables used	X
Staff costs	X
Depreciation and amortisation expense	X
Other operating expenses	X
Total operating expenses	(X)
Profit from operating activities	X

81 The change in finished goods and work in progress during the period represents an adjustment to production expenses to reflect the fact that either production has increased inventory levels or that sales in excess of production have reduced inventory levels. In some jurisdictions, an increase in finished goods and work in progress during the period is presented immediately following revenue in the above analysis. However, the presentation used should not imply that such amounts represent income.

82 The second analysis is referred to as the function of expense or 'cost of sales' method and classifies expenses according to their function as part of cost of sales, distribution or administrative activities. This presentation often provides more relevant information to users than the classification of expenses by nature, but the allocation of costs to functions can be arbitrary and involves considerable judgement. An example of a classification using the function of expense method is as follows:

Revenue	X
Cost of sales	(X)
Gross profit	X
Other operating income	X
Distribution costs	(X)
Administrative expenses	(X)
Other operating expenses	(X)
Profit from operating activities	X

83 *Enterprises classifying expenses by function should disclose additional information on the nature of expenses, including depreciation and amortisation expense and staff costs.*

84 The choice of analysis between the cost of sales method and the nature of expenditure method depends on both historical and industry factors and the nature of the organisation. Both methods provide an indication of those costs which might be expected to vary, directly or indirectly, with the level of sales or production of the enterprise. Because each method of presentation has merit for different types of enterprise, this Standard requires a choice between classifications based on that which most fairly presents the elements of the enterprise's performance. However, because information on the nature of expenses is useful in predicting future cash flows, additional disclosure is required when the cost of sales classification is used.

85 *An enterprise should disclose, either on the face of the income statement or in the notes, the amount of dividends per share, declared or proposed, for the period covered by the financial statements.*

Changes in Equity

86 *An enterprise should present, as a separate component of its financial statements, a statement showing:*
(a) the net profit or loss for the period;

(b) each item of income and expense, gain or loss which, as required by other Standards, is recognised directly in equity, and the total of these items; and

(c) the cumulative effect of changes in accounting policy and the correction of fundamental errors dealt with under the Benchmark treatments in IAS 8.

In addition, an enterprise should present, either within this statement or in the notes:

(d) capital transactions with owners and distributions to owners;

(e) the balance of accumulated profit or loss at the beginning of the period and at the balance sheet date, and the movements for the period; and

(f) a reconciliation between the carrying amount of each class of equity capital, share premium and each reserve at the beginning and the end of the period, separately disclosing each movement.

Changes in an enterprise's equity between two balance sheet dates reflect the increase **87** or decrease in its net assets or wealth during the period, under the particular measurement principles adopted and disclosed in the financial statements. Except for changes resulting from transactions with shareholders, such as capital contributions and dividends, the overall change in equity represents the total gains and losses generated by the enterprises activities during the period.

IAS 8 requires all items of income and expense recognised in a period to be included in **88** the determination of net profit or loss for the period unless an IAS requires or permits otherwise. Other Standards require gains and losses, such as revaluation surpluses and deficits and certain foreign exchange differences, to be recognised directly as changes in equity along with capital transactions with and distributions to the enterprise's owners. Since it is important to take into consideration all gains and losses in assessing the changes in an enterprise's financial position between two balance sheet dates, this Standard requires a separate component of the financial statements which highlights an enterprise's total gains and losses, including those that are recognised directly in equity.

The requirements in paragraph 86 may be met in a number of ways. The approach **89** adopted in many jurisdictions follows a columnar format which reconciles between the opening and closing balances of each element within shareholders' equity, including items (a) to (f). An alternative is to present a separate component of the financial statements which presents only items (a) to (c). Under this approach, the items described in (d) to (f) are shown in the notes to the financial statements. Both approaches are illustrated in the appendix to this Standard. Whichever approach is adopted, paragraph 86 requires a sub–total of the items in (b) to enable users to derive the total gains and losses arising from the enterprise's activities during the period.

Cash Flow Statement

IAS 7 sets out requirements for the presentation of the cash flow statement and related **90** disclosures. ...

Notes to the Financial Statements

Structure

The notes to the financial statements of an enterprise should: **91**

(a) present information about the basis of preparation of the financial statements and the specific accounting policies selected and applied for significant transactions and events;

(b) *disclose the information required by IASs that is not presented elsewhere in the financial statements; and*

(c) *provide additional information which is not presented on the face of the financial statements but that is necessary for a fair presentation.*

92 *Notes to the financial statements should be presented in a systematic manner. Each item on the face of the balance sheet, income statement and cash flow statement should be cross–referenced to any related information in the notes.*

93 Notes to the financial statements include narrative descriptions or more detailed analyses of amounts shown on the face of the balance sheet, income statement, cash flow statement and statement of changes in equity, as well as additional information such as contingent liabilities and commitments. They include information required and encouraged to be disclosed by IASs, and other disclosures necessary to achieve a fair presentation.

94 Notes are normally presented in the following order which assists users in understanding the financial statements and comparing them with those of other enterprises:

(a) statement of compliance with IASs (see paragraph 11);

(b) statement of the measurement basis (bases) and accounting policies applied;

(c) supporting information for items presented on the face of each financial statement in the order in which each line item and each financial statement is presented; and

(d) other disclosures, including:

(i) contingencies, commitments and other financial disclosures; and

(ii) non–financial disclosures.

95 [Not printed]

96 Information about the basis of preparation of the financial statements and specific accounting policies may be presented as a separate component of the financial statements.

Presentation of Accounting Policies

97 *The accounting policies section of the notes to the financial statements should describe the following:*

(a) the measurement basis (or bases) used in preparing the financial statements; and

(b) each specific accounting policy that is necessary for a proper understanding of the financial statements.

98 In addition to the specific accounting policies used in the financial statements, it is important for users to be aware of the measurement basis (bases) used (historical cost, current cost, realisable value, fair value or present value) because they form the basis on which the whole of the financial statements are prepared. When more than one measurement basis is used in the financial statements, for example when certain non–current assets are revalued, it is sufficient to provide an indication of the categories of assets and liabilities to which each measurement basis is applied.

99 In deciding whether a specific accounting policy should be disclosed, management considers whether disclosure would assist users in understanding the way in which transactions and events are reflected in the reported performance and financial position. The accounting policies that an enterprise might consider presenting include, but are not restricted to, the following:

(a) revenue recognition;

(b) consolidation principles, including subsidiaries and associates;
(c) business combinations;
(d) joint ventures;
(e) recognition and depreciation/amortisation of tangible and intangible assets;
(f) capitalisation of borrowing costs and other expenditure;
(g) construction contracts;
(h) investment properties;
(i) financial instruments and investments;
(j) leases;
(k) research and development costs;
(l) inventories;
(m) taxes, including deferred taxes;
(n) provisions;
(o) employee benefit costs;
(p) foreign currency translation and hedging;
(q) definition of business and geographical segments and the basis for allocation of costs between segments;
(r) definition of cash and cash equivalents;
(s) inflation accounting; and
(t) government grants.

...

[Not printed]   **100**

An accounting policy may be significant even if amounts shown for current and prior **101** periods are not material. It is also appropriate to disclose an accounting policy for each policy not covered by existing IASs, but selected and applied in accordance with paragraph 20.

Other Disclosures

An enterprise should disclose the following if not disclosed elsewhere in information **102** *published with the financial statements:*
(a) the domicile and legal form of the enterprise, its country of incorporation and the address of the registered office (or principal place of business, if different from the registered office);
(b) a description of the nature of the enterprise's operations and its principal activities;
(c) the name of the parent enterprise and the ultimate parent enterprise of the group; and
(d) either the number of employees at the end of the period or the average for the period.

Effective Date

[Not printed]   **103–104**

Appendix

Illustrative Financial Statement Structure

...

XYZ GROUP – BALANCE SHEET AS AT 31 DECEMBER 20–2
(in thousands of currency units)

	20–2	20–2	20–1	20–1
ASSETS				
Non–current assets				
Property, plant and equipment	X		X	
Goodwill	X		X	
Manufacturing licences	X		X	
Investments in associates	X		X	
Other financial assets	X		X	
		X		X
Current assets				
Inventories	X		X	
Trade and other receivables	X		X	
Prepayments	X		X	
Cash and cash equivalents	X		X	
		X		X
Total assets		X		X
EQUITY AND LIABILITIES				
Capital and reserves				
Issued capital	X		X	
Reserves	X		X	
Accumulated profits/(losses)	X		X	
		X		X
Minority interest		X		X
Non–current liabilities				
Interest bearing borrowings	X		X	
Deferred tax	X		X	
Retirement benefit obligation	X		X	
		X		X
Current liabilities				
Trade and other payables	X		X	
Short–term borrowings	X		X	
Current portion of interest– bearing borrowings	X		X	
Warranty provision	X		X	
		X		X
Total equity and liabilities		X		X

XYZ GROUP – INCOME STATEMENT FOR THE YEAR ENDED 31 DECEMBER 20–2

(illustrating the classification of expenses by function)

(in thousands of currency units)

	20–2	20–1
Revenue	X	X
Cost of sales	(X)	(X)
Gross profit	X	X
Other operating income	X	X
Distribution costs	(X)	(X)
Administrative expenses	(X)	(X)
Other operating expenses	(X)	(X)
Profit from operations	X	X
Finance cost	(X)	(X)
Income from associates	X	X
Profit before tax	X	X
Income tax expense	(X)	(X)
Profit after tax	X	X
Minority interest	(X)	(X)
Net profit from ordinary activities	X	X
Extraordinary items	X	(X)
Net profit for the period	X	X

XYZ GROUP – INCOME STATEMENT FOR THE YEAR ENDED 31 DECEMBER 20–2
(illustrating the classification of expenses by nature)
(in thousands of currency units)

	20–2	20–1
Revenue	X	X
Other operating income	X	X
Changes in inventories of finished goods and work in progress	(X)	X
Work performed by the enterprise and capitalised	X	X
Raw material and consumables used	(X)	(X)
Staff costs	(X)	(X)
Depreciation and amortisation expense	(X)	(X)
Other operating expenses	(X)	(X)
Profit from operations	X	X
Finance cost	(X)	(X)
Income from associates	X	X
Profit before tax	X	X
Income tax expense	(X)	(X)
Profit after tax	X	X
Minority interest	(X)	(X)
Net profit or loss from ordinary activities	X	X
Extraordinary items	X	(X)
Net profit for the period	X	X

XYZ GROUP – STATEMENT OF CHANGES IN EQUITY FOR THE YEAR ENDED 31 DECEMBER 20–2

(in thousands of currency units)

	Share capital	Share premium	Revaluation reserve	Translation reserve	Accumulated profit	Total
Balance at 31 December 20–0	X	X	X	(X)	X	X
Changes in accounting policy					(X)	(X)
Restated balance	X	X	X	(X)	X	X
Surplus on revaluation of Properties			X			X
Deficit on revaluation of Investments			(X)			(X)
Currency translation differences				(X)		(X)
Net gains and losses not recognised in the income statement			X	(X)		X
Net profit for the period					X	X
Dividends					(X)	(X)
Issue of share capital	X	X				X
Balance at 31 December 20–1	X	X	X	(X)	X	X
Deficit on revaluation of Properties			(X)			(X)
Surplus on revaluation of Investments			X			X
Currency translation differences				(X)		(X)
Net gains and losses not recognised in the income statement			(X)	(X)		(X)
Net profit for the period					X	X
Dividends					(X)	(X)
Issue of share capital	X	X				X
Balance at 31 December 20–2	X	X	X	(X)	X	X

...

XYZ GROUP – STATEMENT OF RECOGNISED GAINS AND LOSSES FOR THE YEAR ENDED 31 DECEMBER 20–2

(in thousands of currency units)

	20–2	20–1
Surplus/(deficit) on revaluation of properties	(X)	X
Surplus/(deficit) on revaluation of investments	X	(X)
Exchange differences on translation of the financial statements of foreign entities	(X)	(X)
Net gains not recognised in the income statement	X	X
Net profit for the period	X	X
Total recognised gains and losses	X	X
Effect of changes in accounting policy		(X)

...

IAS 2: Inventories

IAS 2: Inventories

- Scope 2.1–3
- Definitions 2.4–5
  - Inventories 2.4
  - Net Realisable Value 2.4
- Effective Date 2.41

Measurement of Inventories 2.6

- Cost of Inventories 2.7–18
  - General 2.7
  - Costs of Purchase 2.8–9
  - Costs of Conversion 2.10–12
  - Other Costs 2.13–15
  - Cost of Inventories of a Service Provider 2.16
  - Cost of Agricultural Produce Harvested from Biological Assets 2.16A
  - Techniques for the Measurement of Cost 2.17–18
- Cost Formulas 2.19–24
  - Benchmark Treatment 2.21–22
  - Allowed Alternative Treatment 2.23–24
- Net Realisable Value 2.25–30

Recognition as an Expense 2.31–33

Disclosure 2.34–40

Scope

1 *This Standard should be applied in financial statements prepared in the context of the historical cost system in accounting for inventories other than:*

 (a) work in progress arising under construction contracts, including directly related service contracts (see IAS 11);

 (b) financial instruments; and

 (c) producers' inventories of livestock, agricultural and forest products, and mineral ores to the extent that they are measured at net realisable value in accordance with well established practices in certain industries.

2–3 [Not printed]

Definitions

4 ...

 <u>Inventories</u> are assets:

 (a) held for sale in the ordinary course of business;

 (b) in the process of production for such sale; or

 (c) in the form of materials or supplies to be consumed in the production process or in the rendering of services.

 <u>Net realisable value</u> is the estimated selling price in the ordinary course of business less the estimated costs of completion and the estimated costs necessary to make the sale.

5 [Not printed]

Measurement of Inventories

6 *Inventories should be measured at the lower of cost and net realisable value.*

Cost of Inventories

7 *The cost of inventories should comprise all costs of purchase, costs of conversion and other costs incurred in bringing the inventories to their present location and condition.*

Costs of Purchase

8 The costs of purchase of inventories comprise the purchase price, import duties and other taxes (other than those subsequently recoverable by the enterprise from the taxing authorities), and transport, handling and other costs directly attributable to the acquisition of finished goods, materials and services. Trade discounts, rebates and other similar items are deducted in determining the costs of purchase.

9 The costs of purchase may include foreign exchange differences which arise directly on the recent acquisition of inventories invoiced in a foreign currency in the rare circumstances permitted in the allowed alternative treatment in IAS 21. These exchange differences are limited to those resulting from a severe devaluation or depreciation of a currency against which there is no practical means of hedging and that affects liabilities which cannot be settled and which arise on the recent acquisition of the inventories.

Costs of Conversion

The costs of conversion of inventories include costs directly related to the units of **10** production, such as direct labour. They also include a systematic allocation of fixed and variable production overheads that are incurred in converting materials into finished goods. Fixed production overheads are those indirect costs of production that remain relatively constant regardless of the volume of production, such as depreciation and maintenance of factory buildings and equipment, and the cost of factory management and administration. Variable production overheads are those indirect costs of production that vary directly, or nearly directly, with the volume of production, such as indirect materials and indirect labour.

The allocation of fixed production overheads to the costs of conversion is based on the **11** normal capacity of the production facilities. Normal capacity is the production expected to be achieved on average over a number of periods or seasons under normal circumstances, taking into account the loss of capacity resulting from planned maintenance. The actual level of production may be used if it approximates normal capacity. The amount of fixed overhead allocated to each unit of production is not increased as a consequence of low production or idle plant. Unallocated overheads are recognised as an expense in the period in which they are incurred. In periods of abnormally high production, the amount of fixed overhead allocated to each unit of production is decreased so that inventories are not measured above cost. Variable production overheads are allocated to each unit of production on the basis of the actual use of the production facilities.

A production process may result in more than one product being produced **12** simultaneously. This is the case, for example, when joint products are produced or when there is a main product and a by–product. When the costs of conversion of each product are not separately identifiable, they are allocated between the products on a rational and consistent basis. The allocation may be based, for example, on the relative sales value of each product either at the stage in the production process when the products become separately identifiable, or at the completion of production. Most by–products, by their nature, are immaterial. When this is the case, they are often measured at net realisable value and this value is deducted from the cost of the main product. As a result, the carrying amount of the main product is not materially different from its cost.

Other Costs

Other costs are included in the cost of inventories only to the extent that they are **13** incurred in bringing the inventories to their present location and condition. For example, it may be appropriate to include non–production overheads or the costs of designing products for specific customers in the cost of inventories.

Examples of costs excluded from the cost of inventories and recognised as expenses in **14** the period in which they are incurred are:
(a) abnormal amounts of wasted materials, labour, or other production costs;
(b) storage costs, unless those costs are necessary in the production process prior to a further production stage;
(c) administrative overheads that do not contribute to bringing inventories to their present location and condition; and
(d) selling costs.

15 [Not printed]

Cost of Inventories of a Service Provider

16 The cost of inventories of a service provider consists primarily of the labour and other costs of personnel directly engaged in providing the service, including supervisory personnel, and attributable overheads. Labour and other costs relating to sales and general administrative personnel are not included but are recognised as expenses in the period in which they are incurred.

Cost of Agricultural Produce Harvested from Biological Assets

16A Under IAS 41 inventories comprising agricultural produce that an enterprise has harvested from its biological assets are measured on initial recognition at their fair value less estimated point–of–sale costs at the point of harvest. This is the cost of the inventories at that date for application of this Standard.

Techniques for the Measurement of Cost

17 Techniques for the measurement of the cost of inventories, such as the standard cost method or the retail method, may be used for convenience if the results approximate cost. Standard costs take into account normal levels of materials and supplies, labour, efficiency and capacity utilisation. They are regularly reviewed and, if necessary, revised in the light of current conditions.

18 The retail method is often used in the retail industry for measuring inventories of large numbers of rapidly changing items, that have similar margins and for which it is impracticable to use other costing methods. The cost of the inventory is determined by reducing the sales value of the inventory by the appropriate percentage gross margin. The percentage used takes into consideration inventory which has been marked down to below its original selling price. An average percentage for each retail department is often used.

Cost Formulas

19 *The cost of inventories of items that are not ordinarily interchangeable and goods or services produced and segregated for specific projects should be assigned by using specific identification of their individual costs.*

20 Specific identification of cost means that specific costs are attributed to identified items of inventory. This is an appropriate treatment for items that are segregated for a specific project, regardless of whether they have been bought or produced. However, specific identification of costs is inappropriate when there are large numbers of items of inventory which are ordinarily interchangeable. In such circumstances, the method of selecting those items that remain in inventories could be used to obtain predetermined effects on the net profit or loss for the period.

Benchmark Treatment

21 *The cost of inventories, other than those dealt with in paragraph 19, should be assigned by using the first–in, first–out (FIFO) or weighted average cost formulas.*

22 The FIFO formula assumes that the items of inventory which were purchased first are sold first, and consequently the items remaining in inventory at the end of the period are those most recently purchased or produced. Under the weighted average cost formula, the cost of each item is determined from the weighted average of the cost of similar items at the beginning of a period and the cost of similar items purchased or produced during the period. The average may be calculated on a periodic basis, or as each additional shipment is received, depending upon the circumstances of the enterprise.

Allowed Alternative Treatment

The cost of inventories, other than those dealt with in paragraph 19, should be **23** *assigned by using the last–in, first–out (LIFO) formula.*

The LIFO formula assumes that the items of inventory which were purchased or **24** produced last are sold first, and consequently the items remaining in inventory at the end of the period are those first purchased or produced.

Net Realisable Value

The cost of inventories may not be recoverable if those inventories are damaged, if they **25** have become wholly or partially obsolete, or if their selling prices have declined. The cost of inventories may also not be recoverable if the estimated costs of completion or the estimated costs to be incurred to make the sale have increased. The practice of writing inventories down below cost to net realisable value is consistent with the view that assets should not be carried in excess of amounts expected to be realised from their sale or use.

[Not printed] **26–29**

A new assessment is made of net realisable value in each subsequent period. When the **30** circumstances which previously caused inventories to be written down below cost no longer exist, the amount of the write–down is reversed so that the new carrying amount is the lower of the cost and the revised net realisable value. ...

Recognition as an Expense

When inventories are sold, the carrying amount of those inventories should be **31** *recognised as an expense in the period in which the related revenue is recognised. The amount of any write–down of inventories to net realisable value and all losses of inventories should be recognised as an expense in the period the write–down or loss occurs. The amount of any reversal of any write–down of inventories, arising from an increase in net realisable value, should be recognised as a reduction in the amount of inventories recognised as an expense in the period in which the reversal occurs.*

[Not printed] **32–33**

Disclosure

The financial statements should disclose: **34**
(a) the accounting policies adopted in measuring inventories, including the cost formula used;
(b) the total carrying amount of inventories and the carrying amount in classifications appropriate to the enterprise;
(c) the carrying amount of inventories carried at net realisable value;
(d) the amount of any reversal of any write–down that is recognised as income in the period in accordance with paragraph 31;

(e) the circumstances or events that led to the reversal of a write–down of inventories in accordance with paragraph 31; and

(f) the carrying amount of inventories pledged as security for liabilities.

35 [Not printed]

36 When the cost of inventories is determined using the LIFO formula in accordance with the allowed alternative treatment in paragraph 23, the financial statements should disclose the difference between the amount of inventories as shown in the balance sheet and either:

(a) the lower of the amount arrived at in accordance with paragraph 21 and net realisable value; or

(b) the lower of current cost at the balance sheet date and net realisable value.

37 The financial statements should disclose either:

(a) the cost of inventories recognised as an expense during the period; or

(b) the operating costs, applicable to revenues, recognised as an expense during the period, classified by their nature.

38–40 [Not printed]

Effective Date

41 *[Not printed]*

IAS 7: Cash Flow Statements

IAS 7: Cash Flow Statements			
Scope 7.1–3	Benefits of Cash Flow Information 7.4–5	Definitions 7.6–9	Effective Date 7.53

Presentation of a Cash Flow Statement 7.10–17		
Operating Activities 7.13–15	Investing Activities 7.16	Financing Activities 7.17

Reporting Cash Flows 7.18–47							
General		**Specifics**					
Reporting Cash Flows from Operating Activities 7.18–20	Reporting Cash Flows from Investing and Financing Activities 7.21	Foreign Currency Cash Flows 7.25–28	Extraordinary Items 7.29–30	Interest and Dividends 7.31–34	Taxes on Income 7.35–36	Investments in Subsidiaries, Associates and Joint Ventures 7.37–38	Acquisitions and Disposals of Subsidiaries and Other Business Units 7.39–42
Reporting Cash Flows on a Net Basis 7.22–24							
Non–Cash Transactions 7.43–44							
Components of Cash and Cash Equivalents 7.45–47							

Other Disclosures 7.48–52

Appendices [Partially not printed]	
Cash Flow Statement for an Enterprise other than a Financial Institution	Cash Flow Statement for a Financial Institution

Scope

An enterprise should prepare a cash flow statement in accordance with the require-   **1**
ments of this Standard and should present it as an integral part of its financial state-
ments for each period for which financial statements are presented.

[Not printed]   **2**

Users of an enterprise's financial statements are interested in how the enterprise   **3**
generates and uses cash and cash equivalents. This is the case regardless of the nature
of the enterprise's activities and irrespective of whether cash can be viewed as the

product of the enterprise, as may be the case with a financial institution. Enterprises need cash for essentially the same reasons however different their principal revenue–producing activities might be. They need cash to conduct their operations, to pay their obligations, and to provide returns to their investors. Accordingly, this Standard requires all enterprises to present a cash flow statement.

Benefits of Cash Flow Information

4   A cash flow statement, when used in conjunction with the rest of the financial statements, provides information that enables users to evaluate the changes in net assets of an enterprise, its financial structure (including its liquidity and solvency) and its ability to affect the amounts and timing of cash flows in order to adapt to changing circumstances and opportunities. Cash flow information is useful in assessing the ability of the enterprise to generate cash and cash equivalents and enables users to develop models to assess and compare the present value of the future cash flows of different enterprises. It also enhances the comparability of the reporting of operating performance by different enterprises because it eliminates the effects of using different accounting treatments for the same transactions and events.

5   Historical cash flow information is often used as an indicator of the amount, timing and certainty of future cash flows. It is also useful in checking the accuracy of past assessments of future cash flows and in examining the relationship between profitability and net cash flow and the impact of changing prices.

Definitions

6   ...
Cash comprises cash on hand and demand deposits.
Cash equivalents are short–term, highly liquid investments that are readily convertible to known amounts of cash and which are subject to an insignificant risk of changes in value.
Cash flows are inflows and outflows of cash and cash equivalents.
Operating activities are the principal revenue–producing activities of the enterprise and other activities that are not investing or financing activities.
Investing activities are the acquisition and disposal of long–term assets and other investments not included in cash equivalents.
Financing activities are activities that result in changes in the size and composition of the equity capital and borrowings of the enterprise.

Cash and Cash Equivalents

7   Cash equivalents are held for the purpose of meeting short–term cash commitments rather than for investment or other purposes. For an investment to qualify as a cash equivalent it must be readily convertible to a known amount of cash and be subject to an insignificant risk of changes in value. Therefore, an investment normally qualifies as a cash equivalent only when it has a short maturity of, say, three months or less from the date of acquisition. Equity investments are excluded from cash equivalents unless they are, in substance, cash equivalents, ...

8   Bank borrowings are generally considered to be financing activities. However, in some countries, bank overdrafts which are repayable on demand form an integral part of an

enterprise's cash management. In these circumstances, bank overdrafts are included as a component of cash and cash equivalents. A characteristic of such banking arrangements is that the bank balance often fluctuates from being positive to overdrawn.

Cash flows exclude movements between items that constitute cash or cash equivalents **9** because these components are part of the cash management of an enterprise rather than part of its operating, investing and financing activities. Cash management includes the investment of excess cash in cash equivalents.

Presentation of a Cash Flow Statement

The cash flow statement should report cash flows during the period classified by **10** *operating, investing and financing activities.*

[Not printed] **11**

A single transaction may include cash flows that are classified differently. For example, **12** when the cash repayment of a loan includes both interest and capital, the interest element may be classified as an operating activity and the capital element is classified as a financing activity.

Operating Activities

The amount of cash flows arising from operating activities is a key indicator of the **13** extent to which the operations of the enterprise have generated sufficient cash flows to repay loans, maintain the operating capability of the enterprise, pay dividends and make new investments without recourse to external sources of financing. ...

Cash flows from operating activities are primarily derived from the principal revenue- **14** producing activities of the enterprise. Therefore, they generally result from the transactions and other events that enter into the determination of net profit or loss. Examples of cash flows from operating activities are:
(a) cash receipts from the sale of goods and the rendering of services;
(b) cash receipts from royalties, fees, commissions and other revenue;
(c) cash payments to suppliers for goods and services;
(d) cash payments to and on behalf of employees;
(e) cash receipts and cash payments of an insurance enterprise for premiums and claims, annuities and other policy benefits;
(f) cash payments or refunds of income taxes unless they can be specifically identified with financing and investing activities; and
(g) cash receipts and payments from contracts held for dealing or trading purposes.
...

[Not printed] **15**

Investing Activities

The separate disclosure of cash flows arising from investing activities is important **16** because the cash flows represent the extent to which expenditures have been made for resources intended to generate future income and cash flows. Examples of cash flows arising from investing activities are:

(a) cash payments to acquire property, plant and equipment, intangibles and other long–term assets. These payments include those relating to capitalised development costs and self–constructed property, plant and equipment;

(b) cash receipts from sales of property, plant and equipment, intangibles and other long–term assets;

(c) cash payments to acquire equity or debt instruments of other enterprises and interests in joint ventures (other than payments for those instruments considered to be cash equivalents or those held for dealing or trading purposes);

(d) cash receipts from sales of equity or debt instruments of other enterprises and interests in joint ventures (other than receipts for those instruments considered to be cash equivalents and those held for dealing or trading purposes);

(e) cash advances and loans made to other parties (other than advances and loans made by a financial institution);

(f) cash receipts from the repayment of advances and loans made to other parties (other than advances and loans of a financial institution);

(g) cash payments for futures contracts, forward contracts, option contracts and swap contracts except when the contracts are held for dealing or trading purposes, or the payments are classified as financing activities; and

(h) cash receipts from futures contracts, forward contracts, option contracts and swap contracts except when the contracts are held for dealing or trading purposes, or the receipts are classified as financing activities.

...

Financing Activities

17 The separate disclosure of cash flows arising from financing activities is important because it is useful in predicting claims on future cash flows by providers of capital to the enterprise. Examples of cash flows arising from financing activities are:

(a) cash proceeds from issuing shares or other equity instruments;

(b) cash payments to owners to acquire or redeem the enterprise's shares;

(c) cash proceeds from issuing debentures, loans, notes, bonds, mortgages and other short or long–term borrowings;

(d) cash repayments of amounts borrowed; and

(e) cash payments by a lessee for the reduction of the outstanding liability relating to a finance lease.

Reporting Cash Flows from Operating Activities

18 *An enterprise should report cash flows from operating activities using either:*

(a) the direct method, whereby major classes of gross cash receipts and gross cash payments are disclosed; or

(b) the indirect method, whereby net profit or loss is adjusted for the effects of transactions of a non–cash nature, any deferrals or accruals of past or future operating cash receipts or payments, and items of income or expense associated with investing or financing cash flows.

19 Enterprises are encouraged to report cash flows from operating activities using the direct method. The direct method provides information which may be useful in estimating future cash flows and which is not available under the indirect method. Under the direct method, information about major classes of gross cash receipts and gross cash payments may be obtained either:

(a) from the accounting records of the enterprise; or

(b) by adjusting sales, cost of sales (interest and similar income and interest expense and similar charges for a financial institution) and other items in the income statement for:

    (i) changes during the period in inventories and operating receivables and payables;

    (ii) other non–cash items; and

    (iii) other items for which the cash effects are investing or financing cash flows.

Under the indirect method, the net cash flow from operating activities is determined **20** by adjusting net profit or loss for the effects of:

(a) changes during the period in inventories and operating receivables and payables;

(b) non–cash items such as depreciation, provisions, deferred taxes, unrealised foreign currency gains and losses, undistributed profits of associates, and minority interests; and

(c) all other items for which the cash effects are investing or financing cash flows.

Alternatively, the net cash flow from operating activities may be presented under the indirect method by showing the revenues and expenses disclosed in the income statement and the changes during the period in inventories and operating receivables and payables.

Reporting Cash Flows from Investing and Financing Activities

An enterprise should report separately major classes of gross cash receipts and gross **21** *cash payments arising from investing and financing activities, except to the extent that cash flows described in paragraphs 22 and 24 are reported on a net basis.*

Reporting Cash Flows on a Net Basis

Cash flows arising from the following operating, investing or financing activities may **22** *be reported on a net basis:*

(a) cash receipts and payments on behalf of customers when the cash flows reflect the activities of the customer rather than those of the enterprise; and

(b) cash receipts and payments for items in which the turnover is quick, the amounts are large, and the maturities are short.

Examples of cash receipts and payments referred to in paragraph 22(a) are: **23**

(a) the acceptance and repayment of demand deposits of a bank;

(b) funds held for customers by an investment enterprise; and

(c) rents collected on behalf of, and paid over to, the owners of properties.

Examples of cash receipts and payments referred to in paragraph 22(b) are advances made for, and the repayment of:

(a) principal amounts relating to credit card customers;

(b) the purchase and sale of investments; and

(c) other short–term borrowings, for example, those which have a maturity period of three months or less.

Cash flows arising from each of the following activities of a financial institution may **24** *be reported on a net basis:*

(a) cash receipts and payments for the acceptance and repayment of deposits with a fixed maturity date;

(b) the placement of deposits with and withdrawal of deposits from other financial institutions; and

(c) cash advances and loans made to customers and the repayment of those advances and loans.

Foreign Currency Cash Flows

25 *Cash flows arising from transactions in a foreign currency should be recorded in an enterprise's reporting currency by applying to the foreign currency amount the exchange rate between the reporting currency and the foreign currency at the date of the cash flow.*

26 *The cash flows of a foreign subsidiary should be translated at the exchange rates between the reporting currency and the foreign currency at the dates of the cash flows.*

27 Cash flows denominated in a foreign currency are reported in a manner consistent with IAS 21. This permits the use of an exchange rate that approximates the actual rate. ...

28 Unrealised gains and losses arising from changes in foreign currency exchange rates are not cash flows. However, the effect of exchange rate changes on cash and cash equivalents held or due in a foreign currency is reported in the cash flow statement in order to reconcile cash and cash equivalents at the beginning and the end of the period. This amount is presented separately from cash flows from operating, investing and financing activities and includes the differences, if any, had those cash flows been reported at end of period exchange rates.

Extraordinary Items

29 *The cash flows associated with extraordinary items should be classified as arising from operating, investing or financing activities as appropriate and separately disclosed.*

30 [Not printed]

Interest and Dividends

31 *Cash flows from interest and dividends received and paid should each be disclosed separately. Each should be classified in a consistent manner from period to period as either operating, investing or financing activities.*

32 The total amount of interest paid during a period is disclosed in the cash flow statement whether it has been recognised as an expense in the income statement or capitalised in accordance with the allowed alternative treatment in IAS 23.

33 Interest paid and interest and dividends received are usually classified as operating cash flows for a financial institution. However, there is no consensus on the classification of these cash flows for other enterprises. Interest paid and interest and dividends received may be classified as operating cash flows because they enter into the determination of net profit or loss. Alternatively, interest paid and interest and dividends received may be classified as financing cash flows and investing cash flows respectively, because they are costs of obtaining financial resources or returns on investments.

Dividends paid may be classified as a financing cash flow because they are a cost of **34** obtaining financial resources. Alternatively, dividends paid may be classified as a component of cash flows from operating activities in order to assist users to determine the ability of an enterprise to pay dividends out of operating cash flows.

Taxes on Income

Cash flows arising from taxes on income should be separately disclosed and should **35** *be classified as cash flows from operating activities unless they can be specifically identified with financing and investing activities.*

[Not printed] **36**

Investments in Subsidiaries, Associates and Joint Ventures

When accounting for an investment in an associate or a subsidiary accounted for by **37** use of the equity or cost method, an investor restricts its reporting in the cash flow statement to the cash flows between itself and the investee, for example, to dividends and advances.

An enterprise which reports its interest in a jointly controlled entity (see IAS 31) using **38** proportionate consolidation, includes in its consolidated cash flow statement its proportionate share of the jointly controlled entity's cash flows. An enterprise which reports such an interest using the equity method includes in its cash flow statement the cash flows in respect of its investments in the jointly controlled entity, and distributions and other payments or receipts between it and the jointly controlled entity.

Acquisitions and Disposals of Subsidiaries and Other Business Units

The aggregate cash flows arising from acquisitions and from disposals of subsidiaries **39** *or other business units should be presented separately and classified as investing activities.*

An enterprise should disclose, in aggregate, in respect of both acquisitions and **40** *disposals of subsidiaries or other business units during the period each of the following:*
(a) the total purchase or disposal consideration;
(b) the portion of the purchase or disposal consideration discharged by means of cash and cash equivalents;
(c) the amount of cash and cash equivalents in the subsidiary or business unit acquired or disposed of; and
(d) the amount of the assets and liabilities other than cash or cash equivalents in the subsidiary or business unit acquired or disposed of, summarised by each major category.

[Not printed] **41**

The aggregate amount of the cash paid or received as purchase or sale consideration is **42** reported in the cash flow statement net of cash and cash equivalents acquired or disposed of.

Non–cash Transactions

43 *Investing and financing transactions that do not require the use of cash or cash equivalents should be excluded from a cash flow statement. Such transactions should be disclosed elsewhere in the financial statements in a way that provides all the relevant information about these investing and financing activities.*

44 Many investing and financing activities do not have a direct impact on current cash flows although they do affect the capital and asset structure of an enterprise. The exclusion of non–cash transactions from the cash flow statement is consistent with the objective of a cash flow statement as these items do not involve cash flows in the current period. Examples of non–cash transactions are:
   (a) the acquisition of assets either by assuming directly related liabilities or by means of a finance lease;
   (b) the acquisition of an enterprise by means of an equity issue; and
   (c) the conversion of debt to equity.

Components of Cash and Cash Equivalents

45 *An enterprise should disclose the components of cash and cash equivalents and should present a reconciliation of the amounts in its cash flow statement with the equivalent items reported in the balance sheet.*

46–47 [Not printed]

Other Disclosures

48 *An enterprise should disclose, together with a commentary by management, the amount of significant cash and cash equivalent balances held by the enterprise that are not available for use by the group.*

49–52 [Not printed]

Effective Date

53 *[Not printed]*

Appendix A

Cash Flow Statement for an Enterprise other than a Financial Institution

...

1 The examples show only current period amounts. Corresponding amounts for the preceding period are required to be presented in accordance with IAS 1.

2 Information from the income statement and balance sheet is provided to show how the statements of cash flows under the direct method and indirect method have been derived. Neither the income statement nor the balance sheet are presented in conformity with the disclosure and presentation requirements of IASs.

3 The following additional information is also relevant for the preparation of the statements of cash flows:

- all of the shares of a subsidiary were acquired for 590. The fair values of assets acquired and liabilities assumed were as follows:

inventories	100
accounts receivable	100
cash	40
property, plant and equipment	650
trade payables	100
long–term debt	200

- 250 was raised from the issue of share capital and a further 250 was raised from long–term borrowings.
- interest expense was 400 of which 170 was paid during the period. 100 relating to interest expense of the prior period was also paid during the period.
- dividends paid were 1,200.
- the liability for tax at the beginning and end of the period was 1,000 and 400 respectively. During the period, a further 200 tax was provided for. Withholding tax on dividends received amounted to 100.
- during the period, the group acquired property, plant and equipment with an aggregate cost of 1,250 of which 900 was acquired by means of finance leases. Cash payments of 350 were made to purchase property, plant and equipment.
- plant with original cost of 80 and accumulated depreciation of 60 was sold for 20.
- accounts receivable as at end of 19–2 include 100 of interest receivable.

Consolidated Income Statement for the period ended 19–2

Sales	30,650
Cost of sales	(26,000)
Gross profit	4,650
Depreciation	(450)
Administrative and selling expenses	(910)
Interest expense	(400)
Investment income	500
Foreign exchange loss	(40)
Net profit before taxation and extraordinary item	3,350
Extraordinary item – Insurance proceeds from earthquake disaster settlement	180
Net profit after extraordinary item	3,530
Taxes on income	(300)
Net profit	3,230

Consolidated Balance Sheet as at end of 19–2

		19–2		19–1
Assets				
Cash and cash equivalents		410		160
Accounts receivable		1,900		1,200
Inventory		1,000		1,950
Portfolio investments		2,500		2,500
Property, plant and equipment at cost	3,730		1,910	
Accumulated depreciation	(1,450)		(1,060)	
Property, plant and equipment net		2,280		850
Total assets		8,090		6,660
Liabilities				
Trade payables		250		1,890
Interest payable		230		100
Income taxes payable		400		1,000
Long term debt		2,300		1,040
Total liabilities		3,180		4,030
Shareholders' Equity				
Share capital		1,500		1,250
Retained earnings		3,410		1,380
Total shareholders equity		4,910		2,630
Total liabilities and shareholders equity		8,090		6,660

Direct Method Cash Flow Statement (paragraph 18a)

		19–2
Cash flows from operating activities		
Cash receipts from customers	30,150	
Cash paid to suppliers and employees	(27,600)	
Cash generated from operations	2,550	
Interest paid	(270)	
Income taxes paid	(900)	
Cash flow before extraordinary item	1,380	
Proceeds from earthquake disaster settlement	180	
Net cash from operating activities		1,560
Cash flows from investing activities		
Acquisition of subsidiary X, net of cash acquired (Note A)	(550)	
Purchase of property, plant and equipment (Note B)	(350)	
Proceeds from sale of equipment	20	
Interest received	200	
Dividends received	200	
Net cash used in investing activities		(480)
Cash flows from financing activities		
Proceeds from issuance of share capital	250	
Proceeds from long–term borrowings	250	
Payment of finance lease liabilities	(90)	
Dividends paid*	(1,200)	
Net cash used in financing activities		(790)
Net increase in cash and cash equivalents		290
Cash and cash equivalents at beginning of period (note C)		120
Cash and cash equivalents at end of period (note C)		410

*This could also be shown as an operating cash flow.

Indirect Method Cash Flow Statement (paragraph 18b)

	19–2	
Cash flows from operating activities		
Net profit before taxation, and extraordinary item.	3,350	
Adjustments for:		
Depreciation	450	
Foreign exchange loss	40	
Investment income	(500)	
Interest expense	400	
	3,740	
Increase in trade and other receivables	(500)	
Decrease in inventories	1,050	
Decrease in trade payables	(1,740)	
Cash generated from operations	2,550	
Interest paid	(270)	
Income taxes paid	(900)	
Cash flow before extraordinary item	1,380	
Proceeds from earthquake disaster settlement	180	
Net cash from operating activities		1,560
Cash flows from investing activities		
Acquisition of subsidiary X net of cash acquired	(550)	
(Note A)		
Purchase of property, plant and equipment (Note B)	(350)	
Proceeds from sale of equipment	20	
Interest received	200	
Dividends received	200	
Net cash used in investing activities		(480)
Cash flows from financing activities		
Proceeds from issuance of share capital	250	
Proceeds from long–term borrowings	250	
Payment of finance lease liabilities	(90)	
Dividends paid*	(1,200)	
Net cash used in financing activities		(790)
Net increase in cash and cash equivalents		290
Cash and cash equivalent at beginning of period (Note C)		120
Cash and cash equivalent at end of period (Note C)		
*This could also be shown as an operating cash flow.		410

Notes to the Cash Flow Statement
(direct method and indirect method)

A Acquisition of Subsidiary

During the period the group acquired subsidiary X. The fair value of assets acquired and liabilities assumed were as follows:

Cash	40
Inventories	100
Accounts receivable	100
Property, plant and equipment	650
Trade payables	(100)
Long–term debt	(200)
Total purchase price	590
Less: Cash of X	(40)
Cash flow on acquisition net of cash acquired	550

B Property, Plant and Equipment

During the period, the Group acquired property, plant and equipment with an aggregate cost of 1,250 of which 900 was acquired by means of finance leases. Cash payments of 350 were made to purchase property, plant and equipment.

C Cash and Cash Equivalents

Cash and cash equivalents consist of cash on hand and balances with banks, and investments in money market instruments. Cash and cash equivalents included in the cash flow statement comprise the following balance sheet amounts:

	19–2	19–1
Cash on hand and balances with banks	40	25
Short–term investments	370	135
Cash and cash equivalents as previously reported	410	160
Effect of exchange rate changes	–	(40)
Cash and cash equivalents as restated	410	120

Cash and cash equivalents at the end of the period include deposits with banks of 100 held by a subsidiary which are not freely remissible to the holding company because of currency exchange restrictions.

The Group has undrawn borrowing facilities of 2,000 of which 700 may be used only for future expansion.

D Segment Information

	Segment A	Segment B	Total
Cash flows from:			
Operating activities	1,700	(140)	1,560
Investing activities	(640)	160	(480)
Financing activities	(570)	(220)	(790)
	490	(200)	290

Alternative Presentation
(indirect method)

As an alternative, in an indirect method cash flow statement, operating profit before working capital changes is sometimes presented as follows:

Revenues excluding investment income	30,650	
Operating expense excluding depreciation	(26,910)	
Operating profit before working capital changes		3,740

Appendix B

Cash Flow Statement for a Financial Institution

[Not printed]

IAS 8: Net Profit or Loss for the Period, Fundamental Errors and Changes in Accounting Policies

IAS 8: Net Profit or Loss for the Period, Fundamental Errors and Changes in Accounting Policies		
Scope 8.1–5	Definitions 8.6	Effective Date 8.58

Net Profit or Loss for the Period 8.7–30		
Extraordinary Items 8.11–15	Profit or Loss from Ordinary Activities 8.16–18	Changes in Accounting Estimates 8.23–30

Fundamental Errors 8.31–40	
Benchmark Treatment 8.34–37	Allowed Alternative Treatment 8.38–40

Changes in Accounting Policy 8.41–57		
Adoption of an International Accounting Standard 8.46–48	Other Changes in Accounting Policies– Benchmark Treatment 8.49–53	Other Changes in Accounting Policies–Allowed Alternative Treatment 8.54–57

Appendix [Not printed]		
Extraordinary Items and Discontinued Operations	Fundamental Errors	Changes in Accounting Policy

Scope

This Standard should be applied in presenting profit or loss from ordinary activities　**1**
and extraordinary items in the income statement and in accounting for changes in
accounting estimates, fundamental errors and changes in accounting policies.

[Not printed]　**2**

This Standard deals with, among other things, the disclosure of certain items of net　**3**
profit or loss for the period. These disclosures are made in addition to any other
disclosures required by other IASs, including IAS 1.

[Deleted]　**4**

[Not printed]　**5**

Definitions

6 ...

Extraordinary items are income or expenses that arise from events or transactions that are clearly distinct from the ordinary activities of the enterprise and therefore are not expected to recur frequently or regularly.

Ordinary activities are any activities which are undertaken by an enterprise as part of its business and such related activities in which the enterprise engages in furtherance of, incidental to, or arising from these activities.

Fundamental errors are errors discovered in the current period that are of such significance that the financial statements of one or more prior periods can no longer be considered to have been reliable at the date of their issue.

Accounting policies are the specific principles, bases, conventions, rules and practices adopted by an enterprise in preparing and presenting financial statements.

Net Profit or Loss for the Period

7 *All items of income and expense recognised in a period should be included in the determination of the net profit or loss for the period unless an IAS requires or permits otherwise.*

8 Normally, all items of income and expense recognised in a period are included in the determination of the net profit or loss for the period. This includes extraordinary items and the effects of changes in accounting estimates. However, circumstances may exist when certain items may be excluded from net profit or loss for the current period. This Standard deals with two such circumstances: the correction of fundamental errors and the effect of changes in accounting policies.

9 Other IASs deal with items which may meet the Framework definitions of income or expense but which are usually excluded from the determination of the net profit or loss. Examples include revaluation surpluses (see IAS 16) and gains and losses arising on the translation of the financial statements of a foreign entity (see IAS 21).

10 *The net profit or loss for the period comprises the following components, each of which should be disclosed on the face of the income statement:*
(a) profit or loss from ordinary activities; and
(b) extraordinary items.

Extraordinary Items

11 *The nature and the amount of each extraordinary item should be separately disclosed.*

12 [Not printed]

13 Whether an event or transaction is clearly distinct from the ordinary activities of the enterprise is determined by the nature of the event or transaction in relation to the business ordinarily carried on by the enterprise rather than by the frequency with which such events are expected to occur. Therefore, an event or transaction may be extraordinary for one enterprise but not extraordinary for another enterprise because of the differences between their respective ordinary activities. ...

14 Examples of events or transactions that generally give rise to extraordinary items for most enterprises are:

(a) the expropriation of assets; or

(b) an earthquake or other natural disaster.

The disclosure of the nature and amount of each extraordinary item may be made on **15** the face of the income statement, or when this disclosure is made in the notes to the financial statements, the total amount of all extraordinary items is disclosed on the face of the income statement.

Profit or Loss from Ordinary Activities

When items of income and expense within profit or loss from ordinary activities are **16** *of such size, nature or incidence that their disclosure is relevant to explain the performance of the enterprise for the period, the nature and amount of such items should be disclosed separately.*

[Not printed] **17**

Circumstances which may give rise to the separate disclosure of items of income and **18** expense in accordance with paragraph 16 include:

(a) the write–down of inventories to net realisable value or property, plant and equipment to recoverable amount, as well as the reversal of such write–downs;

(b) a restructuring of the activities of an enterprise and the reversal of any provisions for the costs of restructuring;

(c) disposals of items of property, plant and equipment;

(d) disposals of long–term investments;

(e) discontinued operations;

(f) litigation settlements; and

(g) other reversals of provisions.

[Deleted – see IAS 35] **19–22**

Changes in Accounting Estimates

As a result of the uncertainties inherent in business activities, many financial statement **23** items cannot be measured with precision but can only be estimated. The estimation process involves judgements based on the latest information available. Estimates may be required, for example, of bad debts, inventory obsolescence or the useful lives or expected pattern of consumption of economic benefits of depreciable assets. The use of reasonable estimates is an essential part of the preparation of financial statements and does not undermine their reliability.

An estimate may have to be revised if changes occur regarding the circumstances on **24** which the estimate was based or as a result of new information, more experience or subsequent developments. By its nature, the revision of the estimate does not bring the adjustment within the definitions of an extraordinary item or a fundamental error.

Sometimes it is difficult to distinguish between a change in accounting policy and a **25** change in an accounting estimate. In such cases, the change is treated as a change in an accounting estimate, with appropriate disclosure.

The effect of a change in an accounting estimate should be included in the **26** *determination of net profit or loss in:*

(a) the period of the change, if the change affects the period only; or

(b) the period of the change and future periods, if the change affects both.

27 [Not printed]

28 *The effect of a change in an accounting estimate should be included in the same income statement classification as was used previously for the estimate.*

29 [Not printed]

30 *The nature and amount of a change in an accounting estimate that has a material effect in the current period or which is expected to have a material effect in subsequent periods should be disclosed. If it is impracticable to quantify the amount, this fact should be disclosed.*

Fundamental Errors

31 Errors in the preparation of the financial statements of one or more prior periods may be discovered in the current period. Errors may occur as a result of mathematical mistakes, mistakes in applying accounting policies, misinterpretation of facts, fraud or oversights. The correction of these errors is normally included in the determination of net profit or loss for the current period.

32 On rare occasions, an error has such a significant effect on the financial statements of one or more prior periods that those financial statements can no longer be considered to have been reliable at the date of their issue. These errors are referred to as fundamental errors. An example of a fundamental error is the inclusion in the financial statements of a previous period of material amounts of work in progress and receivables in respect of fraudulent contracts which cannot be enforced. The correction of fundamental errors that relate to prior periods requires the restatement of the comparative information or the presentation of additional pro forma information.

33 The correction of fundamental errors can be distinguished from changes in accounting estimates. Accounting estimates by their nature are approximations that may need revision as additional information becomes known. For example, the gain or loss recognised on the outcome of a contingency which previously could not be estimated reliably does not constitute the correction of a fundamental error.

Benchmark Treatment

34 *The amount of the correction of a fundamental error that relates to prior periods should be reported by adjusting the opening balance of retained earnings. Comparative information should be restated, unless it is impracticable to do so.*

35 The financial statements, including the comparative information for prior periods, are presented as if the fundamental error had been corrected in the period in which it was made. Therefore, the amount of the correction that relates to each period presented is included within the net profit or loss for that period. The amount of the correction relating to periods prior to those included in the comparative information in the financial statements is adjusted against the opening balance of retained earnings in the earliest period presented. Any other information reported with respect to prior periods, such as historical summaries of financial data, is also restated.

36 The restatement of comparative information does not necessarily give rise to the amendment of financial statements which have been approved by shareholders or registered or filed with regulatory authorities. However, national laws may require the amendment of such financial statements.

An enterprise should disclose the following: **37**
(a) the nature of the fundamental error;
(b) the amount of the correction for the current period and for each prior period presented;
(c) the amount of the correction relating to periods prior to those included in the comparative information; and
(d) the fact that comparative information has been restated or that it is impracticable to do so.

Allowed Alternative Treatment

The amount of the correction of a fundamental error should be included in the **38**
determination of net profit or loss for the current period. Comparative information should be presented as reported in the financial statements of the prior period. Additional pro forma information, prepared in accordance with paragraph 34, should be presented unless it is impracticable to do so.

[Not printed] **39**

An enterprise should disclose the following: **40**
(a) the nature of the fundamental error;
(b) the amount of the correction recognised in net profit or loss for the current period; and
(c) the amount of the correction included in each period for which pro forma information is presented and the amount of the correction relating to periods prior to those included in the pro forma information. If it is impracticable to present pro forma information, this fact should be disclosed.

Changes in Accounting Policies

Users need to be able to compare the financial statements of an enterprise over a period **41**
of time to identify trends in its financial position, performance and cash flows.
Therefore, the same accounting policies are normally adopted in each period.

A change in accounting policy should be made only if required by statute, or by an **42**
accounting standard setting body, or if the change will result in a more appropriate presentation of events or transactions in the financial statements of the enterprise.

[Not printed] **43**

The following are not changes in accounting policies: **44**
(a) the adoption of an accounting policy for events or transactions that differ in substance from previously occurring events or transactions; and
(b) the adoption of a new accounting policy for events or transactions which did not occur previously or that were immaterial. ...

A change in accounting policy is applied retrospectively or prospectively in accordance **45**
with the requirements of this Standard. Retrospective application results in the new
accounting policy being applied to events and transactions as if the new accounting
policy had always been in use. Therefore, the accounting policy is applied to events
and transactions from the date of origin of such items. Prospective application means
that the new accounting policy is applied to the events and transactions occurring after
the date of the change. No adjustments relating to prior periods are made either to the

opening balance of retained earnings or in reporting the net profit or loss for the current period because existing balances are not recalculated. However, the new accounting policy is applied to existing balances as from the date of the change. ...

Adoption of an IAS

46 *A change in accounting policy which is made on the adoption of an IAS should be accounted for in accordance with the specific transitional provisions, if any, in that IAS. In the absence of any transitional provisions, the change in accounting policy should be applied in accordance with the benchmark treatment in paragraphs 49, 52 and 53 or the allowed alternative treatment in paragraphs 54, 56 and 57.*

47–48 [Not printed]

Other Changes in Accounting Policies – Benchmark Treatment

49 *A change in accounting policy should be applied retrospectively unless the amount of any resulting adjustment that relates to prior periods is not reasonably determinable. Any resulting adjustment should be reported as an adjustment to the opening balance of retained earnings. Comparative information should be restated unless it is impracticable to do so.*

50 The financial statements, including the comparative information for prior periods, are presented as if the new accounting policy had always been in use. Therefore, comparative information is restated in order to reflect the new accounting policy. The amount of the adjustment relating to periods prior to those included in the financial statements is adjusted against the opening balance of retained earnings of the earliest period presented. Any other information with respect to prior periods, such as historical summaries of financial data, is also restated.

51 The restatement of comparative information does not necessarily give rise to the amendment of financial statements which have been approved by shareholders or registered or filed with regulatory authorities. However, national laws may require the amendment of such financial statements.

52 *The change in accounting policy should be applied prospectively when the amount of the adjustment to the opening balance of retained earnings required by paragraph 49 cannot be reasonably determined.*

53 *When a change in accounting policy has a material effect on the current period or any prior period presented, or may have a material effect in subsequent periods, an enterprise should disclose the following:*
(a) the reasons for the change;
(b) the amount of the adjustment for the current period and for each period presented;
(c) the amount of the adjustment relating to periods prior to those included in the comparative information; and
(d) the fact that comparative information has been restated or that it is impracticable to do so.

Other Changes in Accounting Policies – Allowed Alternative Treatment

54 *A change in accounting policy should be applied retrospectively unless the amount of* *any resulting adjustment that relates to prior periods is not reasonably determinable. Any resulting adjustment should be included in the determination of the net profit or loss for the current period. Comparative information should be presented as reported in the financial statements of the prior period. Additional pro forma comparative information, prepared in accordance with paragraph 49, should be presented unless it is impracticable to do so.*

[Not printed]   55

*The change in accounting policy should be applied prospectively when the amount to   56
be included in net profit or loss for the current period required by paragraph 54
cannot be reasonably determined.*

*When a change in accounting policy has a material effect on the current period or   57
any prior period presented, or may have a material effect in subsequent periods, an
enterprise should disclose the following:*
(a) the reasons for the change;
*(b) the amount of the adjustment recognised in net profit or loss in the current
    period; and*
*(c) the amount of the adjustment included in each period for which pro forma
    information is presented and the amount of the adjustment relating to periods
    prior to those included in the financial statements. If it is impracticable to
    present pro forma information, this fact should be disclosed.*

Effective Date

[Not printed]   58

Appendix

Extraordinary Items

[Not printed]

Fundamental Errors

[Not printed]

Changes in Accounting Policy

[Not printed]

IAS 10: Events After the Balance Sheet Date

IAS 10: Events After the Balance Sheet Date		
Scope 10.1	Definitions 10.2–6	Effective Date 10.22–23

Recognition and Measurement 10.7–12		
Events After The Balance Sheet Date 10.7–10		Dividends 10.11–12
Adjusting 10.7–8	Non-Adjusting 10.9–10	

Going Concern 10.13–15

Disclosure 10.16–21		
Date of Authorisation for Issue 10.16–17	Updating Disclosure about Conditions at the Balance Sheet Date 10.18–19	Non-Adjusting Events After the Balance Sheet Date 10.20–21

Scope

1   *This Standard should be applied in the accounting for, and disclosure of, events after the balance sheet date.*

Definitions

2   ...

Events after the balance sheet date *are those events, both favourable and unfavourable, that occur between the balance sheet date and the date when the financial statements are authorised for issue. Two types of events can be identified:*
   (a) those that provide evidence of conditions that existed at the balance sheet date (adjusting events after the balance sheet date); and
   (b) those that are indicative of conditions that arose after the balance sheet date (non-adjusting events after the balance sheet date).

3   [Not printed]

4   In some cases, an enterprise is required to submit its financial statements to its shareholders for approval after the financial statements have already been issued. In such cases, the financial statements are authorised for issue on the date of original issuance, not on the date when shareholders approve the financial statements.
   ...

5   In some cases, the management of an enterprise is required to issue its financial statements to a supervisory board (made up solely of non-executives) for approval. In

such cases, the financial statements are authorised for issue when the management authorises them for issue to the supervisory board.

...

Events after the balance sheet date include all events up to the date when the financial **6** statements are authorised for issue, even if those events occur after the publication of a profit announcement or of other selected financial information.

Recognition and Measurement

Adjusting Events After the Balance Sheet Date

An enterprise should adjust the amounts recognised in its financial statements to **7** *reflect adjusting events after the balance sheet date.*

The following are examples of adjusting events after the balance sheet date that require **8** an enterprise to adjust the amounts recognised in its financial statements, or to recognise items that were not previously recognised:
(a) the resolution after the balance sheet date of a court case which, because it confirms that an enterprise already had a present obligation at the balance sheet date, requires the enterprise to adjust a provision already recognised, or to recognise a provision instead of merely disclosing a contingent liability;
(b) the receipt of information after the balance sheet date indicating that an asset was impaired at the balance sheet date, or that the amount of a previously recognised impairment loss for that asset needs to be adjusted. For example:
    (i) the bankruptcy of a customer which occurs after the balance sheet date usually confirms that a loss already existed at the balance sheet date on a trade receivable account and that the enterprise needs to adjust the carrying amount of the trade receivable account; and
    (ii) the sale of inventories after the balance sheet date may give evidence about their net realisable value at the balance sheet date;
(c) the determination after the balance sheet date of the cost of assets purchased, or the proceeds from assets sold, before the balance sheet date;
(d) the determination after the balance sheet date of the amount of profit sharing or bonus payments, if the enterprise had a present legal or constructive obligation at the balance sheet date to make such payments as a result of events before that date (see IAS 19); and
(e) the discovery of fraud or errors that show that the financial statements were incorrect.

Non-Adjusting Events After the Balance Sheet Date

An enterprise should not adjust the amounts recognised in its financial statements **9** *to reflect non-adjusting events after the balance sheet date.*

An example of a non-adjusting event after the balance sheet date is a decline in market **10** value of investments between the balance sheet date and the date when the financial statements are authorised for issue. The fall in market value does not normally relate to the condition of the investments at the balance sheet date, but reflects circumstances that have arisen in the following period. Therefore, an enterprise does not adjust the amounts recognised in its financial statements for the investments. Similarly, the enterprise does not update the amounts disclosed for the investments as at the balance sheet date, although it may need to give additional disclosure under paragraph 20.

Dividends

11   *If dividends to holders of equity instruments (as defined in IAS 32) are proposed or declared after the balance sheet date, an enterprise should not recognise those dividends as a liability at the balance sheet date.*

12   IAS 1 requires an enterprise to disclose the amount of dividends that were proposed or declared after the balance sheet date but before the financial statements were authorised for issue. IAS 1 permits an enterprise to make this disclosure either:
      (a) on the face of the balance sheet as a separate component of equity; or
      (b) in the notes to the financial statements.

Going Concern

13   *An enterprise should not prepare its financial statements on a going concern basis if management determines after the balance sheet date either that it intends to liquidate the enterprise or to cease trading, or that it has no realistic alternative but to do so.*

14   Deterioration in operating results and financial position after the balance sheet date may indicate a need to consider whether the going concern assumption is still appropriate. If the going concern assumption is no longer appropriate, the effect is so pervasive that this Standard requires a fundamental change in the basis of accounting, rather than an adjustment to the amounts recognised within the original basis of accounting.

15   IAS 1 requires certain disclosures if:
      (a) the financial statements are not prepared on a going concern basis; or
      (b) management is aware of material uncertainties related to events or conditions that may cast significant doubt upon the enterprise's ability to continue as a going concern. The events or conditions requiring disclosure may arise after the balance sheet date.

Disclosure

Date of Authorisation for Issue

16   *An enterprise should disclose the date when the financial statements were authorised for issue and who gave that authorisation. If the enterprise's owners or others have the power to amend the financial statements after issuance, the enterprise should disclose that fact.*

17   [Not printed]

Updating Disclosure about Conditions at the Balance Sheet Date

18   *If an enterprise receives information after the balance sheet date about conditions that existed at the balance sheet date, the enterprise should update disclosures that relate to these conditions, in the light of the new information.*

In some cases, an enterprise needs to update the disclosures in its financial statements **19** to reflect information received after the balance sheet date, even when the information does not affect the amounts that the enterprise recognises in its financial statements. ...

Non-Adjusting Events After the Balance Sheet Date

Where non-adjusting events after the balance sheet date are of such importance that **20** *non-disclosure would affect the ability of the users of the financial statements to make proper evaluations and decisions, an enterprise should disclose the following information for each significant category of non-adjusting event after the balance sheet date:*

(a) the nature of the event; and

(b) an estimate of its financial effect, or a statement that such an estimate cannot be made.

The following are examples of non-adjusting events after the balance sheet date that **21** may be of such importance that non-disclosure would affect the ability of the users of the financial statements to make proper evaluations and decisions:

(a) a major business combination after the balance sheet date (IAS 22 requires specific disclosures in such cases) or disposing of a major subsidiary;

(b) announcing a plan to discontinue an operation, disposing of assets or settling liabilities attributable to a discontinuing operation or entering into binding agreements to sell such assets or settle such liabilities (see IAS 35);

(c) major purchases and disposals of assets, or expropriation of major assets by government;

(d) the destruction of a major production plant by a fire after the balance sheet date;

(e) announcing, or commencing the implementation of, a major restructuring (see IAS 37);

(f) major ordinary share transactions and potential ordinary share transactions after the balance sheet date (IAS 33 encourages an enterprise to disclose a description of such transactions, other than capitalisation issues and share splits);

(g) abnormally large changes after the balance sheet date in asset prices or foreign exchange rates;

(h) changes in tax rates or tax laws enacted or announced after the balance sheet date that have a significant effect on current and deferred tax assets and liabilities (see IAS 12);

(i) entering into significant commitments or contingent liabilities, for example, by issuing significant guarantees; and

(j) commencing major litigation arising solely out of events that occurred after the balance sheet date.

Effective Date

[Not printed]   **22–23**

IAS 11: Construction Contracts

IAS 11: Construction Contracts		
Scope 11.1–2	Definitions 11.3–6	Effective Date 11.46

Combining and Segmenting Construction Contracts 11.7–10

Contract Revenue and Contract Costs 11.11–21	
Contract Revenue 11.11–15	Contract Costs 11.16–21

Recognition of Contract Revenue and Expenses 11.22–35

Recognition of Expected Losses 11.36–37

Changes in Estimates (Reference to IAS 8) 11.38

Disclosure 11.39–45

Appendix [Not printed]		
Disclosure of Accounting Policies	The Determination of Contract Revenue and Expenses	Contract Disclosures

Scope

1 *This Standard should be applied in accounting for construction contracts in the financial statements of contractors.*

2 [Not printed]

Definitions

3 ...

A *construction contract* is a contract specifically negotiated for the construction of an asset or a combination of assets that are closely interrelated or interdependent in terms of their design, technology and function or their ultimate purpose or use.

A *fixed price contract* is a construction contract in which the contractor agrees to a fixed contract price, or a fixed rate per unit of output, which in some cases is subject to cost escalation clauses.

A *cost plus contract* is a construction contract in which the contractor is reimbursed for allowable or otherwise defined costs, plus a percentage of these costs or a fixed fee.

4 [Not printed]

5 For the purposes of this Standard, construction contracts include:

(a) contracts for the rendering of services which are directly related to the construction of the asset, for example, those for the services of project managers and architects; and_

(b) contracts for the destruction or restoration of assets, and the restoration of the environment following the demolition of assets.

Construction contracts are formulated in a number of ways which, for the purposes of **6** this Standard, are classified as fixed price contracts and cost plus contracts. Some construction contracts may contain characteristics of both a fixed price contract and a cost plus contract, for example in the case of a cost plus contract with an agreed maximum price. In such circumstances, a contractor needs to consider all the conditions in paragraphs 23 and 24 in order to determine when to recognise contract revenue and expenses.

Combining and Segmenting Construction Contracts

[Not printed]   **7**

When a contract covers a number of assets, the construction of each asset should be **8** *treated as a separate construction contract when:*
(a) separate proposals have been submitted for each asset;
(b) each asset has been subject to separate negotiation and the contractor and customer have been able to accept or reject that part of the contract relating to each asset; and
(c) the costs and revenues of each asset can be identified.

A group of contracts, whether with a single customer or with several customers, **9** *should be treated as a single construction contract when:*
(a) the group of contracts is negotiated as a single package;
(b) the contracts are so closely interrelated that they are, in effect, part of a single project with an overall profit margin; and
(c) the contracts are performed concurrently or in a continuous sequence.

A contract may provide for the construction of an additional asset at the option of **10** *the customer or may be amended to include the construction of an additional asset. The construction of the additional asset should be treated as a separate construction contract when:*
(a) the asset differs significantly in design, technology or function from the asset or assets covered by the original contract; or

(b) the price of the asset is negotiated without regard to the original contract price.

Contract Revenue

Contract revenue should comprise: **11**
(a) the initial amount of revenue agreed in the contract; and
(b) variations in contract work, claims and incentive payments:
    (i) to the extent that it is probable that they will result in revenue; and
    (ii) they are capable of being reliably measured.

Contract revenue is measured at the fair value of the consideration received or **12** receivable. The measurement of contract revenue is affected by a variety of uncertainties that depend on the outcome of future events. The estimates often need to be revised as events occur and uncertainties are resolved. Therefore, the amount of contract revenue may increase or decrease from one period to the next. ...

13　A variation is an instruction by the customer for a change in the scope of the work to be performed under the contract. A variation may lead to an increase or a decrease in contract revenue. ...

14　A claim is an amount that the contractor seeks to collect from the customer or another party as reimbursement for costs not included in the contract price. ...

15　Incentive payments are additional amounts paid to the contractor if specified performance standards are met or exceeded. ...

Contract Costs

16　*Contract costs should comprise:*
   (a) costs that relate directly to the specific contract;
   (b) costs that are attributable to contract activity in general and can be allocated to the contract; and
   (c) such other costs as are specifically chargeable to the customer under the terms of the contract.

17　Costs that relate directly to a specific contract include:
   (a) site labour costs, including site supervision;
   (b) costs of materials used in construction;
   (c) depreciation of plant and equipment used on the contract;
   (d) costs of moving plant, equipment and materials to and from the contract site;
   (e) costs of hiring plant and equipment;
   (f) costs of design and technical assistance that is directly related to the contract;
   (g) the estimated costs of rectification and guarantee work, including expected warranty costs; and
   (h) claims from third parties.
   These costs may be reduced by any incidental income that is not included in contract revenue, for example income from the sale of surplus materials and the disposal of plant and equipment at the end of the contract.

18　Costs that may be attributable to contract activity in general and can be allocated to specific contracts include:
   (a) insurance;
   (b) costs of design and technical assistance that is not directly related to a specific contract; and
   (c) construction overheads.
   Such costs are allocated using methods that are systematic and rational and are applied consistently to all costs having similar characteristics. The allocation is based on the normal level of construction activity. Construction overheads include costs such as the preparation and processing of construction personnel payroll. Costs that may be attributable to contract activity in general and can be allocated to specific contracts also include borrowing costs when the contractor adopts the allowed alternative treatment in IAS 23.

19　Costs that are specifically chargeable to the customer under the terms of the contract may include some general administration costs and development costs for which reimbursement is specified in the terms of the contract.

Costs that cannot be attributed to contract activity or cannot be allocated to a contract **20** are excluded from the costs of a construction contract. Such costs include:

(a) general administration costs for which reimbursement is not specified in the contract;

(b) selling costs;

(c) research and development costs for which reimbursement is not specified in the contract; and

(d) depreciation of idle plant and equipment that is not used on a particular contract.

Contract costs include the costs attributable to a contract for the period from the date **21** of securing the contract to the final completion of the contract. However, costs that relate directly to a contract and which are incurred in securing the contract are also included as part of the contract costs if they can be separately identified and measured reliably and it is probable that the contract will be obtained. When costs incurred in securing a contract are recognised as an expense in the period in which they are incurred, they are not included in contract costs when the contract is obtained in a subsequent period.

Recognition of Contract Revenue and Expenses

When the outcome of a construction contract can be estimated reliably, contract **22** *revenue and contract costs associated with the construction contract should be recognised as revenue and expenses respectively by reference to the stage of completion of the contract activity at the balance sheet date. An expected loss on the construction contract should be recognised as an expense immediately in accordance with paragraph 36.*

In the case of a fixed price contract, the outcome of a construction contract can be **23** *estimated reliably when all the following conditions are satisfied:*

(a) total contract revenue can be measured reliably;

(b) it is probable that the economic benefits associated with the contract will flow to the enterprise;

(c) both the contract costs to complete the contract and the stage of contract completion at the balance sheet date can be measured reliably; and

(d) the contract costs attributable to the contract can be clearly identified and measured reliably so that actual contract costs incurred can be compared with prior estimates.

In the case of a cost plus contract, the outcome of a construction contract can be **24** *estimated reliably when all the following conditions are satisfied:*

(a) it is probable that the economic benefits associated with the contract will flow to the enterprise; and

(b) the contract costs attributable to the contract, whether or not specifically reimbursable, can be clearly identified and measured reliably.

The recognition of revenue and expenses by reference to the stage of completion of a **25** contract is often referred to as the percentage of completion method. Under this method, contract revenue is matched with the contract costs incurred in reaching the stage of completion, resulting in the reporting of revenue, expenses and profit which can be attributed to the proportion of work completed. This method provides useful information on the extent of contract activity and performance during a period.

26 Under the percentage of completion method, contract revenue is recognised as revenue in the income statement in the accounting periods in which the work is performed. Contract costs are usually recognised as an expense in the income statement in the accounting periods in which the work to which they relate is performed. However, any expected excess of total contract costs over total contract revenue for the contract is recognised as an expense immediately in accordance with paragraph 36.

27 A contractor may have incurred contract costs that relate to future activity on the contract. Such contract costs are recognised as an asset provided it is probable that they will be recovered. Such costs represent an amount due from the customer and are often classified as contract work in progress.

28 The outcome of a construction contract can only be estimated reliably when it is probable that the economic benefits associated with the contract will flow to the enterprise. However, when an uncertainty arises about the collectability of an amount already included in contract revenue, and already recognised in the income statement, the uncollectable amount or the amount in respect of which recovery has ceased to be probable is recognised as an expense rather than as an adjustment of the amount of contract revenue.

29 An enterprise is generally able to make reliable estimates after it has agreed to a contract which establishes:
  (a) each party's enforceable rights regarding the asset to be constructed;
  (b) the consideration to be exchanged; and
  (c) the manner and terms of settlement.
  ...

30 The stage of completion of a contract may be determined in a variety of ways. The enterprise uses the method that measures reliably the work performed. Depending on the nature of the contract, the methods may include:
  (a) the proportion that contract costs incurred for work performed to date bear to the estimated total contract costs;
  (b) surveys of work performed; or
  (c) completion of a physical proportion of the contract work.
  Progress payments and advances received from customers often do not reflect the work performed.

31 When the stage of completion is determined by reference to the contract costs incurred to date, only those contract costs that reflect work performed are included in costs incurred to date. Examples of contract costs which are excluded are:
  (a) contract costs that relate to future activity on the contract, such as costs of materials that have been delivered to a contract site or set aside for use in a contract but not yet installed, used or applied during contract performance, unless the materials have been made specially for the contract; and
  (b) payments made to subcontractors in advance of work performed under the subcontract.

32 *When the outcome of a construction contract cannot be estimated reliably:*
  (a) revenue should be recognised only to the extent of contract costs incurred that it is probable will be recoverable; and
  (b) contract costs should be recognised as an expense in the period in which they are incurred.
  An expected loss on the construction contract should be recognised as an expense immediately in accordance with paragraph 36.

[Not printed]   33

Contract costs that are not probable of being recovered are recognised as an expense   34
immediately. Examples of circumstances in which the recoverability of contract costs
incurred may not be probable and in which contract costs may need to be recognised
as an expense immediately include contracts:
(a) which are not fully enforceable, that is, their validity is seriously in question;
(b) the completion of which is subject to the outcome of pending litigation or
    legislation;
(c) relating to properties that are likely to be condemned or expropriated;
(d) where the customer is unable to meet its obligations; or
(e) where the contractor is unable to complete the contract or otherwise meet its
    obligations under the contract.

When the uncertainties that prevented the outcome of the contract being estimated   35
reliably no longer exist, revenue and expenses associated with the construction
contract should be recognised in accordance with paragraph 22 rather than in
accordance with paragraph 32.

Recognition of Expected Losses

When it is probable that total contract costs will exceed total contract revenue, the   36
expected loss should be recognised as an expense immediately.

The amount of such a loss is determined irrespective of: 37
(a) whether or not work has commenced on the contract;
(b) the stage of completion of contract activity; or
(c) the amount of profits expected to arise on other contracts which are not treated as
    a single construction contract in accordance with paragraph 9.

Changes in Estimates

The percentage of completion method is applied on a cumulative basis in each   38
accounting period to the current estimates of contract revenue and contract costs.
Therefore, the effect of a change in the estimate of contract revenue or contract costs,
or the effect of a change in the estimate of the outcome of a contract, is accounted for
as a change in accounting estimate (see IAS 8). The changed estimates are used in the
determination of the amount of revenue and expenses recognised in the income
statement in the period in which the change is made and in subsequent periods.

Disclosure

An enterprise should disclose: 39
(a) the amount of contract revenue recognised as revenue in the period;
(b) the methods used to determine the contract revenue recognised in the period; and
(c) the methods used to determine the stage of completion of contracts in progress.

An enterprise should disclose each of the following for contracts in progress at the   40
balance sheet date:
(a) the aggregate amount of costs incurred and recognised profits (less recognised
*   losses) to date;*

(b) the amount of advances received; and
(c) the amount of retentions.

41 Retentions are amounts of progress billings which are not paid until the satisfaction of conditions specified in the contract for the payment of such amounts or until defects have been rectified. Progress billings are amounts billed for work performed on a contract whether or not they have been paid by the customer. Advances are amounts received by the contractor before the related work is performed.

42 *An enterprise should present:*
    (a) the gross amount due from customers for contract work as an asset; and
    (b) the gross amount due to customers for contract work as a liability.

43 The gross amount due from customers for contract work is the net amount of:
    (a) costs incurred plus recognised profits; less
    (b) the sum of recognised losses and progress billings
    for all contracts in progress for which costs incurred plus recognised profits (less recognised losses) exceeds progress billings.

44 The gross amount due to customers for contract work is the net amount of:
    (a) costs incurred plus recognised profits; less
    (b) the sum of recognised losses and progress billings
    for all contracts in progress for which progress billings exceed costs incurred plus recognised profits (less recognised losses).

45 [Not printed]

Effective Date

46 *[Not printed]*

Appendix

Disclosure of Accounting Policies

[Not printed]

The Determination of Contract Revenue and Expenses

[Not printed]

Contract Disclosures

[Not printed]

IAS 12: Income Taxes

IAS 12: Income Taxes			
Scope 12.1–4	Definitions 12.5–11	Effective Date 12.89–91	Related Interpretations: SIC–21, 25
	Tax Base 12.7–11		

Recognition of Current Tax Liabilities and Current Tax Assets 12.12–14

Recognition of Deferred Tax Liabilities and Deferred Tax Assets 12.15–45				
Taxable Temporary Differences 12.15–23	Deductible Temporary Differences 12.24–33	Unused Tax Losses and Unused Tax Credits 12.34–36	Re-assessment of Unrecognised Deferred Tax Assets 12.37	Investments in Subsidiaries, Branches and Associates and Interests in Joint Ventures 12.38–45

Measurement 12.46–56

Recognition of Current and Deferred Tax 12.57–68		
Income Statement 12.58–60	Items Credited or Charged Directly to Equity 12.61–65A	Deferred Tax Arising from a Business Combination 12.66–68

Presentation 12.69–78		
Tax Assets and Tax Liabilities 12.69–76	Tax Expense 12.77–78	
Offset 12.71–76	Tax Expense (Income) Related to Profit or Loss from Ordinary Activities 12.77	Exchange Differences on Deferred Foreign Tax Liabilities or Assets 12.78

Disclosure 12.79–88

Appendices [Not printed]	
Examples of Temporary Differences	Illustrative Computations and Presentation

Scope

1   *This Standard should be applied in accounting for income taxes.*

2   For the purposes of this Standard, income taxes include all domestic and foreign taxes which are based on taxable profits.   Income taxes also include taxes, such as withholding taxes, which are payable by a subsidiary, associate or joint venture on distributions to the reporting enterprise.

3   [Deleted]

4   This Standard does not deal with the methods of accounting for government grants (see IAS 20) or investment tax credits. However, this Standard does deal with the accounting for temporary differences that may arise from such grants or investment tax credits.

Definitions

5   ...

Accounting profit is net profit or loss for a period before deducting tax expense.

Taxable profit (tax loss) is the profit (loss) for a period, determined in accordance with the rules established by the taxation authorities, upon which income taxes are payable (recoverable).

Tax expense (tax income) is the aggregate amount included in the determination of net profit or loss for the period in respect of current tax and deferred tax.

Current tax is the amount of income taxes payable (recoverable) in respect of the taxable profit (tax loss) for a period.

Deferred tax liabilities are the amounts of income taxes payable in future periods in respect of taxable temporary differences.

Deferred tax assets are the amounts of income taxes recoverable in future periods in respect of:

(a) deductible temporary differences;

(b) the carryforward of unused tax losses; and

(c) the carryforward of unused tax credits.

Temporary differences are differences between the carrying amount of an asset or liability in the balance sheet and its tax base. Temporary differences may be either:

(a) taxable temporary differences, which are temporary differences that will result in taxable amounts in determining taxable profit (tax loss) of future periods when the carrying amount of the asset or liability is recovered or settled; or

(b) deductible temporary differences, which are temporary differences that will result in amounts that are deductible in determining taxable profit (tax loss) of future periods when the carrying amount of the asset or liability is recovered or settled.

The tax base of an asset or liability is the amount attributed to that asset or liability for tax purposes.

6   Tax expense (tax income) comprises current tax expense (current tax income) and deferred tax expense (deferred tax income).

Tax Base

7   The tax base of an asset is the amount that will be deductible for tax purposes against any taxable economic benefits that will flow to an enterprise when it recovers the carrying amount of the asset. If those economic benefits will not be taxable, the tax base of the asset is equal to its carrying amount.

...

The tax base of a liability is its carrying amount, less any amount that will be deductible **8** for tax purposes in respect of that liability in future periods. In the case of revenue which is received in advance, the tax base of the resulting liability is its carrying amount, less any amount of the revenue that will not be taxable in future periods.

...

Some items have a tax base but are not recognised as assets and liabilities in the balance **9** sheet. For example, research costs are recognised as an expense in determining accounting profit in the period in which they are incurred but may not be permitted as a deduction in determining taxable profit (tax loss) until a later period. The difference between the tax base of the research costs, being the amount the taxation authorities will permit as a deduction in future periods, and the carrying amount of nil is a deductible temporary difference that results in a deferred tax asset.

Where the tax base of an asset or liability is not immediately apparent, it is helpful to **10** consider the fundamental principle upon which this Standard is based: that an enterprise should, with certain limited exceptions, recognise a deferred tax liability (asset) whenever recovery or settlement of the carrying amount of an asset or liability would make future tax payments larger (smaller) than they would be if such recovery or settlement were to have no tax consequences. ...

In consolidated financial statements, temporary differences are determined by **11** comparing the carrying amounts of assets and liabilities in the consolidated financial statements with the appropriate tax base. The tax base is determined by reference to a consolidated tax return in those jurisdictions in which such a return is filed. In other jurisdictions, the tax base is determined by reference to the tax returns of each enterprise in the group.

Recognition of Current Tax Liabilities and Current Tax Assets

Current tax for current and prior periods should, to the extent unpaid, be recognised **12** *as a liability. If the amount already paid in respect of current and prior periods exceeds the amount due for those periods, the excess should be recognised as an asset.*

The benefit relating to a tax loss that can be carried back to recover current tax of a **13** *previous period should be recognised as an asset.*

When a tax loss is used to recover current tax of a previous period, an enterprise **14** recognises the benefit as an asset in the period in which the tax loss occurs because it is probable that the benefit will flow to the enterprise and the benefit can be reliably measured.

Recognition of Deferred Tax Liabilities and Deferred Tax Assets

Taxable Temporary Differences

A deferred tax liability should be recognised for all taxable temporary differences, **15** *unless the deferred tax liability arises from:*
(a) goodwill for which amortisation is not deductible for tax purposes; or
(b) the initial recognition of an asset or liability in a transaction which:
  (i) is not a business combination; and

(ii) at the time of the transaction, affects neither accounting profit nor taxable profit (tax loss).
However, for taxable temporary differences associated with investments in subsidiaries, branches and associates, and interests in joint ventures, a deferred tax liability should be recognised in accordance with paragraph 39.

16 It is inherent in the recognition of an asset that its carrying amount will be recovered in the form of economic benefits that flow to the enterprise in future periods. When the carrying amount of the asset exceeds its tax base, the amount of taxable economic benefits will exceed the amount that will be allowed as a deduction for tax purposes. This difference is a taxable temporary difference and the obligation to pay the resulting income taxes in future periods is a deferred tax liability. As the enterprise recovers the carrying amount of the asset, the taxable temporary difference will reverse and the enterprise will have taxable profit. This makes it probable that economic benefits will flow from the enterprise in the form of tax payments. Therefore, this Standard requires the recognition of all deferred tax liabilities, except in certain circumstances described in paragraphs 15 and 39.

...

17 Some temporary differences arise when income or expense is included in accounting profit in one period but is included in taxable profit in a different period. Such temporary differences are often described as timing differences. The following are examples of temporary differences of this kind which are taxable temporary differences and which therefore result in deferred tax liabilities:

(a) interest revenue is included in accounting profit on a time proportion basis but may, in some jurisdictions, be included in taxable profit when cash is collected. The tax base of any receivable recognised in the balance sheet with respect to such revenues is nil because the revenues do not affect taxable profit until cash is collected;

(b) depreciation used in determining taxable profit (tax loss) may differ from that used in determining accounting profit. The temporary difference is the difference between the carrying amount of the asset and its tax base which is the original cost of the asset less all deductions in respect of that asset permitted by the taxation authorities in determining taxable profit of the current and prior periods. A taxable temporary difference arises, and results in a deferred tax liability, when tax depreciation is accelerated (if tax depreciation is less rapid than accounting depreciation, a deductible temporary difference arises, and results in a deferred tax asset); and

(c) development costs may be capitalised and amortised over future periods in determining accounting profit but deducted in determining taxable profit in the period in which they are incurred. Such development costs have a tax base of nil as they have already been deducted from taxable profit. The temporary difference is the difference between the carrying amount of the development costs and their tax base of nil.

18 Temporary differences also arise when:

(a) the cost of a business combination that is an acquisition is allocated to the identifiable assets and liabilities acquired by reference to their fair values but no equivalent adjustment is made for tax purposes (see paragraph 19);

(b) assets are revalued and no equivalent adjustment is made for tax purposes (see paragraph 20);

(c) goodwill or negative goodwill arises on consolidation (see paragraphs 21 and 32);

(d) the tax base of an asset or liability on initial recognition differs from its initial carrying amount, for example when an enterprise benefits from non–taxable government grants related to assets (see paragraphs 22 and 33); or

(e) the carrying amount of investments in subsidiaries, branches and associates or interests in joint ventures becomes different from the tax base of the investment or interest (see paragraphs 38–45).

Business Combinations

In a business combination that is an acquisition, the cost of the acquisition is allocated **19** to the identifiable assets and liabilities acquired by reference to their fair values at the date of the exchange transaction. Temporary differences arise when the tax bases of the identifiable assets and liabilities acquired are not affected by the business combination or are affected differently. ...

Assets Carried at Fair Value

IASs permit certain assets to be carried at fair value or to be revalued (see, for example, **20** IAS 16, IAS 38, IAS 39, and IAS 40). In some jurisdictions, the revaluation or other restatement of an asset to fair value affects taxable profit (tax loss) for the current period. As a result, the tax base of the asset is adjusted and no temporary difference arises. In other jurisdictions, the revaluation or restatement of an asset does not affect taxable profit in the period of the revaluation or restatement and, consequently, the tax base of the asset is not adjusted. Nevertheless, the future recovery of the carrying amount will result in a taxable flow of economic benefits to the enterprise and the amount that will be deductible for tax purposes will differ from the amount of those economic benefits. The difference between the carrying amount of a revalued asset and its tax base is a temporary difference and gives rise to a deferred tax liability or asset. This is true even if:

(a) the enterprise does not intend to dispose of the asset. In such cases, the revalued carrying amount of the asset will be recovered through use and this will generate taxable income which exceeds the depreciation that will be allowable for tax purposes in future periods; or

(b) tax on capital gains is deferred if the proceeds of the disposal of the asset are invested in similar assets. In such cases, the tax will ultimately become payable on sale or use of the similar assets.

Goodwill

Goodwill is the excess of the cost of an acquisition over the acquirer's interest in the **21** fair value of the identifiable assets and liabilities acquired. Many taxation authorities do not allow the amortisation of goodwill as a deductible expense in determining taxable profit. Moreover, in such jurisdictions, the cost of goodwill is often not deductible when a subsidiary disposes of its underlying business. In such jurisdictions, goodwill has a tax base of nil. Any difference between the carrying amount of goodwill and its tax base of nil is a taxable temporary difference. However, this Standard does not permit the recognition of the resulting deferred tax liability because goodwill is a residual and the recognition of the deferred tax liability would increase the carrying amount of goodwill.

Initial Recognition of an Asset or Liability

22 A temporary difference may arise on initial recognition of an asset or liability, for example if part or all of the cost of an asset will not be deductible for tax purposes. The method of accounting for such a temporary difference depends on the nature of the transaction which led to the initial recognition of the asset:

(a) in a business combination, an enterprise recognises any deferred tax liability or asset and this affects the amount of goodwill or negative goodwill (see paragraph 19);

(b) if the transaction affects either accounting profit or taxable profit, an enterprise recognises any deferred tax liability or asset and recognises the resulting deferred tax expense or income in the income statement (see paragraph 59);

(c) if the transaction is not a business combination, and affects neither accounting profit nor taxable profit, an enterprise would, in the absence of the exemption provided by paragraphs 15 and 24, recognise the resulting deferred tax liability or asset and adjust the carrying amount of the asset or liability by the same amount. Such adjustments would make the financial statements less transparent. Therefore, this Standard does not permit an enterprise to recognise the resulting deferred tax liability or asset, either on initial recognition or subsequently (see example on next page). Furthermore, an enterprise does not recognise subsequent changes in the unrecognised deferred tax liability or asset as the asset is depreciated.

23 [Not printed]

Deductible Temporary Differences

24 *A deferred tax asset should be recognised for all deductible temporary differences to the extent that it is probable that taxable profit will be available against which the deductible temporary difference can be utilised, unless the deferred tax asset arises from:*

(a) negative goodwill which is treated as deferred income in accordance with IAS 22; or

(b) the initial recognition of an asset or liability in a transaction which:

(i) is not a business combination; and

(ii) at the time of the transaction, affects neither accounting profit nor taxable profit (tax loss).

However, for deductible temporary differences associated with investments in subsidiaries, branches and associates, and interests in joint ventures, a deferred tax asset should be recognised in accordance with paragraph 44.

25 It is inherent in the recognition of a liability that the carrying amount will be settled in future periods through an outflow from the enterprise of resources embodying economic benefits. When resources flow from the enterprise, part or all of their amounts may be deductible in determining taxable profit of a period later than the period in which the liability is recognised. In such cases, a temporary difference exists between the carrying amount of the liability and its tax base. Accordingly, a deferred tax asset arises in respect of the income taxes that will be recoverable in the future periods when that part of the liability is allowed as a deduction in determining taxable profit. Similarly, if the carrying amount of an asset is less than its tax base, the difference gives rise to a deferred tax asset in respect of the income taxes that will be recoverable in future periods.

...

[Not printed]   **26**

The reversal of deductible temporary differences results in deductions in determining **27** taxable profits of future periods. However, economic benefits in the form of reductions in tax payments will flow to the enterprise only if it earns sufficient taxable profits against which the deductions can be offset. Therefore, an enterprise recognises deferred tax assets only when it is probable that taxable profits will be available against which the deductible temporary differences can be utilised.

It is probable that taxable profit will be available against which a deductible temporary **28** difference can be utilised when there are sufficient taxable temporary differences relating to the same taxation authority and the same taxable entity which are expected to reverse:
(a) in the same period as the expected reversal of the deductible temporary difference; or
(b) in periods into which a tax loss arising from the deferred tax asset can be carried back or forward.
In such circumstances, the deferred tax asset is recognised in the period in which the deductible temporary differences arise.

When there are insufficient taxable temporary differences relating to the same taxation **29** authority and the same taxable entity, the deferred tax asset is recognised to the extent that:
(a) it is probable that the enterprise will have sufficient taxable profit relating to the same taxation authority and the same taxable entity in the same period as the reversal of the deductible temporary difference (or in the periods into which a tax loss arising from the deferred tax asset can be carried back or forward). In evaluating whether it will have sufficient taxable profit in future periods, an enterprise ignores taxable amounts arising from deductible temporary differences that are expected to originate in future periods, because the deferred tax asset arising from these deductible temporary differences will itself require future taxable profit in order to be utilised; or
(b) tax planning opportunities are available to the enterprise that will create taxable profit in appropriate periods.

Tax planning opportunities are actions that the enterprise would take in order to create **30** or increase taxable income in a particular period before the expiry of a tax loss or tax credit carryforward. ...

Where tax planning opportunities advance taxable profit from a later period to an earlier period, the utilisation of a tax loss or tax credit carryforward still depends on the existence of future taxable profit from sources other than future originating temporary differences.

[Not printed]   **31**

Negative Goodwill

This Standard does not permit the recognition of a deferred tax asset arising from **32** deductible temporary differences associated with negative goodwill which is treated as deferred income in accordance with IAS 22, because negative goodwill is a residual and the recognition of the deferred tax asset would increase the carrying amount of negative goodwill.

Initial Recognition of an Asset or Liability

33 One case when a deferred tax asset arises on initial recognition of an asset is when a non–taxable government grant related to an asset is deducted in arriving at the carrying amount of the asset but, for tax purposes, is not deducted from the asset's depreciable amount (in other words its tax base); the carrying amount of the asset is less than its tax base and this gives rise to a deductible temporary difference. Government grants may also be set up as deferred income in which case the difference between the deferred income and its tax base of nil is a deductible temporary difference. Whichever method of presentation an enterprise adopts, the enterprise does not recognise the resulting deferred tax asset, for the reason given in paragraph 22.

Unused Tax Losses and Unused Tax Credits

34 *A deferred tax asset should be recognised for the carryforward of unused tax losses and unused tax credits to the extent that it is probable that future taxable profit will be available against which the unused tax losses and unused tax credits can be utilised.*

35 The criteria for recognising deferred tax assets arising from the carryforward of unused tax losses and tax credits are the same as the criteria for recognising deferred tax assets arising from deductible temporary differences. ...

36 An enterprise considers the following criteria in assessing the probability that taxable profit will be available against which the unused tax losses or unused tax credits can be utilised:
    (a) whether the enterprise has sufficient taxable temporary differences relating to the same taxation authority and the same taxable entity, which will result in taxable amounts against which the unused tax losses or unused tax credits can be utilised before they expire;
    (b) whether it is probable that the enterprise will have taxable profits before the unused tax losses or unused tax credits expire;
    (c) whether the unused tax losses result from identifiable causes which are unlikely to recur; and
    (d) whether tax planning opportunities (see paragraph 30) are available to the enterprise that will create taxable profit in the period in which the unused tax losses or unused tax credits can be utilised.
    To the extent that it is not probable that taxable profit will be available against which the unused tax losses or unused tax credits can be utilised, the deferred tax asset is not recognised.

Re–assessment of Unrecognised Deferred Tax Assets

37 At each balance sheet date, an enterprise re–assesses unrecognised deferred tax assets. The enterprise recognises a previously unrecognised deferred tax asset to the extent that it has become probable that future taxable profit will allow the deferred tax asset to be recovered. ...

Investments in Subsidiaries, Branches and Associates and Interests in Joint Ventures

Temporary differences arise when the carrying amount of investments in subsidiaries, **38** branches and associates or interests in joint ventures (namely the parent or investor's share of the net assets of the subsidiary, branch, associate or investee, including the carrying amount of goodwill) becomes different from the tax base (which is often cost) of the investment or interest. Such differences may arise in a number of different circumstances, for example:

(a) the existence of undistributed profits of subsidiaries, branches, associates and joint ventures;

(b) changes in foreign exchange rates when a parent and its subsidiary are based in different countries; and

(c) a reduction in the carrying amount of an investment in an associate to its recoverable amount.

In consolidated financial statements, the temporary difference may be different from the temporary difference associated with that investment in the parent's separate financial statements if the parent carries the investment in its separate financial statements at cost or revalued amount.

An enterprise should recognise a deferred tax liability for all taxable temporary **39** *differences associated with investments in subsidiaries, branches and associates, and interests in joint ventures, except to the extent that both of the following conditions are satisfied:*

(a) the parent, investor or venturer is able to control the timing of the reversal of the temporary difference; and

(b) it is probable that the temporary difference will not reverse in the foreseeable future.

[Not printed] **40–43**

An enterprise should recognise a deferred tax asset for all deductible temporary **44** *differences arising from investments in subsidiaries, branches and associates, and interests in joint ventures, to the extent that, and only to the extent that, it is probable that:*

(a) the temporary difference will reverse in the foreseeable future; and

(b) taxable profit will be available against which the temporary difference can be utilised.

[Not printed] **45**

Measurement

Current tax liabilities (assets) for the current and prior periods should be measured **46** *at the amount expected to be paid to (recovered from) the taxation authorities, using the tax rates (and tax laws) that have been enacted or substantively enacted by the balance sheet date.*

Deferred tax assets and liabilities should be measured at the tax rates that are **47** *expected to apply to the period when the asset is realised or the liability is settled, based on tax rates (and tax laws) that have been enacted or substantively enacted by the balance sheet date.*

48 [Not printed]

49 When different tax rates apply to different levels of taxable income, deferred tax assets and liabilities are measured using the average rates that are expected to apply to the taxable profit (tax loss) of the periods in which the temporary differences are expected to reverse.

50 [Deleted]

51 *The measurement of deferred tax liabilities and deferred tax assets should reflect the tax consequences that would follow from the manner in which the enterprise expects, at the balance sheet date, to recover or settle the carrying amount of its assets and liabilities.*

52 In some jurisdictions, the manner in which an enterprise recovers (settles) the carrying amount of an asset (liability) may affect either or both of:
(a) the tax rate applicable when the enterprise recovers (settles) the carrying amount of the asset (liability); and
(b) the tax base of the asset (liability).
In such cases, an enterprise measures deferred tax liabilities and deferred tax assets using the tax rate and the tax base that are consistent with the expected manner of recovery or settlement.
...

52A–B [Not printed]

53 *Deferred tax assets and liabilities should not be discounted.*

54 [Not printed]

55 Temporary differences are determined by reference to the carrying amount of an asset or liability. ...

56 *The carrying amount of a deferred tax asset should be reviewed at each balance sheet date. An enterprise should reduce the carrying amount of a deferred tax asset to the extent that it is no longer probable that sufficient taxable profit will be available to allow the benefit of part or all of that deferred tax asset to be utilised. Any such reduction should be reversed to the extent that it becomes probable that sufficient taxable profit will be available.*

Recognition of Current and Deferred Tax

57 Accounting for the current and deferred tax effects of a transaction or other event is consistent with the accounting for the transaction or event itself. Paragraphs 58 to 68 implement this principle.

Income Statement

58 *Current and deferred tax should be recognised as income or an expense and included in the net profit or loss for the period, except to the extent that the tax arises from:*
(a) *a transaction or event which is recognised, in the same or a different period, directly in equity (see paragraphs 61 to 65); or*
(b) *a business combination that is an acquisition (see paragraphs 66 to 68).*

Most deferred tax liabilities and deferred tax assets arise where income or expense is **59** included in accounting profit in one period, but is included in taxable profit (tax loss) in a different period. The resulting deferred tax is recognised in the income statement. ...

The carrying amount of deferred tax assets and liabilities may change even though there **60** is no change in the amount of the related temporary differences. ...

The resulting deferred tax is recognised in the income statement, except to the extent that it relates to items previously charged or credited to equity (see paragraph 63).

Items Credited or Charged Directly to Equity

Current tax and deferred tax should be charged or credited directly to equity if the **61** *tax relates to items that are credited or charged, in the same or a different period, directly to equity.*

IASs require or permit certain items to be credited or charged directly to equity. **62** Examples of such items are:
(a) a change in carrying amount arising from the revaluation of property, plant and equipment (see IAS 16);
(b) an adjustment to the opening balance of retained earnings resulting from either a change in accounting policy that is applied retrospectively or the correction of a fundamental error (see IAS 8);
(c) exchange differences arising on the translation of the financial statements of a foreign entity (see IAS 21); and
(d) amounts arising on initial recognition of the equity component of a compound financial instrument (see paragraph 23).

In exceptional circumstances it may be difficult to determine the amount of current and **63** deferred tax that relates to items credited or charged to equity. ...

In such cases, the current and deferred tax related to items that are credited or charged to equity is based on a reasonable pro rata allocation of the current and deferred tax of the entity in the tax jurisdiction concerned, or other method that achieves a more appropriate allocation in the circumstances.

[Not printed] **64**

When an asset is revalued for tax purposes and that revaluation is related to an **65** accounting revaluation of an earlier period, or to one that is expected to be carried out in a future period, the tax effects of both the asset revaluation and the adjustment of the tax base are credited or charged to equity in the periods in which they occur. However, if the revaluation for tax purposes is not related to an accounting revaluation of an earlier period, or to one that is expected to be carried out in a future period, the tax effects of the adjustment of the tax base are recognised in the income statement.

When an enterprise pays dividends to its shareholders, it may be required to pay a **65A** portion of the dividends to taxation authorities on behalf of shareholders. In many jurisdictions, this amount is referred to as a withholding tax. Such an amount paid or payable to taxation authorities is charged to equity as a part of the dividends.

Deferred Tax Arising from a Business Combination

66 As explained in paragraphs 19 and 26(c), temporary differences may arise in a business combination that is an acquisition. In accordance with IAS 22 an enterprise recognises any resulting deferred tax assets (to the extent that they meet the recognition criteria in paragraph 24) or deferred tax liabilities as identifiable assets and liabilities at the date of the acquisition. Consequently, those deferred tax assets and liabilities affect goodwill or negative goodwill. However, in accordance with paragraphs 15(a) and 24(a), an enterprise does not recognise deferred tax liabilities arising from goodwill itself (if amortisation of the goodwill is not deductible for tax purposes) and deferred tax assets arising from non–taxable negative goodwill which is treated as deferred income.

67 As a result of a business combination, an acquirer may consider it probable that it will recover its own deferred tax asset that was not recognised prior to the business combination. For example, the acquirer may be able to utilise the benefit of its unused tax losses against the future taxable profit of the acquiree. In such cases, the acquirer recognises a deferred tax asset and takes this into account in determining the goodwill or negative goodwill arising on the acquisition.

68 When an acquirer did not recognise a deferred tax asset of the acquiree as an identifiable asset at the date of a business combination and that deferred tax asset is subsequently recognised in the acquirer's consolidated financial statements, the resulting deferred tax income is recognised in the income statement. In addition, the acquirer:

(a) adjusts the gross carrying amount of the goodwill and the related accumulated amortisation to the amounts that would have been recorded if the deferred tax asset had been recognised as an identifiable asset at the date of the business combination; and

(b) recognises the reduction in the net carrying amount of the goodwill as an expense.

However, the acquirer does not recognise negative goodwill, nor does it increase the carrying amount of negative goodwill.

...

Presentation

Tax Assets and Tax Liabilities

69 *Tax assets and tax liabilities should be presented separately from other assets and liabilities in the balance sheet. Deferred tax assets and liabilities should be distinguished from current tax assets and liabilities.*

70 *When an enterprise makes a distinction between current and non–current assets and liabilities in its financial statements, it should not classify deferred tax assets (liabilities) as current assets (liabilities).*

Offset

71 *An enterprise should offset current tax assets and current tax liabilities if, and only if, the enterprise:*

(a) *has a legally enforceable right to set off the recognised amounts; and*

(b) *intends either to settle on a net basis, or to realise the asset and settle the liability simultaneously.*

[Not printed]   72

In consolidated financial statements, a current tax asset of one enterprise in a group is   73
offset against a current tax liability of another enterprise in the group if, and only if,
the enterprises concerned have a legally enforceable right to make or receive a single
net payment and the enterprises intend to make or receive such a net payment or to
recover the asset and settle the liability simultaneously.

An enterprise should offset deferred tax assets and deferred tax liabilities if, and only   74
if:
(a) *the enterprise has a legally enforceable right to set off current tax assets against*
    current tax liabilities; and
(b) *the deferred tax assets and the deferred tax liabilities relate to income taxes levied*
    by the same taxation authority on either:
    (i) *the same taxable entity; or*
    (ii) *different taxable entities which intend either to settle current tax liabilities*
         and assets on a net basis, or to realise the assets and settle the liabilities
         simultaneously, in each future period in which significant amounts of
         deferred tax liabilities or assets are expected to be settled or recovered.

[Not printed]   75–76

Tax Expense

Tax Expense (Income) related to Profit or Loss from Ordinary Activities

The tax expense (income) related to profit or loss from ordinary activities should be   77
presented on the face of the income statement.

Exchange Differences on Deferred Foreign Tax Liabilities or Assets

IAS 21 requires certain exchange differences to be recognised as income or expense but   78
does not specify where such differences should be presented in the income statement.
Accordingly, where exchange differences on deferred foreign tax liabilities or assets are
recognised in the income statement, such differences may be classified as deferred tax
expense (income) if that presentation is considered to be the most useful to financial
statement users.

Disclosure

The major components of tax expense (income) should be disclosed separately.   79

Components of tax expense (income) may include: 80
(a) current tax expense (income);
(b) any adjustments recognised in the period for current tax of prior periods;
(c) the amount of deferred tax expense (income) relating to the origination and reversal
    of temporary differences;
(d) the amount of deferred tax expense (income) relating to changes in tax rates or the
    imposition of new taxes;
(e) the amount of the benefit arising from a previously unrecognised tax loss, tax credit
    or temporary difference of a prior period that is used to reduce current tax expense;
(f) the amount of the benefit from a previously unrecognised tax loss, tax credit or
    temporary difference of a prior period that is used to reduce deferred tax expense;

(g) deferred tax expense arising from the write–down, or reversal of a previous write–down, of a deferred tax asset in accordance with paragraph 56; and

(h) the amount of tax expense (income) relating to those changes in accounting policies and fundamental errors which are included in the determination of net profit or loss for the period in accordance with the allowed alternative treatment in IAS 8.

81 *The following should also be disclosed separately:*

(a) *the aggregate current and deferred tax relating to items that are charged or credited to equity;*

(b) *tax expense (income) relating to extraordinary items recognised during the period;*

(c) *an explanation of the relationship between tax expense (income) and accounting profit in either or both of the following forms:*

    (i) *a numerical reconciliation between tax expense (income) and the product of accounting profit multiplied by the applicable tax rate(s), disclosing also the basis on which the applicable tax rate(s) is (are) computed; or*

    (ii) *a numerical reconciliation between the average effective tax rate and the applicable tax rate, disclosing also the basis on which the applicable tax rate is computed;*

(d) *an explanation of changes in the applicable tax rate(s) compared to the previous accounting period;*

(e) *the amount (and expiry date, if any) of deductible temporary differences, unused tax losses, and unused tax credits for which no deferred tax asset is recognised in the balance sheet;*

(f) *the aggregate amount of temporary differences associated with investments in subsidiaries, branches and associates and interests in joint ventures, for which deferred tax liabilities have not been recognised (see paragraph 39);*

(g) *in respect of each type of temporary difference, and in respect of each type of unused tax losses and unused tax credits:*

    (i) *the amount of the deferred tax assets and liabilities recognised in the balance sheet for each period presented;*

    (ii) *the amount of the deferred tax income or expense recognised in the income statement, if this is not apparent from the changes in the amounts recognised in the balance sheet;*

(h) *in respect of discontinued operations, the tax expense relating to:*

    (i) *the gain or loss on discontinuance; and*

    (ii) *the profit or loss from the ordinary activities of the discontinued operation for the period, together with the corresponding amounts for each prior period presented; and*

(i) *the amount of income tax consequences of dividends to shareholders of the enterprise that were proposed or declared before the financial statements were authorised for issue, but are not recognised as a liability in the financial statements.*

82 *An enterprise should disclose the amount of a deferred tax asset and the nature of the evidence supporting its recognition, when:*

(a) *the utilisation of the deferred tax asset is dependent on future taxable profits in excess of the profits arising from the reversal of existing taxable temporary differences; and*

(b) *the enterprise has suffered a loss in either the current or preceding period in the tax jurisdiction to which the deferred tax asset relates.*

[Not printed]   82A

An enterprise discloses the nature and amount of each extraordinary item either on the   83
face of the income statement or in the notes to the financial statements. When this
disclosure is made in the notes to the financial statements, the total amount of all
extraordinary items is disclosed on the face of the income statement, net of the
aggregate related tax expense (income). Although financial statement users may find
the disclosure of the tax expense (income) related to each extraordinary item useful, it
is sometimes difficult to allocate tax expense (income) between such items. Under these
circumstances tax expense (income) relating to extraordinary items may be disclosed in
the aggregate.

[Not printed]   84–85

The average effective tax rate is the tax expense (income) divided by the accounting   86
profit.

It would often be impracticable to compute the amount of unrecognised deferred tax   87
liabilities arising from investments in subsidiaries, branches and associates and interests
in joint ventures (see paragraph 39). Therefore, this Standard requires an enterprise to
disclose the aggregate amount of the underlying temporary differences but does not
require disclosure of the deferred tax liabilities. Nevertheless, where practicable,
enterprises are encouraged to disclose the amounts of the unrecognised deferred tax
liabilities because financial statement users may find such information useful.

[Not printed]   87A–C

An enterprise discloses any tax–related contingent liabilities and contingent assets in   88
accordance with IAS 37. Contingent liabilities and contingent assets may arise, for
example, from unresolved disputes with the taxation authorities. Similarly, where
changes in tax rates or tax laws are enacted or announced after the balance sheet date,
an enterprise discloses any significant effect of those changes on its current and deferred
tax assets and liabilities (see IAS 10).

...

Effective Date

[Not printed]   89–91

Appendix A

Examples of Temporary Differences

[Not printed]

Appendix B

Illustrative Computations and Presentation

[Not printed]

IAS 14: Segment Reporting

IAS 14: Segment Reporting				
	Definitions 14.8–25			
Scope 14.1–7	From Other IASs 14.8	Business Segment and Geographical Segment 14.9–15	Segment Revenue, Expense, Result, Assets, and Liabilities 14.16–25	Effective Date 14.84

Identifying Reportable Segments 14.26–43		
Primary and Secondary Segment Reporting Formats 14.26–30	Business and Geographical Segments 14.31–33	Reportable Segments 14.34–43

Segment Accounting Policies 14.44–48

Disclosure 14.49–83			
Primary Reporting Format 14.50–67	Secondary Segment Information 14.68–72	Illustrative Segment Disclosures 14.73	Other Disclosure Matters 14.74–83

Appendices [Partially not printed]		
A. Segment Definition Decision Tree	B. Illustrative Segment Disclosures	C. Summary of Required Disclosure

Scope

1 This Standard should be applied in complete sets of published financial statements that comply with IASs.

2 A complete set of financial statements includes a balance sheet, income statement, cash flow statement, a statement showing changes in equity, and notes, as provided in IAS 1.

3 This Standard should be applied by enterprises whose equity or debt securities are publicly traded and by enterprises that are in the process of issuing equity or debt securities in public securities markets.

4 If an enterprise whose securities are not publicly traded prepares financial statements that comply with IASs, that enterprise is encouraged to disclose financial information by segment voluntarily.

If an enterprise whose securities are not publicly traded chooses to disclose segment 5
information voluntarily in financial statements that comply with IASs, that
enterprise should comply fully with the requirements of this Standard.

If a single financial report contains both consolidated financial statements of an 6
enterprise whose securities are publicly traded and the separate financial statements
of the parent or one or more subsidiaries, segment information need be presented only
on the basis of the consolidated financial statements. If a subsidiary is itself an
enterprise whose securities are publicly traded, it will present segment information in
its own separate financial report.

Similarly, if a single financial report contains both the financial statements of an 7
enterprise whose securities are publicly traded and the separate financial statements
of an equity method associate or joint venture in which the enterprise has a financial
interest, segment information need be presented only on the basis of the enterprise's
financial statements. If the equity method associate or joint venture is itself an
enterprise whose securities are publicly traded, it will present segment information in
its own separate financial report.

Definitions

Definitions from Other IASs

The following terms are used in this Standard with the meanings specified in IAS 7, 8
IAS 8 and IAS 18:
<u>*Operating activities*</u> *are the principal revenue–producing activities of an enterprise*
and other activities that are not investing or financing activities.
<u>*Accounting policies*</u> *are the specific principles, bases, conventions, rules and practices*
adopted by an enterprise in preparing and presenting financial statements.
<u>*Revenue*</u> *is the gross inflow of economic benefits during the period arising in the course*
of the ordinary activities of an enterprise when those inflows result in increases in
equity, other than increases relating to contributions from equity participants.

Definitions of Business Segment and Geographical Segment

... 9
A <u>*business segment*</u> *is a distinguishable component of an enterprise that is engaged*
in providing an individual product or service or a group of related products or services
and that is subject to risks and returns that are different from those of other business
segments. Factors that should be considered in determining whether products and
services are related include:
(a) the nature of the products or services;
(b) the nature of the production processes;
(c) the type or class of customer for the products or services;
(d) the methods used to distribute the products or provide the services; and
(e) if applicable, the nature of the regulatory environment, for example, banking,
insurance, or public utilities.
A <u>*geographical segment*</u> *is a distinguishable component of an enterprise that is*
engaged in providing products or services within a particular economic environment
and that is subject to risks and returns that are different from those of components

operating in other economic environments. Factors that should be considered in identifying geographical segments include:

(a) similarity of economic and political conditions;

(b) relationships between operations in different geographical areas;

(c) proximity of operations;

(d) special risks associated with operations in a particular area;

(e) exchange control regulations; and

(f) the underlying currency risks.

A reportable segment is a business segment or a geographical segment identified based on the foregoing definitions for which segment information is required to be disclosed by this Standard.

10 The factors in paragraph 9 for identifying business segments and geographical segments are not listed in any particular order.

11 A single business segment does not include products and services with significantly differing risks and returns. While there may be dissimilarities with respect to one or several of the factors in the definition of a business segment, the products and services included in a single business segment are expected to be similar with respect to a majority of the factors.

12 Similarly, a geographical segment does not include operations in economic environments with significantly differing risks and returns. A geographical segment may be a single country, a group of two or more countries, or a region within a country.

13 The predominant sources of risks affect how most enterprises are organised and managed. Therefore, paragraph 27 of this Standard provides that an enterprise's organisational structure and its internal financial reporting system is the basis for identifying its segments. The risks and returns of an enterprise are influenced both by the geographical *location of its operations* (where its products are produced or where its service delivery activities are based) and also by the *location of its markets* (where its products are sold or services are rendered). The definition allows geographical segments to be based on either:

(a) the location of an enterprise's production or service facilities and other assets; or

(b) the location of its markets and customers.

14 An enterprise's organisational and internal reporting structure will normally provide evidence of whether its dominant source of geographical risks results from the location of its assets (the origin of its sales) or the location of its customers (the destination of its sales). Accordingly, an enterprise looks to this structure to determine whether its geographical segments should be based on the location of its assets or on the location of its customers.

15 Determining the composition of a business or geographical segment involves a certain amount of judgement. In making that judgement, enterprise management takes into account the objective of reporting financial information by segment as set forth in this Standard and the qualitative characteristics of financial statements as identified in the IASC Framework for the Preparation and Presentation of Financial Statements. Those qualitative characteristics include the relevance, reliability, and comparability over time of financial information that is reported about an enterprise's different groups of products and services and about its operations in particular geographical areas, and the

usefulness of that information for assessing the risks and returns of the enterprise as a whole.

Definitions of Segment Revenue, Expense, Result, Assets, and Liabilities

...   16

Segment revenue is revenue reported in the enterprise's income statement that is directly attributable to a segment and the relevant portion of enterprise revenue that can be allocated on a reasonable basis to a segment, whether from sales to external customers or from transactions with other segments of the same enterprise. Segment revenue does not include:

(a) extraordinary items;

(b) interest or dividend income, including interest earned on advances or loans to other segments, unless the segment's operations are primarily of a financial nature; or

(c) gains on sales of investments or gains on extinguishment of debt unless the segment's operations are primarily of a financial nature.

Segment revenue includes an enterprise's share of profits or losses of associates, joint ventures, or other investments accounted for under the equity method only if those items are included in consolidated or total enterprise revenue.

Segment revenue includes a joint venturer's share of the revenue of a jointly controlled entity that is accounted for by proportionate consolidation in accordance with IAS 31.

Segment expense is expense resulting from the operating activities of a segment that is directly attributable to the segment and the relevant portion of an expense that can be allocated on a reasonable basis to the segment, including expenses relating to sales to external customers and expenses relating to transactions with other segments of the same enterprise. Segment expense does not include:

(a) extraordinary items;

(b) interest, including interest incurred on advances or loans from other segments, unless the segment's operations are primarily of a financial nature;

(c) losses on sales of investments or losses on extinguishment of debt unless the segment's operations are primarily of a financial nature;

(d) an enterprise's share of losses of associates, joint ventures, or other investments accounted for under the equity method;

(e) income tax expense; or

(f) general administrative expenses, head–office expenses, and other expenses that arise at the enterprise level and relate to the enterprise as a whole. However, costs are sometimes incurred at the enterprise level on behalf of a segment. Such costs are segment expenses if they relate to the segment's operating activities and they can be directly attributed or allocated to the segment on a reasonable basis.

Segment expense includes a joint venturer's share of the expenses of a jointly controlled entity that is accounted for by proportionate consolidation in accordance with IAS 31.

For a segment's operations that are primarily of a financial nature, interest income and interest expense may be reported as a single net amount for segment reporting purposes only if those items are netted in the consolidated or enterprise financial statements.

Segment result is segment revenue less segment expense. Segment result is determined before any adjustments for minority interest.

Segment assets are those operating assets that are employed by a segment in its operating activities and that either are directly attributable to the segment or can be allocated to the segment on a reasonable basis.

If a segment's segment result includes interest or dividend income, its segment assets include the related receivables, loans, investments, or other income–producing assets. Segment assets do not include income tax assets.

Segment assets include investments accounted for under the equity method only if the profit or loss from such investments is included in segment revenue. Segment assets include a joint venturer's share of the operating assets of a jointly controlled entity that is accounted for by proportionate consolidation in accordance with IAS 31.

Segment assets are determined after deducting related allowances that are reported as direct offsets in the enterprise's balance sheet.

Segment liabilities are those operating liabilities that result from the operating activities of a segment and that either are directly attributable to the segment or can be allocated to the segment on a reasonable basis.

If a segment's segment result includes interest expense, its segment liabilities include the related interest–bearing liabilities.

Segment liabilities include a joint venturer's share of the liabilities of a jointly controlled entity that is accounted for by proportionate consolidation in accordance with IAS 31.

Segment liabilities do not include income tax liabilities.

Segment accounting policies are the accounting policies adopted for preparing and presenting the financial statements of the consolidated group or enterprise as well as those accounting policies that relate specifically to segment reporting.

17 The definitions of segment revenue, segment expense, segment assets, and segment liabilities include amounts of such items that are directly attributable to a segment and amounts of such items that can be allocated to a segment on a reasonable basis. An enterprise looks to its internal financial reporting system as the starting point for identifying those items that can be directly attributed, or reasonably allocated, to segments. That is, there is a presumption that amounts that have been identified with segments for internal financial reporting purposes are directly attributable or reasonably allocable to segments for the purpose of measuring the segment revenue, segment expense, segment assets, and segment liabilities of reportable segments.

18 In some cases, however, a revenue, expense, asset, or liability may have been allocated to segments for internal financial reporting purposes on a basis that is understood by enterprise management but that could be deemed subjective, arbitrary, or difficult to understand by external users of financial statements. Such an allocation would not constitute a reasonable basis under the definitions of segment revenue, segment expense, segment assets, and segment liabilities in this Standard. Conversely, an enterprise may choose not to allocate some item of revenue, expense, asset, or liability for internal financial reporting purposes, even though a reasonable basis for doing so exists. Such an item is allocated pursuant to the definitions of segment revenue, segment expense, segment assets, and segment liabilities in this Standard.

19 Examples of segment assets include current assets that are used in the operating activities of the segment, property, plant, and equipment, assets that are the subject of finance leases (IAS 17), and intangible assets. If a particular item of depreciation or amortisation is included in segment expense, the related asset is also included in segment assets. Segment assets do not include assets used for general enterprise or

head–office purposes. Segment assets include operating assets shared by two or more segments if a reasonable basis for allocation exists. Segment assets include goodwill that is directly attributable to a segment or that can be allocated to a segment on a reasonable basis, and segment expense includes related amortisation of goodwill.

Examples of segment liabilities include trade and other payables, accrued liabilities, **20** customer advances, product warranty provisions, and other claims relating to the provision of goods and services. Segment liabilities do not include borrowings, liabilities related to assets that are the subject of finance leases (IAS 17), and other liabilities that are incurred for financing rather than operating purposes. If interest expense is included in segment result, the related interest–bearing liability is included in segment liabilities. The liabilities of segments whose operations are not primarily of a financial nature do not include borrowings and similar liabilities because segment result represents an operating, rather than a net–of–financing, profit or loss. Further, because debt is often issued at the head–office level on an enterprise–wide basis, it is often not possible to directly attribute, or reasonably allocate, the interest–bearing liability to the segment.

Measurements of segment assets and liabilities include adjustments to the prior carrying **21** amounts of the identifiable segment assets and segment liabilities of a company acquired in a business combination accounted for as a purchase, even if those adjustments are made only for the purpose of preparing consolidated financial statements and are not recorded in either the parent's or the subsidiary's separate financial statements. Similarly, if property, plant, and equipment has been revalued subsequent to acquisition in accordance with the alternative accounting treatment allowed by IAS 16, then measurements of segment assets reflect those revaluations.

Some guidance for cost allocation can be found in other IASs. For example, paragraphs **22** 8–16 of IAS 2 provide guidance for attributing and allocating costs to inventories, and paragraphs 16–21 of IAS 11 provide guidance for attributing and allocating costs to contracts. That guidance may be useful in attributing or allocating costs to segments.

[Not printed] **23**

Segment revenue, segment expense, segment assets, and segment liabilities are **24** determined before intra–group balances and intra–group transactions are eliminated as part of the consolidation process, except to the extent that such intra–group balances and transactions are between group enterprises within a single segment.

While the accounting policies used in preparing and presenting the financial statements **25** of the enterprise as a whole are also the fundamental segment accounting policies, segment accounting policies include, in addition, policies that relate specifically to segment reporting, such as identification of segments, method of pricing inter–segment transfers, and basis for allocating revenues and expenses to segments.

Identifying Reportable Segments

Primary and Secondary Segment Reporting Formats

The dominant source and nature of an enterprise's risks and returns should govern **26** *whether its primary segment reporting format will be business segments or geographical segments. If the enterprise's risks and rates of return are affected predominantly by differences in the products and services it produces, its primary* *format for reporting segment information should be business segments, with secondary information reported geographically. Similarly, if the enterprise's risks and rates of return are affected predominantly by the fact that it operates in different countries or other geographical areas, its primary format for reporting segment information should be geographical segments, with secondary information reported for groups of related products and services.*

27 *An enterprise's internal organisational and management structure and its system of internal financial reporting to the board of directors and the chief executive officer should normally be the basis for identifying the predominant source and nature of risks and differing rates of return facing the enterprise and, therefore, for determining which reporting format is primary and which is secondary, except as provided in subparagraphs (a) and (b) below:*

(a) *if an enterprise's risks and rates of return are strongly affected both by differences in the products and services it produces and by differences in the geographical areas in which it operates, as evidenced by a "matrix approach" to managing the company and to reporting internally to the board of directors and the chief executive officer, then the enterprise should use business segments as its primary segment reporting format and geographical segments as its secondary reporting format; and*

(b) *if an enterprise's internal organisational and management structure and its system of internal financial reporting to the board of directors and the chief executive officer are based neither on individual products or services or on groups of related products/services nor on geography, the directors and management of the enterprise should determine whether the enterprise's risks and returns are related more to the products and services it produces or more to the geographical areas in which it operates and, as a consequence, should choose either business segments or geographical segments as the enterprise's primary segment reporting format, with the other as its secondary reporting format.*

28–30 [Not printed]

Business and Geographical Segments

31 *An enterprise's business and geographical segments for external reporting purposes should be those organisational units for which information is reported to the board of directors and to the chief executive officer for the purpose of evaluating the unit's past performance and for making decisions about future allocations of resources, except as provided in paragraph 32.*

32 *If an enterprise's internal organisational and management structure and its system of internal financial reporting to the board of directors and the chief executive officer are based neither on individual products or services or on groups of related products/ services nor on geography, paragraph 27(b) requires that the directors and management of the enterprise should choose either business segments or geographical segments as the enterprise's primary segment reporting format based on their assessment of which reflects the primary source of the enterprise's risks and returns, with the other its secondary reporting format. In that case, the directors and management of the enterprise must determine its business segments and geographical segments for external reporting purposes based on the factors in the definitions in paragraph 9 of this Standard, rather than on the basis of its system of internal*

financial reporting to the board of directors and chief executive officer, consistent with the following:
(a) *if one or more of the segments reported internally to the directors and management is a business segment or a geographical segment based on the factors in the definitions in paragraph 9 but others are not, subparagraph (b) below should be applied only to those internal segments that do not meet the definitions in paragraph 9 (that is, an internally reported segment that meets the definition should not be further segmented);*
(b) *for those segments reported internally to the directors and management that do not satisfy the definitions in paragraph 9, management of the enterprise should look to the next lower level of internal segmentation that reports information along product and service lines or geographical lines, as appropriate under the definitions in paragraph 9; and*
(c) *if such an internally reported lower–level segment meets the definition of business segment or geographical segment based on the factors in paragraph 9, the criteria in paragraphs 34 and 35 for identifying reportable segments should be applied to that segment.*

[Not printed]   **33**

Reportable Segments

Two or more internally reported business segments or geographical segments that are **34** *substantially similar may be combined as a single business segment or geographical segment. Two or more business segments or geographical segments are substantially similar only if:*
(a) *they exhibit similar long–term financial performance; and*
(b) *they are similar in all of the factors in the appropriate definition in paragraph 9.*

A business segment or geographical segment should be identified as a reportable **35** *segment if a majority of its revenue is earned from sales to external customers and:*
(a) *its revenue from sales to external customers and from transactions with other segments is 10 per cent or more of the total revenue, external and internal, of all segments; or*
(b) *its segment result, whether profit or loss, is 10 per cent or more of the combined result of all segments in profit or the combined result of all segments in loss, whichever is the greater in absolute amount; or*
(c) *its assets are 10 per cent or more of the total assets of all segments.*

If an internally reported segment is below all of the thresholds of significance in **36** *paragraph 35:*
(a) *that segment may be designated as a reportable segment despite its size;*
(b) *if not designated as a reportable segment despite its size, that segment may be combined into a separately reportable segment with one or more other similar internally reported segment(s) that are also below all of the thresholds of significance in paragraph 35 (two or more business segments or geographical segments are similar if they share a majority of the factors in the appropriate definition in paragraph 9); and*
(c) *if that segment is not separately reported or combined, it should be included as an unallocated reconciling item.*

37 *If total external revenue attributable to reportable segments constitutes less than 75 per cent of the total consolidated or enterprise revenue, additional segments should be identified as reportable segments, even if they do not meet the 10 per cent thresholds in paragraph 35, until at least 75 per cent of total consolidated or enterprise revenue is included in reportable segments.*

38 The 10 per cent thresholds in this Standard are not intended to be a guide for determining materiality for any aspect of financial reporting other than identifying reportable business and geographical segments.

39–40 [Not printed]

41 *If an enterprise's internal reporting system treats vertically integrated activities as separate segments and the enterprise does not choose to report them externally as business segments, the selling segment should be combined into the buying segment(s) in identifying externally reportable business segments unless there is no reasonable basis for doing so, in which case the selling segment would be included as an unallocated reconciling item.*

42 *A segment identified as a reportable segment in the immediately preceding period because it satisfied the relevant 10 per cent thresholds should continue to be a reportable segment for the current period notwithstanding that its revenue, result, and assets all no longer exceed the 10 per cent thresholds, if the management of the enterprise judges the segment to be of continuing significance.*

43 *If a segment is identified as a reportable segment in the current period because it satisfies the relevant 10 per cent thresholds, prior period segment data that is presented for comparative purposes should be restated to reflect the newly reportable segment as a separate segment, even if that segment did not satisfy the 10 per cent thresholds in the prior period, unless it is impracticable to do so.*

Segment Accounting Policies

44 *Segment information should be prepared in conformity with the accounting policies adopted for preparing and presenting the financial statements of the consolidated group or enterprise.*

45 [Not printed]

46 This Standard does not prohibit the disclosure of additional segment information that is prepared on a basis other than the accounting policies adopted for the consolidated or enterprise financial statements provided that (a) the information is reported internally to the board of directors and the chief executive officer for purposes of making decisions about allocating resources to the segment and assessing its performance and (b) the basis of measurement for this additional information is clearly described.

47 *Assets that are jointly used by two or more segments should be allocated to segments if, and only if, their related revenues and expenses also are allocated to those segments.*

48 [Not printed]

Disclosure

[Not printed]   49

Primary Reporting Format

The disclosure requirements in paragraphs 51–67 should be applied to each reportable   50
segment based on an enterprise's primary reporting format.

An enterprise should disclose segment revenue for each reportable segment. Segment   51
revenue from sales to external customers and segment revenue from transactions with
other segments should be separately reported.

An enterprise should disclose segment result for each reportable segment.   52

[Not printed]   53–54

An enterprise should disclose the total carrying amount of segment assets for each   55
reportable segment.

An enterprise should disclose segment liabilities for each reportable segment.   56

An enterprise should disclose the total cost incurred during the period to acquire   57
segment assets that are expected to be used during more than one period (property,
plant, equipment, and intangible assets) for each reportable segment. While this
sometimes is referred to as capital additions or capital expenditure, the measurement
required by this principle should be on an accrual basis, not a cash basis.

An enterprise should disclose the total amount of expense included in segment result 58
for depreciation and amortisation of segment assets for the period for each reportable
segment.

An enterprise is encouraged, but not required to disclose the nature and amount of   59
any items of segment revenue and segment expense that are of such size, nature, or
incidence that their disclosure is relevant to explain the performance of each
reportable segment for the period.

[Not printed]   60

An enterprise should disclose, for each reportable segment, the total amount of   61
significant non–cash expenses, other than depreciation and amortisation for which
separate disclosure is required by paragraph 58, that were included in segment
expense and, therefore, deducted in measuring segment result.

... This Standard also encourages the segment cash flow disclosures that are encouraged   62
by IAS 7. Additionally, it encourages disclosure of significant non–cash revenues that
were included in segment revenue and, therefore, added in measuring segment result.

An enterprise that provides the segment cash flow disclosures that are encouraged by 63
IAS 7 need not also disclose depreciation and amortisation expense pursuant to
paragraph 58 or non–cash expenses pursuant to paragraph 61.

An enterprise should disclose, for each reportable segment, the aggregate of the   64
enterprise's share of the net profit or loss of associates, joint ventures, or other
investments accounted for under the equity method if substantially all of those
associates' operations are within that single segment.

65 [Not printed]

66 *If an enterprise's aggregate share of the net profit or loss of associates, joint ventures, or other investments accounted for under the equity method is disclosed by reportable segment, the aggregate investments in those associates and joint ventures should also be disclosed by reportable segment.*

67 *An enterprise should present a reconciliation between the information disclosed for reportable segments and the aggregated information in the consolidated or enterprise financial statements. In presenting the reconciliation, segment revenue should be reconciled to enterprise revenue from external customers (including disclosure of the amount of enterprise revenue from external customers not included in any segment's revenue); segment result should be reconciled to a comparable measure of enterprise operating profit or loss as well as to enterprise net profit or loss; segment assets should be reconciled to enterprise assets; and segment liabilities should be reconciled to enterprise liabilities.*

Secondary Segment Information

68 [Not printed]

69 *If an enterprise's primary format for reporting segment information is business segments, it should also report the following information:*
(a) segment revenue from external customers by geographical area based on the geographical location of its customers, for each geographical segment whose revenue from sales to external customers is 10 per cent or more of total enterprise revenue from sales to all external customers;
(b) the total carrying amount of segment assets by geographical location of assets, for each geographical segment whose segment assets are 10 per cent or more of the total assets of all geographical segments; and
(c) the total cost incurred during the period to acquire segment assets that are expected to be used during more than one period (property, plant, equipment, and intangible assets) by geographical location of assets, for each geographical segment whose segment assets are 10 per cent or more of the total assets of all geographical segments.

70 *If an enterprise's primary format for reporting segment information is geographical segments (whether based on location of assets or location of customers), it should also report the following segment information for each business segment whose revenue from sales to external customers is 10 per cent or more of total enterprise revenue from sales to all external customers or whose segment assets are 10 per cent or more of the total assets of all business segments:*
(a) segment revenue from external customers;
(b) the total carrying amount of segment assets; and
(c) the total cost incurred during the period to acquire segment assets that are expected to be used during more than one period (property, plant, equipment, and intangible assets).

71 *If an enterprise's primary format for reporting segment information is geographical segments that are based on location of assets, and if the location of its customers is different from the location of its assets, then the enterprise should also report revenue from sales to external customers for each customer–based geographical segment whose* revenue from sales to external customers is 10 per cent or more of total enterprise revenue from sales to all external customers.

If an enterprise's primary format for reporting segment information is geographical **72** *segments that are based on location of customers, and if the enterprise's assets are located in different geographical areas from its customers, then the enterprise should also report the following segment information for each asset–based geographical segment whose revenue from sales to external customers or segment assets are 10 per cent or more of related consolidated or total enterprise amounts:*

(a) *the total carrying amount of segment assets by geographical location of the assets; and*

(b) *the total cost incurred during the period to acquire segment assets that are expected to be used during more than one period (property, plant, equipment, and intangible assets) by location of the assets.*

Illustrative Segment Disclosures

Appendix B to this Standard presents an illustration of the disclosures for primary and **73** secondary reporting formats that are required by this Standard.

Other Disclosure Matters

If a business segment or geographical segment for which information is reported to **74** *the board of directors and chief executive officer is not a reportable segment because it earns a majority of its revenue from sales to other segments, but nonetheless its revenue from sales to external customers is 10 per cent or more of total enterprise revenue from sales to all external customers, the enterprise should disclose that fact and the amounts of revenue from (a) sales to external customers and (b) internal sales to other segments.*

In measuring and reporting segment revenue from transactions with other segments, **75** *inter–segment transfers should be measured on the basis that the enterprise actually used to price those transfers. The basis of pricing inter–segment transfers and any change therein should be disclosed in the financial statements.*

Changes in accounting policies adopted for segment reporting that have a material **76** *effect on segment information should be disclosed, and prior period segment information presented for comparative purposes should be restated unless it is impracticable to do so. Such disclosure should include a description of the nature of the change, the reasons for the change, the fact that comparative information has been restated or that it is impracticable to do so, and the financial effect of the change, if it is reasonably determinable. If an enterprise changes the identification of its segments and it does not restate prior period segment information on the new basis because it is impracticable to do so, then for the purpose of comparison the enterprise should report segment data for both the old and the new bases of segmentation in the year in which it changes the identification of its segments.*

[Not printed] **77**

Changes in accounting policies adopted at the enterprise level that affect segment **78** information are dealt with in accordance with IAS 8. ...

Some changes in accounting policies relate specifically to segment reporting. ... Such **79** changes can have a significant impact on the segment information reported but will not change aggregate financial information reported for the enterprise. To enable users to understand the changes and to assess trends, prior period segment information that is included in the financial statements for comparative purposes is restated, if practicable, to reflect the new accounting policy.

80 [Not printed]

81 *An enterprise should indicate the types of products and services included in each reported business segment and indicate the composition of each reported geographical segment, both primary and secondary, if not otherwise disclosed in the financial statements or elsewhere in the financial report.*

82 [Not printed]

83 Previously reported segments that no longer satisfy the quantitative thresholds are not reported separately. ...

Effective Date

84 *[Not printed]*

Appendix A: Segment Definition Decision Tree

The purpose of this appendix is to illustrate the application of paragraphs 31–43.

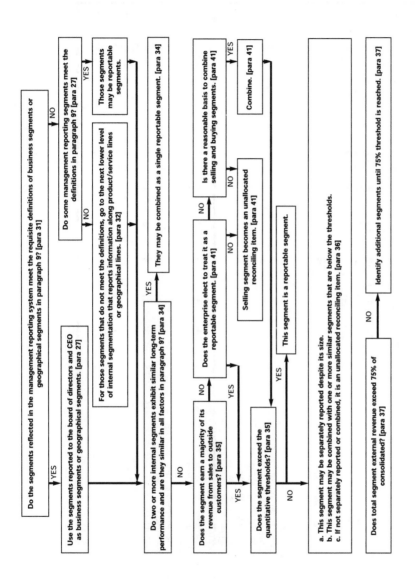

a. This segment may be separately reported despite its size.
b. This segment may be combined with one or more similar segments that are below the thresholds.
c. If not separately reported or combined, it is an unallocated reconciling item. [para 36]

Appendix B: Illustrative Segment Disclosures

...

Schedule A – INFORMATION ABOUT BUSINESS SEGMENTS (...)
(All amounts million)

	Paper Products 20x2	Paper Products 20x1	Office Products 20x2	Office Products 20x1	Publishing 20x2	Publishing 20x1	Other Operations 20x2	Other Operations 20x1	Eliminations 20x2	Eliminations 20x1	Consolidated 20x2	Consolidated 20x1
REVENUE												
External sales	55	50	20	17	19	16	7	7			101	90
Inter-segment sales	15	10	10	14	2	4	2	2	(29)	(30)		
Total revenue	70	60	30	31	21	20	9	9	(29)	(30)	101	90
RESULT												
Segment result	20	17	9	7	2	1	0	0	(1)	(1)	30	24
Unallocated corporate expenses											(7)	(9)
Operating profit											23	15
Interest expense											(4)	(4)
Interest income											2	3
Share of net profits of associates	6	5					2	2			8	7
Income taxes											(7)	(4)
Profit from ordinary activities											22	17
Extraordinary loss: uninsured earthquake damage to factory		(3)										(3)
Net profit											22	14
OTHER INFORMATION												
Segment assets	54	50	34	30	10	10	10	9			108	99
Investment in equity method associates	20	16					12	10			32	26
Unallocated corporate assets											35	30
Consolidated total assets											175	155
Segment liabilities	25	15	8	11	8	8	1	1			42	35
Unallocated corporate liabilities											40	55
Consolidated total liabilities											82	90
Capital expenditure	12	10	3	5	5	3	4	3				
Depreciation	9	7	9	7	5	3	3	4				
Non-cash expenses other than depreciation	8	2	7	3	2	2	2	1				

...

Appendix C: Summary of Required Disclosure

[Not printed]

IAS 15: *Information Reflecting the Effects of Changing Prices*

IAS 15: Information Reflecting the Effects of Changing Prices			
Board Statement October 1989	Scope 15.1–5	Explanation 15.6–7	Effective Date 15.27

Responding to Changing Prices 15.8–26				
Approaches 15.11–18			Disclosures 15.21–26	
General Purchasing Power Approach 15.11	Current Cost Approach 15.12–18	Current Status 15.19–20	Minimum 15.21–25	Other 15.26

Board Statement October 1989

At its meeting in October 1989, the Board of IASC approved the following statement to be added to IAS 15:

"The international consensus on the disclosure of information reflecting the effects of changing prices that was anticipated when IAS 15 was issued has not been reached. As a result, the Board of IASC has decided that enterprises need not disclose the information required by IAS 15 in order that their financial statements conform with IASs. However, the Board encourages enterprises to present such information and urges those that do to disclose the items required by IAS 15."

Scope

This Standard should be applied in reflecting the effects of changing prices on the **1** *measurements used in the determination of an enterprise's results of operation and financial position.*

[Not printed] **2**

This Standard applies to enterprises whose levels of revenues, profit, assets or **3** employment are significant in the economic environment in which they operate. When both parent company and consolidated financial statements are presented, the information called for by this Standard need only be presented on the basis of consolidated information.

[Not printed] **4–5**

Explanation

[Not printed] **6**

In most countries financial statements are prepared on the historical cost basis of **7** accounting without regard either to changes in the general level of prices or to changes in specific prices of assets held, except to the extent that property, plant and equipment may have been revalued or inventories or other current assets reduced to net realisable value. The information required by this Standard is designed to make users of an enterprise's financial statements aware of the effects of changing prices on the results of its operations. Financial statements, however, whether prepared under the historical cost method or under a method that reflects the effects of changing prices, are not intended to indicate directly the value of the enterprise as a whole.

Responding to Changing Prices

8 *Enterprises to which this Standard applies should present information disclosing the items set out in paragraphs 21 to 23 using an accounting method reflecting the effects of changing prices.*

9 Financial information intended as a response to the effects of changing prices is prepared in a number of ways. One way shows financial information in terms of general purchasing power. Another way shows current cost in place of historical cost, recognising changes in specific prices of assets. A third way combines features of both these methods.

10 Underlying these responses are two basic approaches to the determination of income. One recognises income after the general purchasing power of the shareholders' equity in the enterprise has been maintained. The other recognises income after the operating capacity of the enterprise has been maintained, and may or may not include a general price level adjustment.

General Purchasing Power Approach

11 The general purchasing power approach involves the restatement of some or all of the items in the financial statements for changes in the general price level. Proposals on this subject emphasise that general purchasing power restatements change the unit of account but do not change the underlying measurement bases. Under this approach, income normally reflects the effects, using an appropriate index, of general price level changes on depreciation, cost of sales and net monetary items and is reported after the general purchasing power of the shareholders' equity in the enterprise has been maintained.

Current Cost Approach

12 The current cost approach is found in a number of different methods. In general, these use replacement cost as the primary measurement basis. If, however, replacement cost is higher than both net realisable value and present value, the higher of net realisable value and present value is usually used as the measurement basis.

13 The replacement cost of a specific asset is normally derived from the current acquisition cost of a similar asset, new or used, or of an equivalent productive capacity or service potential. Net realisable value usually represents the net current selling price of the asset. Present value represents a current estimate of future net receipts attributable to the asset, appropriately discounted.

14 Specific price indices are often used as a means to determine current costs for items, particularly if no recent transaction involving those items has occurred, no price lists are available or the use of price lists is not practical.

[Not printed]   15–18

Current Status

[Not printed]   19–20

Minimum Disclosures

The items to be presented are: 21
(a) the amount of the adjustment to or the adjusted amount of depreciation of property, plant and equipment;
(b) the amount of the adjustment to or the adjusted amount of cost of sales;
(c) the adjustments relating to monetary items, the effect of borrowing, or equity interests when such adjustments have been taken into account in determining income under the accounting method adopted; and
(d) the overall effect on results of the adjustments described in (a) and (b) and, where appropriate, (c), as well as any other items reflecting the effects of changing prices that are reported under the accounting method adopted.

When a current cost method is adopted the current cost of property, plant and 22
equipment, and of inventories, should be disclosed.

Enterprises should describe the methods adopted to compute the information called 23
for in paragraphs 21 and 22, including the nature of any indices used.

The information required by paragraphs 21 to 23 should be provided on a 24
supplementary basis unless such information is presented in the primary financial statements.

[Not printed]   25

Other Disclosures

Enterprises are encouraged to provide additional disclosures, and in particular a   26
discussion of the significance of the information in the circumstances of the enterprise.
Disclosure of any adjustments to tax provisions or tax balances is usually helpful.

Effective Date

[Not printed]   27

IAS 16: Property, Plant and Equipment

IAS 16: Property, Plant and Equipment			
Scope 16.1–5	Definitions 16.6	Effective Date 16.67–68	Related Interpretations: SIC–14, 23

Recognition of Property, Plant and Equipment 16.7–13

Initial Measurement of Property, Plant and Equipment 16.14–22		
Measurement at Cost 16.14	Components of Cost 16.15–20	Exchanges of Assets 16.21–22

Subsequent Expenditure 16.23–27

Measurement Subsequent to Initial Recognition 16.28–52			
Benchmark Treatment 16.28	Allowed Alternative Treatment 16.29–40	Depreciation 16.41–52	
	Revaluations 16.30–40	Review of Useful Life 16.49–51	Review of Depreciation Method 16.52

Recoverability of the Carrying Amount– Impairment Losses 16.53–54

Retirements and Disposals 16.55–59

Disclosure 16.60–66

Scope

1 *This Standard should be applied in accounting for property, plant and equipment except when another IAS requires or permits a different accounting treatment.*

2–5 [Not printed]

Definitions

6 ...

Property, plant and equipment are tangible assets that:
(a) are held by an enterprise for use in the production or supply of goods or services, for rental to others, or for administrative purposes; and
(b) are expected to be used during more than one period.
Depreciation is the systematic allocation of the depreciable amount of an asset over its useful life.

Depreciable amount is the cost of an asset, or other amount substituted for cost in the financial statements, less its residual value.

Useful life is either:

(a) the period of time over which an asset is expected to be used by the enterprise; or

(b) the number of production or similar units expected to be obtained from the asset by the enterprise.

Cost is the amount of cash or cash equivalents paid or the fair value of the other consideration given to acquire an asset at the time of its acquisition or construction.

Residual value is the net amount which the enterprise expects to obtain for an asset at the end of its useful life after deducting the expected costs of disposal.

Fair value is the amount for which an asset could be exchanged between knowledgeable, willing parties in an arm's length transaction.

An impairment loss is the amount by which the carrying amount of an asset exceeds its recoverable amount.

Carrying amount is the amount at which an asset is recognised in the balance sheet after deducting any accumulated depreciation and accumulated impairment losses thereon.

Recognition of Property, Plant and Equipment

An item of property, plant and equipment should be recognised as an asset when: 7

(a) *it is probable that future economic benefits associated with the asset will flow to the enterprise; and*

(b) *the cost of the asset to the enterprise can be measured reliably.*

[Not printed]   8

In determining whether an item satisfies the first criterion for recognition, an enterprise   9 needs to assess the degree of certainty attaching to the flow of future economic benefits on the basis of the available evidence at the time of initial recognition. Existence of sufficient certainty that the future economic benefits will flow to the enterprise necessitates an assurance that the enterprise will receive the rewards attaching to the asset and will undertake the associated risks. This assurance is usually only available when the risks and rewards have passed to the enterprise. Before this occurs, the transaction to acquire the asset can usually be cancelled without significant penalty and, therefore, the asset is not recognised.

The second criterion for recognition is usually readily satisfied because the exchange   10 transaction evidencing the purchase of the asset identifies its cost. In the case of a self–constructed asset, a reliable measurement of the cost can be made from the transactions with parties external to the enterprise for the acquisition of the materials, labour and other inputs used during the construction process.

In identifying what constitutes a separate item of property, plant and equipment,   11 judgement is required in applying the criteria in the definition to specific circumstances or specific types of enterprises. It may be appropriate to aggregate individually insignificant items, such as moulds, tools and dies, and to apply the criteria to the aggregate value. Most spare parts and servicing equipment are usually carried as inventory and recognised as an expense as consumed. However, major spare parts and stand–by equipment qualify as property, plant and equipment when the enterprise expects to use them during more than one period. Similarly, if the spare parts and servicing equipment can be used only in connection with an item of property, plant and equipment and their use is expected to be irregular, they are accounted for as property, plant and equipment and are depreciated over a time period not exceeding the useful life of the related asset.

12 In certain circumstances, it is appropriate to allocate the total expenditure on an asset to its component parts and account for each component separately. This is the case when the component assets have different useful lives or provide benefits to the enterprise in a different pattern thus necessitating use of different depreciation rates and methods. ...

13 Property, plant and equipment may be acquired for safety or environmental reasons. The acquisition of such property, plant and equipment, while not directly increasing the future economic benefits of any particular existing item of property, plant and equipment may be necessary in order for the enterprise to obtain the future economic benefits from its other assets. When this is the case, such acquisitions of property, plant and equipment qualify for recognition as assets, in that they enable future economic benefits from related assets to be derived by the enterprise in excess of what it could derive if they had not been acquired. However, such assets are only recognised to the extent that the resulting carrying amount of such an asset and related assets does not exceed the total recoverable amount of that asset and its related assets. ...

Initial Measurement of Property, Plant and Equipment

14 *An item of property, plant and equipment which qualifies for recognition as an asset should initially be measured at its cost.*

Components of Cost

15 The cost of an item of property, plant and equipment comprises its purchase price, including import duties and non–refundable purchase taxes, and any directly attributable costs of bringing the asset to working condition for its intended use; any trade discounts and rebates are deducted in arriving at the purchase price. Examples of directly attributable costs are:
   (a) the cost of site preparation;
   (b) initial delivery and handling costs;
   (c) installation costs;
   (d) professional fees such as for architects and engineers; and
   (e) the estimated cost of dismantling and removing the asset and restoring the site, to the extent that it is recognised as a provision under IAS 37.

16 When payment for an item of property, plant and equipment is deferred beyond normal credit terms, its cost is the cash price equivalent; the difference between this amount and the total payments is recognised as interest expense over the period of credit unless it is capitalised in accordance with the allowed alternative treatment in IAS 23.

17 Administration and other general overhead costs are not a component of the cost of property, plant and equipment unless they can be directly attributed to the acquisition of the asset or bringing the asset to its working condition. Similarly, start–up and similar pre–production costs do not form part of the cost of an asset unless they are necessary to bring the asset to its working condition. Initial operating losses incurred prior to an asset achieving planned performance are recognised as an expense.

The cost of a self–constructed asset is determined using the same principles as for an **18** acquired asset. If an enterprise makes similar assets for sale in the normal course of business, the cost of the asset is usually the same as the cost of producing the assets for sale (see IAS 2). Therefore, any internal profits are eliminated in arriving at such costs. Similarly, the cost of abnormal amounts of wasted material, labour, or other resources incurred in the production of a self–constructed asset is not included in the cost of the asset. IAS 23 establishes criteria which need to be satisfied before interest costs can be recognised as a component of property, plant and equipment cost.

The cost of an asset held by a lessee under a finance lease is determined using the **19** principles set out in IAS 17.

The carrying amount of property, plant and equipment may be reduced by applicable **20** government grants in accordance with IAS 20.

Exchanges of Assets

An item of property, plant and equipment may be acquired in exchange or part **21** exchange for a dissimilar item of property, plant and equipment or other asset. The cost of such an item is measured at the fair value of the asset received, which is equivalent to the fair value of the asset given up adjusted by the amount of any cash or cash equivalents transferred.

An item of property, plant and equipment may be acquired in exchange for a similar **22** asset that has a similar use in the same line of business and which has a similar fair value. An item of property, plant and equipment may also be sold in exchange for an equity interest in a similar asset. In both cases, since the earnings process is incomplete, no gain or loss is recognised on the transaction. Instead, the cost of the new asset is the carrying amount of the asset given up. However, the fair value of the asset received may provide evidence of an impairment in the asset given up. Under these circumstances the asset given up is written down and this written down value assigned to the new asset. ... If other assets such as cash are included as part of the exchange transaction this may indicate that the items exchanged do not have a similar value.

Subsequent Expenditure

Subsequent expenditure relating to an item of property, plant and equipment that has **23** *already been recognised should be added to the carrying amount of the asset when it is probable that future economic benefits, in excess of the originally assessed standard of performance of the existing asset, will flow to the enterprise. All other subsequent expenditure should be recognised as an expense in the period in which it is incurred.*

Subsequent expenditure on property plant and equipment is only recognised as an asset **24** when the expenditure improves the condition of the asset beyond its originally assessed standard of performance. Examples of improvements which result in increased future economic benefits include:
(a) modification of an item of plant to extend its useful life, including an increase in its capacity;
(b) upgrading machine parts to achieve a substantial improvement in the quality of output; and
(c) adoption of new production processes enabling a substantial reduction in previously assessed operating costs.

25 Expenditure on repairs or maintenance of property, plant and equipment is made to restore or maintain the future economic benefits that an enterprise can expect from the originally assessed standard of performance of the asset. As such, it is usually recognised as an expense when incurred. ...

26 The appropriate accounting treatment for expenditure incurred subsequent to the acquisition of an item of property, plant and equipment depends on the circumstances which were taken into account on the initial measurement and recognition of the related item of property, plant and equipment and whether the subsequent expenditure is recoverable. For instance, when the carrying amount of the item of property, plant and equipment already takes into account a loss in economic benefits, the subsequent expenditure to restore the future economic benefits expected from the asset is capitalised provided that the carrying amount does not exceed the recoverable amount of the asset. This is also the case when the purchase price of an asset already reflects the enterprise's obligation to incur expenditure in the future which is necessary to bring the asset to its working condition. ...

27 Major components of some items of property, plant and equipment may require replacement at regular intervals. ... The components are accounted for as separate assets because they have useful lives different from those of the items of property, plant and equipment to which they relate. Therefore, provided the recognition criteria in paragraph 7 are satisfied, the expenditure incurred in replacing or renewing the component is accounted for as the acquisition of a separate asset and the replaced asset is written off.

Measurement Subsequent to Initial Recognition

Benchmark Treatment

28 *Subsequent to initial recognition as an asset, an item of property, plant and equipment should be carried at its cost less any accumulated depreciation and any accumulated impairment losses.*

Allowed Alternative Treatment

29 *Subsequent to initial recognition as an asset, an item of property, plant and equipment should be carried at a revalued amount, being its fair value at the date of the revaluation less any subsequent accumulated depreciation and subsequent accumulated impairment losses. Revaluations should be made with sufficient regularity such that the carrying amount does not differ materially from that which would be determined using fair value at the balance sheet date.*

Revaluations

30 The fair value of land and buildings is usually its market value. This value is determined by appraisal normally undertaken by professionally qualified valuers.

31 The fair value of items of plant and equipment is usually their market value determined by appraisal. When there is no evidence of market value because of the specialised nature of the plant and equipment and because these items are rarely sold, except as part of a continuing business, they are valued at their depreciated replacement cost.

The frequency of revaluations depends upon the movements in the fair values of the **32** items of property, plant and equipment being revalued. When the fair value of a revalued asset differs materially from its carrying amount, a further revaluation is necessary. Some items of property, plant and equipment may experience significant and volatile movements in fair value thus necessitating annual revaluation. Such frequent revaluations are unnecessary for items of property, plant and equipment with only insignificant movements in fair value. Instead, revaluation every three or five years may be sufficient.

When an item of property, plant and equipment is revalued, any accumulated **33** depreciation at the date of the revaluation is either:
(a) restated proportionately with the change in the gross carrying amount of the asset so that the carrying amount of the asset after revaluation equals its revalued amount. This method is often used when an asset is revalued by means of an index to its depreciated replacement cost; or
(b) eliminated against the gross carrying amount of the asset and the net amount restated to the revalued amount of the asset. For example, this method is used for buildings which are revalued to their market value.

The amount of the adjustment arising on the restatement or elimination of accumulated depreciation forms part of the increase or decrease in carrying amount which is dealt with in accordance with paragraphs 37 and 38.

When an item of property, plant and equipment is revalued, the entire class of **34** *property, plant and equipment to which that asset belongs should be revalued.*

A class of property, plant and equipment is a grouping of assets of a similar nature and **35** use in an enterprise's operations. The following are examples of separate classes:
(a) land;
(b) land and buildings;
(c) machinery;
(d) ships;
(e) aircraft;
(f) motor vehicles;
(g) furniture and fixtures; and
(h) office equipment.

The items within a class of property, plant and equipment are revalued simultaneously **36** in order to avoid selective revaluation of assets and the reporting of amounts in the financial statements which are a mixture of costs and values as at different dates. However, a class of assets may be revalued on a rolling basis provided revaluation of the class of assets is completed within a short period of time and provided the revaluations are kept up to date.

When an asset's carrying amount is increased as a result of a revaluation, the **37** *increase should be credited directly to equity under the heading of revaluation surplus. However, a revaluation increase should be recognised as income to the extent that it reverses a revaluation decrease of the same asset previously recognised as an expense.*

When an asset's carrying amount is decreased as a result of a revaluation, the **38** *decrease should be recognised as an expense. However, a revaluation decrease should be charged directly against any related revaluation surplus to the extent that the* *decrease does not exceed the amount held in the revaluation surplus in respect of that same asset.*

39   The revaluation surplus included in equity may be transferred directly to retained earnings when the surplus is realised. The whole surplus may be realised on the retirement or disposal of the asset. However, some of the surplus may be realised as the asset is used by the enterprise; in such a case, the amount of the surplus realised is the difference between depreciation based on the revalued carrying amount of the asset and depreciation based on the asset's original cost. The transfer from revaluation surplus to retained earnings is not made through the income statement.

40   [Not printed]

Depreciation

41   *The depreciable amount of an item of property, plant and equipment should be allocated on a systematic basis over its useful life. The depreciation method used should reflect the pattern in which the asset's economic benefits are consumed by the enterprise. The depreciation charge for each period should be recognised as an expense unless it is included in the carrying amount of another asset.*

42   As the economic benefits embodied in an asset are consumed by the enterprise, the carrying amount of the asset is reduced to reflect this consumption, normally by charging an expense for depreciation. A depreciation charge is made even if the value of the asset exceeds its carrying amount.

43   The economic benefits embodied in an item of property, plant and equipment are consumed by the enterprise principally through the use of the asset. However, other factors such as technical obsolescence and wear and tear while an asset remains idle often result in the diminution of the economic benefits that might have been expected to be available from the asset. Consequently, all the following factors need to be considered in determining the useful life of an asset:

(a)   the expected usage of the asset by the enterprise. Usage is assessed by reference to the asset's expected capacity or physical output;

(b)   the expected physical wear and tear, which depends on operational factors such as the number of shifts for which the asset is to be used and the repair and maintenance programme of the enterprise, and the care and maintenance of the asset while idle;

(c)   technical obsolescence arising from changes or improvements in production, or from a change in the market demand for the product or service output of the asset; and

(d)   legal or similar limits on the use of the asset, such as the expiry dates of related leases.

44   The useful life of an asset is defined in terms of the asset's expected utility to the enterprise. The asset management policy of an enterprise may involve the disposal of assets after a specified time or after consumption of a certain proportion of the economic benefits embodied in the asset. Therefore, the useful life of an asset may be shorter than its economic life. The estimation of the useful life of an item of property, plant and equipment is a matter of judgement based on the experience of the enterprise with similar assets.

45   Land and buildings are separable assets and are dealt with separately for accounting purposes, even when they are acquired together. Land normally has an unlimited life

and, therefore, is not depreciated. Buildings have a limited life and, therefore, are depreciable assets. An increase in the value of the land on which a building stands does not affect the determination of the useful life of the building.

The depreciable amount of an asset is determined after deducting the residual value of **46** the asset. In practice, the residual value of an asset is often insignificant and therefore is immaterial in the calculation of the depreciable amount. When the benchmark treatment is adopted and the residual value is likely to be significant, the residual value is estimated at the date of acquisition and is not subsequently increased for changes in prices. However, when the allowed alternative treatment is adopted, a new estimate is made at the date of any subsequent revaluation of the asset. The estimate is based on the residual value prevailing at the date of the estimate for similar assets which have reached the end of their useful lives and which have operated under conditions similar to those in which the asset will be used.

A variety of depreciation methods can be used to allocate the depreciable amount of an **47** asset on a systematic basis over its useful life. These methods include the straight–line method, the diminishing balance method and the sum–of–the–units method. Straight–line depreciation results in a constant charge over the useful life of the asset. The diminishing balance method results in a decreasing charge over the useful life of the asset. The sum–of–the–units method results in a charge based on the expected use or output of the asset. The method used for an asset is selected based on the expected pattern of economic benefits and is consistently applied from period to period unless there is a change in the expected pattern of economic benefits from that asset.

The depreciation charge for a period is usually recognised as an expense. However, in **48** some circumstances, the economic benefits embodied in an asset are absorbed by the enterprise in producing other assets rather than giving rise to an expense. In this case, the depreciation charge comprises part of the cost of the other asset and is included in its carrying amount. ...

Review of Useful Life

The useful life of an item of property, plant and equipment should be reviewed **49** *periodically and, if expectations are significantly different from previous estimates, the depreciation charge for the current and future periods should be adjusted.*

During the life of an asset it may become apparent that the estimate of the useful life **50** is inappropriate. For example, the useful life may be extended by subsequent expenditure on the asset which improves the condition of the asset beyond its originally assessed standard of performance. Alternatively, technological changes or changes in the market for the products may reduce the useful life of the asset. In such cases, the useful life and, therefore, the depreciation rate is adjusted for the current and future periods.

The repair and maintenance policy of the enterprise may also affect the useful life of **51** an asset. The policy may result in an extension of the useful life of the asset or an increase in its residual value. However, the adoption of such a policy does not negate the need to charge depreciation.

Review of Depreciation Method

The depreciation method applied to property, plant and equipment should be reviewed **52** *periodically and, if there has been a significant change in the expected pattern of* *economic benefits from those assets, the method should be changed to reflect the changed pattern. When such a change in depreciation method is necessary the change should be accounted for as a change in accounting estimate and the depreciation charge for the current and future periods should be adjusted.*

Recoverability of the Carrying Amount – Impairment Losses

53 To determine whether an item of property, plant and equipment is impaired, an enterprise applies IAS 36. ...

54 [Not printed]

Retirements and Disposals

55 *An item of property, plant and equipment should be eliminated from the balance sheet on disposal or when the asset is permanently withdrawn from use and no future economic benefits are expected from its disposal.*

56 *Gains or losses arising from the retirement or disposal of an item of property, plant and equipment should be determined as the difference between the estimated net disposal proceeds and the carrying amount of the asset and should be recognised as income or expense in the income statement.*

57 When an item of property, plant and equipment is exchanged for a similar asset, under the circumstances described in paragraph 22, the cost of the acquired asset is equal to the carrying amount of the asset disposed of and no gain or loss results.

58 [Not printed]

59 Property, plant and equipment that is retired from active use and held for disposal is carried at its carrying amount at the date when the asset is retired from active use. At least at each financial year end, an enterprise tests the asset for impairment under IAS 36.

Disclosure

60 *The financial statements should disclose, for each class of property, plant and equipment:*
   (a) the measurement bases used for determining the gross carrying amount. When more than one basis has been used, the gross carrying amount for that basis in each category should be disclosed;
   (b) the depreciation methods used;
   (c) the useful lives or the depreciation rates used;
   (d) the gross carrying amount and the accumulated depreciation (aggregated with accumulated impairment losses) at the beginning and end of the period;
   (e) a reconciliation of the carrying amount at the beginning and end of the period showing:
      (i) additions;
      (ii) disposals;
      (iii) acquisitions through business combinations;
      (iv) increases or decreases during the period resulting from revaluations under paragraphs 29, 37 and 38 and from impairment losses recognised or reversed directly in equity under IAS 36 (if any);

(v) impairment losses recognised in the income statement during the period under IAS 36 (if any);

(vi) impairment losses reversed in the income statement during the period under IAS 36 (if any);

(vii)depreciation;

(viii)the net exchange differences arising on the translation of the financial statements of a foreign entity; and

(ix) other movements.

Comparative information is not required for the reconciliation in (e) above.

The financial statements should also disclose: **61**

(a) the existence and amounts of restrictions on title, and property, plant and equipment pledged as security for liabilities;

(b) the accounting policy for the estimated costs of restoring the site of items of property, plant or equipment;

(c) the amount of expenditures on account of property, plant and equipment in the course of construction; and

(d) the amount of commitments for the acquisition of property, plant and equipment.

[Not printed]   **62**

An enterprise discloses the nature and effect of a change in an accounting estimate that **63** has a material effect in the current period or which is expected to have a material effect in subsequent periods in accordance with IAS 8. Such disclosure may arise from changes in estimate with respect to:

(a) residual values;

(b) the estimated costs of dismantling and removing items of property, plant or equipment and restoring the site;

(c) useful lives; and

(d) depreciation method.

When items of property, plant and equipment are stated at revalued amounts the **64** *following should be disclosed:*

(a) the basis used to revalue the assets;

(b) the effective date of the revaluation;

(c) whether an independent valuer was involved;

(d) the nature of any indices used to determine replacement cost;

(e) the carrying amount of each class of property, plant and equipment that would have been included in the financial statements had the assets been carried under the benchmark treatment in paragraph 28; and

(f) the revaluation surplus, indicating the movement for the period and any restrictions on the distribution of the balance to shareholders.

An enterprise discloses information on impaired property, plant and equipment under **65** IAS 36 in addition to the information required by paragraph 60(e)(iv) to (vi).

Financial statement users also find the following information relevant to their needs: **66**

(a) the carrying amount of temporarily idle property, plant and equipment;

(b) the gross carrying amount of any fully depreciated property, plant and equipment that is still in use;

(c) the carrying amount of property, plant and equipment retired from active use and held for disposal; and

(d) when the benchmark treatment is used, the fair value of property, plant and equipment when this is materially different from the carrying amount.

Therefore, enterprises are encouraged to disclose these amounts.

Effective Date

67–68 [Not printed]

IAS 17: Leases

IAS 17: Leases					
Scope 17.1–2	Definitions 17.3–4	Classification of Leases 17.5–11	Transitional Provisions 17.58	Effective Date 17.59–60	Related Interpretation: SIC–15

Leases in the Financial Statements of Lessees 17.12–27	
Finance Leases 17.12–24	Operating Leases 17.25–27

Leases in the Financial Statements of Lessors 17.28–48A	
Finance Leases 17.28–40	Operating Leases 17.41–48A

Sale and Leaseback Transactions 17.49–57

Appendix [Not printed]
Sale and Leaseback Transactions that Result in Operating Leases

Scope

This Standard should be applied in accounting for all leases other than: **1**
(a) lease agreements to explore for or use minerals, oil, natural gas and similar non-regenerative resources; and
(b) licensing agreements for such items as motion picture films, video recordings, plays, manuscripts, patents and copyrights.
However, this Standard should not be applied to the measurement by:
(a) lessees of investment property held under finance leases (See IAS 40);
(b) lessors of investment property leased out under operating leases (see IAS 40);
(c) lessees of biological assets held under finance leases (see IAS 41); or
(d) lessors of biological assets leased out under operating leases (see IAS 41).

This Standard applies to agreements that transfer the right to use assets even though **2** substantial services by the lessor may be called for in connection with the operation or maintenance of such assets. On the other hand, this Standard does not apply to agreements that are contracts for services that do not transfer the right to use assets from one contracting party to the other.

Definitions

... **3**

A *lease* is an agreement whereby the lessor conveys to the lessee in return for a payment or series of payments the right to use an asset for an agreed period of time. A *finance lease* is a lease that transfers substantially all the risks and rewards incident to ownership of an asset. Title may or may not eventually be transferred. An operating lease is a lease other than a finance lease.

A *non–cancellable lease* is a lease that is cancellable only:

(a) upon the occurrence of some remote contingency;

(b) with the permission of the lessor;

(c) if the lessee enters into a new lease for the same or an equivalent asset with the same lessor; or

(d) upon payment by the lessee of an additional amount such that, at inception, continuation of the lease is reasonably certain.

The *inception of the lease* is the earlier of the date of the lease agreement or of a commitment by the parties to the principal provisions of the lease.

The *lease term* is the non–cancellable period for which the lessee has contracted to lease the asset together with any further terms for which the lessee has the option to continue to lease the asset, with or without further payment, which option at the inception of the lease it is reasonably certain that the lessee will exercise.

Minimum lease payments are the payments over the lease term that the lessee is, or can be required, to make excluding contingent rent, costs for services and taxes to be paid by and reimbursed to the lessor, together with:

(a) in the case of the lessee, any amounts guaranteed by the lessee or by a party related to the lessee; or

(b) in the case of the lessor, any residual value guaranteed to the lessor by either:

    (i) the lessee;

    (ii) a party related to the lessee; or

    (iii)an independent third party financially capable of meeting this guarantee.

However, if the lessee has an option to purchase the asset at a price which is expected to be sufficiently lower than the fair value at the date the option becomes exercisable that, at the inception of the lease, is reasonably certain to be exercised, the minimum lease payments comprise the minimum payments payable over the lease term and the payment required to exercise this purchase option.

Fair value is the amount for which an asset could be exchanged or a liability settled, between knowledgeable, willing parties in an arm's length transaction.

Economic life is either:

(a) the period over which an asset is expected to be economically usable by one or more users; or

(b) the number of production or similar units expected to be obtained from the asset by one or more users.

Useful life is the estimated remaining period, from the beginning of the lease term, without limitation by the lease term, over which the economic benefits embodied in the asset are expected to be consumed by the enterprise.

Guaranteed residual value is:

(a) in the case of the lessee, that part of the residual value which is guaranteed by the lessee or by a party related to the lessee (the amount of the guarantee being the maximum amount that could, in any event, become payable); and

(b) in the case of the lessor, that part of the residual value which is guaranteed by the lessee or by a third party unrelated to the lessor who is financially capable of discharging the obligations under the guarantee.

Unguaranteed residual value is that portion of the residual value of the leased asset, the realisation of which by the lessor is not assured or is guaranteed solely by a party related to the lessor.

Gross investment in the lease is the aggregate of the minimum lease payments under a finance lease from the standpoint of the lessor and any unguaranteed residual value accruing to the lessor.

Unearned finance income is the difference between:

(a) the aggregate of the minimum lease payments under a finance lease from the standpoint of the lessor and any unguaranteed residual value accruing to the lessor; and

(b) the present value of (a) above, at the interest rate implicit in the lease.

Net investment in the lease is the gross investment in the lease less unearned finance income.

The interest rate implicit in the lease is the discount rate that, at the inception of the lease, causes the aggregate present value of (a) the minimum lease payments and (b) the unguaranteed residual value to be equal to the fair value of the leased asset.

The lessee's incremental borrowing rate of interest is the rate of interest the lessee would have to pay on a similar lease or, if that is not determinable, the rate that, at the inception of the lease, the lessee would incur to borrow over a similar term, and with a similar security, the funds necessary to purchase the asset.

Contingent rent is that portion of the lease payments that is not fixed in amount but is based on a factor other than just the passage of time (e.g., percentage of sales, amount of usage, price indices, market rates of interest).

The definition of a lease includes contracts for the hire of an asset which contain a **4** provision giving the hirer an option to acquire title to the asset upon the fulfilment of agreed conditions. These contracts are sometimes known as hire purchase contracts.

Classification of Leases

The classification of leases adopted in this Standard is based on the extent to which **5** risks and rewards incident to ownership of a leased asset lie with the lessor or the lessee. Risks include the possibilities of losses from idle capacity or technological obsolescence and of variations in return due to changing economic conditions. Rewards may be represented by the expectation of profitable operation over the asset's economic life and of gain from appreciation in value or realisation of a residual value.

A lease is classified as a finance lease if it transfers substantially all the risks and rewards **6** incident to ownership. A lease is classified as an operating lease if it does not transfer substantially all the risks and rewards incident to ownership.

[Not printed] **7**

Whether a lease is a finance lease or an operating lease depends on the substance of the **8** transaction rather than the form of the contract. Examples of situations which would normally lead to a lease being classified as a finance lease are:

(a) the lease transfers ownership of the asset to the lessee by the end of the lease term;

(b) the lessee has the option to purchase the asset at a price which is expected to be sufficiently lower than the fair value at the date the option becomes exercisable such that, at the inception of the lease, it is reasonably certain that the option will be exercised;

(c) the lease term is for the major part of the economic life of the asset even if title is not transferred;

(d) at the inception of the lease the present value of the minimum lease payments amounts to at least substantially all of the fair value of the leased asset; and

(e) the leased assets are of a specialised nature such that only the lessee can use them without major modifications being made.

9 Indicators of situations which individually or in combination could also lead to a lease being classified as a finance lease are:

(a) if the lessee can cancel the lease, the lessor's losses associated with the cancellation are borne by the lessee;

(b) gains or losses from the fluctuation in the fair value of the residual fall to the lessee (for example in the form of a rent rebate equalling most of the sales proceeds at the end of the lease); and

(c) the lessee has the ability to continue the lease for a secondary period at a rent which is substantially lower than market rent.

10 Lease classification is made at the inception of the lease. If at any time the lessee and the lessor agree to change the provisions of the lease, other than by renewing the lease, in a manner that would have resulted in a different classification of the lease under the criteria in paragraphs 5 to 9 had the changed terms been in effect at the inception of the lease, the revised agreement is considered as a new agreement over its term. Changes in estimates (for example, changes in estimates of the economic life or of the residual value of the leased property) or changes in circumstances (for example, default by the lessee), however, do not give rise to a new classification of a lease for accounting purposes.

11 Leases of land and buildings are classified as operating or finance leases in the same way as leases of other assets. However, a characteristic of land is that it normally has an indefinite economic life and, if title is not expected to pass to the lessee by the end of the lease term, the lessee does not receive substantially all of the risks and rewards incident to ownership. A premium paid for such a leasehold represents pre–paid lease payments which are amortised over the lease term in accordance with the pattern of benefits provided.

Leases in the Financial Statements of Lessees

Finance Leases

12 *Lessees should recognise finance leases as assets and liabilities in their balance sheets at amounts equal at the inception of the lease to the fair value of the leased property or, if lower, at the present value of the minimum lease payments. In calculating the present value of the minimum lease payments the discount factor is the interest rate implicit in the lease, if this is practicable to determine; if not, the lessee's incremental borrowing rate should be used.*

13 [Not printed]

14 ... At the inception of the lease, the asset and the liability for the future lease payments are recognised in the balance sheet at the same amounts.

15 It is not appropriate for the liabilities for leased assets to be presented in the financial statements as a deduction from the leased assets. If for the presentation of liabilities on

142

the face of the balance sheet a distinction is made between current and non–current liabilities, the same distinction is made for lease liabilities.

Initial direct costs are often incurred in connection with specific leasing activities, as in **16** negotiating and securing leasing arrangements. The costs identified as directly attributable to activities performed by the lessee for a finance lease, are included as part of the amount recognised as an asset under the lease.

Lease payments should be apportioned between the finance charge and the reduction **17** *of the outstanding liability. The finance charge should be allocated to periods during the lease term so as to produce a constant periodic rate of interest on the remaining balance of the liability for each period.*

In practice, in allocating the finance charge to periods during the lease term, some form **18** of approximation may be used to simplify the calculation.

A finance lease gives rise to a depreciation expense for depreciable assets as well as a **19** *finance expense for each accounting period. The depreciation policy for depreciable leased assets should be consistent with that for depreciable assets which are owned, and the depreciation recognised should be calculated on the basis set out in IAS 16 and IAS 38. If there is no reasonable certainty that the lessee will obtain ownership by the end of the lease term, the asset should be fully depreciated over the shorter of the lease term or its useful life.*

The depreciable amount of a leased asset is allocated to each accounting period during **20** the period of expected use on a systematic basis consistent with the depreciation policy the lessee adopts for depreciable assets that are owned. If there is reasonable certainty that the lessee will obtain ownership by the end of the lease term, the period of expected use is the useful life of the asset; otherwise the asset is depreciated over the shorter of the lease term or its useful life.

[Not printed] **21**

To determine whether a leased asset has become impaired, that is when the expected **22** future economic benefits from that asset are lower than its carrying amount, an enterprise applies the IAS dealing with impairment of assets, …

Lessees should, in addition to the requirements of IAS 32 make the following **23** *disclosures for finance leases:*
(a) for each class of asset, the net carrying amount at the balance sheet date;
(b) a reconciliation between the total of minimum lease payments at the balance sheet date, and their present value. In addition, an enterprise should disclose the total of minimum lease payments at the balance sheet date, and their present value, for each of the following periods:
  (i) not later than one year;
  (ii) later than one year and not later than five years;
  (iii) later than five years;
(c) contingent rents recognised in income for the period;
(d) the total of future minimum sublease payments expected to be received under non–cancellable subleases at the balance sheet date; and
(e) a general description of the lessee's significant leasing arrangements including, but not limited to, the following:
  (i) the basis on which contingent rent payments are determined;

    (ii) the existence and terms of renewal or purchase options and escalation clauses; and

    (iii) restrictions imposed by lease arrangements, such as those concerning dividends, additional debt, and further leasing.

24   In addition, the requirements on disclosure under IAS 16, IAS 36, IAS 38, IAS 40 and IAS 41 apply to the amounts of leased assets under finance leases that are accounted for by the lessee as acquisitions of assets.

Operating Leases

25   *Lease payments under an operating lease should be recognised as an expense in the income statement on a straight line basis over the lease term unless another systematic basis is more representative of the time pattern of the user's benefit.*

26   For operating leases, lease payments (excluding costs for services such as insurance and maintenance) are recognised as an expense in the income statement on a straight line basis unless another systematic basis is representative of the time pattern of the user's benefit, even if the payments are not on that basis.

27   *Lessees should, in addition to the requirements of IAS 32 make the following disclosures for operating leases:*

    (a) the total of future minimum lease payments under non–cancellable operating leases for each of the following periods:

      (i) not later than one year;

      (ii) later than one year and not later than five years;

      (iii) later than five years;

    (b) the total of future minimum sublease payments expected to be received under non–cancellable subleases at the balance sheet date;

    (c) lease and sublease payments recognised in income for the period, with separate amounts for minimum lease payments, contingent rents, and sublease payments;

    (d) a general description of the lessee's significant leasing arrangements including, but not limited to, the following:

      (i) the basis on which contingent rent payments are determined;

      (ii) the existence and terms of renewal or purchase options and escalation clauses; and

      (iii) restrictions imposed by lease arrangements, such as those concerning dividends, additional debt, and further leasing.

Leases in the Financial Statements of Lessors

Finance Leases

28   *Lessors should recognise assets held under a finance lease in their balance sheets and present them as a receivable at an amount equal to the net investment in the lease.*

29   [Not printed]

30   *The recognition of finance income should be based on a pattern reflecting a constant periodic rate of return on the lessor's net investment outstanding in respect of the finance lease.*

A lessor aims to allocate finance income over the lease term on a systematic and rational **31** basis. This income allocation is based on a pattern reflecting a constant periodic return on the lessor's net investment outstanding in respect of the finance lease. Lease payments relating to the accounting period, excluding costs for services, are applied against the gross investment in the lease to reduce both the principal and the unearned finance income.

Estimated unguaranteed residual values used in computing the lessor's gross investment **32** in a lease are reviewed regularly. If there has been a reduction in the estimated unguaranteed residual value, the income allocation over the lease term is revised and any reduction in respect of amounts already accrued is recognised immediately.

Initial direct costs, such as commissions and legal fees, are often incurred by lessors in **33** negotiating and arranging a lease. For finance leases, these initial direct costs are incurred to produce finance income and are either recognised immediately in income or allocated against this income over the lease term. The latter may be achieved by recognising as an expense the cost as incurred and recognising as income in the same period a portion of the unearned finance income equal to the initial direct costs.

Manufacturer or dealer lessors should recognise selling profit or loss in income for the **34** *period, in accordance with the policy followed by the enterprise for outright sales. If artificially low rates of interest are quoted, selling profit should be restricted to that which would apply if a commercial rate of interest were charged. Initial direct costs should be recognised as an expense in the income statement at the inception of the lease.*

Manufacturers or dealers often offer to customers the choice of either buying or leasing **35** an asset. A finance lease of an asset by a manufacturer or dealer lessor gives rise to two types of income:

(a) the profit or loss equivalent to the profit or loss resulting from an outright sale of the asset being leased, at normal selling prices, reflecting any applicable volume or trade discounts; and

(b) the finance income over the lease term.

The sales revenue recorded at the commencement of a finance lease term by a **36** manufacturer or dealer lessor is the fair value of the asset, or, if lower, the present value of the minimum lease payments accruing to the lessor, computed at a commercial rate of interest. The cost of sale recognised at the commencement of the lease term is the cost, or carrying amount if different, of the leased property less the present value of the unguaranteed residual value. The difference between the sales revenue and the cost of sale is the selling profit, which is recognised in accordance with the policy followed by the enterprise for sales.

Manufacturer or dealer lessors sometimes quote artificially low rates of interest in order **37** to attract customers. The use of such a rate would result in an excessive portion of the total income from the transaction being recognised at the time of sale. If artificially low rates of interest are quoted, selling profit would be restricted to that which would apply if a commercial rate of interest were charged.

Initial direct costs are recognised as an expense at the commencement of the lease term **38** because they are mainly related to earning the manufacturer's or dealer's selling profit.

Lessors should, in addition to the requirements in IAS 32 make the following **39** *disclosures for finance leases:*

(a) *a reconciliation between the total gross investment in the lease at the balance sheet date, and the present value of minimum lease payments receivable at the balance sheet date. In addition, an enterprise should disclose the total gross investment in the lease and the present value of minimum lease payments receivable at the balance sheet date, for each of the following periods:*

   (i) *not later than one year;*

   (ii) *later than one year and not later than five years;*

   (iii)*later than five years;*

(b) *unearned finance income;*

(c) *the unguaranteed residual values accruing to the benefit of the lessor;*

(d) *the accumulated allowance for uncollectible minimum lease payments receivable;*

(e) *contingent rents recognised in income; and*

(f) *a general description of the lessor's significant leasing arrangements.*

40 As an indicator of growth it is often useful to also disclose the gross investment less unearned income in new business added during the accounting period, after deducting the relevant amounts for cancelled leases.

Operating Leases

41 *Lessors should present assets subject to operating leases in their balance sheets according to the nature of the asset.*

42 *Lease income from operating leases should be recognised in income on a straight line basis over the lease term, unless another systematic basis is more representative of the time pattern in which use benefit derived from the leased asset is diminished.*

43 Costs, including depreciation, incurred in earning the lease income are recognised as an expense. Lease income (excluding receipts for services provided such as insurance and maintenance) is recognised in income on a straight line basis over the lease term even if the receipts are not on such a basis, unless another systematic basis is more representative of the time pattern in which use benefit derived from the leased asset is diminished.

44 Initial direct costs incurred specifically to earn revenues from an operating lease are either deferred and allocated to income over the lease term in proportion to the recognition of rent income, or are recognised as an expense in the income statement in the period in which they are incurred.

45 *The depreciation of depreciable leased assets should be on a basis consistent with the lessor's normal depreciation policy for similar assets, and the depreciation charge should be calculated on the basis set out in IAS 16 and IAS 38.*

46 To determine whether a leased asset has become impaired, that is when the expected future economic benefits from that asset are lower than its carrying amount, an enterprise applies the IAS dealing with impairment of assets ...

47 A manufacturer or dealer lessor does not recognise any selling profit on entering into an operating lease because it is not the equivalent of a sale.

48 *Lessors should, in addition to the requirements of IAS 32 make the following disclosures for operating leases:*

   (a) *the future minimum lease payments under non–cancellable operating leases in the aggregate and for each of the following periods:*

(i) not later than one year;
(ii) later than one year and not later than five years;
(iii) later than five years;
(b) total contingent rents recognised in income; and
(c) a general description of the lessor's significant leasing arrangements.

In addition, the requirements on disclosure under IAS 16, IAS 36, IAS 38, IAS 40 and **48A** IAS 41 apply to assets leased out under operating leases.

Sale and Leaseback Transactions

A sale and leaseback transaction involves the sale of an asset by the vendor and the **49** leasing of the same asset back to the vendor. The lease payment and the sale price are usually interdependent as they are negotiated as a package. The accounting treatment of a sale and leaseback transaction depends upon the type of lease involved.

If a sale and leaseback transaction results in a finance lease, any excess of sales **50** *proceeds over the carrying amount should not be immediately recognised as income in the financial statements of a seller–lessee. Instead, it should be deferred and amortised over the lease term.*

If the leaseback is a finance lease, the transaction is a means whereby the lessor provides **51** finance to the lessee, with the asset as security. For this reason it is not appropriate to regard an excess of sales proceeds over the carrying amount as income. Such excess, is deferred and amortised over the lease term.

If a sale and leaseback transaction results in an operating lease, and it is clear that **52** *the transaction is established at fair value, any profit or loss should be recognised immediately. If the sale price is below fair value, any profit or loss should be recognised immediately except that, if the loss is compensated by future lease payments at below market price, it should be deferred and amortised in proportion to the lease payments over the period for which the asset is expected to be used. If the sale price is above fair value, the excess over fair value should be deferred and amortised over the period for which the asset is expected to be used.*

If the leaseback is an operating lease, and the lease payments and the sale price are **53** established at fair value, there has in effect been a normal sale transaction and any profit or loss is recognised immediately.

For operating leases, if the fair value at the time of a sale and leaseback transaction **54** *is less than the carrying amount of the asset, a loss equal to the amount of the difference between the carrying amount and fair value should be recognised immediately.*

For finance leases, no such adjustment is necessary unless there has been an impairment **55** in value, in which case the carrying amount is reduced to recoverable amount in accordance with the IAS dealing with impairment of assets.

Disclosure requirements for lessees and lessors apply equally to sale and leaseback **56** transactions. The required description of the significant leasing arrangements leads to disclosure of unique or unusual provisions of the agreement or terms of the sale and leaseback transactions.

57 Sale and leaseback transactions may meet the separate disclosure criteria in IAS 8 paragraph 16.

Transitional Provisions

58 *[Not printed]*

Effective Date

59–60 [Not printed]

Appendix

Sale and Leaseback Transactions that Result in Operating Leases

[Not printed]

IAS 18: Revenue

IAS 18: Revenue		
Scope 18.1–6	Definitions 18.7–8	Effective Date 18.37

Measurement of Revenue 18.9–12

Identification of the Transaction 18.13

Sale of Goods 18.14–19

Rendering of Services 18.20–28

Interest, Royalties and Dividends 18.29–34

Disclosure 18.35–36

Appendix [Not printed]		
Sale of Goods	Rendering of Services	Interest, Royalties and Dividends

Scope

This Standard should be applied in accounting for revenue arising from the following **1**
transactions and events:
(a) the sale of goods;
(b) the rendering of services; and
(c) the use by others of enterprise assets yielding interest, royalties and dividends.

[Not printed] **2**

Goods includes goods produced by the enterprise for the purpose of sale and goods **3**
purchased for resale, such as merchandise purchased by a retailer or land and other
property held for resale.

The rendering of services typically involves the performance by the enterprise of a **4**
contractually agreed task over an agreed period of time. The services may be rendered
within a single period or over more than one period. Some contracts for the rendering
of services are directly related to construction contracts, for example, those for the
services of project managers and architects. Revenue arising from these contracts is not
dealt with in this Standard but is dealt with in accordance with the requirements for
construction contracts as specified in IAS 11.

The use by others of enterprise assets gives rise to revenue in the form of: **5**

(a) interest – charges for the use of cash or cash equivalents or amounts due to the enterprise;

(b) royalties – charges for the use of long–term assets of the enterprise, for example, patents, trademarks, copyrights and computer software; and

(c) dividends – distributions of profits to holders of equity investments in proportion to their holdings of a particular class of capital.

6 This Standard does not deal with revenue arising from:
   (a) lease agreements (see IAS 17);
   (b) dividends arising from investments which are accounted for under the equity method (see IAS 28);
   (c) insurance contracts of insurance enterprises;
   (d) changes in the fair value of financial assets and financial liabilities or their disposal (see IAS 39);
   (e) changes in the value of other current assets;
   (f) initial recognition and from changes in the fair value of biological assets related to agricultural activity (see IAS 41);
   (g) initial recognition of agricultural produce (see IAS 41); and
   (h) the extraction of mineral ores.

Definitions

7 ...

   Revenue is the gross inflow of economic benefits during the period arising in the course of the ordinary activities of an enterprise when those inflows result in increases in equity, other than increases relating to contributions from equity participants.

   Fair value is the amount for which an asset could be exchanged, or a liability settled, between knowledgeable, willing parties in an arm's length transaction.

8 [Not printed]

Measurement of Revenue

9 *Revenue should be measured at the fair value of the consideration received or receivable.*

10 The amount of revenue arising on a transaction is usually determined by agreement between the enterprise and the buyer or user of the asset. It is measured at the fair value of the consideration received or receivable taking into account the amount of any trade discounts and volume rebates allowed by the enterprise.

11 In most cases, the consideration is in the form of cash or cash equivalents and the amount of revenue is the amount of cash or cash equivalents received or receivable. However, when the inflow of cash or cash equivalents is deferred, the fair value of the consideration may be less than the nominal amount of cash received or receivable. ... When the arrangement effectively constitutes a financing transaction, the fair value of the consideration is determined by discounting all future receipts using an imputed rate of interest. The imputed rate of interest is the more clearly determinable of either:
   (a) the prevailing rate for a similar instrument of an issuer with a similar credit rating; or
   (b) a rate of interest that discounts the nominal amount of the instrument to the current cash sales price of the goods or services.

The difference between the fair value and the nominal amount of the consideration is recognised as interest revenue in accordance with paragraphs 29 and 30 and in accordance with IAS 39.

When goods or services are exchanged or swapped for goods or services which are of a **12** similar nature and value, the exchange is not regarded as a transaction which generates revenue. ... When goods are sold or services are rendered in exchange for dissimilar goods or services, the exchange is regarded as a transaction which generates revenue. The revenue is measured at the fair value of the goods or services received, adjusted by the amount of any cash or cash equivalents transferred. When the fair value of the goods or services received cannot be measured reliably, the revenue is measured at the fair value of the goods or services given up, adjusted by the amount of any cash or cash equivalents transferred.

Identification of the Transaction

The recognition criteria in this Standard are usually applied separately to each **13** transaction. However, in certain circumstances, it is necessary to apply the recognition criteria to the separately identifiable components of a single transaction in order to reflect the substance of the transaction. ... Conversely, the recognition criteria are applied to two or more transactions together when they are linked in such a way that the commercial effect cannot be understood without reference to the series of transactions as a whole. ...

Sale of Goods

Revenue from the sale of goods should be recognised when all the following conditions **14** *have been satisfied:*
(a) the enterprise has transferred to the buyer the significant risks and rewards of ownership of the goods;
(b) the enterprise retains neither continuing managerial involvement to the degree usually associated with ownership nor effective control over the goods sold;
(c) the amount of revenue can be measured reliably;
(d) it is probable that the economic benefits associated with the transaction will flow to the enterprise; and
(e) the costs incurred or to be incurred in respect of the transaction can be measured reliably.

[Not printed]   **15**

If the enterprise retains significant risks of ownership, the transaction is not a sale and **16** revenue is not recognised. An enterprise may retain a significant risk of ownership in a number of ways. Examples of situations in which the enterprise may retain the significant risks and rewards of ownership are:
(a) when the enterprise retains an obligation for unsatisfactory performance not covered by normal warranty provisions;
(b) when the receipt of the revenue from a particular sale is contingent on the derivation of revenue by the buyer from its sale of the goods;
(c) when the goods are shipped subject to installation and the installation is a significant part of the contract which has not yet been completed by the enterprise; and

(d) when the buyer has the right to rescind the purchase for a reason specified in the sales contract and the enterprise is uncertain about the probability of return.

17 If an enterprise retains only an insignificant risk of ownership, the transaction is a sale and revenue is recognised. ...

18 Revenue is recognised only when it is probable that the economic benefits associated with the transaction will flow to the enterprise. ... However, when an uncertainty arises about the collectability of an amount already included in revenue, the uncollectable amount or the amount in respect of which recovery has ceased to be probable is recognised as an expense, rather than as an adjustment of the amount of revenue originally recognised.

19 Revenue and expenses that relate to the same transaction or other event are recognised simultaneously; this process is commonly referred to as the matching of revenues and expenses. Expenses, including warranties and other costs to be incurred after the shipment of the goods can normally be measured reliably when the other conditions for the recognition of revenue have been satisfied. However, revenue cannot be recognised when the expenses cannot be measured reliably; in such circumstances, any consideration already received for the sale of the goods is recognised as a liability.

Rendering of Services

20 *When the outcome of a transaction involving the rendering of services can be estimated reliably, revenue associated with the transaction should be recognised by reference to the stage of completion of the transaction at the balance sheet date. The outcome of a transaction can be estimated reliably when all the following conditions are satisfied:*
(a) *the amount of revenue can be measured reliably;*
(b) *it is probable that the economic benefits associated with the transaction will flow to the enterprise;*
(c) *the stage of completion of the transaction at the balance sheet date can be measured reliably; and*
(d) *the costs incurred for the transaction and the costs to complete the transaction can be measured reliably.*

21 The recognition of revenue by reference to the stage of completion of a transaction is often referred to as the percentage of completion method. Under this method, revenue is recognised in the accounting periods in which the services are rendered. The recognition of revenue on this basis provides useful information on the extent of service activity and performance during a period. IAS 11 also requires the recognition of revenue on this basis. ...

22 Revenue is recognised only when it is probable that the economic benefits associated with the transaction will flow to the enterprise. However, when an uncertainty arises about the collectability of an amount already included in revenue, the uncollectable amount, or the amount in respect of which recovery has ceased to be probable, is recognised as an expense, rather than as an adjustment of the amount of revenue originally recognised.

23 An enterprise is generally able to make reliable estimates after it has agreed to the following with the other parties to the transaction:

(a) each party's enforceable rights regarding the service to be provided and received by the parties;

(b) the consideration to be exchanged; and

(c) the manner and terms of settlement.

It is also usually necessary for the enterprise to have an effective internal financial budgeting and reporting system. The enterprise reviews and, when necessary, revises the estimates of revenue as the service is performed. The need for such revisions does not necessarily indicate that the outcome of the transaction cannot be estimated reliably.

The stage of completion of a transaction may be determined by a variety of methods. **24** An enterprise uses the method that measures reliably the services performed. Depending on the nature of the transaction, the methods may include:

(a) surveys of work performed;

services performed to date as a percentage of total services to be performed; or

(c) the proportion that costs incurred to date bear to the estimated total costs of the transaction. Only costs that reflect services performed to date are included in costs incurred to date. Only costs that reflect services performed or to be performed are included in the estimated total costs of the transaction.

Progress payments and advances received from customers often do not reflect the services performed.

For practical purposes, when services are performed by an indeterminate number of acts **25** over a specified period of time, revenue is recognised on a straight line basis over the specified period unless there is evidence that some other method better represents the stage of completion. When a specific act is much more significant than any other acts, the recognition of revenue is postponed until the significant act is executed.

When the outcome of the transaction involving the rendering of services cannot be **26** *estimated reliably, revenue should be recognised only to the extent of the expenses recognised that are recoverable.*

[Not printed] **27**

When the outcome of a transaction cannot be estimated reliably and it is not probable **28** that the costs incurred will be recovered, revenue is not recognised and the costs incurred are recognised as an expense. ...

Interest, Royalties and Dividends

Revenue arising from the use by others of enterprise assets yielding interest, royalties **29** *and dividends should be recognised on the bases set out in paragraph 30 when:*

(a) it is probable that the economic benefits associated with the transaction will flow to the enterprise; and

(b) the amount of the revenue can be measured reliably.

Revenue should be recognised on the following bases: **30**

(a) interest should be recognised on a time proportion basis that takes into account the effective yield on the asset;

(b) royalties should be recognised on an accrual basis in accordance with the substance of the relevant agreement; and

(c) dividends should be recognised when the shareholder's right to receive payment is established.

31 The effective yield on an asset is the rate of interest required to discount the stream of future cash receipts expected over the life of the asset to equate to the initial carrying amount of the asset. Interest revenue includes the amount of amortisation of any discount, premium or other difference between the initial carrying amount of a debt security and its amount at maturity.

32 When unpaid interest has accrued before the acquisition of an interest–bearing investment, the subsequent receipt of interest is allocated between pre–acquisition and post–acquisition periods; only the post–acquisition portion is recognised as revenue. When dividends on equity securities are declared from pre–acquisition net income, those dividends are deducted from the cost of the securities. If it is difficult to make such an allocation except on an arbitrary basis, dividends are recognised as revenue unless they clearly represent a recovery of part of the cost of the equity securities.

33 Royalties accrue in accordance with the terms of the relevant agreement and are usually recognised on that basis unless, having regard to the substance of the agreement, it is more appropriate to recognise revenue on some other systematic and rational basis.

34 Revenue is recognised only when it is probable that the economic benefits associated with the transaction will flow to the enterprise. However, when an uncertainty arises about the collectability of an amount already included in revenue, the uncollectable amount, or the amount in respect of which recovery has ceased to be probable, is recognised as an expense, rather than as an adjustment of the amount of revenue originally recognised.

Disclosure

35 *An enterprise should disclose:*
   (a) the accounting policies adopted for the recognition of revenue including the methods adopted to determine the stage of completion of transactions involving the rendering of services;
   (b) the amount of each significant category of revenue recognised during the period including revenue arising from:
      (i) the sale of goods;
      (ii) the rendering of services;
      (iii) interest;
      (iv) royalties;
      (v) dividends; and
   (c) the amount of revenue arising from exchanges of goods or services included in each significant category of revenue.

36 An enterprise discloses any contingent liabilities and contingent assets in accordance with IAS 37. ...

Effective Date

37 *[Not printed]*

Appendix

Sale of Goods

[Not printed]

Rendering of Services

[Not printed]

Interest, Royalties and Dividends

[Not printed]

IAS 19: Employee Benefits

IAS 19: Employee Benefits			
Scope 19.1–6	Definitions 19.7	Transitional Provisions 19.153–156	Effective Date 19.157–160

Short-term Employee Benefits 19.8–23			
Recognition and Measurement 19.10–22			Disclosure 19.23
All Short-term Employee Benefits 19.10	Short-term Compensated Absences 19.11–16	Profit Sharing and Bonus Plans 19.17–22	Disclosure 19.23

Post-employment Benefits: Distinction between Defined Contribution Plans and Defined Benefit Plans 19.24–42		
Multi-employer Plans 19.29–35	State Plans 19.36–38	Insured Benefits 19.39–42

Post-employment Benefits: Defined Contribution Plans 19.43–47	
Recognition and Measurement 19.44–45	Disclosure 19.46–47

Post-employment Benefits: Defined Benefit Plans 19.48–125						
Recognition and Measurement 19.49–107						
Recognition and Measurement 19.49–62	Present Value of Defined Benefit Obligations and Current Service Cost 19.63–101	Plan Assets 19.102–107	Business Combinations 19.108	Curtailments and Settlements 19.109 –115	Presentation 19.116 –119	Disclosure 19.120 –125

Other Long-Term Employee Benefits 19.128–131	
Recognition and Measurement 19.126–130	Disclosure 19.131

Termination Benefits 19.132–143		
Recognition 19.133–138	Measurement 19.139–140	Disclosure 19.141–143

Equity Compensation Benefits 19.144–152	
Recognition and Measurement 19.145	Disclosure 19.146–152

Appendices A–F [Not printed]					
Illustrative Example	Illustrative Disclosures	Illustration of the Application of Paragraph 58A	Basis for Conclusions	Approval of 2002 Amendment by the Board	Dissenting Opinion (2002 Amendment)

Scope

This Standard should be applied by an employer in accounting for employee benefits.   1

[Not printed]   2

This Standard applies to all employee benefits, including those provided: 3
(a) under formal plans or other formal agreements between an enterprise and individual employees, groups of employees or their representatives;
(b) under legislative requirements, or through industry arrangements, whereby enterprises are required to contribute to national, state, industry or other multi-employer plans; or
(c) by those informal practices that give rise to a constructive obligation. Informal practices give rise to a constructive obligation where the enterprise has no realistic alternative but to pay employee benefits. An example of a constructive obligation is where a change in the enterprise's informal practices would cause unacceptable damage to its relationship with employees.

Employee benefits include: 4
(a) short-term employee benefits, such as wages, salaries and social security contributions, paid annual leave and paid sick leave, profit sharing and bonuses (if payable within twelve months of the end of the period) and non-monetary benefits (such as medical care, housing, cars and free or subsidised goods or services) for current employees;
(b) post-employment benefits such as pensions, other retirement benefits, post-employment life insurance and post-employment medical care;
(c) other long-term employee benefits, including long-service leave or sabbatical leave, jubilee or other long-service benefits, long-term disability benefits and, if they are not payable wholly within twelve months after the end of the period, profit sharing, bonuses and deferred compensation;
(d) termination benefits; and

(e) equity compensation benefits.

Because each category identified in (a) to (e) above has different characteristics, this Standard establishes separate requirements for each category.

5   Employee benefits include benefits provided to either employees or their dependants and may be settled by payments (or the provision of goods or services) made either directly to the employees, to their spouses, children or other dependants or to others, such as insurance companies.

6   .... For the purpose of this Standard, employees include directors and other management personnel.

Definitions

7   ...

Employee benefits are all forms of consideration given by an enterprise in exchange for service rendered by employees.

Short-term employee benefits are employee benefits (other than termination benefits and equity compensation benefits) which fall due wholly within twelve months after the end of the period in which the employees render the related service.

Post-employment benefits are employee benefits (other than termination benefits and equity compensation benefits) which are payable after the completion of employment.

Post-employment benefit plans are formal or informal arrangements under which an enterprise provides post-employment benefits for one or more employees.

Defined contribution plans are post-employment benefit plans under which an enterprise pays fixed contributions into a separate entity (a fund) and will have no legal or constructive obligation to pay further contributions if the fund does not hold sufficient assets to pay all employee benefits relating to employee service in the current and prior periods.

Defined benefit plans are post-employment benefit plans other than defined contribution plans.

Multi-employer plans are defined contribution plans (other than state plans) or defined benefit plans (other than state plans) that:

(a) pool the assets contributed by various enterprises that are not under common control; and

(b) use those assets to provide benefits to employees of more than one enterprise, on the basis that contribution and benefit levels are determined without regard to the identity of the enterprise that employs the employees concerned.

Other long-term employee benefits are employee benefits (other than post-employment benefits, termination benefits and equity compensation benefits) which do not fall due wholly within twelve months after the end of the period in which the employees render the related service.

Termination benefits are employee benefits payable as a result of either:

(a) an enterprise's decision to terminate an employee's employment before the normal retirement date; or

(b) an employee's decision to accept voluntary redundancy in exchange for those benefits.

Equity compensation benefits are employee benefits under which either:

(a) employees are entitled to receive equity financial instruments issued by the enterprise (or its parent); or

(b) the amount of the enterprise's obligation to employees depends on the future price of equity financial instruments issued by the enterprise.

Equity compensation plans are formal or informal arrangements under which an enterprise provides equity compensation benefits for one or more employees.

Vested employee benefits are employee benefits that are not conditional on future employment.

The _present value of a defined benefit obligation_ is the present value, without deducting any plan assets, of expected future payments required to settle the obligation resulting from employee service in the current and prior periods.

Current service cost is the increase in the present value of the defined benefit obligation resulting from employee service in the current period.

Interest cost is the increase during a period in the present value of a defined benefit obligation which arises because the benefits are one period closer to settlement.

Plan assets comprise:

(a) assets held by a long-term employee benefit fund; and

(b) qualifying insurance policies.

Assets held by a long-term employee benefit fund are assets (other than non-transferable financial instruments issued by the reporting enterprise) that:

(a) are held by an entity (a fund) that is legally separate from the reporting enterprise and exists solely to pay or fund employee benefits; and

(b) are available to be used only to pay or fund employee benefits, are not available to the reporting enterprise's own creditors (even in bankruptcy), and cannot be returned to the reporting enterprise, unless either:

    (i) the remaining assets of the fund are sufficient to meet all the related employee benefit obligations of the plan or the reporting enterprise; or

    (ii) the assets are returned to the reporting enterprise to reimburse it for employee benefits already paid.

A _qualifying insurance policy_ is an insurance policy issued by an insurer that is not a related party (as defined in IAS 24) of the reporting enterprise, if the proceeds of the policy:

(a) can be used only to pay or fund employee benefits under a defined benefit plan; and

(b) are not available to the reporting enterprise's own creditors (even in bankruptcy) and cannot be paid to the reporting enterprise, unless either:

    (i) the proceeds represent surplus assets that are not needed for the policy to meet all the related employee benefit obligations; or

    the proceeds are returned to the reporting enterprise to reimburse it for employee benefits already paid.

Fair value is the amount for which an asset could be exchanged or a liability settled between knowledgeable, willing parties in an arm's length transaction.

The _return on plan assets_ is interest, dividends and other revenue derived from the plan assets, together with realised and unrealised gains or losses on the plan assets, less any costs of administering the plan and less any tax payable by the plan itself.

Actuarial gains and losses comprise:

(a) experience adjustments (the effects of differences between the previous actuarial assumptions and what has actually occurred); and

(b) the effects of changes in actuarial assumptions.

Past service cost is the increase in the present value of the defined benefit obligation for employee service in prior periods, resulting in the current period from the introduction of, or changes to, post-employment benefits or other long-term employee *benefits. Past service cost may be either positive (where benefits are introduced or improved) or negative (where existing benefits are reduced).*

Short-term Employee Benefits

8 Short-term employee benefits include items such as:
(a) wages, salaries and social security contributions;
(b) short-term compensated absences (such as paid annual leave and paid sick leave) where the absences are expected to occur within twelve months after the end of the period in which the employees render the related employee service;
(c) profit sharing and bonuses payable within twelve months after the end of the period in which the employees render the related service; and
(d) non-monetary benefits (such as medical care, housing, cars and free or subsidised goods or services) for current employees.

9 Accounting for short-term employee benefits is generally straightforward because no actuarial assumptions are required to measure the obligation or the cost and there is no possibility of any actuarial gain or loss. Moreover, short-term employee benefit obligations are measured on an undiscounted basis.

Recognition and Measurement

All Short-term Employee Benefits

10 *When an employee has rendered service to an enterprise during an accounting period, the enterprise should recognise the undiscounted amount of short-term employee benefits expected to be paid in exchange for that service:*
(a) as a liability (accrued expense), after deducting any amount already paid. If the amount already paid exceeds the undiscounted amount of the benefits, an enterprise should recognise that excess as an asset (prepaid expense) to the extent that the prepayment will lead to, for example, a reduction in future payments or a cash refund; and
(b) as an expense, unless another IAS requires or permits the inclusion of the benefits in the cost of an asset (see, for example, IAS 2 and IAS 16).
Paragraphs 11, 14 and 17 explain how an enterprise should apply this requirement to short-term employee benefits in the form of compensated absences and profit sharing and bonus plans.

Short-term Compensated Absences

11 *An enterprise should recognise the expected cost of short-term employee benefits in the form of compensated absences under paragraph 10 as follows:*
(a) in the case of accumulating compensated absences, when the employees render service that increases their entitlement to future compensated absences; and
(b) in the case of non-accumulating compensated absences, when the absences occur.

12 [Not printed]

13 Accumulating compensated absences are those that are carried forward and can be used in future periods if the current period's entitlement is not used in full. Accumulating compensated absences may be either vesting (in other words, employees are entitled to a cash payment for unused entitlement on leaving the enterprise) or non-vesting (when employees are not entitled to a cash payment for unused entitlement on leaving). An obligation arises as employees render service that increases their entitlement to future compensated absences. The obligation exists, and is recognised, even if the compensated absences are non-vesting, although the possibility that employees may leave before they use an accumulated non-vesting entitlement affects the measurement of that obligation.

An enterprise should measure the expected cost of accumulating compensated 14 *absences as the additional amount that the enterprise expects to pay as a result of the unused entitlement that has accumulated at the balance sheet date.*

The method specified in the previous paragraph measures the obligation at the amount 15 of the additional payments that are expected to arise solely from the fact that the benefit accumulates. ...

Non-accumulating compensated absences do not carry forward: they lapse if the current 16 period's entitlement is not used in full and do not entitle employees to a cash payment for unused entitlement on leaving the enterprise. This is commonly the case for sick pay (to the extent that unused past entitlement does not increase future entitlement), maternity or paternity leave and compensated absences for jury service or military service. An enterprise recognises no liability or expense until the time of the absence, because employee service does not increase the amount of the benefit.

Profit Sharing and Bonus Plans

An enterprise should recognise the expected cost of profit sharing and bonus payments 17 *under paragraph 10 when, and only when:*
(a) the enterprise has a present legal or constructive obligation to make such payments as a result of past events; and
(b) a reliable estimate of the obligation can be made.
A present obligation exists when, and only when, the enterprise has no realistic alternative but to make the payments.

[Not printed]   18–19

An enterprise can make a reliable estimate of its legal or constructive obligation under 20 a profit sharing or bonus plan when, and only when:
(a) the formal terms of the plan contain a formula for determining the amount of the benefit;
(b) the enterprise determines the amounts to be paid before the financial statements are authorised for issue; or
(c) past practice gives clear evidence of the amount of the enterprise's constructive obligation.

[Not printed]   21

If profit sharing and bonus payments are not due wholly within twelve months after 22 the end of the period in which the employees render the related service, those payments are other long-term employee benefits (see paragraphs 126-131). If profit sharing and bonus payments meet the definition of equity compensation benefits, an enterprise treats them under paragraphs 144-152.

Disclosure

Although this Standard does not require specific disclosures about short-term employee 23 benefits, other IASs may require disclosures. For example, where required by IAS 24 an enterprise discloses information about employee benefits for key management personnel. IAS 1 requires that an enterprise should disclose staff costs.

Post-employment Benefits: Distinction between Defined Contribution Plans and Defined Benefit Plans

24 Post-employment benefits include, for example:
   (a) retirement benefits, such as pensions; and
   (b) other post-employment benefits, such as post-employment life insurance and post-employment medical care.
   Arrangements whereby an enterprise provides post-employment benefits are post-employment benefit plans. An enterprise applies this Standard to all such arrangements whether or not they involve the establishment of a separate entity to receive contributions and to pay benefits.

25 Post-employment benefit plans are classified as either defined contribution plans or defined benefit plans, depending on the economic substance of the plan as derived from its principal terms and conditions. Under defined contribution plans:
   (a) the enterprise's legal or constructive obligation is limited to the amount that it agrees to contribute to the fund. Thus, the amount of the post-employment benefits received by the employee is determined by the amount of contributions paid by an enterprise (and perhaps also the employee) to a post-employment benefit plan or to an insurance company, together with investment returns arising from the contributions; and
   (b) in consequence, actuarial risk (that benefits will be less than expected) and investment risk (that assets invested will be insufficient to meet expected benefits) fall on the employee.

26 [Not printed]

27 Under defined benefit plans:
   (a) the enterprise's obligation is to provide the agreed benefits to current and former employees; and
   (b) actuarial risk (that benefits will cost more than expected) and investment risk fall, in substance, on the enterprise. If actuarial or investment experience are worse than expected, the enterprise's obligation may be increased.

28 [Not printed]

Multi-employer Plans

29 *An enterprise should classify a multi-employer plan as a defined contribution plan or a defined benefit plan under the terms of the plan (including any constructive obligation that goes beyond the formal terms). Where a multi-employer plan is a defined benefit plan, an enterprise should:*
   (a) *account for its proportionate share of the defined benefit obligation, plan assets and cost associated with the plan in the same way as for any other defined benefit plan; and*
   (b) *disclose the information required by paragraph 120.*

30 *When sufficient information is not available to use defined benefit accounting for a multi-employer plan that is a defined benefit plan, an enterprise should:*

(a) account for the plan under paragraphs 44-46 as if it were a defined contribution plan;

(b) disclose:

   (i) the fact that the plan is a defined benefit plan; and

   (ii) the reason why sufficient information is not available to enable the enterprise to account for the plan as a defined benefit plan; and

(c) to the extent that a surplus or deficit in the plan may affect the amount of future contributions, disclose in addition:

   (i) any available information about that surplus or deficit;

   (ii) the basis used to determine that surplus or deficit; and

   (iii) the implications, if any, for the enterprise.

[Not printed] **31**

Where sufficient information is available about a multi-employer plan which is a **32** defined benefit plan, an enterprise accounts for its proportionate share of the defined benefit obligation, plan assets and post-employment benefit cost associated with the plan in the same way as for any other defined benefit plan. However, in some cases, an enterprise may not be able to identify its share of the underlying financial position and performance of the plan with sufficient reliability for accounting purposes. This may occur if:

   (a) the enterprise does not have access to information about the plan that satisfies the requirements of this Standard; or

   (b) the plan exposes the participating enterprises to actuarial risks associated with the current and former employees of other enterprises, with the result that there is no consistent and reliable basis for allocating the obligation, plan assets and cost to individual enterprises participating in the plan.

In those cases, an enterprise accounts for the plan as if it were a defined contribution plan and discloses the additional information required by paragraph 30.

Multi-employer plans are distinct from group administration plans. A group **33** administration plan is merely an aggregation of single employer plans combined to allow participating employers to pool their assets for investment purposes and reduce investment management and administration costs, but the claims of different employers are segregated for the sole benefit of their own employees. Group administration plans pose no particular accounting problems because information is readily available to treat them in the same way as any other single employer plan and because such plans do not expose the participating enterprises to actuarial risks associated with the current and former employees of other enterprises. The definitions in this Standard require an enterprise to classify a group administration plan as a defined contribution plan or a defined benefit plan in accordance with the terms of the plan (including any constructive obligation that goes beyond the formal terms).

Defined benefit plans that pool the assets contributed by various enterprises under **34** common control, for example a parent and its subsidiaries, are not multi-employer plans. Therefore, an enterprise treats all such plans as defined benefit plans.

IAS 37 requires an enterprise to recognise, or disclose information about, certain **35** contingent liabilities. In the context of a multi-employer plan, a contingent liability may arise from, for example:

   (a) actuarial losses relating to other participating enterprises because each enterprise that participates in a multi-employer plan shares in the actuarial risks of every other participating enterprise; or

(b) any responsibility under the terms of a plan to finance any shortfall in the plan if other enterprises cease to participate.

State Plans

36 *An enterprise should account for a state plan in the same way as for a multi-employer plan (see paragraphs 29 and 30).*

37 State plans are established by legislation to cover all enterprises (or all enterprises in a particular category, for example a specific industry) and are operated by national or local government or by another body (for example an autonomous agency created specifically for this purpose) which is not subject to control or influence by the reporting enterprise. Some plans established by an enterprise provide both compulsory benefits which substitute for benefits that would otherwise be covered under a state plan and additional voluntary benefits. Such plans are not state plans.

38 State plans are characterised as defined benefit or defined contribution in nature based on the enterprise's obligation under the plan. ...

Insured Benefits

39 *An enterprise may pay insurance premiums to fund a post-employment benefit plan. The enterprise should treat such a plan as a defined contribution plan unless the enterprise will have (either directly, or indirectly through the plan) a legal or constructive obligation to either:*
(a) pay the employee benefits directly when they fall due; or
(b) pay further amounts if the insurer does not pay all future employee benefits relating to employee service in the current and prior periods.
If the enterprise retains such a legal or constructive obligation, the enterprise should treat the plan as a defined benefit plan.

40 [Not printed]

41 Where an enterprise funds a post-employment benefit obligation by contributing to an insurance policy under which the enterprise (...) retains a legal or constructive obligation, the payment of the premiums does not amount to a defined contribution arrangement. It follows that the enterprise:
(a) accounts for a qualifying insurance policy as a plan asset (see paragraph 7); and
(b) recognises other insurance policies as reimbursement rights (if the policies satisfy the criteria in paragraph 104A).

42 Where an insurance policy is in the name of a specified plan participant or a group of plan participants and the enterprise does not have any legal or constructive obligation to cover any loss on the policy, the enterprise has no obligation to pay benefits to the employees and the insurer has sole responsibility for paying the benefits. The payment of fixed premiums under such contracts is, in substance, the settlement of the employee benefit obligation, rather than an investment to meet the obligation. Consequently, the enterprise no longer has an asset or a liability. Therefore, an enterprise treats such payments as contributions to a defined contribution plan.

Post-employment Benefits: Defined Contribution Plans

Accounting for defined contribution plans is straightforward because the reporting **43** enterprise's obligation for each period is determined by the amounts to be contributed for that period. Consequently, no actuarial assumptions are required to measure the obligation or the expense and there is no possibility of any actuarial gain or loss. Moreover, the obligations are measured on an undiscounted basis, except where they do not fall due wholly within twelve months after the end of the period in which the employees render the related service.

Recognition and Measurement

When an employee has rendered service to an enterprise during a period, the **44** *enterprise should recognise the contribution payable to a defined contribution plan in exchange for that service:*
(a) as a liability (accrued expense), after deducting any contribution already paid. If the contribution already paid exceeds the contribution due for service before the balance sheet date, an enterprise should recognise that excess as an asset (prepaid expense) to the extent that the prepayment will lead to, for example, a reduction in future payments or a cash refund; and
(b) as an expense, unless another IAS requires or permits the inclusion of the contribution in the cost of an asset (see, for example, IAS 2 and IAS 16).

Where contributions to a defined contribution plan do not fall due wholly within **45** *twelve months after the end of the period in which the employees render the related service, they should be discounted using the discount rate specified in paragraph 78.*

Disclosure

An enterprise should disclose the amount recognised as an expense for defined **46** *contribution plans.*

[Not printed] **47**

Post-employment Benefits: Defined Benefit Plans

Accounting for defined benefit plans is complex because actuarial assumptions are **48** required to measure the obligation and the expense and there is a possibility of actuarial gains and losses. Moreover, the obligations are measured on a discounted basis because they may be settled many years after the employees render the related service.

Recognition and Measurement

[Not printed] **49**

Accounting by an enterprise for defined benefit plans involves the following steps: **50**
(a) using actuarial techniques to make a reliable estimate of the amount of benefit that employees have earned in return for their service in the current and prior periods. This requires an enterprise to determine how much benefit is attributable to the current and prior periods (see paragraphs 67-71) and to make estimates (actuarial assumptions) about demographic variables (such as employee turnover and mortality) and financial variables (such as future increases in salaries and medical costs) that will influence the cost of the benefit (see paragraphs 72-91);

(b) discounting that benefit using the Projected Unit Credit Method in order to determine the present value of the defined benefit obligation and the current service cost (see paragraphs 64-66);

(c) determining the fair value of any plan assets (see paragraphs 102-104);

(d) determining the total amount of actuarial gains and losses and the amount of those actuarial gains and losses that should be recognised (see paragraphs 92-95);

(e) where a plan has been introduced or changed, determining the resulting past service cost (see paragraphs 96-101); and

(f) where a plan has been curtailed or settled, determining the resulting gain or loss (see paragraphs 109-115).

...

51 [Not printed]

Accounting for the Constructive Obligation

52 *An enterprise should account not only for its legal obligation under the formal terms of a defined benefit plan, but also for any constructive obligation that arises from the enterprise's informal practices. Informal practices give rise to a constructive obligation where the enterprise has no realistic alternative but to pay employee benefits. ...*

53 [Not printed]

Balance Sheet

54 *The amount recognised as a defined benefit liability should be the net total of the following amounts:*

(a) *the present value of the defined benefit obligation at the balance sheet date (see paragraph 64);*

(b) *plus any actuarial gains (less any actuarial losses) not recognised because of the treatment set out in paragraphs 92-93;*

(c) *minus any past service cost not yet recognised (see paragraph 96);*

(d) *minus the fair value at the balance sheet date of plan assets (if any) out of which the obligations are to be settled directly (see paragraphs 102-104).*

55 The present value of the defined benefit obligation is the gross obligation, before deducting the fair value of any plan assets.

56 *An enterprise should determine the present value of defined benefit obligations and the fair value of any plan assets with sufficient regularity that the amounts recognised in the financial statements do not differ materially from the amounts that would be determined at the balance sheet date.*

57 [Not printed]

58 *The amount determined under paragraph 54 may be negative (an asset). An enterprise should measure the resulting asset at the lower of:*

(a) *the amount determined under paragraph 54; and*

(b) *the total of:*

(i) *any cumulative unrecognised net actuarial losses and past service cost (see paragraphs 92, 93 and 96); and*

(ii) *the present value of any economic benefits available in the form of refunds from the plan or reductions in future contributions to the plan. The present* value of these economic benefits should be determined using the discount rate specified in paragraph 78.

The application of paragraph 58 should not result in a gain being recognised solely **58A** as a result of an actuarial loss or past service cost in the current period or in a loss being recognised solely as a result of an actuarial gain in the current period. The enterprise should therefore recognise immediately under paragraph 54 the following, to the extent that they arise while the defined benefit asset is determined in accordance with paragraph 58(b):
(a) net actuarial losses of the current period and past service cost of the current period to the extent that they exceed any reduction in the present value of the economic benefits specified in paragraph 58(b)(ii). If there is no change or an increase in the present value of the economic benefits, the entire net actuarial losses of the current period and past service cost of the current period should be recognised immediately under paragraph 54.
(b) net actuarial gains of the current period after the deduction of past service cost of the current period to the extent that they exceed any increase in the present value of the economic benefits specified in paragraph 58(b)(ii). If there is no change or a decrease in the present value of the economic benefits, the entire net actuarial gains of the current period after the deduction of past service cost of the current period should be recognised immediately under paragraph 54.

Paragraph 58A applies to an enterprise only if it has, at the beginning or end of the **58B** accounting period, a surplus ... in a defined benefit plan and cannot, based on the current terms of the plan, recover that surplus fully through refunds or reductions in future contributions. In such cases, past service cost and actuarial losses that arise in the period, the recognition of which is deferred under paragraph 54, will increase the amount specified in paragraph 58(b)(i). If that increase is not offset by an equal decrease in the present value of economic benefits that qualify for recognition under paragraph 58(b)(ii), there will be an increase in the net total specified by paragraph 58(b) and, hence, a recognised gain. Paragraph 58A prohibits the recognition of a gain in these circumstances. The opposite effect arises with actuarial gains that arise in the period, the recognition of which is deferred under paragraph 54, to the extent that the actuarial gains reduce cumulative unrecognised actuarial losses. Paragraph 58A prohibits the recognition of a loss in these circumstances. ...

An asset may arise where a defined benefit plan has been overfunded or in certain cases **59** where actuarial gains are recognised. An enterprise recognises an asset in such cases because:
(a) the enterprise controls a resource, which is the ability to use the surplus to generate future benefits;
(b) that control is a result of past events (contributions paid by the enterprise and service rendered by the employee); and
(c) future economic benefits are available to the enterprise in the form of a reduction in future contributions or a cash refund, either directly to the enterprise or indirectly to another plan in deficit.

The limit in paragraph 58(b) does not over-ride the delayed recognition of certain **60** actuarial losses (see paragraphs 92 and 93) and certain past service cost (see paragraph 96), other than as specified in paragraph 58A. However, that limit does over-ride the

transitional option in paragraph 155(b). Paragraph 120(c)(vi) requires an enterprise to disclose any amount not recognised as an asset because of the limit in paragraph 58(b).
...

Income Statement

61 *An enterprise should recognise the net total of the following amounts as expense or (subject to the limit in paragraph 58(b)) income, except to the extent that another IAS requires or permits their inclusion in the cost of an asset:*

(a) current service cost (see paragraph 63-91);

(b) interest cost (see paragraph 82);

(c) the expected return on any plan assets (see paragraphs 105-107) and on any reimbursement rights (paragraph 104A);

(d) actuarial gains and losses, to the extent that they are recognised under paragraphs 92 and 93;

(e) past service cost, to the extent that paragraph 96 requires an enterprise to recognise it; and

(f) the effect of any curtailments or settlements (see paragraphs 109 and 110).

62 Other IASs require the inclusion of certain employee benefit costs within the cost of assets such as inventories or property, plant and equipment (see IAS 2 and IAS 16). Any post-employment benefit costs included in the cost of such assets include the appropriate proportion of the components listed in paragraph 61.

Recognition and Measurement: Present Value of Defined Benefit Obligations and Current Service Cost

63 The ultimate cost of a defined benefit plan may be influenced by many variables, such as final salaries, employee turnover and mortality, medical cost trends and, for a funded plan, the investment earnings on the plan assets. The ultimate cost of the plan is uncertain and this uncertainty is likely to persist over a long period of time. In order to measure the present value of the post-employment benefit obligations and the related current service cost, it is necessary to:

(a) apply an actuarial valuation method (see paragraphs 64-66);

(b) attribute benefit to periods of service (see paragraphs 67-71); and

(c) make actuarial assumptions (see paragraphs 72-91).

Actuarial Valuation Method

64 *An enterprise should use the Projected Unit Credit Method to determine the present value of its defined benefit obligations and the related current service cost and, where applicable, past service cost.*

65 The Projected Unit Credit Method (sometimes known as the accrued benefit method pro-rated on service or as the benefit/years of service method) sees each period of service as giving rise to an additional unit of benefit entitlement (see paragraphs 67-71) and measures each unit separately to build up the final obligation (see paragraphs 72-91).

66 An enterprise discounts the whole of a post-employment benefit obligation, even if part of the obligation falls due within twelve months of the balance sheet date.
...

Attributing Benefit to Periods of Service

In determining the present value of its defined benefit obligations and the related **67**
current service cost and, where applicable, past service cost, an enterprise should
attribute benefit to periods of service under the plan's benefit formula. However, if
an employee's service in later years will lead to a materially higher level of benefit
than in earlier years, an enterprise should attribute benefit on a straight-line basis
from:
(a) the date when service by the employee first leads to benefits under the plan
    (whether or not the benefits are conditional on further service); until
(b) the date when further service by the employee will lead to no material amount of
    further benefits under the plan, other than from further salary increases.

The Projected Unit Credit Method requires an enterprise to attribute benefit to the **68**
current period (in order to determine current service cost) and the current and prior
periods (in order to determine the present value of defined benefit obligations). An
enterprise attributes benefit to periods in which the obligation to provide post-
employment benefits arises. That obligation arises as employees render services in
return for post-employment benefits which an enterprise expects to pay in future
reporting periods. Actuarial techniques allow an enterprise to measure that obligation
with sufficient reliability to justify recognition of a liability.

...

[Not printed] **69**

The obligation increases until the date when further service by the employee will lead **70**
to no material amount of further benefits. Therefore, all benefit is attributed to periods
ending on or before that date. Benefit is attributed to individual accounting periods
under the plan's benefit formula. However, if an employee's service in later years will
lead to a materially higher level of benefit than in earlier years, an enterprise attributes
benefit on a straight-line basis until the date when further service by the employee will
lead to no material amount of further benefits. That is because the employee's service
throughout the entire period will ultimately lead to benefit at that higher level.

...

Where the amount of a benefit is a constant proportion of final salary for each year of **71**
service, future salary increases will affect the amount required to settle the obligation
that exists for service before the balance sheet date, but do not create an additional
obligation. Therefore:
(a) for the purpose of paragraph 67(b), salary increases do not lead to further benefits,
    even though the amount of the benefits is dependent on final salary; and
(b) the amount of benefit attributed to each period is a constant proportion of the
    salary to which the benefit is linked.

...

Actuarial Assumptions

Actuarial assumptions should be unbiased and mutually compatible. **72**

Actuarial assumptions are an enterprise's best estimates of the variables that will **73**
determine the ultimate cost of providing post-employment benefits. Actuarial
assumptions comprise:

    (a) demographic assumptions about the future characteristics of current and former employees (and their dependants) who are eligible for benefits. Demographic assumptions deal with matters such as:

      (i) mortality, both during and after employment;

      (ii) rates of employee turnover, disability and early retirement;

      (iii) the proportion of plan members with dependants who will be eligible for benefits; and

      (iv) claim rates under medical plans; and

    (b) financial assumptions, dealing with items such as:

      (i) the discount rate (see paragraphs 78-82);

      (ii) future salary and benefit levels (see paragraphs 83-87);

      (iii) in the case of medical benefits, future medical costs, including, where material, the cost of administering claims and benefit payments (see paragraphs 88-91); and

      (iv) the expected rate of return on plan assets (see paragraphs 105-107).

74 Actuarial assumptions are unbiased if they are neither imprudent nor excessively conservative.

75 Actuarial assumptions are mutually compatible if they reflect the economic relationships between factors such as inflation, rates of salary increase, the return on plan assets and discount rates. For example, all assumptions which depend on a particular inflation level (such as assumptions about interest rates and salary and benefit increases) in any given future period assume the same inflation level in that period.

76 An enterprise determines the discount rate and other financial assumptions in nominal (stated) terms, unless estimates in real (inflation-adjusted) terms are more reliable, for example, in a hyper-inflationary economy (see IAS 29), or where the benefit is index-linked and there is a deep market in index-linked bonds of the same currency and term.

77 *Financial assumptions should be based on market expectations, at the balance sheet date, for the period over which the obligations are to be settled.*

Actuarial Assumptions: Discount Rate

78 *The rate used to discount post-employment benefit obligations (both funded and unfunded) should be determined by reference to market yields at the balance sheet date on high quality corporate bonds. In countries where there is no deep market in such bonds, the market yields (at the balance sheet date) on government bonds should be used. The currency and term of the corporate bonds or government bonds should be consistent with the currency and estimated term of the post-employment benefit obligations.*

79 One actuarial assumption which has a material effect is the discount rate. The discount rate reflects the time value of money but not the actuarial or investment risk. Furthermore, the discount rate does not reflect the enterprise-specific credit risk borne by the enterprise's creditors, nor does it reflect the risk that future experience may differ from actuarial assumptions.

80 The discount rate reflects the estimated timing of benefit payments. In practice, an enterprise often achieves this by applying a single weighted average discount rate that reflects the estimated timing and amount of benefit payments and the currency in which the benefits are to be paid.

81 [Not printed]

Interest cost is computed by multiplying the discount rate as determined at the start of **82** the period by the present value of the defined benefit obligation throughout that period, taking account of any material changes in the obligation. ...

Actuarial Assumptions: Salaries, Benefits and Medical Costs

Post-employment benefit obligations should be measured on a basis that reflects: **83**
(a) estimated future salary increases;
(b) the benefits set out in the terms of the plan (or resulting from any constructive obligation that goes beyond those terms) at the balance sheet date; and
(c) estimated future changes in the level of any state benefits that affect the benefits payable under a defined benefit plan, if, and only if, either:
  (i) those changes were enacted before the balance sheet date; or
  (ii) past history, or other reliable evidence, indicates that those state benefits will change in some predictable manner, ...

[Not printed] **84**

If the formal terms of a plan (or a constructive obligation that goes beyond those terms) **85** require an enterprise to change benefits in future periods, the measurement of the obligation reflects those changes. ...

Actuarial assumptions do not reflect future benefit changes that are not set out in the **86** formal terms of the plan (or a constructive obligation) at the balance sheet date. Such changes will result in:
(a) past service cost, to the extent that they change benefits for service before the change; and
(b) current service cost for periods after the change, to the extent that they change benefits for service after the change.

[Not printed] **87**

Assumptions about medical costs should take account of estimated future changes in **88** *the cost of medical services, resulting from both inflation and specific changes in medical costs.*

Measurement of post-employment medical benefits requires assumptions about the **89** level and frequency of future claims and the cost of meeting those claims. An enterprise estimates future medical costs on the basis of historical data about the enterprise's own experience, supplemented where necessary by historical data from other enterprises, insurance companies, medical providers or other sources. Estimates of future medical costs consider the effect of technological advances, changes in health care utilisation or delivery patterns and changes in the health status of plan participants.

The level and frequency of claims is particularly sensitive to the age, health status and **90** sex of employees (and their dependants) and may be sensitive to other factors such as geographical location. Therefore, historical data is adjusted to the extent that the demographic mix of the population differs from that of the population used as a basis for the historical data. It is also adjusted where there is reliable evidence that historical trends will not continue.

[Not printed] **91**

Actuarial Gains and Losses

92 *In measuring its defined benefit liability under paragraph 54, an enterprise should, subject to paragraph 58A, recognise a portion (as specified in paragraph 93) of its actuarial gains and losses as income or expense if the net cumulative unrecognised actuarial gains and losses at the end of the previous reporting period exceeded the greater of:*

(a) 10% of the present value of the defined benefit obligation at that date (before deducting plan assets); and

(b) 10% of the fair value of any plan assets at that date.

These limits should be calculated and applied separately for each defined benefit plan.

93 *The portion of actuarial gains and losses to be recognised for each defined benefit plan is the excess determined under paragraph 92, divided by the expected average remaining working lives of the employees participating in that plan. However, an enterprise may adopt any systematic method that results in faster recognition of actuarial gains and losses, provided that the same basis is applied to both gains and losses and the basis is applied consistently from period to period. An enterprise may apply such systematic methods to actuarial gains and losses even if they fall within the limits specified in paragraph 92.*

94 Actuarial gains and losses may result from increases or decreases in either the present value of a defined benefit obligation or the fair value of any related plan assets. Causes of actuarial gains and losses include, for example:

(a) unexpectedly high or low rates of employee turnover, early retirement or mortality or of increases in salaries, benefits (if the formal or constructive terms of a plan provide for inflationary benefit increases) or medical costs;

(b) the effect of changes in estimates of future employee turnover, early retirement or mortality or of increases in salaries, benefits (if the formal or constructive terms of a plan provide for inflationary benefit increases) or medical costs;

(c) the effect of changes in the discount rate; and

(d) differences between the actual return on plan assets and the expected return on plan assets (see paragraphs 105-107).

95 In the long term, actuarial gains and losses may offset one another. Therefore, estimates of post-employment benefit obligations are best viewed as a range (or 'corridor') around the best estimate. An enterprise is permitted, but not required, to recognise actuarial gains and losses that fall within that range. This Standard requires an enterprise to recognise, as a minimum, a specified portion of the actuarial gains and losses that fall outside a 'corridor' of plus or minus 10%. [...] The Standard also permits systematic methods of faster recognition, provided that those methods satisfy the conditions set out in paragraph 93. Such permitted methods include, for example, immediate recognition of all actuarial gains and losses, both within and outside the 'corridor'. Paragraph 155(b)(iii) explains the need to consider any unrecognised part of the transitional liability in accounting for subsequent actuarial gains.

Past Service Cost

96 *In measuring its defined benefit liability under paragraph 54, an enterprise should, subject to paragraph 58A, recognise past service cost as an expense on a straight-line basis over the average period until the benefits become vested. To the extent that the*

172

benefits are already vested immediately following the introduction of, or changes to, a defined benefit plan, an enterprise should recognise past service cost immediately.

Past service cost arises when an enterprise introduces a defined benefit plan or changes **97** the benefits payable under an existing defined benefit plan. Such changes are in return for employee service over the period until the benefits concerned are vested. Therefore, past service cost is recognised over that period, regardless of the fact that the cost refers to employee service in previous periods. Past service cost is measured as the change in the liability resulting from the amendment (see paragraph 64).

...

Past service cost excludes: **98**
(a) the effect of differences between actual and previously assumed salary increases on the obligation to pay benefits for service in prior years (there is no past service cost because actuarial assumptions allow for projected salaries);
(b) under and over estimates of discretionary pension increases where an enterprise has a constructive obligation to grant such increases (there is no past service cost because actuarial assumptions allow for such increases);
(c) estimates of benefit improvements that result from actuarial gains that have already been recognised in the financial statements if the enterprise is obliged, by either the formal terms of a plan (or a constructive obligation that goes beyond those terms) or legislation, to use any surplus in the plan for the benefit of plan participants, even if the benefit increase has not yet been formally awarded (the resulting increase in the obligation is an actuarial loss and not past service cost, see paragraph 85(b));
(d) the increase in vested benefits when, in the absence of new or improved benefits, employees complete vesting requirements (there is no past service cost because the estimated cost of benefits was recognised as current service cost as the service was rendered); and
(e) the effect of plan amendments that reduce benefits for future service (a curtailment).

An enterprise establishes the amortisation schedule for past service cost when the **99** benefits are introduced or changed. ... Therefore, an enterprise amends the amortisation schedule for past service cost only if there is a curtailment or settlement.

Where an enterprise reduces benefits payable under an existing defined benefit plan, **100** the resulting reduction in the defined benefit liability is recognised as (negative) past service cost over the average period until the reduced portion of the benefits becomes vested.

Where an enterprise reduces certain benefits payable under an existing defined benefit **101** plan and, at the same time, increases other benefits payable under the plan for the same employees, the enterprise treats the change as a single net change.

Recognition and Measurement: Plan Assets

Fair Value of Plan Assets

The fair value of any plan assets is deducted in determining the amount recognised in **102** the balance sheet under paragraph 54. When no market price is available, the fair value of plan assets is estimated; for example, by discounting expected future cash flows using a discount rate that reflects both the risk associated with the plan assets and the maturity or expected disposal date of those assets (or, if they have no maturity, the expected period until the settlement of the related obligation).

103 Plan assets exclude unpaid contributions due from the reporting enterprise to the fund, as well as any non-transferable financial instruments issued by the enterprise and held by the fund. Plan assets are reduced by any liabilities of the fund that do not relate to employee benefits, for example, trade and other payables and liabilities resulting from derivative financial instruments.

104 Where plan assets include qualifying insurance policies that exactly match the amount and timing of some or all of the benefits payable under the plan, the fair value of those insurance policies is deemed to be the present value of the related obligations, as described in paragraph 54 (subject to any reduction required if the amounts receivable under the insurance policies are not recoverable in full).

Reimbursements

104A *When, and only when, it is virtually certain that another party will reimburse some or all of the expenditure required to settle a defined benefit obligation, an enterprise should recognise its right to reimbursement as a separate asset. The enterprise should measure the asset at fair value. In all other respects, an enterprise should treat that asset in the same way as plan assets. In the income statement, the expense relating to a defined benefit plan may be presented net of the amount recognised for a reimbursement.*

104B [Not printed]

104C When an insurance policy is not a qualifying insurance policy, that insurance policy is not a plan asset. Paragraph 104A deals with such cases: the enterprise recognises its right to reimbursement under the insurance policy as a separate asset, rather than as a deduction in determining the defined benefit liability recognised under paragraph 54; in all other respects, the enterprise treats that asset in the same way as plan assets. In particular, the defined benefit liability recognised under paragraph 54 is increased (reduced) to the extent that net cumulative actuarial gains (losses) on the defined benefit obligation and on the related reimbursement right remain unrecognised under paragraphs 92 and 93. ...

104D If the right to reimbursement arises under an insurance policy that exactly matches the amount and timing of some or all of the benefits payable under a defined benefit plan, the fair value of the reimbursement right is deemed to be the present value of the related obligation, as described in paragraph 54 (subject to any reduction required if the reimbursement is not recoverable in full).

Return on Plan Assets

105 The expected return on plan assets is one component of the expense recognised in the income statement. The difference between the expected return on plan assets and the actual return on plan assets is an actuarial gain or loss; it is included with the actuarial gains and losses on the defined benefit obligation in determining the net amount that is compared with the limits of the 10% 'corridor' specified in paragraph 92.

106 The expected return on plan assets is based on market expectations, at the beginning of the period, for returns over the entire life of the related obligation. The expected return on plan assets reflects changes in the fair value of plan assets held during the

period as a result of actual contributions paid into the fund and actual benefits paid out of the fund.

In determining the expected and actual return on plan assets, an enterprise deducts **107** expected administration costs, other than those included in the actuarial assumptions used to measure the obligation.

...

Business Combinations

In a business combination that is an acquisition, an enterprise recognises assets and **108** liabilities arising from post-employment benefits at the present value of the obligation less the fair value of any plan assets (see IAS 22). The present value of the obligation includes all of the following, even if the acquiree had not yet recognised them at the date of the acquisition:

(a) actuarial gains and losses that arose before the date of the acquisition (whether or not they fell inside the 10% 'corridor');

(b) past service cost that arose from benefit changes, or the introduction of a plan, before the date of the acquisition; and

(c) amounts that, under the transitional provisions of paragraph 155(b), the acquiree had not recognised.

Curtailments and Settlements

An enterprise should recognise gains or losses on the curtailment or settlement of a **109** *defined benefit plan when the curtailment or settlement occurs. The gain or loss on a curtailment or settlement should comprise:*

(a) any resulting change in the present value of the defined benefit obligation;

(b) any resulting change in the fair value of the plan assets;

(c) any related actuarial gains and losses and past service cost that, under paragraphs 92 and 96, had not previously been recognised.

Before determining the effect of a curtailment or settlement, an enterprise should **110** *remeasure the obligation (and the related plan assets, if any) using current actuarial assumptions (including current market interest rates and other current market prices).*

A curtailment occurs when an enterprise either: **111**

(a) is demonstrably committed to make a material reduction in the number of employees covered by a plan; or

(b) amends the terms of a defined benefit plan such that a material element of future service by current employees will no longer qualify for benefits, or will qualify only for reduced benefits.

A curtailment may arise from an isolated event, such as the closing of a plant, discontinuance of an operation or termination or suspension of a plan. An event is material enough to qualify as a curtailment if the recognition of a curtailment gain or loss would have a material effect on the financial statements. Curtailments are often linked with a restructuring. Therefore, an enterprise accounts for a curtailment at the same time as for a related restructuring.

A settlement occurs when an enterprise enters into a transaction that eliminates all **112** further legal or constructive obligation for part or all of the benefits provided under a defined benefit plan, ...

113 [Not printed]

114 A settlement occurs together with a curtailment if a plan is terminated such that the obligation is settled and the plan ceases to exist. However, the termination of a plan is not a curtailment or settlement if the plan is replaced by a new plan that offers benefits that are, in substance, identical.

115 Where a curtailment relates to only some of the employees covered by a plan, or where only part of an obligation is settled, the gain or loss includes a proportionate share of the previously unrecognised past service cost and actuarial gains and losses (and of transitional amounts remaining unrecognised under paragraph 155(b)). The proportionate share is determined on the basis of the present value of the obligations before and after the curtailment or settlement, unless another basis is more rational in the circumstances. ...

Presentation

Offset

116 *An enterprise should offset an asset relating to one plan against a liability relating to another plan when, and only when, the enterprise:*
   (a) has a legally enforceable right to use a surplus in one plan to settle obligations under the other plan; and
   (b) intends either to settle the obligations on a net basis, or to realise the surplus in one plan and settle its obligation under the other plan simultaneously.

117 [Not printed]

Current / Non-current Distinction

118 [Not printed]

Financial Components of Post-employment Benefit Costs

119 [Not printed]

Disclosure

120 *An enterprise should disclose the following information about defined benefit plans:*
   (a) the enterprise's accounting policy for recognising actuarial gains and losses;
   (b) a general description of the type of plan;
   (c) a reconciliation of the assets and liabilities recognised in the balance sheet, showing at least:
      (i) the present value at the balance sheet date of defined benefit obligations that are wholly unfunded;
      (ii) the present value (before deducting the fair value of plan assets) at the balance sheet date of defined benefit obligations that are wholly or partly funded;
      (iii) the fair value of any plan assets at the balance sheet date;
      (iv) the net actuarial gains or losses not recognised in the balance sheet (see paragraph 92);
      (v) the past service cost not yet recognised in the balance sheet (see paragraph 96);
      (vi) any amount not recognised as an asset, because of the limit in paragraph 58(b);

(vii)the fair value at the balance sheet date of any reimbursement right recognised as an asset under paragraph 104A (with a brief description of the link between the reimbursement right and the related obligation); and

(viii)the othe amounts recognised in the balance sheet;

(d) the amounts included in the fair value of plan assets for:
   (i) each category of the reporting enterprise's own financial instruments; and
   (ii) any property occupied by, or other assets used by, the reporting enterprise;

(e) a reconciliation showing the movements during the period in the net liability (or asset) recognised in the balance sheet;

(f) the total expense recognised in the income statement for each of the following, and the line item(s) of the income statement in which they are included:
   (i) current service cost;
   (ii) interest cost;
   (iii)expected return on plan assets;
   (iv) expected return on any reimbursement right recognised as an asset under paragraph 104A;
   (v) actuarial gains and losses;
   (vi) past service cost; and
   (vii)the effect of any curtailment or settlement;

(g) the actual return on plan assets, as well as the actual return on any reimbursement right recognised as an asset under paragraph 104A; and

(h) the principal actuarial assumptions used as at the balance sheet date, including, where applicable:
   (i) the discount rates;
   (ii) the expected rates of return on any plan assets for the periods presented in the financial statements;
   (iii) the expected rates of return for the periods presented in the financial statements on any reimbursement right recognised as an asset under paragraph 104A;
   (iv) the expected rates of salary increases (and of changes in an index or other variable specified in the formal or constructive terms of a plan as the basis for future benefit increases);
   (v) medical cost trend rates; and
   (vi) any other material actuarial assumptions used.

An enterprise should disclose each actuarial assumption in absolute terms (for example as an absolute percentage) and not just as a margin between different percentages or other variables.

[Not printed]   121–125

Other Long-term Employee Benefits

Other long-term employee benefits include, for example: 126

(a) long-term compensated absences such as long-service or sabbatical leave;

(b) jubilee or other long-service benefits;

(c) long-term disability benefits;

(d) profit sharing and bonuses payable twelve months or more after the end of the period in which the employees render the related service; and

(e) deferred compensation paid twelve months or more after the end of the period in which it is earned.

127 The measurement of other long-term employee benefits is not usually subject to the same degree of uncertainty as the measurement of post-employment benefits. Furthermore, the introduction of, or changes to, other long-term employee benefits rarely causes a material amount of past service cost. For these reasons, this Standard requires a simplified method of accounting for other long-term employee benefits. This method differs from the accounting required for post-employment benefits as follows:

(a) actuarial gains and losses are recognised immediately and no 'corridor' is applied; and

(b) all past service cost is recognised immediately.

Recognition and Measurement

128 *The amount recognised as a liability for other long-term employee benefits should be the net total of the following amounts:*

(a) the present value of the defined benefit obligation at the balance sheet date (see paragraph 64);

(b) minus the fair value at the balance sheet date of plan assets (if any) out of which the obligations are to be settled directly (see paragraphs 102-104).

In measuring the liability, an enterprise should apply paragraphs 49-91, excluding paragraphs 54 and 61. An enterprise should apply paragraph 104A in recognising and measuring any reimbursement right.

129 *For other long-term employee benefits, an enterprise should recognise the net total of the following amounts as expense or (subject to paragraph 58) income, except to the extent that another IAS requires or permits their inclusion in the cost of an asset:*

(a) current service cost (see paragraphs 63-91);

(b) interest cost (see paragraph 82);

(c) the expected return on any plan assets (see paragraphs 105-107) and on any reimbursement right recognised as an asset (see paragraph 104A);

(d) actuarial gains and losses, which should all be recognised immediately;

(e) past service cost, which should all be recognised immediately; and

(f) the effect of any curtailments or settlements (see paragraphs 109 and 110).

130 One form of other long-term employee benefit is long-term disability benefit. If the level of benefit depends on the length of service, an obligation arises when the service is rendered. Measurement of that obligation reflects the probability that payment will be required and the length of time for which payment is expected to be made. If the level of benefit is the same for any disabled employee regardless of years of service, the expected cost of those benefits is recognised when an event occurs that causes a long-term disability.

Disclosure

131 Although this Standard does not require specific disclosures about other long-term employee benefits, other IASs may require disclosures, ...

Termination Benefits

132 [Not printed]

Recognition

An enterprise should recognise termination benefits as a liability and an expense 133
when, and only when, the enterprise is demonstrably committed to either:
(a) terminate the employment of an employee or group of employees before the
*   normal retirement date; or*
(b) provide termination benefits as a result of an offer made in order to encourage
*   voluntary redundancy.*

An enterprise is demonstrably committed to a termination when, and only when, the 134
enterprise has a detailed formal plan for the termination and is without realistic
possibility of withdrawal. The detailed plan should include, as a minimum:
(a) the location, function, and approximate number of employees whose services are
*   to be terminated;*
(b) the termination benefits for each job classification or function; and
(c) the time at which the plan will be implemented. Implementation should begin
*   as soon as possible and the period of time to complete implementation should be*
*   such that material changes to the plan are not likely.*

An enterprise may be committed, by legislation, by contractual or other agreements 135
with employees or their representatives or by a constructive obligation based on
business practice, custom or a desire to act equitably, to make payments (or provide
other benefits) to employees when it terminates their employment. Such payments are
termination benefits. ...

Some employee benefits are payable regardless of the reason for the employee's 136
departure. The payment of such benefits is certain (subject to any vesting or minimum
service requirements) but the timing of their payment is uncertain. Although such
benefits are described in some countries as termination indemnities, or termination
gratuities, they are post-employment benefits, rather than termination benefits and an
enterprise accounts for them as post-employment benefits. Some enterprises provide a
lower level of benefit for voluntary termination at the request of the employee (in
substance, a post-employment benefit) than for involuntary termination at the request
of the enterprise. The additional benefit payable on involuntary termination is a
termination benefit.

Termination benefits do not provide an enterprise with future economic benefits and 137
are recognised as an expense immediately.

[Not printed] 138

Measurement

Where termination benefits fall due more than 12 months after the balance sheet 139
date, they should be discounted using the discount rate specified in paragraph 78.

In the case of an offer made to encourage voluntary redundancy, the measurement of 140
termination benefits should be based on the number of employees expected to accept
the offer.

Disclosure

Where there is uncertainty about the number of employees who will accept an offer of 141
termination benefits, a contingent liability exists. As required by IAS 37 an enterprise

discloses information about the contingent liability unless the possibility of an outflow in settlement is remote.

142 As required by IAS 8 an enterprise discloses the nature and amount of an expense if it is of such size, nature or incidence that its disclosure is relevant to explain the performance of the enterprise for the period. Termination benefits may result in an expense needing disclosure in order to comply with this requirement.

143 Where required by IAS 24 an enterprise discloses information about termination benefits for key management personnel.

Equity Compensation Benefits

144 Equity compensation benefits include benefits in such forms as:
   (a) shares, share options, and other equity instruments, issued to employees at less than the fair value at which those instruments would be issued to a third party; and
   (b) cash payments, the amount of which will depend on the future market price of the reporting enterprise's shares.

Recognition and Measurement

145 This Standard does not specify recognition and measurement requirements for equity compensation benefits.

Disclosure

146 The disclosures required below are intended to enable users of financial statements to assess the effect of equity compensation benefits on an enterprise's financial position, performance and cash flows. Equity compensation benefits may affect:
   (a) an enterprise's financial position by requiring the enterprise to issue equity financial instruments or convert financial instruments, for example when employees, or employee compensation plans, hold share options or have partially satisfied the vesting provisions that will enable them to acquire share options in the future; and
   (b) an enterprise's performance and cash flows by reducing the amount of cash or other employee benefits that the enterprise provides to employees in exchange for their services.

147 *An enterprise should disclose:*
   (a) the nature and terms (including any vesting provisions) of equity compensation plans;
   (b) the accounting policy for equity compensation plans;
   (c) the amounts recognised in the financial statements for equity compensation plans;
   (d) the number and terms (including, where applicable, dividend and voting rights, conversion rights, exercise dates, exercise prices and expiry dates) of the enterprise's own equity financial instruments which are held by equity compensation plans (and, in the case of share options, by employees) at the beginning and end of the period. The extent to which employees' entitlements to those instruments are vested at the beginning and end of the period should be specified;
   (e) the number and terms (including, where applicable, dividend and voting rights, conversion rights, exercise dates, exercise prices and expiry dates) of equity

financial instruments issued by the enterprise to equity compensation plans or to employees (or of the enterprise's own equity financial instruments distributed by equity compensation plans to employees) during the period and the fair value of any consideration received from the equity compensation plans or the employees;

(f) the number, exercise dates and exercise prices of share options exercised under equity compensation plans during the period;

(g) the number of share options held by equity compensation plans, or held by employees under such plans, that lapsed during the period; and

(h) the amount, and principal terms, of any loans or guarantees granted by the reporting enterprise to, or on behalf of, equity compensation plans.

An enterprise should also disclose: **148**

(a) the fair value, at the beginning and end of the period, of the enterprise's own equity financial instruments (other than share options) held by equity compensation plans; and

(b) the fair value, at the date of issue, of the enterprise's own equity financial instruments (other than share options) issued by the enterprise to equity compensation plans or to employees, or by equity compensation plans to employees, during the period.

If it is not practicable to determine the fair value of the equity financial instruments (other than share options), that fact should be disclosed.

When an enterprise has more than one equity compensation plan, disclosures may be **149** made in total, separately for each plan, or in such groupings as are considered most useful for assessing the enterprise's obligations to issue equity financial instruments under such plans and the changes in those obligations during the current period. Such groupings may distinguish, for example, the location and seniority of the employee groups covered. When an enterprise provides disclosures in total for a grouping of plans, such disclosures are provided in the form of weighted averages or of relatively narrow ranges.

When an enterprise has issued share options to employees, or to employee **150** compensation plans, disclosures may be made in total, or in such groupings as are considered most useful for assessing the number and timing of shares that may be issued and the cash that may be received as a result. ...

The disclosures required by paragraphs 147 and 148 are intended to meet the objectives **151** of this Standard. Additional disclosure may be required to satisfy the requirements of IAS 24 if an enterprise:

(a) provides equity compensation benefits to key management personnel;

(b) provides equity compensation benefits in the form of instruments issued by the enterprise's parent; or

(c) enters into related party transactions with equity compensation plans.

[Not printed] **152**

Transitional Provisions

[Not printed] **153–156**

Effective Date

[Not printed] **157–160**

Appendix A

Illustrative Example

[Not printed]

Appendix B

Illustrative Disclosures

[Not printed]

Appendix C

Illustration of the Application of Paragraph 58A

[Not printed]

Appendix D

Basis for Conclusions

[Not printed]

Appendix E

Approval of 2002 Amendment by the Board

[Not printed]

Appendix F

Dissenting Opinion (2002 Amendment)

[Not printed]

IAS 20: Accounting for Government Grants and Disclosure of Government Assistance

IAS 20: Accounting for Government Grants and Disclosure of Government Assistance				
Scope 20.1–2	Definitions 20.3–6	Transitional Provisions 20.40	Effective Date 20.41	Related Interpretation: SIC–10

Government Grants 20.7–33			
Non-monetary Government Grants 20.23	Presentation of Grants Related to Assets 20.24–28	Presentation of Grants Related to Income 20.29–31	Repayment of Government Grants 20.32–33

Government Assistance 20.34–38

Disclosure 20.39

Scope

This Standard should be applied in accounting for, and in the disclosure of, **1** *government grants and in the disclosure of other forms of government assistance.*

This Standard does not deal with: **2**
(a) the special problems arising in accounting for government grants in financial statements reflecting the effects of changing prices or in supplementary information of a similar nature;
(b) government assistance that is provided for an enterprise in the form of benefits that are available in determining taxable income or are determined or limited on the basis of income tax liability (such as income tax holidays, investment tax credits, accelerated depreciation allowances and reduced income tax rates);
(c) government participation in the ownership of the enterprise;
(d) government grants covered by IAS 41.

Definitions

... **3**

Government refers to government, government agencies and similar bodies whether local, national or international.

Government assistance is action by government designed to provide an economic benefit specific to an enterprise or range of enterprises qualifying under certain criteria. Government assistance for the purpose of this Standard does not include benefits provided only indirectly through action affecting general trading conditions, such as the provision of infrastructure in development areas or the imposition of trading constraints on competitors.

Government grants are assistance by government in the form of transfers of resources to an enterprise in return for past or future compliance with certain conditions relating to the operating activities of the enterprise. They exclude those forms of government assistance which cannot reasonably have a value placed upon them and transactions with government which cannot be distinguished from the normal trading transactions of the enterprise.

Grants related to assets are government grants whose primary condition is that an enterprise qualifying for them should purchase, construct or otherwise acquire long-term assets. Subsidiary conditions may also be attached restricting the type or location of the assets or the periods during which they are to be acquired or held.

Grants related to income are government grants other than those related to assets.

Forgivable loans are loans which the lender undertakes to waive repayment of under certain prescribed conditions.

Fair value is the amount for which an asset could be exchanged between a knowledgeable, willing buyer and a knowledgeable, willing seller in an arm's length transaction.

4–6 [Not printed]

Government Grants

7 *Government grants, including non-monetary grants at fair value, should not be recognised until there is reasonable assurance that:*
(a) the enterprise will comply with the conditions attaching to them; and
(b) the grants will be received.

8–9 [Not printed]

10 A forgivable loan from government is treated as a government grant when there is reasonable assurance that the enterprise will meet the terms for forgiveness of the loan.

11 [Not printed]

12 *Government grants should be recognised as income over the periods necessary to match them with the related costs which they are intended to compensate, on a systematic basis. They should not be credited directly to shareholders' interests.*

13–16 [Not printed]

17 In most cases the periods over which an enterprise recognises the costs or expenses related to a government grant are readily ascertainable and thus grants in recognition of specific expenses are recognised as income in the same period as the relevant expense. Similarly, grants related to depreciable assets are usually recognised as income over the periods and in the proportions in which depreciation on those assets is charged.

18 Grants related to non-depreciable assets may also require the fulfilment of certain obligations and would then be recognised as income over the periods which bear the cost of meeting the obligations. ...

19 [Not printed]

A government grant that becomes receivable as compensation for expenses or losses **20**
already incurred or for the purpose of giving immediate financial support to the
enterprise with no future related costs should be recognised as income of the period
in which it becomes receivable, as an extraordinary item if appropriate (see IAS 8).

[Not printed] **21**

A government grant may become receivable by an enterprise as compensation for **22**
expenses or losses incurred in a previous accounting period. Such a grant is recognised
as income of the period in which it becomes receivable, as an extraordinary item if
appropriate, with disclosure to ensure that its effect is clearly understood.

Non-monetary Government Grants

A government grant may take the form of a transfer of a non-monetary asset, such as **23**
land or other resources, for the use of the enterprise. In these circumstances it is usual
to assess the fair value of the non-monetary asset and to account for both grant and
asset at that fair value. An alternative course that is sometimes followed is to record
both asset and grant at a nominal amount.

Presentation of Grants Related to Assets

Government grants related to assets, including non-monetary grants at fair value, **24**
should be presented in the balance sheet either by setting up the grant as deferred
income or by deducting the grant in arriving at the carrying amount of the asset.

[Not printed] **25**

One method sets up the grant as deferred income which is recognised as income on a **26**
systematic and rational basis over the useful life of the asset.

The other method deducts the grant in arriving at the carrying amount of the asset. **27**
The grant is recognised as income over the life of a depreciable asset by way of a reduced
depreciation charge.

The purchase of assets and the receipt of related grants can cause major movements in **28**
the cash flow of an enterprise. For this reason and in order to show the gross
investment in assets, such movements are often disclosed as separate items in the cash
flow statement regardless of whether or not the grant is deducted from the related asset
for the purpose of balance sheet presentation.

Presentation of Grants Related to Income

Grants related to income are sometimes presented as a credit in the income statement, **29**
either separately or under a general heading such as "Other income"; alternatively, they
are deducted in reporting the related expense.

[Not printed] **30**

Both methods are regarded as acceptable for the presentation of grants related to **31**
income. Disclosure of the grant may be necessary for a proper understanding of the
financial statements. Disclosure of the effect of the grants on any item of income or
expense which is required to be separately disclosed is usually appropriate.

Repayment of Government Grants

32 *A government grant that becomes repayable should be accounted for as a revision to an accounting estimate (see IAS 8). Repayment of a grant related to income should be applied first against any unamortised deferred credit set up in respect of the grant. To the extent that the repayment exceeds any such deferred credit, or where no deferred credit exists, the repayment should be recognised immediately as an expense. Repayment of a grant related to an asset should be recorded by increasing the carrying amount of the asset or reducing the deferred income balance by the amount repayable. The cumulative additional depreciation that would have been recognised to date as an expense in the absence of the grant should be recognised immediately as an expense.*

33 Circumstances giving rise to repayment of a grant related to an asset may require consideration to be given to the possible impairment of the new carrying amount of the asset.

Government Assistance

34 Excluded from the definition of government grants in paragraph 3 are certain forms of government assistance which cannot reasonably have a value placed upon them and transactions with government which cannot be distinguished from the normal trading transactions of the enterprise.

35–36 [Not printed]

37 Loans at nil or low interest rates are a form of government assistance, but the benefit is not quantified by the imputation of interest.

38 In this Standard, government assistance does not include the provision of infrastructure by improvement to the general transport and communication network and the supply of improved facilities such as irrigation or water reticulation which is available on an ongoing indeterminate basis for the benefit of an entire local community.

Disclosure

39 *The following matters should be disclosed:*
    (a) the accounting policy adopted for government grants, including the methods of presentation adopted in the financial statements;
    (b) the nature and extent of government grants recognised in the financial statements and an indication of other forms of government assistance from which the enterprise has directly benefited; and
    (c) unfulfilled conditions and other contingencies attaching to government assistance that has been recognised.

Transitional Provisions

40 [Not printed]

Effective Date

41 *[Not printed]*

IAS 21: The Effects of Changes in Foreign Exchange Rates

IAS 21: The Effects of Changes in Foreign Exchange Rates				
Scope 21.1–6	Definitions 21.7	Transitional Provisions 21.48	Effective Date 21.49	Related Interpretations: SIC–7, 11, 19 and 30

Foreign Currency Transactions 21.8–22							
		Reporting at Subsequent Balance Sheet Dates 21.11–12			Recognition of Exchange Differences 21.13–22		
			Non-Monetary Items				
Initial Recognition 21.8–10	Monetary Items: Closing Rate	Carried in Terms of Historical Cost: Exchange Rate at Transaction Date	Carried at Fair Value: Exchange Rate that Existed when Values Were Determined	Bench-mark Treat-ment 21.13–15	Net Invest-ment in a Foreign Entity 21.17–19	Allowed Alterna-tive Treat-ment 21.20–22

Financial Statements of Foreign Operations 21.23–40					
	Foreign Operations that Are Integral to the Opera-tions of the Reporting Enterprise 21.27–29	Foreign Entities 21.30–38			Change in the Classification of a Foreign Operation 21.39–40
Classification of Foreign Operations 21.23–26		Assets and Liabilities: Closing Rate	Income and Expense: Exchange Rate at Transaction Date	Resulting Exchange Differences: Equity	

Tax Effects of Exchange Differences 21.41

Disclosure 21.42–47

Scope

This Standard should be applied:　　　　　　　　　　　　　　　　　　　　　　1

(a) in accounting for transactions in foreign currencies; and

(b) in translating the financial statements of foreign operations that are included in the financial statements of the enterprise by consolidation, proportionate consolidation or by the equity method.

2 This Standard does not deal with hedge accounting for foreign currency items other than the classification of exchange differences arising on a foreign currency liability accounted for as a hedge of a net investment in a foreign entity. Other aspects of hedge accounting, including the criteria to use hedge accounting, are dealt with in IAS 39.

3 [Not printed]

4 This Standard does not specify the currency in which an enterprise presents its financial statements. However, an enterprise normally uses the currency of the country in which it is domiciled. If it uses a different currency, this Standard requires disclosure of the reason for using that currency. This Standard also requires disclosure of the reason for any change in the reporting currency.

5 This Standard does not deal with the restatement of an enterprise's financial statements from its reporting currency into another currency for the convenience of users accustomed to that currency or for similar purposes.

6 This Standard does not deal with the presentation in a cash flow statement of cash flows arising from transactions in a foreign currency and the translation of cash flows of a foreign operation (see IAS 7).

Definitions

7 ...

Foreign operation is a subsidiary, associate, joint venture or branch of the reporting enterprise, the activities of which are based or conducted in a country other than the country of the reporting enterprise.

Foreign entity is a foreign operation, the activities of which are not an integral part of those of the reporting enterprise.

Reporting currency is the currency used in presenting the financial statements.

Foreign currency is a currency other than the reporting currency of an enterprise.

Exchange rate is the ratio for exchange of two currencies.

Exchange difference is the difference resulting from reporting the same number of units of a foreign currency in the reporting currency at different exchange rates.

Closing rate is the spot exchange rate at the balance sheet date.

Net investment in a foreign entity is the reporting enterprise's share in the net assets of that entity.

Monetary items are money held and assets and liabilities to be received or paid in fixed or determinable amounts of money.

Fair value is the amount for which an asset could be exchanged, or a liability settled, between knowledgeable, willing parties in an arm's length transaction.

Foreign Currency Transactions

Initial Recognition

8 A foreign currency transaction is a transaction which is denominated in or requires settlement in a foreign currency, including transactions arising when an enterprise either:

(a) buys or sells goods or services whose price is denominated in a foreign currency;

(b) borrows or lends funds when the amounts payable or receivable are denominated in a foreign currency;

188

(c) becomes a party to an unperformed foreign exchange contract; or

(d) otherwise acquires or disposes of assets, or incurs or settles liabilities, denominated in a foreign currency.

A foreign currency transaction should be recorded, on initial recognition in the **9** *reporting currency, by applying to the foreign currency amount the exchange rate between the reporting currency and the foreign currency at the date of the transaction.*

The exchange rate at the date of the transaction is often referred to as the spot rate. **10** For practical reasons, a rate that approximates the actual rate at the date of the transaction is often used, for example, an average rate for a week or a month might be used for all transactions in each foreign currency occurring during that period. However, if exchange rates fluctuate significantly, the use of the average rate for a period is unreliable.

Reporting at Subsequent Balance Sheet Dates

At each balance sheet date: **11**

(a) foreign currency monetary items should be reported using the closing rate;

(b) non-monetary items which are carried in terms of historical cost denominated in a foreign currency should be reported using the exchange rate at the date of the transaction; and

(c) non-monetary items which are carried at fair value denominated in a foreign currency should be reported using the exchange rates that existed when the values were determined.

[Not printed] **12**

Recognition of Exchange Differences

[Not printed] **13–14**

Exchange differences arising on the settlement of monetary items or on reporting an **15** *enterprise's monetary items at rates different from those at which they were initially recorded during the period, or reported in previous financial statements, should be recognised as income or as expenses in the period in which they arise, with the exception of exchange differences dealt with in accordance with paragraphs 17 and 19.*

An exchange difference results when there is a change in the exchange rate between **16** the transaction date and the date of settlement of any monetary items arising from a foreign currency transaction. When the transaction is settled within the same accounting period as that in which it occurred, all the exchange difference is recognised in that period. However, when the transaction is settled in a subsequent accounting period, the exchange difference recognised in each intervening period up to the period of settlement is determined by the change in exchange rates during that period.

Net Investment in a Foreign Entity

Exchange differences arising on a monetary item that, in substance, forms part of **17** *an enterprise's net investment in a foreign entity should be classified as equity in the enterprise's financial statements until the disposal of the net investment, at which* *time they should be recognised as income or as expenses in accordance with paragraph 37.*

18   An enterprise may have a monetary item that is receivable from, or payable to, a foreign entity.   An item for which settlement is neither planned nor likely to occur in the foreseeable future is, in substance, an extension to, or deduction from, the enterprise's net investment in that foreign entity.   Such monetary items may include long-term receivables or loans but do not include trade receivables or trade payables.

19   *Exchange differences arising on a foreign currency liability accounted for as a hedge of an enterprise's net investment in a foreign entity should be classified as equity in the enterprise's financial statements until the disposal of the net investment, at which time they should be recognised as income or as expenses in accordance with paragraph 37.*

Allowed Alternative Treatment

20   [Not printed]

21   *Exchange differences may result from a severe devaluation or depreciation of a currency against which there is no practical means of hedging and that affects liabilities which cannot be settled and which arise directly on the recent acquisition of an asset invoiced in a foreign currency.   Such exchange differences should be included in the carrying amount of the related asset, provided that the adjusted carrying amount does not exceed the lower of the replacement cost and the amount recoverable from the sale or use of the asset.*

22   Exchange differences are not included in the carrying amount of an asset when the enterprise is able to settle or hedge the foreign currency liability arising on the acquisition of the asset.   However, exchange losses are part of the directly attributable costs of the asset when the liability cannot be settled and there is no practical means of hedging, for example when, as a result of exchange controls, there is a delay in obtaining foreign currency.   Therefore, under the allowed alternative treatment, the cost of an asset invoiced in a foreign currency is regarded as the amount of reporting currency that the enterprise ultimately has to pay to settle its liabilities arising directly on the recent acquisition of the asset.

Financial Statements of Foreign Operations

Classification of Foreign Operations

23   The method used to translate the financial statements of a foreign operation depends on the way in which it is financed and operates in relation to the reporting enterprise. For this purpose, foreign operations are classified as either "foreign operations that are integral to the operations of the reporting enterprise" or "foreign entities".

24   A foreign operation that is integral to the operations of the reporting enterprise carries on its business as if it were an extension of the reporting enterprise's operations.   ... Therefore, the change in the exchange rate affects the individual monetary items held by the foreign operation rather than the reporting enterprise's net investment in that operation.

25   In contrast, a foreign entity accumulates cash and other monetary items, incurs expenses, generates income and perhaps arranges borrowings, all substantially in its

local currency. It may also enter into transactions in foreign currencies, including transactions in the reporting currency. When there is a change in the exchange rate between the reporting currency and the local currency, there is little or no direct effect on the present and future cash flows from operations of either the foreign entity or the reporting enterprise. The change in the exchange rate affects the reporting enterprise's net investment in the foreign entity rather than the individual monetary and non-monetary items held by the foreign entity.

The following are indications that a foreign operation is a foreign entity rather than a **26** foreign operation that is integral to the operations of the reporting enterprise:
(a) while the reporting enterprise may control the foreign operation, the activities of the foreign operation are carried out with a significant degree of autonomy from those of the reporting enterprise;
(b) transactions with the reporting enterprise are not a high proportion of the foreign operation's activities;
(c) the activities of the foreign operation are financed mainly from its own operations or local borrowings rather than from the reporting enterprise;
(d) costs of labour, material and other components of the foreign operation's products or services are primarily paid or settled in the local currency rather than in the reporting currency;
(e) the foreign operation's sales are mainly in currencies other than the reporting currency; and
(f) cash flows of the reporting enterprise are insulated from the day-to-day activities of the foreign operation rather than being directly affected by the activities of the foreign operation.
...

Foreign Operations that are Integral to the Operations of the Reporting Enterprise

The financial statements of a foreign operation that is integral to the operations of **27** *the reporting enterprise should be translated using the standards and procedures in paragraphs 8 to 22 as if the transactions of the foreign operation had been those of the reporting enterprise itself.*

The individual items in the financial statements of the foreign operation are translated **28** as if all its transactions had been entered into by the reporting enterprise itself. The cost and depreciation of property, plant and equipment is translated using the exchange rate at the date of purchase of the asset or, if the asset is carried at fair value, using the rate that existed on the date of the valuation. The cost of inventories is translated at the exchange rates that existed when those costs were incurred. The recoverable amount or realisable value of an asset is translated using the exchange rate that existed when the recoverable amount or net realisable value was determined. For example, when the net realisable value of an item of inventory is determined in a foreign currency, that value is translated using the exchange rate at the date as at which the net realisable value is determined. The rate used is therefore usually the closing rate. An adjustment may be required to reduce the carrying amount of an asset in the financial statements of the reporting enterprise to its recoverable amount or net realisable value even when no such adjustment is necessary in the financial statements of the foreign operation. Alternatively, an adjustment in the financial statements of the foreign operation may need to be reversed in the financial statements of the reporting enterprise.

29 For practical reasons, a rate that approximates the actual rate at the date of the transaction is often used, for example, an average rate for a week or a month might be used for all transactions in each foreign currency occurring during that period. However, if exchange rates fluctuate significantly, the use of the average rate for a period is unreliable.

Foreign Entities

30 *In translating the financial statements of a foreign entity for incorporation in its financial statements, the reporting enterprise should use the following procedures:*
    (a) *the assets and liabilities, both monetary and non-monetary, of the foreign entity should be translated at the closing rate;*
    (b) *income and expense items of the foreign entity should be translated at exchange rates at the dates of the transactions, except when the foreign entity reports in the currency of a hyperinflationary economy, in which case income and expense items should be translated at the closing rate; and*
    (c) *all resulting exchange differences should be classified as equity until the disposal of the net investment.*

31 For practical reasons, a rate that approximates the actual exchange rates, for example an average rate for the period, is often used to translate income and expense items of a foreign operation.

32 The translation of the financial statements of a foreign entity results in the recognition of exchange differences arising from:
    (a) translating income and expense items at the exchange rates at the dates of transactions and assets and liabilities at the closing rate;
    (b) translating the opening net investment in the foreign entity at an exchange rate different from that at which it was previously reported; and
    (c) other changes to equity in the foreign entity.
    These exchange differences are not recognised as income or expenses for the period because the changes in the exchange rates have little or no direct effect on the present and future cash flows from operations of either the foreign entity or the reporting enterprise. When a foreign entity is consolidated but is not wholly owned, accumulated exchange differences arising from translation and attributable to minority interests are allocated to, and reported as part of, the minority interest in the consolidated balance sheet.

33 Any goodwill arising on the acquisition of a foreign entity and any fair value adjustments to the carrying amounts of assets and liabilities arising on the acquisition of that foreign entity are treated as either:
    (a) assets and liabilities of the foreign entity and translated at the closing rate in accordance with paragraph 30; or
    (b) assets and liabilities of the reporting entity which either are already expressed in the reporting currency or are non-monetary foreign currency items which are reported using the exchange rate at the date of the transaction in accordance with paragraph 11(b).

34 The incorporation of the financial statements of a foreign entity in those of the reporting enterprise follows normal consolidation procedures, such as the elimination

of intra-group balances and intra-group transactions of a subsidiary (see IAS 27 and IAS 31). However, an exchange difference arising on an intra-group monetary item, whether short-term or long-term, cannot be eliminated against a corresponding amount arising on other intra-group balances because the monetary item represents a commitment to convert one currency into another and exposes the reporting enterprise to a gain or loss through currency fluctuations. Accordingly, in the consolidated financial statements of the reporting enterprise, such an exchange difference continues to be recognised as income or an expense or, if it arises from the circumstances described in paragraphs 17 and 19, it is classified as equity until the disposal of the net investment.

When the financial statements of a foreign entity are drawn up to a different reporting **35** date from that of the reporting enterprise, the foreign entity often prepares, for purposes of incorporation in the financial statements of the reporting enterprise, statements as at the same date as the reporting enterprise. When it is impracticable to do this, IAS 27 allows the use of financial statements drawn up to a different reporting date provided that the difference is no greater than three months. In such a case, the assets and liabilities of the foreign entity are translated at the exchange rate at the balance sheet date of the foreign entity. Adjustments are made when appropriate for significant movements in exchange rates up to the balance sheet date of the reporting enterprise in accordance with IAS 27 and IAS 28.

The financial statements of a foreign entity that reports in the currency of a **36** *hyperinflationary economy should be restated in accordance with IAS 29 before they are translated into the reporting currency of the reporting enterprise. When the economy ceases to be hyperinflationary and the foreign entity discontinues the preparation and presentation of financial statements prepared in accordance with IAS 29 it should use the amounts expressed in the measuring unit current at the date of discontinuation as the historical costs for translation into the reporting currency of the reporting enterprise.*

Disposal of a Foreign Entity

On the disposal of a foreign entity, the cumulative amount of the exchange differences **37** *which have been deferred and which relate to that foreign entity should be recognised as income or as expenses in the same period in which the gain or loss on disposal is recognised.*

An enterprise may dispose of its interest in a foreign entity through sale, liquidation, **38** repayment of share capital, or abandonment of all, or part of, that entity. The payment of a dividend forms part of a disposal only when it constitutes a return of the investment. In the case of a partial disposal, only the proportionate share of the related accumulated exchange differences is included in the gain or loss. A write-down of the carrying amount of a foreign entity does not constitute a partial disposal. Accordingly, no part of the deferred foreign exchange gain or loss is recognised at the time of a write-down.

Change in the Classification of a Foreign Operation

When there is a change in the classification of a foreign operation, the translation **39** *procedures applicable to the revised classification should be applied from the date of the change in the classification.*

40 A change in the way in which a foreign operation is financed and operates in relation to the reporting enterprise may lead to a change in the classification of that foreign operation. When a foreign operation that is integral to the operations of the reporting enterprise is reclassified as a foreign entity, exchange differences arising on the translation of non-monetary assets at the date of the reclassification are classified as equity. When a foreign entity is reclassified as a foreign operation that is integral to the operation of the reporting enterprise, the translated amounts for non-monetary items at the date of the change are treated as the historical cost for those items in the period of change and subsequent periods. Exchange differences which have been deferred are not recognised as income or expenses until the disposal of the operation.

All Changes in Foreign Exchange Rates

Tax Effects of Exchange Differences

41 Gains and losses on foreign currency transactions and exchange differences arising on the translation of the financial statements of foreign operations may have associated tax effects which are accounted for in accordance with IAS 12.

Disclosure

42 *An enterprise should disclose:*
   (a) the amount of exchange differences included in the net profit or loss for the period;
   (b) net exchange differences classified as equity as a separate component of equity, and a reconciliation of the amount of such exchange differences at the beginning and end of the period; and
   (c) the amount of exchange differences arising during the period which is included in the carrying amount of an asset in accordance with the allowed alternative treatment in paragraph 21.

43 *When the reporting currency is different from the currency of the country in which the enterprise is domiciled, the reason for using a different currency should be disclosed. The reason for any change in the reporting currency should also be disclosed.*

44 *When there is a change in the classification of a significant foreign operation, an enterprise should disclose:*
   (a) the nature of the change in classification;
   (b) the reason for the change;
   (c) the impact of the change in classification on shareholders' equity; and
   (d) the impact on net profit or loss for each prior period presented had the change in classification occurred at the beginning of the earliest period presented.

45 *An enterprise should disclose the method selected in accordance with paragraph 33 to translate goodwill and fair value adjustments arising on the acquisition of a foreign entity.*

46 An enterprise discloses the effect on foreign currency monetary items or on the financial statements of a foreign operation of a change in exchange rates occurring after the balance sheet date if the change is of such importance that non-disclosure would affect

the ability of users of the financial statements to make proper evaluations and decisions (see IAS 10).

Disclosure is also encouraged of an enterprise's foreign currency risk management **47** policy.

Transitional Provisions

On the first occasion that an enterprise applies this Standard, the enterprise should, **48** *except when the amount is not reasonably determinable, classify separately and disclose the cumulative balance, at the beginning of the period, of exchange differences deferred and classified as equity in previous periods.*

Effective Date

[Not printed] **49**

IAS 22: Business Combinations

IAS 22: Business Combinations				
Scope 22.1–7	Definitions 22.8	Transitional Provisions 22.99–101	Effective Date 22.102–103	Related Interpretations: SIC–9, 22

Nature of a Business Combination 22.9–16	
Acquisitions 22.10–12	Unitings of Interests 22.13–16
Reverse Acquisitions 22.10	

Accounting for Acquisitions: General 22.17–40

Account-ing for Acquisi-tions 22.17–18	Date of Acquisi-tion 22.19–20	Cost of Acquisi-tion 22.21–25	Recogni-tion of Identifia-ble Assets and Liabilities 22.26–31	Allocation of Cost of Acquisition 22.32–35		Succes-sive Share Purchases 22.36–38	Determin-ing the Fair Values of Identifia-ble Assets and Liabilities Acquired 22.39–40
				Bench-mark-Treat-ment 22.32–33	Allowed Alterna-tive Treatment 22.34–35		

Accounting for Acquisitions: Other 22.41–76

Goodwill Arising on Acquisition 22.41–58			Negative Goodwill Arising on Acquisition 22.59–64		Adjust-ment to Purchase Consider-ation Contin-gent on Future Events 22.65–67	Subse-quent Changes in Cost of Acquisi-tion 22.68–70	Subse-quent Identifi-cation or Changes in Value of Identi-fiable Assets and Liabilities 22.71–76
Recogni-tion and Measure-ment 22.41–43	Amortisa-tion 22.44–54	Impair-ment Losses 22.55–58	Recogni-tion and Measure-ment 22.59–63	Presenta-tion 22.64			

Unitings of Interests 22.77–83
Accounting for Unitings of Interests 22.77–83

All Business Combinations 22.84–85
Taxes on Income 22.84–85

Disclosure 22.86–98

Appendix [Not printed]

Scope

This Standard should be applied in accounting for business combinations. 1

A business combination may be structured in a variety of ways which are determined 2
for legal, taxation or other reasons. It may involve the purchase by an enterprise of
the equity of another enterprise or the purchase of the net assets of a business
enterprise. It may be effected by the issue of shares or by the transfer of cash, cash
equivalents or other assets. The transaction may be between the shareholders of the
combining enterprises or between one enterprise and the shareholders of the other
enterprise. The business combination may involve the establishment of a new
enterprise to have control over the combining enterprises, the transfer of the net
assets of one or more of the combining enterprises to another enterprise or the
dissolution of one or more of the combining enterprises. When the substance of the
transaction is consistent with the definition of a business combination in this
Standard, the accounting and disclosure requirements contained in this Standard are
appropriate irrespective of the particular structure adopted for the combination.

A business combination may result in a parent-subsidiary relationship in which the 3
acquirer is the parent and the acquiree a subsidiary of the acquirer. In such
circumstances, the acquirer applies this Standard in its consolidated financial
statements. It includes its interest in the acquiree in its separate financial statements
as an investment in a subsidiary (see IAS 27).

A business combination may involve the purchase of the net assets, including any 4
goodwill, of another enterprise rather than the purchase of the shares in the other
enterprise. Such a business combination does not result in a parent-subsidiary
relationship. In such circumstances, the acquirer applies this Standard in its separate
financial statements and consequently in its consolidated financial statements.

A business combination may give rise to a legal merger. While the requirements for 5
legal mergers differ among countries, a legal merger is usually a merger between two
companies in which either:
(a) the assets and liabilities of one company are transferred to the other company and
the first company is dissolved; or
(b) the assets and liabilities of both companies are transferred to a new company and
both the original companies are dissolved.
...

This Standard does not deal with the separate financial statements of a parent other 6
than in the circumstances described in paragraph 4. ...

This Standard does not deal with: 7
(a) transactions among enterprises under common control; and
(b) interests in joint ventures (see IAS 31) and the financial statements of joint
ventures.

Definitions

... 8

A *business combination* is the bringing together of separate enterprises into one
economic entity as a result of one enterprise uniting with or obtaining control over
the net assets and operations of another enterprise.

An acquisition is a business combination in which one of the enterprises, the acquirer, obtains control over the net assets and operations of another enterprise, the acquiree, in exchange for the transfer of assets, incurrence of a liability or issue of equity.

A uniting of interests is a business combination in which the shareholders of the combining enterprises combine control over the whole, or effectively the whole, of their net assets and operations to achieve a continuing mutual sharing in the risks and benefits attaching to the combined entity such that neither party can be identified as the acquirer.

Control is the power to govern the financial and operating policies of an enterprise so as to obtain benefits from its activities.

A parent is an enterprise that has one or more subsidiaries.

A subsidiary is an enterprise that is controlled by another enterprise (known as the parent).

Minority interest is that part of the net results of operations and of net assets of a subsidiary attributable to interests which are not owned, directly or indirectly through subsidiaries, by the parent.

Fair value is the amount for which an asset could be exchanged or a liability settled between knowledgeable, willing parties in an arm's length transaction.

Monetary assets are money held and assets to be received in fixed or determinable amounts of money.

Date of acquisition is the date on which control of the net assets and operations of the acquiree is effectively transferred to the acquirer.

Nature of a Business Combination

9   In accounting for a business combination, an acquisition is in substance different from a uniting of interests and the substance of the transaction needs to be reflected in the financial statements. ...

Acquisitions

10   In virtually all business combinations one of the combining enterprises obtains control over the other combining enterprise, thereby enabling an acquirer to be identified.   Control is presumed to be obtained when one of the combining enterprises acquires more than one half of the voting rights of the other combining enterprise unless, in exceptional circumstances, it can be clearly demonstrated that such ownership does not constitute control.   Even when one of the combining enterprises does not acquire more than one half of the voting rights of the other combining enterprise, it may still be possible to identify an acquirer when one of the combining enterprises, as a result of the business combination, acquires:

(a) power over more than one half of the voting rights of the other enterprise by virtue of an agreement with other investors;

(b) power to govern the financial and operating policies of the other enterprise under a statute or an agreement;

(c) power to appoint or remove the majority of the members of the board of directors or equivalent governing body of the other enterprise; or

(d) power to cast the majority of votes at meetings of the board of directors or equivalent governing body of the other enterprise.

Although it may sometimes be difficult to identify an acquirer, there are usually **11**
indications that one exists. For example:
(a) the fair value of one enterprise is significantly greater than that of the other
combining enterprise. In such cases, the larger enterprise is the acquirer;
(b) the business combination is effected through an exchange of voting common
shares for cash. In such cases, the enterprise giving up cash is the acquirer; or
(c) the business combination results in the management of one enterprise being able
to dominate the selection of the management team of the resulting combined
enterprise. In such cases the dominant enterprise is the acquirer.

Reverse Acquisitions

Occasionally an enterprise obtains ownership of the shares of another enterprise but **12**
as part of the exchange transaction issues enough voting shares, as consideration,
such that control of the combined enterprise passes to the owners of the enterprise
whose shares have been acquired. This situation is described as a reverse acquisition.
Although legally the enterprise issuing the shares may be regarded as the parent or
continuing enterprise, the enterprise whose shareholders now control the combined
enterprise is the acquirer enjoying the voting or other powers identified in paragraph
10. The enterprise issuing the shares is deemed to have been acquired by the other
enterprise; the latter enterprise is deemed to be the acquirer and applies the purchase
method to the assets and liabilities of the enterprise issuing the shares.

Unitings of Interests

In exceptional circumstances, it may not be possible to identify an acquirer. Instead **13**
of a dominant party emerging, the shareholders of the combining enterprises join in
a substantially equal arrangement to share control over the whole, or effectively the
whole, of their net assets and operations. In addition, the managements of the
combining enterprises participate in the management of the combined entity. As a
result, the shareholders of the combining enterprises share mutually in the risks and
benefits of the combined entity. Such a business combination is accounted for as a
uniting of interests.

A mutual sharing of risks and benefits is usually not possible without a substantially **14**
equal exchange of voting common shares between the combining enterprises. Such
an exchange ensures that the relative ownership interests of the combining
enterprises, and consequently their relative risks and benefits in the combined
enterprise, are maintained and the decision-making powers of the parties are
preserved. However, for a substantially equal share exchange to be effective in this
regard there cannot be a significant reduction in the rights attaching to the shares of
one of the combining enterprises, otherwise the influence of that party is weakened.

In order to achieve a mutual sharing of the risks and benefits of the combined entity: **15**
(a) the substantial majority, if not all, of the voting common shares of the combining
enterprises are exchanged or pooled;
(b) the fair value of one enterprise is not significantly different from that of the other
enterprise; and
(c) the shareholders of each enterprise maintain substantially the same voting rights
and interest in the combined entity, relative to each other, after the combination
as before.

16 The mutual sharing of the risks and benefits of the combined entity diminishes and the likelihood that an acquirer can be identified increases when:
   (a) the relative equality in fair values of the combining enterprises is reduced and the percentage of voting common shares exchanged decreases;
   (b) financial arrangements provide a relative advantage to one group of shareholders over the other shareholders. ... and
   (c) one party's share of the equity in the combined entity depends on how the business which it previously controlled performs subsequent to the business combination.

Acquisitions

Accounting for Acquisitions

17 *A business combination which is an acquisition should be accounted for by use of the purchase method of accounting as set out in the standards contained in paragraphs 19 to 76.*

18 The use of the purchase method results in an acquisition of an enterprise being accounted for similarly to the purchase of other assets. This is appropriate since an acquisition involves a transaction in which assets are transferred, liabilities are incurred or capital is issued in exchange for control of the net assets and operations of another enterprise. The purchase method uses cost as the basis for recording the acquisition and relies on the exchange transaction underlying the acquisition for determination of the cost.

Date of Acquisition

19 *As from the date of acquisition, an acquirer should:*
   (a) incorporate into the income statement the results of operations of the acquiree; and
   (b) recognise in the balance sheet the identifiable assets and liabilities of the acquiree and any goodwill or negative goodwill arising on the acquisition.

20 The date of acquisition is the date on which control of the net assets and operations of the acquiree is effectively transferred to the acquirer and the date when application of the purchase method commences. The results of operations of an acquired business are included in the financial statements of the acquirer as from the date of acquisition, which is the date on which control of the acquiree is effectively transferred to the acquirer. In substance, the date of acquisition is the date from when the acquirer has the power to govern the financial and operating policies of an enterprise so as to obtain benefits from its activities. Control is not deemed to have been transferred to the acquirer until all conditions necessary to protect the interests of the parties involved have been satisfied. However, this does not necessitate a transaction being closed or finalised at law before control effectively passes to the acquirer. In assessing whether control has effectively been transferred, the substance of the acquisition needs to be considered.

Cost of Acquisition

An acquisition should be accounted for at its cost, being the amount of cash or cash **21**
equivalents paid or the fair value, at the date of exchange, of the other purchase
consideration given by the acquirer in exchange for control over the net assets of the
other enterprise, plus any costs directly attributable to the acquisition.

When an acquisition involves more than one exchange transaction the cost of the **22**
acquisition is the aggregate cost of the individual transactions. When an acquisition
is achieved in stages, the distinction between the date of acquisition and the date of
the exchange transaction is important. While accounting for the acquisition
commences as from the date of acquisition, it uses cost and fair value information
determined as at the date of each exchange transaction.

Monetary assets given and liabilities incurred are measured at their fair values at the **23**
date of the exchange transaction. When settlement of the purchase consideration is
deferred, the cost of the acquisition is the present value of the consideration, taking
into account any premium or discount likely to be incurred in settlement, and not
the nominal value of the payable.

In determining the cost of the acquisition, marketable securities issued by the acquirer **24**
are measured at their fair value which is their market price as at the date of the
exchange transaction, provided that undue fluctuations or the narrowness of the
market do not make the market price an unreliable indicator. When the market price
on one particular date is not a reliable indicator, price movements for a reasonable
period before and after the announcement of the terms of the acquisition need to be
considered. When the market is unreliable or no quotation exists, the fair value of
the securities issued by the acquirer is estimated by reference to their proportional
interest in the fair value of the acquirer's enterprise or by reference to the proportional
interest in the fair value of the enterprise acquired, whichever is the more clearly
evident. Purchase consideration which is paid in cash to shareholders of the acquiree
as an alternative to securities may also provide evidence of the total fair value given.
All aspects of the acquisition, including significant factors influencing the
negotiations, need to be considered, and independent valuations may be used as an
aid in determining the fair value of securities issued.

In addition to the purchase consideration, the acquirer may incur direct costs relating **25**
to the acquisition. These include the costs of registering and issuing equity securities,
and professional fees paid to accountants, legal advisers, valuers and other consultants
to effect the acquisition. General administrative costs, including the costs of
maintaining an acquisitions department, and other costs which cannot be directly
attributed to the particular acquisition being accounted for, are not included in the
cost of the acquisition but are recognised as an expense as incurred.

Recognition of Identifiable Assets and Liabilities

The identifiable assets and liabilities acquired that are recognised under **26**
paragraph 19 should be those of the acquiree that existed at the date of acquisition
together with any liabilities recognised under paragraph 31. They should be
recognised separately as at the date of acquisition if, and only if:
(a) it is probable that any associated future economic benefits will flow to, or
resources embodying economic benefits will flow from, the acquirer; and
(b) a reliable measure is available of their cost or fair value.

27 Assets and liabilities that are recognised under paragraph 26 are described in this Standard as identifiable assets and liabilities. To the extent that assets and liabilities are purchased which do not satisfy these recognition criteria there is a resultant impact on the amount of goodwill or negative goodwill arising on the acquisition, because goodwill or negative goodwill is determined as the residual cost of acquisition after recognising the identifiable assets and liabilities.

28 The identifiable assets and liabilities over which the acquirer obtains control may include assets and liabilities which were not previously recognised in the financial statements of the acquiree. This may be because they did not qualify for recognition prior to the acquisition. ...

29 *Subject to paragraph 31, liabilities should not be recognised at the date of acquisition if they result from the acquirer's intentions or actions. Liabilities should also not be recognised for future losses or other costs expected to be incurred as a result of the acquisition, whether they relate to the acquirer or the acquiree.*

30 The liabilities referred to in paragraph 29 are not liabilities of the acquiree at the date of acquisition. Therefore, they are not relevant in allocating the cost of acquisition. Nonetheless, this Standard contains one specific exception to this general principle. This exception applies if the acquirer has developed plans that relate to the acquiree's business and an obligation comes into existence as a direct consequence of the acquisition. Because these plans are an integral part of the acquirer's plan for the acquisition, this Standard requires an enterprise to recognise a provision for the resulting costs (see paragraph 31). For the purpose of this Standard, identifiable assets and liabilities acquired include the provisions recognised under paragraph 31. Paragraph 31 lays down strict conditions designed to ensure that the plans were an integral part of the acquisition and that within a short time – the earlier of three months after the date of acquisition and the date when the financial statements are authorised for issue the acquirer has developed the plans in a way that requires the enterprise to recognise a restructuring provision under IAS 37. This Standard also requires an enterprise to reverse such provisions if the plan is not implemented in the manner expected or within the time originally expected (see paragraph 75) and to disclose information on such provisions (see paragraph 92).

31 *At the date of acquisition, the acquirer should recognise a provision that was not a liability of the acquiree at that date if, and only if, the acquirer has:*
    (a) at, or before, the date of acquisition, developed the main features of a plan that involves terminating or reducing the activities of the acquiree and that relates to:
        (i) compensating employees of the acquiree for termination of their employment;
        (ii) closing facilities of the acquiree;
        (iii) eliminating product lines of the acquiree; or
        (iv) terminating contracts of the acquiree that have become onerous because the acquirer has communicated to the other party at, or before, the date of acquisition that the contract will be terminated;
    (b) by announcing the main features of the plan at, or before, the date of acquisition, raised a valid expectation in those affected by the plan that it will implement the plan; and

(c) by the earlier of three months after the date of acquisition and the date when the annual financial statements are authorised for issue, developed those main features into a detailed formal plan identifying at least:

(i)   the business or part of a business concerned;

(ii) the principal locations affected;

(iii) the location, function, and approximate number of employees who will be compensated for terminating their services;

(iv) the expenditures that will be undertaken; and

(v) when the plan will be implemented.

Any provision recognised under this paragraph should cover only the costs of the items listed in (a)(i) to (iv) above.

Allocation of Cost of Acquisition

Benchmark Treatment

The identifiable assets and liabilities recognised under paragraph 26 should be **32** *measured at the aggregate of:*

(a) the fair value of the identifiable assets and liabilities acquired as at the date of the exchange transaction to the extent of the acquirer's interest obtained in the exchange transaction; and

(b) the minority's proportion of the pre-acquisition carrying amounts of the identifiable assets and liabilities of the subsidiary.

Any goodwill or negative goodwill should be accounted for under this Standard.

The cost of an acquisition is allocated to the identifiable assets and liabilities **33** recognised under paragraph 26 by reference to their fair values at the date of the exchange transaction.   However, the cost of the acquisition only relates to the percentage of the identifiable assets and liabilities purchased by the acquirer. Consequently, when an acquirer purchases less than all the shares of the other enterprise, the resulting minority interest is stated at the minority's proportion of the pre-acquisition carrying amounts of the net identifiable assets of the subsidiary.   This is because the minority's proportion has not been part of the exchange transaction to effect the acquisition.

Allowed Alternative Treatment

The identifiable assets and liabilities recognised under paragraph 26 should be **34** *measured at their fair values as at the date of acquisition. Any goodwill or negative goodwill should be accounted for under this Standard. Any minority interest should be stated at the minority's proportion of the fair values of the identifiable assets and liabilities recognised under paragraph 26.*

Under this approach, the net identifiable assets over which the acquirer has obtained **35** control are stated at their fair values, regardless of whether the acquirer has acquired all or only some of the capital of the other enterprise or has acquired the assets directly.   Consequently, any minority interest is stated at the minority's proportion of the fair values of the net identifiable assets of the subsidiary.

Successive Share Purchases

36 An acquisition may involve more than one exchange transaction, as for example when it is achieved in stages by successive purchases on a stock exchange. When this occurs, each significant transaction is treated separately for the purpose of determining the fair values of the identifiable assets and liabilities acquired and for determining the amount of any goodwill or negative goodwill on that transaction. This results in a step-by-step comparison of the cost of the individual investments with the acquirer's percentage interest in the fair values of the identifiable assets and liabilities acquired at each significant step.

37 When an acquisition is achieved by successive purchases, the fair values of the identifiable assets and liabilities may vary at the date of each exchange transaction. If all the identifiable assets and liabilities relating to an acquisition are restated to fair values at the time of successive purchases, any adjustment relating to the previously held interest of the acquirer is a revaluation and is accounted for as such.

38 Prior to qualifying as an acquisition, a transaction may qualify as an investment in an associate and be accounted for by use of the equity method under IAS 28. If so, the determination of fair values for the identifiable assets and liabilities acquired and the recognition of goodwill or negative goodwill occurs notionally as from the date when the equity method is applied. When the investment did not qualify previously as an associate, the fair values of the identifiable assets and liabilities are determined as at the date of each significant step and goodwill or negative goodwill is recognised from the date of acquisition.

Determining the Fair Values of Identifiable Assets and Liabilities Acquired

39 General guidelines for arriving at the fair values of identifiable assets and liabilities acquired are as follows:
(a) marketable securities at their current market values;
(b) non-marketable securities at estimated values that take into consideration features such as price earnings ratios, dividend yields and expected growth rates of comparable securities of enterprises with similar characteristics;
(c) receivables at the present values of the amounts to be received, determined at appropriate current interest rates, less allowances for uncollectability and collection costs, if necessary. However, discounting is not required for short-term receivables when the difference between the nominal amount of the receivable and the discounted amount is not material;
(d) inventories:
   (i) finished goods and merchandise at selling prices less the sum of (a) the costs of disposal and (b) a reasonable profit allowance for the selling effort of the acquirer based on profit for similar finished goods and merchandise;
   (ii) work in progress at selling prices of finished goods less the sum of (a) costs to complete, (b) costs of disposal and (c) a reasonable profit allowance for the completing and selling effort based on profit for similar finished goods; and
   (iii) raw materials at current replacement costs;
(e) land and buildings at their market value;
(f) plant and equipment at market value, normally determined by appraisal. When there is no evidence of market value because of the specialised nature of the plant and equipment or because the items are rarely sold, except as part of a continuing business, they are valued at their depreciated replacement cost;

(g) intangible assets, as defined in IAS 38 at fair value determined:
   (i) by reference to an active market as defined in IAS 38; and
   (ii) if no active market exists, on a basis that reflects the amount that the enterprise would have paid for the asset in an arm's length transaction between knowledgeable willing parties, based on the best information available (see IAS 38 for further guidance on determining the fair value of an intangible asset acquired in a business combination);

(h) net employee benefit assets or liabilities for defined benefit plans at the present value of the defined benefit obligation less the fair value of any plan assets. However, an asset is only recognised to the extent that it is probable that it will be available to the enterprise in the form of refunds from the plan or a reduction in future contributions;

(i) tax assets and liabilities at the amount of the tax benefit arising from tax losses or the taxes payable in respect of the net profit or loss, assessed from the perspective of the combined entity or group resulting from the acquisition. The tax asset or liability is determined after allowing for the tax effect of restating identifiable assets and liabilities to their fair values and is not discounted. The tax assets include any deferred tax asset of the acquirer that was not recognised prior to the business combination, but which, as a consequence of the business combination, now satisfies the recognition criteria in IAS 12;

   (j) accounts and notes payable, long-term debt, liabilities, accruals and other claims payable at the present values of amounts to be disbursed in meeting the liability determined at appropriate current interest rates. However, discounting is not required for short-term liabilities when the difference between the nominal amount of the liability and the discounted amount is not material;

(k) onerous contracts and other identifiable liabilities of the acquiree at the present values of amounts to be disbursed in meeting the obligation determined at appropriate current interest rates; and

(l) provisions for terminating or reducing activities of the acquiree that are recognised under paragraph 31, at an amount determined under IAS 37.

Certain of the guidelines above assume that fair values will be determined by the use of discounting. When the guidelines do not refer to the use of discounting, discounting may or may not be used in determining the fair values of identifiable assets and liabilities.

If the fair value of an intangible asset cannot be measured by reference to an active **40** *market (as defined in IAS 38), the amount recognised for that intangible asset at the date of the acquisition should be limited to an amount that does not create or increase negative goodwill that arises on the acquisition (see paragraph 59).*

Goodwill Arising on Acquisition

Recognition and Measurement

Any excess of the cost of the acquisition over the acquirer's interest in the fair value **41** *of the identifiable assets and liabilities acquired as at the date of the exchange transaction should be described as goodwill and recognised as an asset.*

Goodwill arising on acquisition represents a payment made by the acquirer in **42** anticipation of future economic benefits. The future economic benefits may result from synergy between the identifiable assets acquired or from assets which, individually, do not qualify for recognition in the financial statements but for which the acquirer is prepared to make a payment in the acquisition.

43 *Goodwill should be carried at cost less any accumulated amortisation and any accumulated impairment losses.*

Amortisation

44 *Goodwill should be amortised on a systematic basis over its useful life. The amortisation period should reflect the best estimate of the period during which future economic benefits are expected to flow to the enterprise. There is a rebuttable presumption that the useful life of goodwill will not exceed twenty years from initial recognition.*

45 *The amortisation method used should reflect the pattern in which the future economic benefits arising from goodwill are expected to be consumed. The straight-line method should be adopted unless there is persuasive evidence that another method is more appropriate in the circumstances.*

46 *The amortisation for each period should be recognised as an expense.*

47 With the passage of time, goodwill diminishes, reflecting the fact that its service potential is decreasing. In some cases, the value of goodwill may appear not to decrease over time. This is because the potential for economic benefits that was purchased initially is being progressively replaced by the potential for economic benefits resulting from subsequent enhancements of goodwill. In other words, the goodwill that was purchased is being replaced by internally generated goodwill. IAS 38 prohibits the recognition of internally generated goodwill as an asset. Therefore, it is appropriate that goodwill is amortised on a systematic basis over the best estimate of its useful life.

48 Many factors need to be considered in estimating the useful life of goodwill including:
(a) the nature and foreseeable life of the acquired business;
(b) the stability and foreseeable life of the industry to which the goodwill relates;
(c) public information on the characteristics of goodwill in similar businesses or industries and typical life cycles of similar businesses;
(d) the effects of product obsolescence, changes in demand and other economic factors on the acquired business;
(e) the service life expectancies of key individuals or groups of employees and whether the acquired business could be efficiently managed by another management team;
(f) the level of maintenance expenditure or of funding required to obtain the expected future economic benefits from the acquired business and the company's ability and intent to reach such a level;
(g) expected actions by competitors or potential competitors; and
(h) the period of control over the acquired business and legal, regulatory or contractual provisions affecting its useful life.

49 Because goodwill represents, among other things, future economic benefits from synergy or assets that cannot be recognised separately, it is difficult to estimate its useful life. Estimates of its useful life become less reliable as the length of the useful life increases. The presumption in this Standard is that goodwill does not normally have a useful life in excess of twenty years from initial recognition.

In rare cases, there may be persuasive evidence that the useful life of goodwill will be **50** a specific period longer than twenty years. Although examples are difficult to find, this may occur when the goodwill is so clearly related to an identifiable asset or a group of identifiable assets that it can reasonably be expected to benefit the acquirer over the useful life of the identifiable asset or group of assets. In these cases, the presumption that the useful life of goodwill will not exceed twenty years is rebutted and the enterprise:

(a) amortises the goodwill over the best estimate of its useful life;

(b) estimates the recoverable amount of the goodwill at least annually to identify any impairment loss (see paragraph 56); and

(c) discloses the reasons why the presumption is rebutted and the factor(s) that played a significant role in determining the useful life of the goodwill (see paragraph 88(b)).

The useful life of goodwill is always finite. Uncertainty justifies estimating the useful **51** life of goodwill on a prudent basis, but it does not justify estimating a useful life that is unrealistically short.

There will rarely, if ever, be persuasive evidence to support an amortisation method **52** for goodwill other than the straight-line basis, especially if that other method results in a lower amount of accumulated amortisation than under the straight-line method. The amortisation method is applied consistently from period to period unless there is a change in the expected pattern of economic benefits from goodwill.

When accounting for an acquisition, there may be circumstances in which the **53** goodwill on acquisition does not reflect future economic benefits that are expected to flow to the acquirer. For example, since negotiating the purchase consideration, there may have been a decline in the expected future cash flows from the net identifiable assets acquired. In this case, an enterprise tests the goodwill for impairment under IAS 36 and accounts for any impairment loss accordingly.

The amortisation period and the amortisation method should be reviewed at least **54** *at each financial year end. If the expected useful life of goodwill is significantly different from previous estimates, the amortisation period should be changed accordingly. If there has been a significant change in the expected pattern of economic benefits from goodwill, the method should be changed to reflect the changed pattern. Such changes should be accounted for as changes in accounting estimates under IAS 8 by adjusting the amortisation charge for the current and future periods.*

Recoverability of the Carrying Amount - Impairment Losses

To determine whether goodwill is impaired, an enterprise applies IAS 36. ... **55**

In addition to following the requirements included in IAS 36 an enterprise should, **56** *at least at each financial year end, estimate in accordance with IAS 36 the recoverable amount of goodwill that is amortised over a period exceeding twenty years from initial recognition, even if there is no indication that it is impaired.*

[Not printed] **57–58**

Negative Goodwill Arising on Acquisition

Recognition and Measurement

59 *Any excess, as at the date of the exchange transaction, of the acquirer's interest in the fair values of the identifiable assets and liabilities acquired over the cost of the acquisition, should be recognised as negative goodwill.*

60 The existence of negative goodwill may indicate that identifiable assets have been overstated and identifiable liabilities have been omitted or understated. It is important to ensure that this is not the case before negative goodwill is recognised.

61 *To the extent that negative goodwill relates to expectations of future losses and expenses that are identified in the acquirer's plan for the acquisition and can be measured reliably, but which do not represent identifiable liabilities at the date of acquisition (see paragraph 26), that portion of negative goodwill should be recognised as income in the income statement when the future losses and expenses are recognised. If these identifiable future losses and expenses are not recognised in the expected period, negative goodwill should be treated under paragraph 62 (a) and (b).*

62 *To the extent that negative goodwill does not relate to identifiable expected future losses and expenses that can be measured reliably at the date of acquisition, negative goodwill should be recognised as income in the income statement as follows:*
   (a) the amount of negative goodwill not exceeding the fair values of acquired identifiable non-monetary assets should be recognised as income on a systematic basis over the remaining weighted average useful life of the identifiable acquired depreciable/
   amortisable assets; and
   (b) the amount of negative goodwill in excess of the fair values of acquired identifiable non-monetary assets should be recognised as income immediately.

63 To the extent that negative goodwill does not relate to expectations of future losses and expenses that have been identified in the acquirer's plan for the acquisition and can be measured reliably, negative goodwill is a gain which is recognised as income when the future economic benefits embodied in the identifiable depreciable/ amortisable assets acquired are consumed. In the case of monetary assets, the gain is recognised as income immediately.

Presentation

64 *Negative goodwill should be presented as a deduction from the assets of the reporting enterprise, in the same balance sheet classification as goodwill.*

Adjustments to Purchase Consideration Contingent on Future Events

65 *When the acquisition agreement provides for an adjustment to the purchase consideration contingent on one or more future events, the amount of the adjustment should be included in the cost of the acquisition as at the date of acquisition if the adjustment is probable and the amount can be measured reliably.*

66–67 [Not printed]

Subsequent Changes in Cost of Acquisition

The cost of the acquisition should be adjusted when a contingency affecting the 68
amount of the purchase consideration is resolved subsequent to the date of the
acquisition, so that payment of the amount is probable and a reliable estimate of
the amount can be made.

[Not printed] 69

In some circumstances, the acquirer may be required to make subsequent payment to 70
the seller as compensation for a reduction in the value of the purchase consideration.
This is the case when the acquirer has guaranteed the market price of securities or
debt issued as consideration and has to make a further issue of securities or debt for
the purpose of restoring the originally determined cost of acquisition. In such cases,
there is no increase in the cost of acquisition and, consequently, no adjustment to
goodwill or negative goodwill. Instead, the increase in securities or debt issued
represents a reduction in the premium or an increase in the discount on the initial
issue.

Subsequent Identification or Changes in Value of Identifiable Assets and Liabilities

Identifiable assets and liabilities, which are acquired but which do not satisfy the 71
criteria in paragraph 26 for separate recognition when the acquisition is initially
accounted for, should be recognised subsequently as and when they satisfy the
criteria. The carrying amounts of identifiable assets and liabilities acquired should
be adjusted when, subsequent to acquisition, additional evidence becomes available
to assist with the estimation of the amounts assigned to those identifiable assets
and liabilities when the acquisition was initially accounted for. The amount
assigned to goodwill or negative goodwill should also be adjusted, when necessary,
to the extent that:
(a) the adjustment does not increase the carrying amount of goodwill above its
    recoverable amount, as defined in IAS 36; and
(b) such adjustment is made by the end of the first annual accounting period
    commencing after acquisition (except for the recognition of an identifiable
    liability under paragraph 31, for which the time-frame in paragraph 31(c)
    applies);
otherwise the adjustments to the identifiable assets and liabilities should be
recognised as income or expense.

Identifiable assets and liabilities of an acquiree may not have been recognised at the 72
time of acquisition because they did not meet the recognition criteria for identifiable
assets and liabilities or the acquirer was unaware of their existence. Similarly, the fair
values assigned at the date of acquisition to the identifiable assets and liabilities
acquired may need to be adjusted as additional evidence becomes available to assist
with the estimation of the value of the identifiable asset or liability at the date of
acquisition. When the identifiable assets or liabilities are recognised or the carrying
amounts are adjusted after the end of the first annual accounting period (excluding
interim periods) commencing after acquisition, income or expense is recognised
rather than an adjustment to goodwill or negative goodwill. This time-limit, while

arbitrary in its length, prevents goodwill and negative goodwill from being reassessed and adjusted indefinitely.

73 [Not printed]

74 When, subsequent to acquisition but prior to the end of the first annual accounting period commencing after acquisition, the acquirer becomes aware of the existence of a liability which had existed at the date of acquisition or of an impairment loss that does not relate to specific events or changes in circumstances occurring after the date of acquisition, goodwill is not increased above its recoverable amount determined under IAS 36.

75 *If provisions for terminating or reducing activities of the acquiree were recognised under paragraph 31, these provisions should be reversed if, and only if:*
(a) the outflow of economic benefits is no longer probable; or
(b) the detailed formal plan is not implemented:
*   (i) in the manner set out in the detailed formal plan; or*
*   (ii) within the time established in the detailed formal plan.*
Such a reversal should be reflected as an adjustment to goodwill or negative goodwill (and minority interests, if appropriate), so that no income or expense is recognised in respect of it. The adjusted amount of goodwill should be amortised prospectively over its remaining useful life. The adjusted amount of negative goodwill should be dealt with under paragraph 62(a) and (b).

76 [Not printed]

Unitings of Interests

Accounting for Unitings of Interests

77 *A uniting of interests should be accounted for by use of the pooling of interests method as set out in paragraphs 78, 79 and 82.*

78 *In applying the pooling of interests method, the financial statement items of the combining enterprises for the period in which the combination occurs and for any comparative periods disclosed should be included in the financial statements of the combined enterprises as if they had been combined from the beginning of the earliest period presented. The financial statements of an enterprise should not incorporate a uniting of interests to which the enterprise is a party if the date of the uniting of interests is after the date of the most recent balance sheet included in the financial statements.*

79 *Any difference between the amount recorded as share capital issued plus any additional consideration in the form of cash or other assets and the amount recorded for the share capital acquired should be adjusted against equity.*

80 The substance of a uniting of interests is that no acquisition has occurred and there has been a continuation of the mutual sharing of risks and benefits that existed prior to the business combination. ...

81 Since a uniting of interests results in a single combined entity, a single uniform set of accounting policies is adopted by that entity. Therefore, the combined entity recognises the assets, liabilities and equity of the combining enterprises at their existing carrying amounts adjusted only as a result of conforming the combining enterprises' accounting policies and applying those policies to all periods presented. There is no recognition of any new goodwill or negative goodwill. Similarly, the effects of all transactions between the combining enterprises, whether occurring before or after the uniting of interests, are eliminated in preparing the financial statements of the combined entity.

Expenditures incurred in relation to a uniting of interests should be recognised as **82** *expenses in the period in which they are incurred.*

[Not printed]   **83**

All Business Combinations

Taxes on Income

In some countries, the accounting treatment for a business combination may differ **84** from that applied under their respective income tax laws. Any resulting deferred tax liabilities and deferred tax assets are recognised under IAS 12.

The potential benefit of income tax loss carryforwards, or other deferred tax assets, of **85** an acquired enterprise, which were not recognised as an identifiable asset by the acquirer at the date of acquisition, may subsequently be realised. When this occurs, the acquirer recognises the benefit as income under IAS 12. In addition, the acquirer:
(a) adjusts the gross carrying amount of the goodwill and the related accumulated amortisation to the amounts that would have been recorded if the deferred tax asset had been recognised as an identifiable asset at the date of the business combination; and
(b) recognises the reduction in the net carrying amount of the goodwill as an expense.
However, this procedure does not create negative goodwill, nor does it increase the carrying amount of negative goodwill.

Disclosure

For all business combinations, the following disclosures should be made in the **86** *financial statements for the period during which the combination has taken place:*
(a) the names and descriptions of the combining enterprises;
(b) the method of accounting for the combination;
(c) the effective date of the combination for accounting purposes; and
(d) any operations resulting from the business combination which the enterprise has decided to dispose of.

For a business combination which is an acquisition, the following additional **87** *disclosures should be made in the financial statements for the period during which the acquisition has taken place:*
(a) the percentage of voting shares acquired; and
(b) the cost of acquisition and a description of the purchase consideration paid or contingently payable.

For goodwill, the financial statements should disclose: **88**
(a) the amortisation period(s) adopted;

(b) *if goodwill is amortised over more than twenty years, the reasons why the presumption that the useful life of goodwill will not exceed twenty years from initial recognition is rebutted. In giving these reasons, the enterprise should describe the factor(s) that played a significant role in determining the useful life of the goodwill;*

(c) *if goodwill is not amortised on the straight-line basis, the basis used and reason why that basis is more appropriate than the straight-line basis;*

(d) *the line item(s) of the income statement in which the amortisation of goodwill is included; and*

(e) *a reconciliation of the carrying amount of goodwill at the beginning and end of the period showing:*

    (i) *the gross amount and the accumulated amortisation (aggregated with accumulated impairment losses), at the beginning of the period;*

    (ii) *any additional goodwill recognised during the period;*

    (iii) *any adjustments resulting from subsequent identification or changes in value of identifiable assets and liabilities;*

    (iv) *any goodwill derecognised on the disposal of all or part of the business to which it relates during the period;*

    (v) *amortisation recognised during the period;*

    (vi) *impairment losses recognised during the period under IAS 36 (if any);*

    (vii) *impairment losses reversed during the period under IAS 36 (if any);*

    (viii) *other changes in the carrying amount during the period (if any); and*

    (ix) *the gross amount and the accumulated amortisation (aggregated with accumulated impairment losses), at the end of the period.*

...

89 [Not printed]

90 An enterprise discloses information on impaired goodwill under IAS 36 in addition to the information required by paragraph 88(e)(vi) and (vii).

91 *For negative goodwill, the financial statements should disclose:*

(a) *to the extent that negative goodwill is treated under paragraph 61, a description, the amount and the timing of the expected future losses and expenses;*

(b) *the period(s) over which negative goodwill is recognised as income;*

(c) *the line item(s) of the income statement in which negative goodwill is recognised as income; and*

(d) *a reconciliation of the carrying amount of negative goodwill at the beginning and end of the period showing:*

    (i) *the gross amount of negative goodwill and the accumulated amount of negative goodwill already recognised as income, at the beginning of the period;*

    (ii) *any additional negative goodwill recognised during the period;*

    (iii) *any adjustments resulting from subsequent identification or changes in value of identifiable assets and liabilities;*

    (iv) *any negative goodwill derecognised on the disposal of all or part of the business to which it relates during the period;*

    (v) *negative goodwill recognised as income during the period, showing separately the portion of negative goodwill recognised as income under paragraph 61 (if any);*

(vi) other changes in the carrying amount during the period (if any); and

(vii) the gross amount of negative goodwill and the accumulated amount of negative goodwill already recognised as income, at the end of the period.

...

The disclosure requirements of IAS 37 apply to provisions recognised under paragraph 31 for terminating or reducing the activities of an acquiree. These provisions should be treated as a separate class of provisions for the purpose of disclosure under IAS 37. In addition, the aggregate carrying amount of these provisions should be disclosed for each individual business combination. **92**

In an acquisition, if the fair values of the identifiable assets and liabilities or the purchase consideration can only be determined on a provisional basis at the end of the period in which the acquisition took place, this should be stated and reasons given. When there are subsequent adjustments to such provisional fair values, those adjustments should be disclosed and explained in the financial statements of the period concerned. **93**

For a business combination which is a uniting of interests, the following additional disclosures should be made in the financial statements for the period during which the uniting of interests has taken place: **94**
(a) description and number of shares issued, together with the percentage of each enterprise's voting shares exchanged to effect the uniting of interests;
(b) amounts of assets and liabilities contributed by each enterprise; and
(c) sales revenue, other operating revenues, extraordinary items and the net profit or loss of each enterprise prior to the date of the combination that are included in the net profit or loss shown by the combined enterprise's financial statements.

[Not printed] **95**

For business combinations effected after the balance sheet date, the information required by paragraphs 86 to 94 should be disclosed. If it is impracticable to disclose any of this information, this fact should be disclosed. **96**

Business combinations which have been effected after the balance sheet date and before the date on which the financial statements of one of the combining enterprises are authorised for issue are disclosed if they are of such importance that non-disclosure would affect the ability of the users of the financial statements to make proper evaluations and decisions (see IAS 10). **97**

[Not printed] **98**

Transitional Provisions

[Not printed] **99–101**

Effective Date

[Not printed] **102–103**

IAS 23: Borrowing Costs

IAS 23: Borrowing Costs				
Scope 23.1–3	Definitions 23.4–6	Transitional Provisions 23.30	Effective Date 23.31	Related Interpretation: SIC–2

Borrowing Costs – Benchmark Treatment 23.7–9	
Recognition 23.7–8	Disclosure 23.9

Borrowing Costs – Allowed Alternative Treatment 23.10–29					
Recognition 23.10–28					Disclosure 23.29
Borrowing Costs Eligible for Capitalisation 23.13–18	Excess of the Carrying Amount of the Qualified Asset over Recoverable Amount 23.19	Commencement of Capitalisation 23.20–22	Suspension of Capitalisation 23.23–24	Cessation of Capitalisation 23.25–28	Disclosure 23.29

Scope

This Standard should be applied in accounting for borrowing costs.   **1**

[Not printed]   **2**

This Standard does not deal with the actual or imputed cost of equity, including **3** preferred capital not classified as a liability.

Definitions

...   **4**

Borrowing costs are interest and other costs incurred by an enterprise in connection with the borrowing of funds.
A qualifying asset is an asset that necessarily takes a substantial period of time to get ready for its intended use or sale.

Borrowing costs may include: **5**
(a) interest on bank overdrafts and short-term and long-term borrowings;
(b) amortisation of discounts or premiums relating to borrowings;
(c) amortisation of ancillary costs incurred in connection with the arrangement of borrowings;

(d) finance charges in respect of finance leases recognised in accordance with IAS 17; and

(e) exchange differences arising from foreign currency borrowings to the extent that they are regarded as an adjustment to interest costs.

6 Examples of qualifying assets are inventories that require a substantial period of time to bring them to a saleable condition, manufacturing plants, power generation facilities and investment properties. Other investments, and those inventories that are routinely manufactured or otherwise produced in large quantities on a repetitive basis over a short period of time, are not qualifying assets. Assets that are ready for their intended use or sale when acquired also are not qualifying assets.

Borrowing Costs - Benchmark Treatment

Recognition

7 *Borrowing costs should be recognised as an expense in the period in which they are incurred.*

8 [Not printed]

Disclosure

9 *The financial statements should disclose the accounting policy adopted for borrowing costs.*

Borrowing Costs - Allowed Alternative Treatment

Recognition

10 *Borrowing costs should be recognised as an expense in the period in which they are incurred, except to the extent that they are capitalised in accordance with paragraph 11.*

11 *Borrowing costs that are directly attributable to the acquisition, construction or production of a qualifying asset should be capitalised as part of the cost of that asset. The amount of borrowing costs eligible for capitalisation should be determined in accordance with this Standard.*

12 ... Such borrowing costs are capitalised as part of the cost of the asset when it is probable that they will result in future economic benefits to the enterprise and the costs can be measured reliably. Other borrowing costs are recognised as an expense in the period in which they are incurred.

Borrowing Costs Eligible for Capitalisation

13 The borrowing costs that are directly attributable to the acquisition, construction or production of a qualifying asset are those borrowing costs that would have been avoided if the expenditure on the qualifying asset had not been made. When an enterprise borrows funds specifically for the purpose of obtaining a particular qualifying asset, the borrowing costs that directly relate to that qualifying asset can be readily identified.

[Not printed]   14

To the extent that funds are borrowed specifically for the purpose of obtaining a   15
qualifying asset, the amount of borrowing costs eligible for capitalisation on that
asset should be determined as the actual borrowing costs incurred on that borrowing
during the period less any investment income on the temporary investment of those
borrowings.

[Not printed]   16

To the extent that funds are borrowed generally and used for the purpose of obtaining   17
a qualifying asset, the amount of borrowing costs eligible for capitalisation should be
determined by applying a capitalisation rate to the expenditures on that asset. The
capitalisation rate should be the weighted average of the borrowing costs applicable
to the borrowings of the enterprise that are outstanding during the period, other than
borrowings made specifically for the purpose of obtaining a qualifying asset. The
amount of borrowing costs capitalised during a period should not exceed the amount
of borrowing costs incurred during that period.

[Not printed]   18

Excess of the Carrying Amount of the Qualifying Asset over Recoverable Amount

When the carrying amount or the expected ultimate cost of the qualifying asset exceeds   19
its recoverable amount or net realisable value, the carrying amount is written down or
written off in accordance with the requirements of other IASs. In certain circumstances,
the amount of the write-down or write-off is written back in accordance with those
other IASs.

Commencement of Capitalisation

The capitalisation of borrowing costs as part of the cost of a qualifying asset should   20
commence when:
(a) expenditures for the asset are being incurred;
(b) borrowing costs are being incurred; and
(c) activities that are necessary to prepare the asset for its intended use or sale are
in progress.

Expenditures on a qualifying asset include only those expenditures that have resulted   21
in payments of cash, transfers of other assets or the assumption of interest-bearing
liabilities. Expenditures are reduced by any progress payments received and grants
received in connection with the asset (see IAS 20). The average carrying amount of the
asset during a period, including borrowing costs previously capitalised, is normally a
reasonable approximation of the expenditures to which the capitalisation rate is applied
in that period.

The activities necessary to prepare the asset for its intended use or sale encompass more   22
than the physical construction of the asset. They include technical and administrative
work prior to the commencement of physical construction, such as the activities
associated with obtaining permits prior to the commencement of the physical
construction. However, such activities exclude the holding of an asset when no
production or development that changes the asset's condition is taking place. ...

Suspension of Capitalisation

23 *Capitalisation of borrowing costs should be suspended during extended periods in which active development is interrupted.*

24 Borrowing costs may be incurred during an extended period in which the activities necessary to prepare an asset for its intended use or sale are interrupted. Such costs are costs of holding partially completed assets and do not qualify for capitalisation. However, capitalisation of borrowing costs is not normally suspended during a period when substantial technical and administrative work is being carried out. Capitalisation of borrowing costs is also not suspended when a temporary delay is a necessary part of the process of getting an asset ready for its intended use or sale. ...

Cessation of Capitalisation

25 *Capitalisation of borrowing costs should cease when substantially all the activities necessary to prepare the qualifying asset for its intended use or sale are complete.*

26 An asset is normally ready for its intended use or sale when the physical construction of the asset is complete even though routine administrative work might still continue. If minor modifications, such as the decoration of a property to the purchaser's or user's specification, are all that are outstanding, this indicates that substantially all the activities are complete.

27 *When the construction of a qualifying asset is completed in parts and each part is capable of being used while construction continues on other parts, capitalisation of borrowing costs should cease when substantially all the activities necessary to prepare that part for its intended use or sale are completed.*

28 [Not printed]

Disclosure

29 *The financial statements should disclose:*
(a) the accounting policy adopted for borrowing costs;
(b) the amount of borrowing costs capitalised during the period; and
(c) the capitalisation rate used to determine the amount of borrowing costs eligible for capitalisation.

Transitional Provisions

30 *[Not printed]*

Effective Date

31 *[Not printed]*

IAS 24: Related Party Disclosures

IAS 24: Related Party Disclosures		
Scope 24.1–4	Definitions 24.5–6	Effective Date 24.26

The Related Party Issue 24.7–17				
General 24.7–11	Methods to Price Transactions between Related Parties 24.12–17			
	Comparable Uncontrolled Price Method 24.13	Resale Price Method 24.14	Cost-Plus Method 24.15	Other 24.16–17

Disclosure 24.18–25

Scope

This Standard should be applied in dealing with related parties and transactions **1**
between a reporting enterprise and its related parties. The requirements of this
Standard apply to the financial statements of each reporting enterprise.

[Not printed] **2**

This Standard deals only with those related party relationships described in (a) to (e) **3**
below:
(a) enterprises that directly, or indirectly through one or more intermediaries, control,
or are controlled by, or are under common control with, the reporting enterprise.
(This includes holding companies, subsidiaries and fellow subsidiaries);
(b) associates (see IAS 28);
(c) individuals owning, directly or indirectly, an interest in the voting power of the
reporting enterprise that gives them significant influence over the enterprise, and
close members of the family of any such individual;
(d) key management personnel, that is, those persons having authority and
responsibility for planning, directing and controlling the activities of the reporting
enterprise, including directors and officers of companies and close members of the
families of such individuals; and
(e) enterprises in which a substantial interest in the voting power is owned, directly or
indirectly, by any person described in (c) or (d) or over which such a person is able
to exercise significant influence. This includes enterprises owned by directors or
major shareholders of the reporting enterprise and enterprises that have a member
of key management in common with the reporting enterprise.
In considering each possible related party relationship, attention is directed to the
substance of the relationship, and not merely the legal form.

No disclosure of transactions is required: **4**
(a) in consolidated financial statements in respect of intra-group transactions;

(b) in parent financial statements when they are made available or published with the consolidated financial statements;

(c) in financial statements of a wholly-owned subsidiary if its parent is incorporated in the same country and provides consolidated financial statements in that country; and

(d) in financial statements of state-controlled enterprises of transactions with other state-controlled enterprises.

Definitions

5 ...

Related party - *parties are considered to be related if one party has the ability to control the other party or exercise significant influence over the other party in making financial and operating decisions.*

Related party transaction - *a transfer of resources or obligations between related parties, regardless of whether a price is charged.*

Control - *ownership, directly, or indirectly through subsidiaries, of more than one half of the voting power of an enterprise, or a substantial interest in voting power and the power to direct, by statute or agreement, the financial and operating policies of the management of the enterprise.*

Significant influence (for the purpose of this Standard) - *participation in the financial and operating policy decisions of an enterprise, but not control of those policies. Significant influence may be exercised in several ways, usually by representation on the board of directors but also by, for example, participation in the policy making process, material intercompany transactions, interchange of managerial personnel or dependence on technical information. Significant influence may be gained by share ownership, statute or agreement. With share ownership, significant influence is presumed in accordance with the definition contained in IAS 28.*

6 In the context of this Standard, the following are deemed not to be related parties:

(a) two companies simply because they have a director in common, notwithstanding paragraphs 3 (d) and (e) above, (but it is necessary to consider the possibility, and to assess the likelihood, that the director would be able to affect the policies of both companies in their mutual dealings);

(b) (i) providers of finance;
(ii) trade unions;
(iii) public utilities;
(iv) government departments and agencies, in the course of their normal dealings with an enterprise by virtue only of those dealings (although they may circumscribe the freedom of action of an enterprise or participate in its decision-making process); and

(c) a single customer, supplier, franchisor, distributor, or general agent with whom an enterprise transacts a significant volume of business merely by virtue of the resulting economic dependence.

The Related Party Issue

7 Related party relationships are a normal feature of commerce and business. ...

8 A related party relationship could have an effect on the financial position and operating results of the reporting enterprise. Related parties may enter into transactions which unrelated parties would not enter into. Also, transactions between related parties may not be effected at the same amounts as between unrelated parties.

The operating results and financial position of an enterprise may be affected by a related **9** party relationship even if related party transactions do not occur. The mere existence of the relationship may be sufficient to affect the transactions of the reporting enterprise with other parties. ... Alternatively, one party may refrain from acting because of the significant influence of another - ...

Because there is an inherent difficulty for management to determine the effect of **10** influences which do not lead to transactions, disclosure of such effects is not required by this Standard.

Accounting recognition of a transfer of resources is normally based on the price agreed **11** between the parties. Between unrelated parties the price is an arm's length price. Related parties may have a degree of flexibility in the price-setting process that is not present in transactions between unrelated parties.

A variety of methods is used to price transactions between related parties. **12**

One way of determining a price for a transaction between related parties is by the **13** comparable uncontrolled price method, which sets the price by reference to comparable goods sold in an economically comparable market to a buyer unrelated to the seller. Where the goods or services supplied in a related party transaction, and the conditions relating thereto, are similar to those in normal trading transactions, this method is often used. It is also often used for determining the cost of finance.

Where goods are transferred between related parties before sale to an independent party, **14** the resale price method is often used. This reduces the resale price by a margin, representing an amount from which the re-seller would seek to cover his costs and make an appropriate profit, to arrive at a transfer price to the re-seller. There are problems of judgement in determining a compensation appropriate to the re-seller's contribution to the process. This method is also used for transfers of other resources, such as rights and services.

Another approach is the cost-plus method, which seeks to add an appropriate mark-up **15** to the supplier's cost. Difficulties may be experienced in determining both the elements of cost attributable and the mark-up. Among the yardsticks that may assist in determining transfer prices are comparable returns in similar industries on turnover or capital employed.

Sometimes prices of related party transactions are not determined under one of the **16** methods described in paragraphs 13 to 15 above. Sometimes, no price is charged - as in the examples of the free provision of management services and the extension of free credit on a debt.

Sometimes, transactions would not have taken place if the relationship had not existed. **17** ...

Disclosure

... IAS 27 and IAS 28 require disclosure of a list of significant subsidiaries and associates. **18** IAS 8 requires disclosure of extraordinary items and items of income and expense within profit or loss from ordinary activities that are of such size, nature or incidence that their disclosure is relevant to explain the performance of the enterprise for the period.

19 The following are examples of situations where related party transactions may lead to disclosures by a reporting enterprise in the period which they affect:
- purchases or sales of goods (finished or unfinished);
- purchases or sales of property and other assets;
- rendering or receiving of services;
- agency arrangements;
- leasing arrangements;
- transfer of research and development;
- licence agreements;
- finance (including loans and equity contributions in cash or in kind);
- guarantees and collaterals; and
- management contracts.

20 *Related party relationships where control exists should be disclosed irrespective of whether there have been transactions between the related parties.*

21 [Not printed]

22 *If there have been transactions between related parties, the reporting enterprise should disclose the nature of the related party relationships as well as the types of transactions and the elements of the transactions necessary for an understanding of the financial statements.*

23 The elements of transactions necessary for an understanding of the financial statements would normally include:
(a) an indication of the volume of the transactions, either as an amount or as an appropriate proportion;
(b) amounts or appropriate proportions of outstanding items; and
(c) pricing policies.

24 *Items of a similar nature may be disclosed in aggregate except when separate disclosure is necessary for an understanding of the effects of related party transactions on the financial statements of the reporting enterprise.*

25 Disclosure of transactions between members of a group is unnecessary in consolidated financial statements because consolidated financial statements present information about the parent and subsidiaries as a single reporting enterprise. Transactions with associated enterprises accounted for under the equity method are not eliminated and therefore require separate disclosure as related party transactions.

Effective Date

26 *[Not printed]*

IAS 26: Accounting and Reporting by Retirement Benefit Plans

IAS 26: Accounting and Reporting by Retirement Benefit Plans		
Scope 26.1–7	Definitions 26.8–12	Effective Date 26.37

Defined Contribution Plans 26.13–16

Defined Benefit Plans 26.17–31			
Report Contents 26.17–22	Actuarial Present Value of Promised Retirement Benefits 26.23–26	Frequency of Actuarial Valuations 26.27	Report Content 26.28–31

All Plans 26.32–36	
Valuation of Plan Assets 26.32–33	Disclosure 26.34–36

Scope

This Standard should be applied in the reports of retirement benefit plans where such **1** *reports are prepared.*

Retirement benefit plans are sometimes referred to by various other names, such as **2** 'pension schemes', 'superannuation schemes' or 'retirement benefit schemes'. This Standard regards a retirement benefit plan as a reporting entity separate from the employers of the participants in the plan. All other IASs apply to the reports of retirement benefit plans to the extent that they are not superseded by this Standard.

This Standard deals with accounting and reporting by the plan to all participants as a **3** group. It does not deal with reports to individual participants about their retirement benefit rights.

[Not printed] **4**

Retirement benefit plans may be defined contribution plans or defined benefit plans. ... **5**

Retirement benefit plans with assets invested with insurance companies are subject to **6** the same accounting and funding requirements as privately invested arrangements. Accordingly, they are within the scope of this Standard unless the contract with the insurance company is in the name of a specified participant or a group of participants and the retirement benefit obligation is solely the responsibility of the insurance company.

This Standard does not deal with other forms of employment benefits such as **7** employment termination indemnities, deferred compensation arrangements, long-service leave benefits, special early retirement or redundancy plans, health and welfare plans or bonus plans. Government social security type arrangements are also excluded from the scope of this Standard.

Definitions

8 ...

Retirement benefit plans are arrangements whereby an enterprise provides benefits for its employees on or after termination of service (either in the form of an annual income or as a lump sum) when such benefits, or the employer's contributions towards them, can be determined or estimated in advance of retirement from the provisions of a document or from the enterprise's practices.

Defined contribution plans are retirement benefit plans under which amounts to be paid as retirement benefits are determined by contributions to a fund together with investment earnings thereon.

Defined benefit plans are retirement benefit plans under which amounts to be paid as retirement benefits are determined by reference to a formula usually based on employees' earnings and/or years of service.

Funding is the transfer of assets to an entity (the fund) separate from the employer's enterprise to meet future obligations for the payment of retirement benefits.

For the purposes of this Standard the following terms are also used:

Participants are the members of a retirement benefit plan and others who are entitled to benefits under the plan.

Net assets available for benefits are the assets of a plan less liabilities other than the actuarial present value of promised retirement benefits.

Actuarial present value of promised retirement benefits is the present value of the expected payments by a retirement benefit plan to existing and past employees, attributable to the service already rendered.

Vested benefits are benefits, the rights to which, under the conditions of a retirement benefit plan, are not conditional on continued employment.

9 Some retirement benefit plans have sponsors other than employers; this Standard also applies to the reports of such plans.

10 [Not printed]

11 Many retirement benefit plans provide for the establishment of separate funds into which contributions are made and out of which benefits are paid. Such funds may be administered by parties who act independently in managing fund assets. Those parties are called trustees in some countries. The term trustee is used in this Standard to describe such parties regardless of whether a trust has been formed.

12 Retirement benefit plans are normally described as either defined contribution plans or defined benefit plans, each having their own distinctive characteristics. Occasionally plans exist that contain characteristics of both. Such hybrid plans are considered to be defined benefit plans for the purposes of this Standard.

Defined Contribution Plans

13 *The report of a defined contribution plan should contain a statement of net assets available for benefits and a description of the funding policy.*

14 Under a defined contribution plan, the amount of a participant's future benefits is determined by the contributions paid by the employer, the participant, or both, and the operating efficiency and investment earnings of the fund. An employer's obligation is usually discharged by contributions to the fund. An actuary's advice is not normally required although such advice is sometimes used to estimate future benefits that may

be achievable based on present contributions and varying levels of future contributions and investment earnings.

The participants are interested in the activities of the plan because they directly affect 15 the level of their future benefits. Participants are interested in knowing whether contributions have been received and proper control has been exercised to protect the rights of beneficiaries. An employer is interested in the efficient and fair operation of the plan.

The objective of reporting by a defined contribution plan is periodically to provide 16 information about the plan and the performance of its investments. That objective is usually achieved by providing a report including the following:
(a) a description of significant activities for the period and the effect of any changes relating to the plan, and its membership and terms and conditions;
(b) statements reporting on the transactions and investment performance for the period and the financial position of the plan at the end of the period; and
(c) a description of the investment policies.

Defined Benefit Plans

The report of a defined benefit plan should contain either: 17
(a) a statement that shows:
  (i) the net assets available for benefits;
  (ii) the actuarial present value of promised retirement benefits, distinguishing between vested benefits and non-vested benefits; and
  (iii) the resulting excess or deficit; or
(b) a statement of net assets available for benefits including either:
  (i) a note disclosing the actuarial present value of promised retirement benefits, distinguishing between vested benefits and non-vested benefits; or
  (ii) a reference to this information in an accompanying actuarial report.
If an actuarial valuation has not been prepared at the date of the report, the most recent valuation should be used as a base and the date of the valuation disclosed.

For the purposes of paragraph 17, the actuarial present value of promised retirement 18 *benefits should be based on the benefits promised under the terms of the plan on service rendered to date using either current salary levels or projected salary levels with disclosure of the basis used. The effect of any changes in actuarial assumptions that have had a significant effect on the actuarial present value of promised retirement benefits should also be disclosed.*

The report should explain the relationship between the actuarial present value of 19 *promised retirement benefits and the net assets available for benefits, and the policy for the funding of promised benefits.*

Under a defined benefit plan, the payment of promised retirement benefits depends on 20 the financial position of the plan and the ability of contributors to make future contributions to the plan as well as the investment performance and operating efficiency of the plan.

[Not printed] 21

The objective of reporting by a defined benefit plan is periodically to provide 22 information about the financial resources and activities of the plan that is useful in assessing the relationships between the accumulation of resources and plan benefits over time. This objective is usually achieved by providing a report including the following:

(a) a description of significant activities for the period and the effect of any changes relating to the plan, and its membership and terms and conditions;

(b) statements reporting on the transactions and investment performance for the period and the financial position of the plan at the end of the period;

(c) actuarial information either as part of the statements or by way of a separate report; and

(d) a description of the investment policies.

Actuarial Present Value of Promised Retirement Benefits

23 The present value of the expected payments by a retirement benefit plan may be calculated and reported using current salary levels or projected salary levels up to the time of retirement of participants.

24–25 [Not printed]

26 The actuarial present value of promised retirement benefits based on current salaries is disclosed in the report of a plan to indicate the obligation for benefits earned to the date of the report. The actuarial present value of promised retirement benefits based on projected salaries is disclosed to indicate the magnitude of the potential obligation on a going concern basis which is generally the basis for funding. In addition to disclosure of the actuarial present value of promised retirement benefits, sufficient explanation may need to be given so as to indicate clearly the context in which the actuarial present value of promised retirement benefits should be read. Such explanation may be in the form of information about the adequacy of the planned future funding and of the funding policy based on salary projections. This may be included in the financial information or in the actuary's report.

Frequency of Actuarial Valuations

27 In many countries, actuarial valuations are not obtained more frequently than every three years. If an actuarial valuation has not been prepared at the date of the report, the most recent valuation is used as a base and the date of the valuation disclosed.

Report Content

28 For defined benefit plans, information is presented in one of the following formats which reflect different practices in the disclosure and presentation of actuarial information:

(a) a statement is included in the report that shows the net assets available for benefits, the actuarial present value of promised retirement benefits, and the resulting excess or deficit. The report of the plan also contains statements of changes in net assets available for benefits and changes in the actuarial present value of promised retirement benefits. The report may include a separate actuary's report supporting the actuarial present value of promised retirement benefits;

(b) a report that includes a statement of net assets available for benefits and a statement of changes in net assets available for benefits. The actuarial present value of promised retirement benefits is disclosed in a note to the statements. The report may also include a report from an actuary supporting the actuarial present value of promised retirement benefits; and

(c) a report that includes a statement of net assets available for benefits and a statement of changes in net assets available for benefits with the actuarial present value of promised retirement benefits contained in a separate actuarial report.

In each format a trustees' report in the nature of a management or directors' report and an investment report may also accompany the statements.

[Not printed]   29–31

All Plans

Valuation of Plan Assets

Retirement benefit plan investments should be carried at fair value. In the case of **32** *marketable securities fair value is market value. Where plan investments are held for which an estimate of fair value is not possible disclosure should be made of the reason why fair value is not used.*

[Not printed]   **33**

Disclosure

The report of a retirement benefit plan, whether defined benefit or defined **34** *contribution, should also contain the following information:*
(a) a statement of changes in net assets available for benefits;
(b) a summary of significant accounting policies; and
(c) a description of the plan and the effect of any changes in the plan during the period.

Reports provided by retirement benefit plans include the following, if applicable: **35**
(a) a statement of net assets available for benefits disclosing:
  (i) assets at the end of the period suitably classified;
  (ii) the basis of valuation of assets;
  (iii) details of any single investment exceeding either 5% of the net assets available for benefits or 5% of any class or type of security;
  (iv) details of any investment in the employer; and
  (v) liabilities other than the actuarial present value of promised retirement benefits;
(b) a statement of changes in net assets available for benefits showing the following:
  (i) employer contributions;
  (ii) employee contributions;
  (iii) investment income such as interest and dividends;
  (iv) other income;
  (v) benefits paid or payable (analysed, for example, as retirement, death and disability benefits, and lump sum payments);
  (vi) administrative expenses;
  (vii)other expenses;
  (viii)taxes on income;
  (ix) profits and losses on disposal of investments and changes in value of investments; and
  (x) transfers from and to other plans;
(c) a description of the funding policy;

(d) for defined benefit plans, the actuarial present value of promised retirement benefits (which may distinguish between vested benefits and non-vested benefits) based on the benefits promised under the terms of the plan, on service rendered to date and using either current salary levels or projected salary levels; this information may be included in an accompanying actuarial report to be read in conjunction with the related financial information; and

(e) for defined benefit plans, a description of the significant actuarial assumptions made and the method used to calculate the actuarial present value of promised retirement benefits.

36 The report of a retirement benefit plan contains a description of the plan, either as part of the financial information or in a separate report. It may contain the following:

(a) the names of the employers and the employee groups covered;

(b) the number of participants receiving benefits and the number of other participants, classified as appropriate;

(c) the type of plan - defined contribution or defined benefit;

(d) a note as to whether participants contribute to the plan;

(e) a description of the retirement benefits promised to participants;

(f) a description of any plan termination terms; and

(g) changes in items (a) to (f) during the period covered by the report.

It is not uncommon to refer to other documents that are readily available to users and in which the plan is described, and to include only information on subsequent changes in the report.

Effective Date

37 *[Not printed]*

IAS 27: Consolidated Financial Statements and Accounting for Investments in Subsidiaries

IAS 27: Consolidated Financial Statements and Accounting for Investments in Subsidiaries			
Scope 27.1–5	Definitions 27.6	Effective Date 27.33	Related Interpretations: SIC–12, 20

Presentation of Consolidated Financial Statements 27.7–10	
General Obligation of a Parent to Present the Consolidated Financial Statements 27.7, 9	Exception 27.8, 10

Scope of Consolidated Financial Statements 27.11–14	
Consolidation of all Subsidiaries 27.11–12	Exceptions 27.13–14

Consolidation Procedures 27.15–28

Accounting for Investments in Subsidiaries in a Parent's Separate Financial Statements 27.29–31	
Investments in Subsidiaries Included in the Consolidated Financial Statements 27.29	Investments in Subsidiaries Excluded from Consolidated Financial Statements 27.30–31

Disclosure 27.32

Scope

This Standard should be applied in the preparation and presentation of 1
consolidated financial statements for a group of enterprises under the control of a parent.

This Standard should also be applied in accounting for investments in subsidiaries 2
in a parent's separate financial statements.

[Not printed] 3–4

This Standard does not deal with: 5
(a) methods of accounting for business combinations and their effects on consolidation, including goodwill arising on a business combination (see IAS 22);

(b) accounting for investments in associates (see IAS 28); and

(c) accounting for investments in joint ventures (see IAS 31).

Definitions

6 ...

Control (for the purpose of this Standard) is the power to govern the financial and operating policies of an enterprise so as to obtain benefits from its activities.

A subsidiary is an enterprise that is controlled by another enterprise (known as the parent).

A parent is an enterprise that has one or more subsidiaries.

A group is a parent and all its subsidiaries.

Consolidated financial statements are the financial statements of a group presented as those of a single enterprise.

Minority interest is that part of the net results of operations and of net assets of a subsidiary attributable to interests which are not owned, directly or indirectly through subsidiaries, by the parent.

Presentation of Consolidated Financial Statements

7 *A parent, other than a parent mentioned in paragraph 8, should present consolidated financial statements.*

8 *A parent that is a wholly owned subsidiary, or is virtually wholly owned, need not present consolidated financial statements provided, in the case of one that is virtually wholly owned, the parent obtains the approval of the owners of the minority interest. Such a parent should disclose the reasons why consolidated financial statements have not been presented together with the bases on which subsidiaries are accounted for in its separate financial statements. The name and registered office of its parent that publishes consolidated financial statements should also be disclosed.*

9 Users of the financial statements of a parent are usually concerned with, and need to be informed about, the financial position, results of operations and changes in financial position of the group as a whole. This need is served by consolidated financial statements, which present financial information about the group as that of a single enterprise without regard for the legal boundaries of the separate legal entities.

10 ... Virtually wholly owned is often taken to mean that the parent owns 90% or more of the voting power.

Scope of Consolidated Financial Statements

11 *A parent which issues consolidated financial statements should consolidate all subsidiaries, foreign and domestic, other than those referred to in paragraph 13.*

12 The consolidated financial statements include all enterprises that are controlled by the parent, other than those subsidiaries excluded for the reasons set out in paragraph 13. Control is presumed to exist when the parent owns, directly or indirectly through subsidiaries, more than one half of the voting power of an enterprise unless, in exceptional circumstances, it can be clearly demonstrated that such ownership does

230

not constitute control. Control also exists even when the parent owns one half or less of the voting power of an enterprise when there is:

(a) power over more than one half of the voting rights by virtue of an agreement with other investors;

(b) power to govern the financial and operating policies of the enterprise under a statute or an agreement;

(c) power to appoint or remove the majority of the members of the board of directors or equivalent governing body; or

(d) power to cast the majority of votes at meetings of the board of directors or equivalent governing body.

A subsidiary should be excluded from consolidation when: 13

(a) control is intended to be temporary because the subsidiary is acquired and held exclusively with a view to its subsequent disposal in the near future; or

(b) it operates under severe long-term restrictions which significantly impair its ability to transfer funds to the parent.

Such subsidiaries should be accounted for in accordance with IAS 39.

A subsidiary is not excluded from consolidation because its business activities are   14 dissimilar from those of the other enterprises within the group. Better information is provided by consolidating such subsidiaries and disclosing additional information in the consolidated financial statements about the different business activities of subsidiaries. ...

Consolidation Procedures

In preparing consolidated financial statements, the financial statements of the parent   15 and its subsidiaries are combined on a line-by-line basis by adding together like items of assets, liabilities, equity, income and expenses. In order that the consolidated financial statements present financial information about the group as that of a single enterprise, the following steps are then taken:

(a) the carrying amount of the parent's investment in each subsidiary and the parent's portion of equity of each subsidiary are eliminated (see IAS 22, which also describes the treatment of any resultant goodwill);

(b) minority interests in the net income of consolidated subsidiaries for the reporting period are identified and adjusted against the income of the group in order to arrive at the net income attributable to the owners of the parent; and

(c) minority interests in the net assets of consolidated subsidiaries are identified and presented in the consolidated balance sheet separately from liabilities and the parent shareholders' equity. Minority interests in the net assets consist of:

(i) the amount at the date of the original combination calculated in accordance with IAS 22; and

(ii) the minority's share of movements in equity since the date of the combination.

Taxes payable by either the parent or its subsidiaries on distribution to the parent of   16 the profits retained in subsidiaries are accounted for in accordance with IAS 12.

Intragroup balances and intragroup transactions and resulting unrealised profits   17 *should be eliminated in full. Unrealised losses resulting from intragroup transactions should also be eliminated unless cost cannot be recovered.*

18 Intragroup balances and intragroup transactions, including sales, expenses and dividends, are eliminated in full. Unrealised profits resulting from intragroup transactions that are included in the carrying amount of assets, such as inventory and fixed assets, are eliminated in full. Unrealised losses resulting from intragroup transactions that are deducted in arriving at the carrying amount of assets are also eliminated unless cost cannot be recovered. Timing differences that arise from the elimination of unrealised profits and losses resulting from intragroup transactions are dealt with in accordance with IAS 12.

19 *When the financial statements used in the consolidation are drawn up to different reporting dates, adjustments should be made for the effects of significant transactions or other events that occur between those dates and the date of the parent's financial statements. In any case the difference between reporting dates should be no more than three months.*

20 The financial statements of the parent and its subsidiaries used in the preparation of the consolidated financial statements are usually drawn up to the same date. When the reporting dates are different, the subsidiary often prepares, for consolidation purposes, statements as at the same date as the group. When it is impracticable to do this, financial statements drawn up to different reporting dates may be used provided the difference is no greater than three months. The consistency principle dictates that the length of the reporting periods and any difference in the reporting dates should be the same from period to period.

21 *Consolidated financial statements should be prepared using uniform accounting policies for like transactions and other events in similar circumstances. If it is not practicable to use uniform accounting policies in preparing the consolidated financial statements, that fact should be disclosed together with the proportions of the items in the consolidated financial statements to which the different accounting policies have been applied.*

22 [Not printed]

23 The results of operations of a subsidiary are included in the consolidated financial statements as from the date of acquisition, which is the date on which control of the acquired subsidiary is effectively transferred to the buyer, in accordance with IAS 22. The results of operations of a subsidiary disposed of are included in the consolidated income statement until the date of disposal which is the date on which the parent ceases to have control of the subsidiary. The difference between the proceeds from the disposal of the subsidiary and the carrying amount of its assets less liabilities as of the date of disposal is recognised in the consolidated income statement as the profit or loss on the disposal of the subsidiary. In order to ensure the comparability of the financial statements from one accounting period to the next, supplementary information is often provided about the effect of the acquisition and disposal of subsidiaries on the financial position at the reporting date and the results for the reporting period and on the corresponding amounts for the preceding period.

24 *An investment in an enterprise should be accounted for in accordance with IAS 39 from the date that it ceases to fall within the definition of a subsidiary and does not become an associate as defined in IAS 28.*

25 The carrying amount of the investment at the date that it ceases to be a subsidiary is regarded as cost thereafter.

Minority interests should be presented in the consolidated balance sheet separately **26**
from liabilities and the parent shareholders' equity. Minority interests in the
income of the group should also be separately presented.

The losses applicable to the minority in a consolidated subsidiary may exceed the **27**
minority interest in the equity of the subsidiary. The excess, and any further losses
applicable to the minority, are charged against the majority interest except to the
extent that the minority has a binding obligation to, and is able to, make good the
losses. If the subsidiary subsequently reports profits, the majority interest is allocated
all such profits until the minority's share of losses previously absorbed by the majority
has been recovered.

If a subsidiary has outstanding cumulative preferred shares which are held outside the **28**
group, the parent computes its share of profits or losses after adjusting for the
subsidiary's preferred dividends, whether or not dividends have been declared.

Accounting for Investments in Subsidiaries in a Parent's Separate Financial Statements

In a parent's separate financial statements, investments in subsidiaries that are **29**
included in the consolidated financial statements should be either:
(a) carried at cost;
(b) accounted for using the equity method as described in IAS 28; or
(c) accounted for as available-for-sale financial assets as described in IAS 39.

Investments in subsidiaries that are excluded from consolidated financial statements **30**
should be either:
(a) carried at cost;
(b) accounted for using the equity method as described in IAS 28; or
(c) accounted for as available-for-sale financial assets as described in IAS 39.

[Not printed] **31**

Disclosure

In addition to those disclosures required by paragraphs 8 and 21, the following **32**
disclosures should be made:
(a) in consolidated financial statements a listing of significant subsidiaries
    including the name, country of incorporation or residence, proportion of
    ownership interest and, if different, proportion of voting power held;
(b) in consolidated financial statements, where applicable:
    (i) the reasons for not consolidating a subsidiary;
    (ii) the nature of the relationship between the parent and a subsidiary of which
         the parent does not own, directly or indirectly through subsidiaries, more
         than one half of the voting power;
    (iii) the name of an enterprise in which more than one half of the voting power
         is owned, directly or indirectly through subsidiaries, but which, because of
         the absence of control, is not a subsidiary; and
    (iv) the effect of the acquisition and disposal of subsidiaries on the financial
         position at the reporting date, the results for the reporting period and on the
         corresponding amounts for the preceding period; and

IAS 28: Accounting for Investments in Associates

IAS 28: Accounting for Investments in Associates						
Scope 28.1–2	Definitions 28.3–7				Effective Date 28.29–31	Related Interpretation: SIC–3
	General 28.3	Significant Influence 28.4–5	Equity Method 28.6	Cost Method 28.7		

Consolidated Financial Statements 28.8–11	
Equity Method and Exceptions 28.8–9	Termination of the Equity Method 28.11

Separate Financial Statements of the Investor 28.12–15	
When Investor Issues Consolidated Financial Statements 28.12–13	When Investor Does Not Issue Consolidated Financial Statements 28.14–15

Application of the Equity Method 28.16–24	
General 28.16–22	Impairment Losses 28.23–24

Income Taxes 28.25 (Reference to IAS 12)

Contingencies 28.26 (Reference to IAS 37)

Disclosure 28.27–28

Scope

This Standard should be applied in accounting by an investor for investments in **1** *associates.*

[Not printed] **2**

Definitions

... **3**

An associate is an enterprise in which the investor has significant influence and which is neither a subsidiary nor a joint venture of the investor.
Significant influence is the power to participate in the financial and operating policy decisions of the investee but is not control over those policies.
Control (for the purpose of this Standard) is the power to govern the financial and operating policies of an enterprise so as to obtain benefits from its activities.

A subsidiary is an enterprise that is controlled by another enterprise (known as the parent).

The equity method is a method of accounting whereby the investment is initially recorded at cost and adjusted thereafter for the post acquisition change in the investor's share of net assets of the investee. The income statement reflects the investor's share of the results of operations of the investee.

The cost method is a method of accounting whereby the investment is recorded at cost. The income statement reflects income from the investment only to the extent that the investor receives distributions from accumulated net profits of the investee arising subsequent to the date of acquisition.

Significant Influence

4   If an investor holds, directly or indirectly through subsidiaries, 20% or more of the voting power of the investee, it is presumed that the investor does have significant influence, unless it can be clearly demonstrated that this is not the case. Conversely, if the investor holds, directly or indirectly through subsidiaries, less than 20% of the voting power of the investee, it is presumed that the investor does not have significant influence, unless such influence can be clearly demonstrated. A substantial or majority ownership by another investor does not necessarily preclude an investor from having significant influence.

5   The existence of significant influence by an investor is usually evidenced in one or more of the following ways:
(a)   representation on the board of directors or equivalent governing body of the investee;
(b)   participation in policy making processes;
(c)   material transactions between the investor and the investee;
(d)   interchange of managerial personnel; or
provision of essential technical information.

Equity Method

6   Under the equity method, the investment is initially recorded at cost and the carrying amount is increased or decreased to recognise the investor's share of the profits or losses of the investee after the date of acquisition. Distributions received from an investee reduce the carrying amount of the investment. Adjustments to the carrying amount may also be necessary for alterations in the investor's proportionate interest in the investee arising from changes in the investee's equity that have not been included in the income statement. Such changes include those arising from the revaluation of property, plant, equipment and investments, from foreign exchange translation differences and from the adjustment of differences arising on business combinations.

Cost Method

7   Under the cost method, an investor records its investment in the investee at cost. The investor recognises income only to the extent that it receives distributions from the accumulated net profits of the investee arising subsequent to the date of acquisition by the investor. Distributions received in excess of such profits are considered a recovery of investment and are recorded as a reduction of the cost of the investment.

Consolidated Financial Statements

An investment in an associate should be accounted for in consolidated financial **8**
statements under the equity method except when:
(a) the investment is acquired and held exclusively with a view to its subsequent
disposal in the near future.; or
(b) it operates under severe long-term restrictions that significantly impair its ability
to transfer funds to the investor.
Such investments should be accounted for in accordance with IAS 39.

[Not printed] **9**

[Deleted] **10**

An investor should discontinue the use of the equity method from the date that: **11**
(a) it ceases to have significant influence in an associate but retains, either in whole
or in part, its investment; or
(b) the use of the equity method is no longer appropriate because the associate
operates under severe long-term restrictions that significantly impair its ability to
transfer funds to the investor.
The carrying amount of the investment at that date should be regarded as cost
thereafter.

Separate Financial Statements of the Investor

An investment in an associate that is included in the separate financial statements **12**
of an investor that issues consolidated financial statements and that is not held
exclusively with a view to its disposal in the near future should be either:
(a) carried at cost;
(b) accounted for using the equity method as described in this Standard; or
(c) accounted for as an available-for-sale financial asset as described in IAS 39.

[Not printed] **13**

An investment in an associate that is included in the financial statements of an **14**
investor that does not issue consolidated financial statements should be either:
(a) carried at cost;
(b) accounted for using the equity method as described in this Standard if the equity
method would be appropriate for the associate if the investor issued consolidated
financial statements; or
(c) accounted for under IAS 39 as an available-for-sale financial asset or a financial
asset held for trading based on the definitions in IAS 39.
[Not printed] **15**

Application of the Equity Method

[Not printed] **16**

An investment in an associate is accounted for under the equity method from the date **17**
on which it falls within the definition of an associate. On acquisition of the investment
any difference (whether positive or negative) between the cost of acquisition and the
investor's share of the fair values of the net identifiable assets of the associate is

accounted for in accordance with IAS 22. Appropriate adjustments to the investor's share of the profits or losses after acquisition are made to account for:

(a) depreciation of the depreciable assets, based on their fair values; and

(b) amortisation of the difference between the cost of the investment and the investor's share of the fair values of the net identifiable assets.

18 The most recent available financial statements of the associate are used by the investor in applying the equity method; they are usually drawn up to the same date as the financial statements of the investor. When the reporting dates of the investor and the associate are different, the associate often prepares, for the use of the investor, statements as at the same date as the financial statements of the investor. When it is impracticable to do this, financial statements drawn up to a different reporting date may be used. The consistency principle dictates that the length of the reporting periods, and any difference in the reporting dates, are consistent from period to period.

19 When financial statements with a different reporting date are used, adjustments are made for the effects of any significant events or transactions between the investor and the associate that occur between the date of the associate's financial statements and the date of the investor's financial statements.

20 The investor's financial statements are usually prepared using uniform accounting policies for like transactions and events in similar circumstances. In many cases, if an associate uses accounting policies other than those adopted by the investor for like transactions and events in similar circumstances, appropriate adjustments are made to the associate's financial statements when they are used by the investor in applying the equity method. If it is not practicable for such adjustments to be calculated, that fact is generally disclosed.

21 If an associate has outstanding cumulative preferred shares, held by outside interests, the investor computes its share of profits or losses after adjusting for the preferred dividends, whether or not the dividends have been declared.

22 If, under the equity method, an investor's share of losses of an associate equals or exceeds the carrying amount of an investment, the investor ordinarily discontinues including its share of further losses. The investment is reported at nil value. Additional losses are provided for to the extent that the investor has incurred obligations or made payments on behalf of the associate to satisfy obligations of the associate that the investor has guaranteed or otherwise committed. If the associate subsequently reports profits, the investor resumes including its share of those profits only after its share of the profits equals the share of net losses not recognised.

Impairment Losses

23 If there is an indication that an investment in an associate may be impaired, an enterprise applies IAS 36. In determining the value in use of the investment, an enterprise estimates:

(a) its share of the present value of the estimated future cash flows expected to be generated by the investee as a whole, including the cash flows from the operations of the investee and the proceeds on the ultimate disposal of the investment; or

(b) the present value of the estimated future cash flows expected to arise from dividends to be received from the investment and from its ultimate disposal.

Under appropriate assumptions, both methods give the same result. Any resulting impairment loss for the investment is allocated in accordance with IAS 36. Therefore, it is allocated first to any remaining goodwill (see paragraph 17).

The recoverable amount of an investment in an associate is assessed for each individual **24** associate, unless an individual associate does not generate cash inflows from continuing use that are largely independent of those from other assets of the reporting enterprise.

Income Taxes

Income taxes arising from investments in associates are accounted for in accordance **25** with IAS 12.

Contingencies

In accordance with IAS 37 the investor discloses: **26**
(a) its share of the contingent liabilities and capital commitments of an associate for which it is also contingently liable; and
(b) those contingent liabilities that arise because the investor is severally liable for all the liabilities of the associate.

Disclosure

The following disclosures should be made: **27**
(a) an appropriate listing and description of significant associates including the proportion of ownership interest and, if different, the proportion of voting power held; and
(b) the methods used to account for such investments.

Investments in associates accounted for using the equity method should be classified **28** *as long-term assets and disclosed as a separate item in the balance sheet. The investor's share of the profits or losses of such investments should be disclosed as a separate item in the income statement. The investor's share of any extraordinary or prior period items should also be separately disclosed.*

Effective Date

[Not printed] **29–31**

IAS 29: Financial Reporting in Hyperinflationary Economies

IAS 29: Financial Reporting in Hyperinflationary Economies		
Scope 29.1–4	Effective Date 29.41	Related Interpretation: SIC–19

The Restatement of Financial Statements 29.5–10								
Financial Statements 29.11–31								Consolidated Financial Statements 29.35–36
Historical Cost 29.11–28			Current Cost 29.29–31			Cash Flow Statement 29.33	Corresponding Figures 29.34	
Balance Sheet 29.11–25	Income Statement 29.26	Gain or Loss 29.27–28	Balance Sheet 29.29	Income Statement 29.30	Gain or Loss 29.31			
Taxes 29.32								
Selection and Use of the General Price Index 29.37								

Economies Ceasing to be Hyperinflationary 29.38

Disclosures 29.39–40

Scope

1 *This Standard should be applied to the primary financial statements, including the consolidated financial statements, of any enterprise that reports in the currency of a hyperinflationary economy.*

2 In a hyperinflationary economy, reporting of operating results and financial position in the local currency without restatement is not useful. Money loses purchasing power at such a rate that comparison of amounts from transactions and other events that have occurred at different times, even within the same accounting period, is misleading.

3 This Standard does not establish an absolute rate at which hyperinflation is deemed to arise. It is a matter of judgement when restatement of financial statements in accordance with this Standard becomes necessary. Hyperinflation is indicated by characteristics of the economic environment of a country which include, but are not limited to, the following:
   (a) the general population prefers to keep its wealth in non-monetary assets or in a relatively stable foreign currency. Amounts of local currency held are immediately invested to maintain purchasing power;
   (b) the general population regards monetary amounts not in terms of the local currency but in terms of a relatively stable foreign currency. Prices may be quoted in that currency;
   (c) sales and purchases on credit take place at prices that compensate for the expected loss of purchasing power during the credit period, even if the period is short;
   (d) interest rates, wages and prices are linked to a price index; and

(e) the cumulative inflation rate over three years is approaching, or exceeds, 100%.

[Not printed]   4

The Restatement of Financial Statements

[Not printed]   5–7

The financial statements of an enterprise that reports in the currency of a **8**
hyperinflationary economy, whether they are based on a historical cost approach or
a current cost approach, should be stated in terms of the measuring unit current at
the balance sheet date. The corresponding figures for the previous period required
by IAS 1 and any information in respect of earlier periods should also be stated in
terms of the measuring unit current at the balance sheet date.

The gain or loss on the net monetary position should be included in net income and **9**
separately disclosed.

The restatement of financial statements in accordance with this Standard requires the **10**
application of certain procedures as well as judgement. The consistent application of
these procedures and judgements from period to period is more important than the
precise accuracy of the resulting amounts included in the restated financial
statements.

Historical Cost Financial Statements

Balance Sheet

Balance sheet amounts not already expressed in terms of the measuring unit current **11**
at the balance sheet date are restated by applying a general price index.

Monetary items are not restated because they are already expressed in terms of the **12**
monetary unit current at the balance sheet date. Monetary items are money held and
items to be received or paid in money.

Assets and liabilities linked by agreement to changes in prices, such as index linked **13**
bonds and loans, are adjusted in accordance with the agreement in order to ascertain
the amount outstanding at the balance sheet date. These items are carried at this
adjusted amount in the restated balance sheet.

All other assets and liabilities are non-monetary. Some non-monetary items are **14**
carried at amounts current at the balance sheet date, such as net realisable value and
market value, so they are not restated. All other non-monetary assets and liabilities
are restated.

Most non-monetary items are carried at cost or cost less depreciation; hence they are **15**
expressed at amounts current at their date of acquisition. The restated cost, or cost
less depreciation, of each item is determined by applying to its historical cost and
accumulated depreciation the change in a general price index from the date of
acquisition to the balance sheet date. Hence, property, plant and equipment,
investments, inventories of raw materials and merchandise, goodwill, patents,
trademarks and similar assets are restated from the dates of their purchase.
Inventories of partly-finished and finished goods are restated from the dates on which
the costs of purchase and of conversion were incurred.

16–17 [Not printed]

18 Some non-monetary items are carried at amounts current at dates other than that of acquisition or that of the balance sheet, for example property, plant and equipment that has been revalued at some earlier date. In these cases, the carrying amounts are restated from the date of the revaluation.

19 The restated amount of a non-monetary item is reduced, in accordance with appropriate IASs, when it exceeds the amount recoverable from the item's future use (including sale or other disposal). Hence, in such cases, restated amounts of property, plant and equipment, goodwill, patents and trademarks are reduced to recoverable amount, restated amounts of inventories are reduced to net realisable value and restated amounts of current investments are reduced to market value.

20 [Not printed]

21 The impact of inflation is usually recognised in borrowing costs. It is not appropriate both to restate the capital expenditure financed by borrowing and to capitalise that part of the borrowing costs that compensates for the inflation during the same period. This part of the borrowing costs is recognised as an expense in the period in which the costs are incurred.

22 An enterprise may acquire assets under an arrangement that permits it to defer payment without incurring an explicit interest charge. Where it is impracticable to impute the amount of interest, such assets are restated from the payment date and not the date of purchase.

23 IAS 21 permits an enterprise to include foreign exchange differences on borrowings in the carrying amount of assets following a severe and recent devaluation. Such a practice is not appropriate for an enterprise reporting in the currency of a hyperinflationary economy when the carrying amount of the asset is restated from the date of its acquisition.

24 At the beginning of the first period of application of this Standard, the components of owners' equity, except retained earnings and any revaluation surplus, are restated by applying a general price index from the dates the components were contributed or otherwise arose. Any revaluation surplus that arose in previous periods is eliminated. Restated retained earnings are derived from all the other amounts in the restated balance sheet.

25 At the end of the first period and in subsequent periods, all components of owners' equity are restated by applying a general price index from the beginning of the period or the date of contribution, if later. The movements for the period in owners' equity are disclosed in accordance with IAS 1.

Income Statement

26 This Standard requires that all items in the income statement are expressed in terms of the measuring unit current at the balance sheet date. Therefore all amounts need to be restated by applying the change in the general price index from the dates when the items of income and expenses were initially recorded in the financial statements.

Gain or Loss on Net Monetary Position

27 In a period of inflation, an enterprise holding an excess of monetary assets over monetary liabilities loses purchasing power and an enterprise with an excess of monetary liabilities over monetary assets gains purchasing power to the extent the assets and liabilities are not linked to a price level. This gain or loss on the net monetary position may be derived as the difference resulting from the restatement of non-monetary assets, owners' equity and income statement items and the adjustment of index linked assets and liabilities. The gain or loss may be estimated by applying the change in a general price index to the weighted average for the period of the difference between monetary assets and monetary liabilities.

The gain or loss on the net monetary position is included in net income. The **28** adjustment to those assets and liabilities linked by agreement to changes in prices made in accordance with paragraph 13 is offset against the gain or loss on net monetary position. Other income statement items, such as interest income and expense, and foreign exchange differences related to invested or borrowed funds, are also associated with the net monetary position. Although such items are separately disclosed, it may be helpful if they are presented together with the gain or loss on net monetary position in the income statement.

Current Cost Financial Statements

Balance Sheet

Items stated at current cost are not restated because they are already expressed in **29** terms of the measuring unit current at the balance sheet date. Other items in the balance sheet are restated in accordance with paragraphs 11 to 25.

Income Statement

The current cost income statement, before restatement, generally reports costs current **30** at the time at which the underlying transactions or events occurred. Cost of sales and depreciation are recorded at current costs at the time of consumption; sales and other expenses are recorded at their money amounts when they occurred. Therefore all amounts need to be restated into the measuring unit current at the balance sheet date by applying a general price index.

Gain or Loss on Net Monetary Position

The gain or loss on the net monetary position is accounted for in accordance with **31** paragraphs 27 and 28. The current cost income statement may, however, already include an adjustment reflecting the effects of changing prices on monetary items in accordance with paragraph 16 of IAS 15. Such an adjustment is part of the gain or loss on net monetary position.

Taxes

The restatement of financial statements in accordance with this Standard may give **32** rise to differences between taxable income and accounting income. These differences are accounted for in accordance with IAS 12.

Cash Flow Statement

This Standard requires that all items in the cash flow statement are expressed in terms **33** of the measuring unit current at the balance sheet date.

Corresponding Figures

34 Corresponding figures for the previous reporting period, whether they were based on a historical cost approach or a current cost approach, are restated by applying a general price index so that the comparative financial statements are presented in terms of the measuring unit current at the end of the reporting period. Information that is disclosed in respect of earlier periods is also expressed in terms of the measuring unit current at the end of the reporting period.

Consolidated Financial Statements

35 A parent that reports in the currency of a hyperinflationary economy may have subsidiaries that also report in the currencies of hyperinflationary economies. The financial statements of any such subsidiary need to be restated by applying a general price index of the country in whose currency it reports before they are included in the consolidated financial statements issued by its parent. Where such a subsidiary is a foreign subsidiary, its restated financial statements are translated at closing rates. The financial statements of subsidiaries that do not report in the currencies of hyperinflationary economies are dealt with in accordance with IAS 21.

36 If financial statements with different reporting dates are consolidated, all items, whether non-monetary or monetary, need to be restated into the measuring unit current at the date of the consolidated financial statements.

Selection and Use of the General Price Index

37 The restatement of financial statements in accordance with this Standard requires the use of a general price index that reflects changes in general purchasing power. It is preferable that all enterprises that report in the currency of the same economy use the same index.

Economies Ceasing to be Hyperinflationary

38 *When an economy ceases to be hyperinflationary and an enterprise discontinues the preparation and presentation of financial statements prepared in accordance with this Standard, it should treat the amounts expressed in the measuring unit current at the end of the previous reporting period as the basis for the carrying amounts in its subsequent financial statements.*

Disclosures

39 *The following disclosures should be made:*
   (a) the fact that the financial statements and the corresponding figures for previous periods have been restated for the changes in the general purchasing power of the reporting currency and, as a result, are stated in terms of the measuring unit current at the balance sheet date;
   (b) whether the financial statements are based on a historical cost approach or a current cost approach; and
   (c) the identity and level of the price index at the balance sheet date and the movement in the index during the current and the previous reporting period.

[Not printed]   **40**

Effective Date

[Not printed]   **41**

IAS 30: Disclosures in the Financial Statements of Banks and Similar Financial Institutions

IAS 30: Disclosures in the Financial Statements of Banks and Similar Financial Institutions		
Scope 30.1–5	Background 30.6–7	Effective Date 30.59

Accounting Policies 30.8		

Income Statement 30.9–17		
General 30.9	Items of Income and Expenses 30.10–12	Offset of Income and Expenses 30.13–17

Balance Sheet 30.18–25			
General 30.18	Assets and Liabilities 30.19–22	Offset of Assets and Liabilities 30.23	Disclosure of Fair Values 30.24–25

Specific Items 30.26–58							
Contingencies and Commitments Including Off-Balance Sheet Items 30.26–29	Maturities of Assets and Liabilities 30.30–39	Concentrations of Assets, Liabilities and Off-Balance Sheet Items 30.40–42	Losses on Loans and Advances 30.43–49	General Banking Risks 30.50–52	Assets Pledged as Security 30.53–54	Trust Activities 30.55	Related Party Transactions 30.56–58

Scope

1 *This Standard should be applied in the financial statements of banks and similar financial institutions (subsequently referred to as banks).*

2 For the purposes of this Standard, the term "bank" includes all financial institutions, one of whose principal activities is to take deposits and borrow with the objective of lending and investing and which are within the scope of banking or similar legislation. The Standard is relevant to such enterprises whether or not they have the word "bank" in their name.

[Not printed] 3

This Standard supplements other IASs which also apply to banks unless they are 4 specifically exempted in a Standard.

This Standard applies to the separate financial statements and the consolidated financial 5 statements of a bank. Where a group undertakes banking operations, this Standard is applicable in respect of those operations on a consolidated basis.

Background

The users of the financial statements of a bank need relevant, reliable and comparable 6 information which assists them in evaluating the financial position and performance of the bank and which is useful to them in making economic decisions. They also need information which gives them a better understanding of the special characteristics of the operations of a bank. Users need such information even though a bank is subject to supervision and provides the regulatory authorities with information that is not always available to the public. Therefore disclosures in the financial statements of a bank need to be sufficiently comprehensive to meet the needs of users, within the constraint of what it is reasonable to require of management.

The users of the financial statements of a bank are interested in its liquidity and 7 solvency and the risks related to the assets and liabilities recognised on its balance sheet and to its off balance sheet items. Liquidity refers to the availability of sufficient funds to meet deposit withdrawals and other financial commitments as they fall due. Solvency refers to the excess of assets over liabilities and, hence, to the adequacy of the bank's capital. A bank is exposed to liquidity risk and to risks arising from currency fluctuations, interest rate movements, changes in market prices and from counterparty failure. These risks may be reflected in the financial statements, but users obtain a better understanding if management provides a commentary on the financial statements which describes the way it manages and controls the risks associated with the operations of the bank.

Accounting Policies

Banks use differing methods for the recognition and measurement of items in their 8 financial statements. While harmonisation of these methods is desirable, it is beyond the scope of this Standard. In order to comply with IAS 1 and thereby enable users to understand the basis on which the financial statements of a bank are prepared, accounting policies dealing with the following items may need to be disclosed:
(a) the recognition of the principal types of income (see paragraphs 10 and 11);
(b) the valuation of investment and dealing securities (see paragraphs 24 and 25);
(c) the distinction between those transactions and other events that result in the recognition of assets and liabilities on the balance sheet and those transactions and other events that only give rise to contingencies and commitments (see paragraphs 26 to 29);
(d) the basis for the determination of losses on loans and advances and for writing off uncollectable loans and advances (see paragraphs 43 to 49); and
(e) the basis for the determination of charges for general banking risks and the accounting treatment of such charges (see paragraphs 50 to 52).
...

Income Statement

9   *A bank should present an income statement which groups income and expenses by nature and discloses the amounts of the principal types of income and expenses.*

10 *In addition to the requirements of other IASs, the disclosures in the income statement or the notes to the financial statements should include, but are not limited to, the following items of income and expenses:*
   Interest and similar income;
   Interest expense and similar charges;
   Dividend income;
   Fee and commission income;
   Fee and commission expense;
   Gains less losses arising from dealing securities;
   Gains less losses arising from investment securities;
   Gains less losses arising from dealing in foreign currencies;
   Other operating income;
   Losses on loans and advances;
   General administrative expenses; and
   Other operating expenses.

11 The principal types of income arising from the operations of a bank include interest, fees for services, commissions and dealing results. Each type of income is separately disclosed in order that users can assess the performance of a bank. Such disclosures are in addition to those of the source of income required by IAS 14.

12 The principal types of expenses arising from the operations of a bank include interest, commissions, losses on loans and advances, charges relating to the reduction in the carrying amount of investments and general administrative expenses. Each type of expense is separately disclosed in order that users can assess the performance of a bank.

13 *Income and expense items should not be offset except for those relating to hedges and to assets and liabilities which have been offset in accordance with paragraph 23.*

14 [Not printed]

15 Gains and losses arising from each of the following are normally reported on a net basis:
   (a) disposals and changes in the carrying amount of dealing securities;
   (b) disposals of investment securities; and
   (c) dealings in foreign currencies.

16 Interest income and interest expense are disclosed separately in order to give a better understanding of the composition of, and reasons for changes in, net interest.

17 Net interest is a product of both interest rates and the amounts of borrowing and lending. It is desirable for management to provide a commentary about average interest rates, average interest earning assets and average interest-bearing liabilities for the period. In some countries, governments provide assistance to banks by making deposits and other credit facilities available at interest rates which are substantially below market rates. In these cases, management's commentary often discloses the extent of these deposits and facilities and their effect on net income.

Balance Sheet

A bank should present a balance sheet that groups assets and liabilities by nature **18**
and lists them in an order that reflects their relative liquidity.

In addition to the requirements of other IASs, the disclosures in the balance sheet or **19**
the notes to the financial statements should include, but are not limited to, the
following assets and liabilities:

Assets

Cash and balances with the central bank;
Treasury bills and other bills eligible for rediscounting with the central bank;
Government and other securities held for dealing purposes;
Placements with, and loans and advances to, other banks;
Other money market placements;
Loans and advances to customers; and
Investment securities.

Liabilities

Deposits from other banks;
Other money market deposits;
Amounts owed to other depositors;
Certificates of deposits;
Promissory notes and other liabilities evidenced by paper; and
Other borrowed funds.

[Not printed]   **20**

The distinction between balances with other banks and those with other parts of the   **21**
money market and from other depositors is relevant information because it gives an
understanding of a bank's relations with, and dependence on, other banks and the
money market. Hence, a bank discloses separately:
(a) balances with the central bank;
(b) placements with other banks;
(c) other money market placements;
(d) deposits from other banks;
(e) other money market deposits; and
(f) other deposits.

A bank generally does not know the holders of its certificates of deposit because they **22**
are usually traded on an open market. Hence, a bank discloses separately deposits that
have been obtained through the issue of its own certificates of deposit or other
negotiable paper.

The amount at which any asset or liability is stated in the balance sheet should not **23**
be offset by the deduction of another liability or asset unless a legal right of set-off
exists and the offsetting represents the expectation as to the realisation or settlement
of the asset or liability.

A bank should disclose the fair values of each class of its financial assets and **24**
liabilities as required by IAS 32 and IAS 39.

[Not printed]   **25**

Contingencies and Commitments Including Off Balance Sheet Items

26 *A bank should disclose the following contingent liabilities and commitments:*

(a) *the nature and amount of commitments to extend credit that are irrevocable because they cannot be withdrawn at the discretion of the bank without the risk of incurring significant penalty or expense; and*

(b) *the nature and amount of contingent liabilities and commitments arising from off balance sheet items including those relating to:*

(i) *direct credit substitutes including general guarantees of indebtedness, bank acceptance guarantees and standby letters of credit serving as financial guarantees for loans and securities;*

(ii) *certain transaction-related contingent liabilities including performance bonds, bid bonds, warranties and standby letters of credit related to particular transactions;*

(iii) *short-term self-liquidating trade-related contingent liabilities arising from the movement of goods, such as documentary credits where the underlying shipment is used as security;*

(iv) *those sale and repurchase agreements not recognised in the balance sheet;*

(v) *interest and foreign exchange rate related items including swaps, options and futures; and*

(vi) *other commitments, note issuance facilities and revolving underwriting facilities.*

27–29 [Not printed]

Maturities of Assets and Liabilities

30 *A bank should disclose an analysis of assets and liabilities into relevant maturity groupings based on the remaining period at the balance sheet date to the contractual maturity date.*

31–32 [Not printed]

33 The maturity groupings applied to individual assets and liabilities differ between banks and in their appropriateness to particular assets and liabilities. Examples of periods used include the following:

(a) up to 1 month;

(b) from 1 month to 3 months;

(c) from 3 months to 1 year;

(d) from 1 year to 5 years; and

(e) from 5 years and over.

Frequently the periods are combined, for example, in the case of loans and advances, by grouping those under one year and those over one year. When repayment is spread over a period of time, each instalment is allocated to the period in which it is contractually agreed or expected to be paid or received.

34 It is essential that the maturity periods adopted by a bank are the same for assets and liabilities. This makes clear the extent to which the maturities are matched and the consequent dependence of the bank on other sources of liquidity.

35 Maturities could be expressed in terms of:

(a) the remaining period to the repayment date;

(b) the original period to the repayment date; or

(c) the remaining period to the next date at which interest rates may be changed.

The analysis of assets and liabilities by their remaining periods to the repayment dates provides the best basis to evaluate the liquidity of a bank. A bank may also disclose repayment maturities based on the original period to the repayment date in order to provide information about its funding and business strategy. In addition, a bank may disclose maturity groupings based on the remaining period to the next date at which interest rates may be changed in order to demonstrate its exposure to interest rate risks. Management may also provide, in its commentary on the financial statements, information about interest rate exposure and about the way it manages and controls such exposures.

[Not printed]   36

Some assets of a bank do not have a contractual maturity date. The period in which   37
these assets are assumed to mature is usually taken as the expected date on which the
assets will be realised.

[Not printed]   38–39

Concentrations of Assets, Liabilities and Off Balance Sheet Items

A bank should disclose any significant concentrations of its assets, liabilities and off   40
balance sheet items. Such disclosures should be made in terms of geographical areas,
customer or industry groups or other concentrations of risk. A bank should also
disclose the amount of significant net foreign currency exposures.

[Not printed]   41–42

Losses on Loans and Advances

A bank should disclose the following: 43
(a) the accounting policy which describes the basis on which uncollectable loans and
*   advances are recognised as an expense and written off;*
(b) details of the movements in the provision for losses on loans and advances during
*   the period. It should disclose separately the amount recognised as an expense in*
*   the period for losses on uncollectable loans and advances, the amount charged in*
*   the period for loans and advances written off and the amount credited in the*
*   period for loans and advances previously written off that have been recovered;*
(c) the aggregate amount of the provision for losses on loans and advances at the
*   balance sheet date; and*
(d) the aggregate amount included in the balance sheet for loans and advances on
*   which interest is not being accrued and the basis used to determine the carrying*
*   amount of such loans and advances.*

Any amounts set aside in respect of losses on loans and advances in addition to those   44
losses that have been specifically identified or potential losses which experience
indicates are present in the portfolio of loans and advances should be accounted for
as appropriations of retained earnings. Any credits resulting from the reduction of
such amounts result in an increase in retained earnings and are not included in the
determination of net profit or loss for the period.

[Not printed]   45–48

49 When loans and advances cannot be recovered, they are written off and charged against the provision for losses. In some cases, they are not written off until all the necessary legal procedures have been completed and the amount of the loss is finally determined. In other cases, they are written off earlier, for example when the borrower has not paid any interest or repaid any principal that was due in a specified period. As the time at which uncollectable loans and advances are written off differs, the gross amount of loans and advances and of the provisions for losses may vary considerably in similar circumstances. As a result, a bank discloses its policy for writing off uncollectable loans and advances.

General Banking Risks

50 *Any amounts set aside for general banking risks, including future losses and other unforeseeable risks or contingencies should be separately disclosed as appropriations of retained earnings. Any credits resulting from the reduction of such amounts result in an increase in retained earnings and should not be included in the determination of net profit or loss for the period.*

51–52 [Not printed]

Assets Pledged as Security

53 *A bank should disclose the aggregate amount of secured liabilities and the nature and carrying amount of the assets pledged as security.*

54 [Not printed]

Trust Activities

55 Banks commonly act as trustees and in other fiduciary capacities that result in the holding or placing of assets on behalf of individuals, trusts, retirement benefit plans and other institutions. Provided the trustee or similar relationship is legally supported, these assets are not assets of the bank and, therefore, are not included in its balance sheet. If the bank is engaged in significant trust activities, disclosure of that fact and an indication of the extent of those activities is made in its financial statements because of the potential liability if it fails in its fiduciary duties. For this purpose, trust activities do not encompass safe custody functions.

Related Party Transactions

56–57 [Not printed]

58 When a bank has entered into transactions with related parties, it is appropriate to disclose the nature of the related party relationship, the types of transactions, and the elements of transactions necessary for an understanding of the financial statements of the bank. The elements that would normally be disclosed to conform with IAS 24 include a bank's lending policy to related parties and, in respect of related party transactions, the amount included in or the proportion of:
(a) each of loans and advances, deposits and acceptances and promissory notes; disclosures may include the aggregate amounts outstanding at the beginning and

end of the period, as well as advances, deposits, repayments and other changes during the period;

(b) each of the principal types of income, interest expense and commissions paid;

(c) the amount of the expense recognised in the period for losses on loans and advances and the amount of the provision at the balance sheet date; and

(d) irrevocable commitments and contingencies and commitments arising from off balance sheet items.

Effective Date

[Not printed]   59

IAS 31: Financial Reporting of Interests in Joint Ventures

IAS 31: Financial Reporting of Interests in Joint Ventures					
Scope 31.1	Definitions 31.2–7			Effective Date 30.50-52	Related Interpre- tation: SIC–13
	Definitions 31.2	Forms of Joint Venture 31.3	Contractual Arrangement 31.4–7		

Jointly Controlled Operations 31.8–12

Jointly Controlled Assets 31.13–18

Jointly Controlled Entities 31.19–38		
Consolidated Financial Statements of a Venturer 31.25–37		
Benchmark Treatment: Proportionate Consolidation 31.25–31	Allowed Alternative Treatment: Equity Method 31.32–34	Separate Financial Statements of a Venturer 31.38
Exceptions to Benchmark and Allowed Alternative Treatments 31.35–37		

Transactions between a Venturer and Joint Venture 31.39–41

Reporting Interests in Joint Ventures in the Financial Statements of an Investor 31.42

Operators of Joint Ventures 31.43–44

Disclosure 31.45–49

Scope

1   *This Standard should be applied in accounting for interests in joint ventures and the reporting of joint venture assets, liabilities, income and expenses in the financial statements of venturers and investors, regardless of the structures or forms under which the joint venture activities take place.*

Definitions

2   ...
A joint venture is a contractual arrangement whereby two or more parties undertake an economic activity which is subject to joint control.
Control is the power to govern the financial and operating policies of an economic activity so as to obtain benefits from it.

Joint control is the contractually agreed sharing of control over an economic activity.

Significant influence is the power to participate in the financial and operating policy decisions of an economic activity but is not control or joint control over those policies.

A *venturer* is a party to a joint venture and has joint control over that joint venture.

An *investor* in a joint venture is a party to a joint venture and does not have joint control over that joint venture.

Proportionate consolidation is a method of accounting and reporting whereby a venturer's share of each of the assets, liabilities, income and expenses of a jointly controlled entity is combined on a line-by-line basis with similar items in the venturer's financial statements or reported as separate line items in the venturer's financial statements.

The *equity method* is a method of accounting and reporting whereby an interest in a jointly controlled entity is initially recorded at cost and adjusted thereafter for the post acquisition change in the venturer's share of net assets of the jointly controlled entity. The income statement reflects the venturer's share of the results of operations of the jointly controlled entity.

Forms of Joint Venture

Joint ventures take many different forms and structures. This Standard identifies three **3** broad types - jointly controlled operations, jointly controlled assets and jointly controlled entities - which are commonly described as, and meet the definition of, joint ventures. The following characteristics are common to all joint ventures:
(a) two or more venturers are bound by a contractual arrangement; and
(b) the contractual arrangement establishes joint control.

Contractual Arrangement

The existence of a contractual arrangement distinguishes interests which involve joint **4** control from investments in associates in which the investor has significant influence (see IAS 28). Activities which have no contractual arrangement to establish joint control are not joint ventures for the purposes of this Standard.

... Whatever its form, the contractual arrangement is usually in writing and deals with **5** such matters as:
(a) the activity, duration and reporting obligations of the joint venture;
(b) the appointment of the board of directors or equivalent governing body of the joint venture and the voting rights of the venturers;
(c) capital contributions by the venturers; and
(d) the sharing by the venturers of the output, income, expenses or results of the joint venture.

The contractual arrangement establishes joint control over the joint venture. Such a **6** requirement ensures that no single venturer is in a position to control unilaterally the activity. The arrangement identifies those decisions in areas essential to the goals of the joint venture which require the consent of all the venturers and those decisions which may require the consent of a specified majority of the venturers.

The contractual arrangement may identify one venturer as the operator or manager **7** of the joint venture. The operator does not control the joint venture but acts within the financial and operating policies which have been agreed by the venturers in accordance with the contractual arrangement and delegated to the operator. If the operator has the power to govern the financial and operating policies of the economic activity, it controls the venture and the venture is a subsidiary of the operator and not a joint venture.

Jointly Controlled Operations

8   The operation of some joint ventures involves the use of the assets and other resources of the venturers rather than the establishment of a corporation, partnership or other entity, or a financial structure that is separate from the venturers themselves. Each venturer uses its own property, plant and equipment and carries its own inventories. It also incurs its own expenses and liabilities and raises its own finance, which represent its own obligations. The joint venture activities may be carried out by the venturer's employees alongside the venturer's similar activities. The joint venture agreement usually provides a means by which the revenue from the sale of the joint product and any expenses incurred in common are shared among the venturers.

9   [Not printed]

10   *In respect of its interests in jointly controlled operations, a venturer should recognise in its separate financial statements and consequently in its consolidated financial statements:*
      (a) the assets that it controls and the liabilities that it incurs; and
      (b) the expenses that it incurs and its share of the income that it earns from the sale of goods or services by the joint venture.

11   Because the assets, liabilities, income and expenses are already recognised in the separate financial statements of the venturer, and consequently in its consolidated financial statements, no adjustments or other consolidation procedures are required in respect of these items when the venturer presents consolidated financial statements.

12   Separate accounting records may not be required for the joint venture itself and financial statements may not be prepared for the joint venture. However, the venturers may prepare management accounts so that they may assess the performance of the joint venture.

Jointly Controlled Assets

13   Some joint ventures involve the joint control, and often the joint ownership, by the venturers of one or more assets contributed to, or acquired for the purpose of, the joint venture and dedicated to the purposes of the joint venture. The assets are used to obtain benefits for the venturers. Each venturer may take a share of the output from the assets and each bears an agreed share of the expenses incurred.

14   These joint ventures do not involve the establishment of a corporation, partnership or other entity, or a financial structure that is separate from the venturers themselves. Each venturer has control over its share of future economic benefits through its share in the jointly controlled asset.

15   [Not printed]

In respect of its interest in jointly controlled assets, a venturer should recognise in **16**
its separate financial statements and consequently in its consolidated financial
statements:
(a) its share of the jointly controlled assets, classified according to the nature of the
    assets;
(b) any liabilities which it has incurred;
(c) its share of any liabilities incurred jointly with the other venturers in relation
    to the joint venture;
(d) any income from the sale or use of its share of the output of the joint venture,
    together with its share of any expenses incurred by the joint venture; and
(e) any expenses which it has incurred in respect of its interest in the joint venture.

[Not printed]   **17–18**

Jointly Controlled Entities

A jointly controlled entity is a joint venture which involves the establishment of a **19**
corporation, partnership or other entity in which each venturer has an interest. The
entity operates in the same way as other enterprises, except that a contractual
arrangement between the venturers establishes joint control over the economic
activity of the entity.

A jointly controlled entity controls the assets of the joint venture, incurs liabilities **20**
and expenses and earns income. It may enter into contracts in its own name and
raise finance for the purposes of the joint venture activity. Each venturer is entitled
to a share of the results of the jointly controlled entity, although some jointly
controlled entities also involve a sharing of the output of the joint venture.

[Not printed]   **21**

Many jointly controlled entities are similar in substance to those joint ventures **22**
referred to as jointly controlled operations or jointly controlled assets. ...

A jointly controlled entity maintains its own accounting records and prepares and **23**
presents financial statements in the same way as other enterprises in conformity with
the appropriate national requirements and IASs.

Each venturer usually contributes cash or other resources to the jointly controlled **24**
entity. These contributions are included in the accounting records of the venturer
and recognised in its separate financial statements as an investment in the jointly
controlled entity.

Consolidated Financial Statements of a Venturer

Benchmark Treatment - Proportionate Consolidation

In its consolidated financial statements, a venturer should report its interest in a **25**
jointly controlled entity using one of the two reporting formats for proportionate
consolidation.

When reporting an interest in a jointly controlled entity in consolidated financial **26**
statements, it is essential that a venturer reflects the substance and economic reality
of the arrangement, rather than the joint venture's particular structure or form. In a

jointly controlled entity, a venturer has control over its share of future economic benefits through its share of the assets and liabilities of the venture. This substance and economic reality is reflected in the consolidated financial statements of the venturer when the venturer reports its interests in the assets, liabilities, income and expenses of the jointly controlled entity by using one of the two reporting formats for proportionate consolidation described in paragraph 28.

27 The application of proportionate consolidation means that the consolidated balance sheet of the venturer includes its share of the assets that it controls jointly and its share of the liabilities for which it is jointly responsible. The consolidated income statement of the venturer includes its share of the income and expenses of the jointly controlled entity. Many of the procedures appropriate for the application of proportionate consolidation are similar to the procedures for the consolidation of investments in subsidiaries, which are set out in IAS 27.

28 Different reporting formats may be used to give effect to proportionate consolidation. The venturer may combine its share of each of the assets, liabilities, income and expenses of the jointly controlled entity with the similar items in its consolidated financial statements on a line-by-line basis. For example, it may combine its share of the jointly controlled entity's inventory with the inventory of the consolidated group and its share of the jointly controlled entity's property, plant and equipment with the same items of the consolidated group. Alternatively, the venturer may include separate line items for its share of the assets, liabilities, income and expenses of the jointly controlled entity in its consolidated financial statements. For example, it may show its share of the current assets of the jointly controlled entity separately as part of the current assets of the consolidated group; it may show its share of the property, plant and equipment of the jointly controlled entity separately as part of the property, plant and equipment of the consolidated group. Both these reporting formats result in the reporting of identical amounts of net income and of each major classification of assets, liabilities, income and expenses; both formats are acceptable for the purposes of this Standard.

29 Whatever format is used to give effect to proportionate consolidation, it is inappropriate to offset any assets or liabilities by the deduction of other liabilities or assets or any income or expenses by the deduction of other expenses or income, unless a legal right of set-off exists and the offsetting represents the expectation as to the realisation of the asset or the settlement of the liability.

30 *A venturer should discontinue the use of proportionate consolidation from the date on which it ceases to have joint control over a jointly controlled entity.*

31 [Not printed]

Allowed Alternative Treatment - Equity Method

32 *In its consolidated financial statements, a venturer should report its interest in a jointly controlled entity using the equity method.*

33 ... The use of the equity method is supported by those who argue that it is inappropriate to combine controlled items with jointly controlled items and by those who believe that venturers have significant influence, rather than joint control, in a jointly controlled entity. This Standard does not recommend the use of the equity method because proportionate consolidation better reflects the substance and economic reality of a venturer's interest in a jointly controlled entity, that is control

over the venturer's share of the future economic benefits. Nevertheless, this Standard permits the use of the equity method, as an allowed alternative treatment, when reporting interests in jointly controlled entities.

A venturer should discontinue the use of the equity method from the date on which   **34** *it ceases to have joint control over, or have significant influence in, a jointly controlled entity.*

Exceptions to Benchmark and Allowed Alternative Treatments

A venturer should account for the following interests in accordance with IAS 39:   **35**
(a) an interest in a jointly controlled entity which is acquired and held exclusively with a view to its subsequent disposal in the near future; and
(b) an interest in a jointly controlled entity which operates under severe long-term restrictions that significantly impair its ability to transfer funds to the venturer.

[Not printed]   **36**

From the date on which a jointly controlled entity becomes a subsidiary of a   **37** *venturer, the venturer accounts for its interest in accordance with IAS 27.*

Separate Financial Statements of a Venturer

In many countries separate financial statements are presented by a venturer in order   **38** to meet legal or other requirements. ... Accordingly, this Standard does not indicate a preference for any particular treatment.

Transactions between a Venturer and a Joint Venture

When a venturer contributes or sells assets to a joint venture, recognition of any   **39** *portion of a gain or loss from the transaction should reflect the substance of the transaction. While the assets are retained by the joint venture, and provided the venturer has transferred the significant risks and rewards of ownership, the venturer should recognise only that portion of the gain or loss which is attributable to the interests of the other venturers. The venturer should recognise the full amount of any loss when the contribution or sale provides evidence of a reduction in the net realisable value of current assets or an impairment loss.*

When a venturer purchases assets from a joint venture, the venturer should not   **40** *recognise its share of the profits of the joint venture from the transaction until it resells the assets to an independent party. A venturer should recognise its share of the losses resulting from these transactions in the same way as profits except that losses should be recognised immediately when they represent a reduction in the net realisable value of current assets or an impairment loss.*

To assess whether a transaction between a venturer and a joint venture provides   **41** evidence of impairment of an asset, the venturer determines the recoverable amount of the asset under IAS 36. In determining value in use, future cash flows from the asset are estimated based on continuing use of the asset and its ultimate disposal by the joint venture.

Reporting Interests in Joint Ventures in the Financial Statements of an Investor

42 *An investor in a joint venture, which does not have joint control, should report its interest in a joint venture in its consolidated financial statements in accordance with IAS 39 or, if it has significant influence in the joint venture, in accordance with IAS 28. In the separate financial statements of an investor that issues consolidated financial statements, it may also report the investment at cost.*

Operators of Joint Ventures

43 *Operators or managers of a joint venture should account for any fees in accordance with IAS 18.*

44 ... The fees are accounted for by the joint venture as an expense.

Disclosure

45 *A venturer should disclose the aggregate amount of the following contingent liabilities, unless the probability of loss is remote, separately from the amount of other contingent liabilities:*
   (a) *any contingent liabilities that the venturer has incurred in relation to its interests in joint ventures and its share in each of the contingent liabilities which have been incurred jointly with other venturers;*
   (b) *its share of the contingent liabilities of the joint ventures themselves for which it is contingently liable; and*
   (c) *those contingent liabilities that arise because the venturer is contingently liable for the liabilities of the other venturers of a joint venture.*

46 *A venturer should disclose the aggregate amount of the following commitments in respect of its interests in joint ventures separately from other commitments:*
   (a) *any capital commitments of the venturer in relation to its interests in joint ventures and its share in the capital commitments that have been incurred jointly with other venturers; and*
   (b) *its share of the capital commitments of the joint ventures themselves.*

47 *A venturer should disclose a listing and description of interests in significant joint ventures and the proportion of ownership interest held in jointly controlled entities. A venturer which reports its interests in jointly controlled entities using the line-by-line reporting format for proportionate consolidation or the equity method should disclose the aggregate amounts of each of current assets, long-term assets, current liabilities, long-term liabilities, income and expenses related to its interests in joint ventures.*

48 *A venturer which does not issue consolidated financial statements, because it does not have subsidiaries, should disclose the information required in paragraphs 45, 46 and 47.*

IAS 32: Financial Instruments: Disclosure and Presentation

IAS 32: Financial Instruments: Disclosure and Presentation				
Scope 32.1–4	Definitions 32.5–17	Transitional Provision 32.95	Effective Date 32.96	Related Interpretations: SIC–5, 16, 17

Presentation 32.18–41			
Liabilities and Equity 32.18–22	Classification of Compound Instruments by the Issuer 32.23–29	Interest, Dividends,Losses and Gains 32.30–32	Offsetting of a Financial Asset and a Financial Liability 32.33–41

Disclosure 32.42–94						
Disclosure of Risk Management Policies 32.43A	Terms, Conditions and Accounting Policies 32.47–55	Interest Rate Risk 32.56–65	Credit Risk 32.66–76	Fair Value 32.77–87	Financial Assets Carried at an Amount in Excess of Fair Value 32.88–90	Other Disclosures 32.94

Appendix - Examples of the Application of the Standard [Not printed]

Scope

1 *This Standard should be applied in presenting and disclosing information about all types of financial instruments, both recognised and unrecognised, other than:*
   (a) interests in subsidiaries, as defined in IAS 27;
   (b) interests in associates, as defined in IAS 28;
   (c) interests in joint ventures, as defined in IAS 31;
   (d) employers' and plans' obligations for post–employment benefits of all types, including employee benefit plans as described in IAS 19 and IAS 26;
   (e) employers' obligations under employee stock option and stock purchase plans as described in IAS 19; and
   (f) obligations arising under insurance contracts.

2 Although this Standard does not apply to an enterprise's interests in subsidiaries, it does apply to all financial instruments included in the consolidated financial statements of a parent, regardless of whether those instruments are held or issued by the parent or by

a subsidiary. Similarly, the Standard applies to financial instruments held or issued by a joint venture and included in the financial statements of a venturer either directly or through proportionate consolidation.

[Not printed]   3–4

Definitions

...   5

A *financial instrument* is any contract that gives rise to both a financial asset of one enterprise and a financial liability or equity instrument of another enterprise.

Commodity-based contracts that give either party the right to settle in cash or some other financial instrument should be accounted for as if they were financial instruments, with the exception of commodity contracts that (a) were entered into and continue to meet the enterprise's expected purchase, sale, or usage requirements, (b) were designated for that purpose at their inception, and (c) are expected to be settled by delivery.

A *financial asset* is any asset that is:

(a) cash;

(b) a contractual right to receive cash or another financial asset from another enterprise;

(c) a contractual right to exchange financial instruments with another enterprise under conditions that are potentially favourable; or

(d) an equity instrument of another enterprise.

A *financial liability* is any liability that is a contractual obligation:

(a) to deliver cash or another financial asset to another enterprise; or

(b) to exchange financial instruments with another enterprise under conditions that are potentially unfavourable.

An enterprise may have a contractual obligation that it can settle either by payment of financial assets or by payment in the form of its own equity securities. In such a case, if the number of equity securities required to settle the obligation varies with changes in their fair value so that the total fair value of the equity securities paid always equals the amount of the contractual obligation, the holder of the obligation is not exposed to gain or loss from fluctuations in the price of its equity securities. Such an obligation should be accounted for as a financial liability of the enterprise.

An *equity instrument* is any contract that evidences a residual interest in the assets of an enterprise after deducting all of its liabilities.

Monetary financial assets and financial liabilities (also referred to as monetary financial instruments) are financial assets and financial liabilities to be received or paid in fixed or determinable amounts of money.

Fair value is the amount for which an asset could be exchanged, or a liability settled, between knowledgeable, willing parties in an arm's length transaction.

Market value is the amount obtainable from the sale, or payable on the acquisition, of a financial instrument in an active market.

In this Standard, the terms "contract" and "contractual" refer to an agreement between   6 two or more parties that has clear economic consequences that the parties have little, if any, discretion to avoid, usually because the agreement is enforceable at law. Contracts, and thus financial instruments, may take a variety of forms and need not be in writing.

7   For purposes of the definitions in paragraph 5, the term "enterprise" includes individuals, partnerships, incorporated bodies and government agencies.

8   [Not printed]

9   Financial instruments include both primary instruments, such as receivables, payables and equity securities, and derivative instruments, such as financial options, futures and forwards, interest rate swaps and currency swaps. Derivative financial instruments, whether recognised or unrecognised, meet the definition of a financial instrument and, accordingly, are subject to this Standard.

10–11   [Not printed]

12   Assets, such as prepaid expenses, for which the future economic benefit is the receipt of goods or services rather than the right to receive cash or another financial asset are not financial assets. Similarly, items such as deferred revenue and most warranty obligations are not financial liabilities because the probable outflow of economic benefits associated with them is the delivery of goods and services rather than cash or another financial asset.

13–14   [Not printed]

15   ... A contingent right and obligation meet the definition of a financial asset and a financial liability, even though many such assets and liabilities do not qualify for recognition in financial statements.

16   An obligation of an enterprise to issue or deliver its own equity instruments, such as a share option or warrant, is itself an equity instrument, not a financial liability, since the enterprise is not obliged to deliver cash or another financial asset. Similarly, the cost incurred by an enterprise to purchase a right to re-acquire its own equity instruments from another party is a deduction from its equity, not a financial asset.

17   The minority interest that may arise on an enterprise's balance sheet from consolidating a subsidiary is not a financial liability or an equity instrument of the enterprise. ...

Presentation

Liabilities and Equity

18   *The issuer of a financial instrument should classify the instrument, or its component parts, as a liability or as equity in accordance with the substance of the contractual arrangement on initial recognition and the definitions of a financial liability and an equity instrument.*

19   The substance of a financial instrument, rather than its legal form, governs its classification on the issuer's balance sheet. While substance and legal form are commonly consistent, this is not always the case. ... That classification continues at each subsequent reporting date until the financial instrument is removed from the enterprise's balance sheet.

20   The critical feature in differentiating a financial liability from an equity instrument is the existence of a contractual obligation on one party to the financial instrument (the issuer) either to deliver cash or another financial asset to the other party (the holder) or to exchange another financial instrument with the holder under conditions that are potentially unfavourable to the issuer. When such a contractual obligation exists, that

instrument meets the definition of a financial liability regardless of the manner in which the contractual obligation will be settled. ...

When a financial instrument does not give rise to a contractual obligation on the part **21** of the issuer to deliver cash or another financial asset or to exchange another financial instrument under conditions that are potentially unfavourable, it is an equity instrument. Although the holder of an equity instrument may be entitled to receive a pro rata share of any dividends or other distributions out of equity, the issuer does not have a contractual obligation to make such distributions.

When a preferred share provides for mandatory redemption by the issuer for a fixed or **22** determinable amount at a fixed or determinable future date or gives the holder the right to require the issuer to redeem the share at or after a particular date for a fixed or determinable amount, the instrument meets the definition of a financial liability and is classified as such. ...

Classification of Compound Instruments by the Issuer

The issuer of a financial instrument that contains both a liability and an equity **23** *element should classify the instrument's component parts separately in accordance with paragraph 18.*

[Not printed] **24**

For purposes of balance sheet presentation, an issuer recognises separately the **25** component parts of a financial instrument that creates a primary financial liability of the issuer and grants an option to the holder of the instrument to convert it into an equity instrument of the issuer. ...

Classification of the liability and equity components of a convertible instrument is not **26** revised as a result of a change in the likelihood that a conversion option will be exercised, even when exercise of the option may appear to have become economically advantageous to some holders. ...

A financial instrument may contain components that are neither financial liabilities nor **27** equity instruments of the issuer. ... The issuer recognises and presents the equity instrument (the exchange option) separately from the liability components of the compound instrument, whether the liabilities are financial or non-financial.

This Standard does not deal with measurement of financial assets, financial liabilities **28** and equity instruments and does not therefore prescribe any particular method for assigning a carrying amount to liability and equity elements contained in a single instrument. Approaches that might be followed include:
(a) assigning to the less easily measurable component (often an equity instrument), the residual amount after deducting from the instrument as a whole the amount separately determined for the component that is more easily measurable; and
(b) measuring the liability and equity components separately and, to the extent necessary, adjusting these amounts on a pro rata basis so that the sum of the components equals the amount of the instrument as a whole.
The sum of the carrying amounts assigned to the liability and equity components on initial recognition is always equal to the carrying amount that would be ascribed to the instrument as a whole. No gain or loss arises from recognising and presenting the components of the instrument separately.

29 [Not printed]

Interest, Dividends, Losses and Gains

30 *Interest, dividends, losses and gains relating to a financial instrument, or a component part, classified as a financial liability should be reported in the income statement as expense or income. Distributions to holders of a financial instrument classified as an equity instrument should be debited by the issuer directly to equity.*

31 [Not printed]

32 Dividends classified as an expense may be presented in the income statement either with interest on other liabilities or as a separate item. Disclosure of interest and dividends is subject to the requirements of IAS 1, IAS 30 and IAS 39. In some circumstances, because of significant differences between interest and dividends with respect to matters such as tax deductibility, it is desirable to disclose them separately within the income statement. Disclosures of the amounts of tax effects are made in accordance with IAS 12.

Offsetting of a Financial Asset and a Financial Liability

33 *A financial asset and a financial liability should be offset and the net amount reported in the balance sheet when an enterprise:*
(a) has a legally enforceable right to set off the recognised amounts; and
(b) intends either to settle on a net basis, or to realise the asset and settle the liability simultaneously.

34–39 [Not printed]

40 The conditions set out in paragraph 33 are generally not satisfied and offsetting is usually inappropriate when:
(a) several different financial instruments are used to emulate the features of a single financial instrument (i.e. a "synthetic instrument");
(b) financial assets and financial liabilities arise from financial instruments having the same primary risk exposure (...) but involve different counterparties;
(c) financial or other assets are pledged as collateral for non-recourse financial liabilities;
(d) financial assets are set aside in trust by a debtor for the purpose of discharging an obligation without those assets having been accepted by the creditor in settlement of the obligation (...); or
(e) obligations incurred as a result of events giving rise to losses are expected to be recovered from a third party by virtue of a claim made under an insurance policy.

41 An enterprise that undertakes a number of financial instrument transactions with a single counterparty may enter into a "master netting arrangement" with that counterparty. Such an agreement provides for a single net settlement of all financial instruments covered by the agreement in the event of default on, or termination of, any one contract. These arrangements are commonly used by financial institutions to provide protection against loss in the event of bankruptcy or other events that result in a counterparty being unable to meet its obligations. A master netting arrangement commonly creates a right of set-off that becomes enforceable and affects the realisation or settlement of individual financial assets and financial liabilities only following a specified event of default or in other circumstances not expected to arise in the normal course of business. A master netting arrangement does not provide a basis for offsetting unless both of the criteria in paragraph 33 are satisfied. When financial assets and financial liabilities subject to a master netting arrangement are not offset, the effect of the arrangement on an enterprise's exposure to credit risk is disclosed in accordance with paragraph 66.

Disclosure

[Not printed] **42**

Transactions in financial instruments may result in an enterprise's assuming or **43** transferring to another party one or more of the financial risks described below. The required disclosures provide information that assists users of financial statements in assessing the extent of risk related to both recognised and unrecognised financial instruments.

(a) Price risk — There are three types of price risk: currency risk, interest rate risk and market risk.

    (i) Currency risk is the risk that the value of a financial instrument will fluctuate due to changes in foreign exchange rates.

    (ii) Interest rate risk is the risk that the value of a financial instrument will fluctuate due to changes in market interest rates.

    (iii) Market risk is the risk that the value of a financial instrument will fluctuate as a result of changes in market prices whether those changes are caused by factors specific to the individual security or its issuer or factors affecting all securities traded in the market.

The term "price risk" embodies not only the potential for loss but also the potential for gain.

(b) Credit risk — Credit risk is the risk that one party to a financial instrument will fail to discharge an obligation and cause the other party to incur a financial loss.

(c) Liquidity risk — Liquidity risk, also referred to as funding risk, is the risk that an enterprise will encounter difficulty in raising funds to meet commitments associated with financial instruments. Liquidity risk may result from an inability to sell a financial asset quickly at close to its fair value.

(d) Cash flow risk — Cash flow risk is the risk that future cash flows associated with a monetary financial instrument will fluctuate in amount. In the case of a floating rate debt instrument, for example, such fluctuations result in a change in the effective interest rate of the financial instrument, usually without a corresponding change in its fair value.

Disclosure of Risk Management Policies

An enterprise should describe its financial risk management objectives and policies, **43A** *including its policy for hedging each major type of forecasted transaction for which hedge accounting is used.*

The standards do not prescribe either the format of the information required to be **44** disclosed or its location within the financial statements. With regard to recognised financial instruments, to the extent that the required information is presented on the face of the balance sheet, it is not necessary for it to be repeated in the notes to the financial statements. With regard to unrecognised financial instruments, however, information in notes or supplementary schedules is the primary means of disclosure.

Disclosures may include a combination of narrative descriptions and specific quantified data, as appropriate to the nature of the instruments and their relative significance to the enterprise.

45 Determination of the level of detail to be disclosed about particular financial instruments is a matter for the exercise of judgement taking into account the relative significance of those instruments. It is necessary to strike a balance between overburdening financial statements with excessive detail that may not assist users of financial statements and obscuring significant information as a result of too much aggregation. ...

46 Management of an enterprise groups financial instruments into classes that are appropriate to the nature of the information to be disclosed, taking into account matters such as the characteristics of the instruments, whether they are recognised or unrecognised and, if they are recognised, the measurement basis that has been applied. In general, classes are determined on a basis that distinguishes items carried on a cost basis from items carried at fair value. When amounts disclosed in notes or supplementary schedules relate to recognised assets and liabilities, sufficient information is provided to permit a reconciliation to relevant line items on the balance sheet. When an enterprise is a party to financial instruments not dealt with by this Standard, ... these instruments constitute a class or classes of financial assets or financial liabilities disclosed separately from those dealt with by this Standard.

Terms, Conditions and Accounting Policies

47 *For each class of financial asset, financial liability and equity instrument, both recognised and unrecognised, an enterprise should disclose:*
   (a) information about the extent and nature of the financial instruments, including significant terms and conditions that may affect the amount, timing and certainty of future cash flows; and
   (b) the accounting policies and methods adopted, including the criteria for recognition and the basis of measurement applied.

48 The contractual terms and conditions of a financial instrument are an important factor affecting the amount, timing and certainty of future cash receipts and payments by the parties to the instrument. When recognised and unrecognised instruments are important, either individually or as a class, in relation to the current financial position of an enterprise or its future operating results, their terms and conditions are disclosed. If no single instrument is individually significant to the future cash flows of a particular enterprise, the essential characteristics of the instruments are described by reference to appropriate groupings of like instruments.

49 When financial instruments held or issued by an enterprise, either individually or as a class, create a potentially significant exposure to the risks described in paragraph 43, terms and conditions that may warrant disclosure include:
   (a) the principal, stated, face or other similar amount which, for some derivative instruments, such as interest rate swaps, may be the amount (referred to as the notional amount) on which future payments are based;
   (b) the date of maturity, expiry or execution;
   (c) early settlement options held by either party to the instrument, including the period in which, or date at which, the options may be exercised and the exercise price or range of prices;

(d) options held by either party to the instrument to convert the instrument into, or exchange it for, another financial instrument or some other asset or liability, including the period in which, or date at which, the options may be exercised and the conversion or exchange ratio(s);

(e) the amount and timing of scheduled future cash receipts or payments of the principal amount of the instrument, including instalment repayments and any sinking fund or similar requirements;

(f) stated rate or amount of interest, dividend or other periodic return on principal and the timing of payments;

(g) collateral held, in the case of a financial asset, or pledged, in the case of a financial liability;

(h) in the case of an instrument for which cash flows are denominated in a currency other than the enterprise's reporting currency, the currency in which receipts or payments are required;

(i) in the case of an instrument that provides for an exchange, information described in items (a) to (h) for the instrument to be acquired in the exchange; and

(j) any condition of the instrument or an associated covenant that, if contravened, would significantly alter any of the other terms (for example, a maximum debt-to-equity ratio in a bond covenant that, if contravened, would make the full principal amount of the bond due and payable immediately).

When the balance sheet presentation of a financial instrument differs from the **50** instrument's legal form, it is desirable for an enterprise to explain in the notes to the financial statements the nature of the instrument.

[Not printed]   **51**

In accordance with IAS 1 an enterprise provides clear and concise disclosure of all **52** significant accounting policies, including both the general principles adopted and the method of applying those principles to significant transactions and circumstances arising in the enterprise's business. In the case of financial instruments, such disclosure includes:

(a) the criteria applied in determining when to recognise a financial asset or financial liability on the balance sheet and when to cease to recognise it;

(b) the basis of measurement applied to financial assets and financial liabilities both on initial recognition and subsequently; and

(c) the basis on which income and expense arising from financial assets and financial liabilities is recognised and measured.

Types of transactions for which it may be necessary to disclose the relevant accounting **53** policies include:

(a) transfers of financial assets when there is a continuing interest in, or involvement with, the assets by the transferor, such as securitisations of financial assets, repurchase agreements and reverse repurchase agreements;

(b) transfers of financial assets to a trust for the purpose of satisfying liabilities when they mature without the obligation of the transferor being discharged at the time of the transfer, such as an in-substance defeasance trust;

(c) acquisition or issuance of separate financial instruments as part of a series of transactions designed to synthesise the effect of acquiring or issuing a single instrument;

(d) acquisition or issuance of financial instruments as hedges of risk exposures; and

(e) acquisition or issuance of monetary financial instruments bearing a stated interest rate that differs from the prevailing market rate at the date of issue.

54 To provide adequate information for users of financial statements to understand the basis on which financial assets and financial liabilities have been measured, disclosures of accounting policies indicate not only whether cost, fair value or some other basis of measurement has been applied to a specific class of asset or liability but also the method of applying that basis. For example, for financial instruments carried on the cost basis, an enterprise may be required to disclose how it accounts for:

(a) costs of acquisition or issuance;

(b) premiums and discounts on monetary financial assets and financial liabilities;

(c) changes in the estimated amount of determinable future cash flows associated with a monetary financial instrument such as a bond indexed to a commodity price;

(d) changes in circumstances that result in significant uncertainty about the timely collection of all contractual amounts due from monetary financial assets;

(e) declines in the fair value of financial assets below their carrying amount; and

(f) restructured financial liabilities.

For financial assets and financial liabilities carried at fair value, an enterprise indicates whether carrying amounts are determined from quoted market prices, independent appraisals, discounted cash flow analysis or another appropriate method, and discloses any significant assumptions made in applying those methods.

55 An enterprise discloses the basis for reporting in the income statement realised and unrealised gains and losses, interest and other items of income and expense associated with financial assets and financial liabilities. This disclosure includes information about the basis on which income and expense arising from financial instruments held for hedging purposes are recognised. When an enterprise presents income and expense items on a net basis even though the corresponding financial assets and financial liabilities on the balance sheet have not been offset, the reason for that presentation is disclosed if the effect is significant.

Interest Rate Risk

56 *For each class of financial asset and financial liability, both recognised and unrecognised, an enterprise should disclose information about its exposure to interest rate risk, including:*

(a) contractual repricing or maturity dates, whichever dates are earlier; and

(b) effective interest rates, when applicable.

57 An enterprise provides information concerning its exposure to the effects of future changes in the prevailing level of interest rates. Changes in market interest rates have a direct effect on the contractually determined cash flows associated with some financial assets and financial liabilities (cash flow risk) and on the fair value of others (price risk).

58 [Not printed]

59 To supplement the information about contractual repricing and maturity dates, an enterprise may elect to disclose information about expected repricing or maturity dates when those dates differ significantly from the contractual dates. Such information may be particularly relevant when, for example, an enterprise is able to predict, with reasonable reliability, the amount of fixed rate mortgage loans that will be repaid prior to maturity and it uses this data as the basis for managing its interest rate risk exposure. The additional information includes disclosure of the fact that it is based on management's expectations of future events and explains the assumptions made about repricing or maturity dates and how those assumptions differ from the contractual dates.

An enterprise indicates which of its financial assets and financial liabilities are: **60**
(a) exposed to interest rate price risk, such as monetary financial assets and financial liabilities with a fixed interest rate;
(b) exposed to interest rate cash flow risk, such as monetary financial assets and financial liabilities with a floating interest rate that is reset as market rates change; and
(c) not exposed to interest rate risk, such as some investments in equity securities.

The effective interest rate (effective yield) of a monetary financial instrument is the rate **61** that, when used in a present value calculation, results in the carrying amount of the instrument. The present value calculation applies the interest rate to the stream of future cash receipts or payments from the reporting date to the next repricing (maturity) date and to the expected carrying amount (principal amount) at that date. The rate is a historical rate for a fixed rate instrument carried at amortised cost and a current market rate for a floating rate instrument or an instrument carried at fair value. The effective interest rate is sometimes termed the level yield to maturity or to the next repricing date, and is the internal rate of return of the instrument for that period.

[Not printed] **62–63**

The nature of an enterprise's business and the extent of its activity in financial **64** instruments will determine whether information about interest rate risk is presented in narrative form, in tables, or by using a combination of the two. When an enterprise has a significant number of financial instruments exposed to interest rate price or cash flow risks, it may adopt one or more of the following approaches to presenting information.
(a) The carrying amounts of financial instruments exposed to interest rate price risk may be presented in tabular form, grouped by those that are contracted to mature or be repriced:
    (i) within one year of the balance sheet date;
    (ii) more than one year and less than five years from the balance sheet date; and
    (iii) five years or more from the balance sheet date.
(b) When the performance of an enterprise is significantly affected by the level of its exposure to interest rate price risk or changes in that exposure, more detailed information is desirable. An enterprise such as a bank may disclose, for example, separate groupings of the carrying amounts of financial instruments contracted to mature or be repriced:
    (i) within one month of the balance sheet date;
    (ii) more than one and less than three months from the balance sheet date; and
    (iii) more than three and less than twelve months from the balance sheet date.
(c) Similarly, an enterprise may indicate its exposure to interest rate cash flow risk through a table indicating the aggregate carrying amount of groups of floating rate financial assets and financial liabilities maturing within various future time periods.
(d) Interest rate information may be disclosed for individual financial instruments or weighted average rates or a range of rates may be presented for each class of financial instrument. An enterprise groups instruments denominated in different

currencies or having substantially different credit risks into separate classes when these factors result in instruments having substantially different effective interest rates.

65 [Not printed]

Credit Risk

66 *For each class of financial asset, both recognised and unrecognised, an enterprise should disclose information about its exposure to credit risk, including:*
(a) *the amount that best represents its maximum credit risk exposure at the balance sheet date, without taking account of the fair value of any collateral, in the event other parties fail to perform their obligations under financial instruments; and*
(b) *significant concentrations of credit risk.*

67 [Not printed]

68 The purposes of disclosing amounts exposed to credit risk without regard to potential recoveries from realisation of collateral ("an enterprise's maximum credit risk exposure") are:
(a) to provide users of financial statements with a consistent measure of the amount exposed to credit risk for both recognised and unrecognised financial assets; and
(b) to take into account the possibility that the maximum exposure to loss may differ from the carrying amount of a recognised financial asset or the fair value of an unrecognised financial asset that is otherwise disclosed in the financial statements.

69 In the case of recognised financial assets exposed to credit risk, the carrying amount of the assets in the balance sheet, net of any applicable provisions for loss, usually represents the amount exposed to credit risk. ...

70 A financial asset subject to a legally enforceable right of set-off against a financial liability is not presented on the balance sheet net of the liability unless settlement is intended to take place on a net basis or simultaneously. Nevertheless, an enterprise discloses the existence of the legal right of set-off when providing information in accordance with paragraph 66. ... To inform financial statement users of the extent to which exposure to credit risk at a particular point in time has been reduced, the enterprise discloses the existence and effect of the right of set-off when the financial asset is expected to be collected in accordance with its terms. When the financial liability against which a right of set-off exists is due to be settled before the financial asset, the enterprise is exposed to credit risk on the full carrying amount of the asset if the counterparty defaults after the liability has been settled.

71 An enterprise may have entered into one or more master netting arrangements that serve to mitigate its exposure to credit loss but do not meet the criteria for offsetting. When a master netting arrangement significantly reduces the credit risk associated with financial assets not offset against financial liabilities with the same counterparty, an enterprise provides additional information concerning the effect of the arrangement. Such disclosure indicates that:
(a) the credit risk associated with financial assets subject to a master netting arrangement is eliminated only to the extent that financial liabilities due to the same counterparty will be settled after the assets are realised; and
(b) the extent to which an enterprise's overall exposure to credit risk is reduced through a master netting arrangement may change substantially within a short period

following the balance sheet date because the exposure is affected by each transaction subject to the arrangement.

It is also desirable for an enterprise to disclose the terms of its master netting arrangements that determine the extent of the reduction in its credit risk.

[Not printed] **72**

Guaranteeing an obligation of another party exposes the guarantor to credit risk that **73** would be taken into account in making the disclosures required by paragraph 66. ...

Concentrations of credit risk are disclosed when they are not apparent from other **74** disclosures about the nature and financial position of the business and they result in a significant exposure to loss in the event of default by other parties. Identification of significant concentrations is a matter for the exercise of judgement by management taking into account the circumstances of the enterprise and its debtors. IAS 14 provides useful guidance in identifying industry and geographic segments within which credit risk concentrations may arise.

[Not printed] **75**

Disclosure of concentrations of credit risk includes a description of the shared **76** characteristic that identifies each concentration and the amount of the maximum credit risk exposure associated with all recognised and unrecognised financial assets sharing that characteristic.

Fair Value

For each class of financial asset and financial liability, both recognised and **77** *unrecognised, an enterprise should disclose information about fair value. When it is not practicable within constraints of timeliness or cost to determine the fair value of a financial asset or financial liability with sufficient reliability, that fact should be disclosed together with information about the principal characteristics of the underlying financial instrument that are pertinent to its fair value.*

[Not printed] **78**

The fair value of a financial asset or financial liability may be determined by one of **79** several generally accepted methods. Disclosure of fair value information includes disclosure of the method adopted and any significant assumptions made in its application.

Underlying the definition of fair value is a presumption that an enterprise is a going **80** concern without any intention or need to liquidate, curtail materially the scale of its operations or undertake a transaction on adverse terms. Fair value is not, therefore, the amount that an enterprise would receive or pay in a forced transaction, involuntary liquidation or distress sale. However, an enterprise takes its current circumstances into account in determining the fair values of its financial assets and financial liabilities. ...

When a financial instrument is traded in an active and liquid market, its quoted market **81** price provides the best evidence of fair value. The appropriate quoted market price for an asset held or liability to be issued is usually the current bid price and, for an asset to be acquired or liability held, the current offer or asking price. When current bid and offer prices are unavailable, the price of the most recent transaction may provide evidence of the current fair value provided that there has not been a significant change in economic circumstances between the transaction date and the reporting date. When an enterprise has matching asset and liability positions, it may appropriately use mid-market prices as a basis for establishing fair values.

82　When there is infrequent activity in a market, the market is not well established (for example, some "over the counter" markets) or small volumes are traded relative to the number of trading units of a financial instrument to be valued, quoted market prices may not be indicative of the fair value of the instrument. In these circumstances, as well as when a quoted market price is not available, estimation techniques may be used to determine fair value with sufficient reliability to satisfy the requirements of this Standard. Techniques that are well established in financial markets include reference to the current market value of another instrument that is substantially the same, discounted cash flow analysis and option pricing models. In applying discounted cash flow analysis, an enterprise uses a discount rate equal to the prevailing market rate of interest for financial instruments having substantially the same terms and characteristics, including the creditworthiness of the debtor, the remaining term over which the contractual interest rate is fixed, the remaining term to repayment of the principal and the currency in which payments are to be made.

83　The fair value to an enterprise of a financial asset or financial liability, whether determined from market value or otherwise, is determined without deduction for the costs that would be incurred to exchange or settle the underlying financial instrument. The costs may be relatively insignificant for instruments traded in organised, liquid markets but may be substantial for other instruments. Transaction costs may include taxes and duties, fees and commissions paid to agents, advisers, brokers or dealers and levies by regulatory agencies or securities exchanges.

84　When an instrument is not traded in an organised financial market, it may not be appropriate for an enterprise to determine and disclose a single amount that represents an estimate of fair value. Instead, it may be more useful to disclose a range of amounts within which the fair value of a financial instrument is reasonably believed to lie.

85　When disclosure of fair value information is omitted because it is not practicable to determine fair value with sufficient reliability, information is provided to assist users of the financial statements in making their own judgements about the extent of possible differences between the carrying amount of financial assets and financial liabilities and their fair value. In addition to an explanation of the reason for the omission and the principal characteristics of the financial instruments that are pertinent to their value, information is provided about the market for the instruments. ...

86　The historical cost carrying amount of receivables and payables subject to normal trade credit terms usually approximates fair value. Similarly, the fair value of a deposit liability without a specified maturity is the amount payable on demand at the reporting date.

87　Fair value information relating to classes of financial assets or financial liabilities that are carried on the balance sheet at other than fair value is provided in a way that permits comparison between the carrying amount and the fair value. Accordingly, the fair values of recognised financial assets and financial liabilities are grouped into classes and offset only to the extent that their related carrying amounts are offset. Fair values of unrecognised financial assets and financial liabilities are presented in a class or classes separate from recognised items and are offset only to the extent that they meet the offsetting criteria for recognised financial assets and financial liabilities.

Financial Assets Carried at an Amount in Excess of Fair Value

When an enterprise carries one or more financial assets at an amount in excess of **88**
their fair value, the enterprise should disclose:
(a) the carrying amount and the fair value of either the individual assets or
appropriate groupings of those individual assets; and
(b) the reasons for not reducing the carrying amount, including the nature of the
evidence that provides the basis for management's belief that the carrying
amount will be recovered.

[Not printed]   **89–90**

[Deleted]   **91–93**

Other Disclosures

Additional disclosures are encouraged when they are likely to enhance financial **94**
statement users' understanding of financial instruments. It may be desirable to disclose
such information as:
(a) the total amount of the change in the fair value of financial assets and financial
    liabilities that has been recognised as income or expense for the period; and
(b) the average aggregate carrying amount during the year of recognised financial assets
    and financial liabilities, the average aggregate principal, stated, notional or other
    similar amount during the year of unrecognised financial assets and financial
    liabilities and the average aggregate fair value during the year of all financial assets
    and financial liabilities, particularly when the amounts on hand at the balance
    sheet date are unrepresentative of amounts on hand during the year.

Transitional Provision

When comparative information for prior periods is not available when this IAS is first **95**
adopted, such information need not be presented.

Effective Date

[Not printed]   **96**

Appendix

Examples of the Application of the Standard

[Not printed]

IAS 33: Earnings Per Share

IAS 33: Earnings Per Share				
Scope 33.1–5				
Enterprises Whose Shares are Publicly Traded 33.1–3	Enterprises Whose Shares are Not Publicly Traded 33.4–5	Definitions 33.6–9	Effective Date 33.53	Related Interpretation: SIC–24

Measurement 33.10–42				
Basic Earnings Per Share 33.10–23		Diluted Earnings Per Share 33.24–42		
Earnings - Basic 33.11–13	Per Share - Basic 33.14–23	Earnings - Diluted 33.26–28	Per Share - Diluted 33.29–37	Dilutive Potential Ordinary Shares 33.38–42

Restatement 33.43–46

Presentation 33.47–48

Disclosure 33.49–52

Scope

Enterprises Whose Shares are Publicly Traded

1 *This Standard should be applied by enterprises whose ordinary shares or potential ordinary shares are publicly traded and by enterprises that are in the process of issuing ordinary shares or potential ordinary shares in public securities markets.*

2 *When both parent and consolidated financial statements are presented, the information called for by this Standard need be presented only on the basis of consolidated information.*

3 [Not printed]

Enterprises Whose Shares are Not Publicly Traded

4 *An enterprise which has neither ordinary shares nor potential ordinary shares which are publicly traded, but which discloses earnings per share, should calculate and disclose earnings per share in accordance with this Standard.*

5 [Not printed]

Definitions

... **6**

An ordinary share is an equity instrument that is subordinate to all other classes of equity instruments.

A potential ordinary share is a financial instrument or other contract that may entitle its holder to ordinary shares.

Warrants or options are financial instruments that give the holder the right to purchase ordinary shares.

Ordinary shares participate in the net profit for the period only after other types of **7** shares such as preference shares. An enterprise may have more than one class of ordinary shares. Ordinary shares of the same class will have the same rights to receive dividends.

Examples of potential ordinary shares are: **8**
(a) debt or equity instruments, including preference shares, that are convertible into ordinary shares;
(b) share warrants and options;
(c) employee plans that allow employees to receive ordinary shares as part of their remuneration and other share purchase plans; and
(d) shares which would be issued upon the satisfaction of certain conditions resulting from contractual arrangements, such as the purchase of a business or other assets.

The following terms are used with the meanings specified in IAS 32: **9**

A financial instrument is any contract that gives rise to both a financial asset of one enterprise and a financial liability or equity instrument of another enterprise.

An equity instrument is any contract that evidences a residual interest in the assets of an enterprise after deducting all of its liabilities.

Fair value is the amount for which an asset could be exchanged, or a liability settled, between knowledgeable, willing parties in an arm's length transaction.

Measurement

Basic Earnings Per Share

Basic earnings per share should be calculated by dividing the net profit or loss for the **10** *period attributable to ordinary shareholders by the weighted average number of ordinary shares outstanding during the period.*

Earnings - Basic

For the purpose of calculating basic earnings per share, the net profit or loss for the **11** *period attributable to ordinary shareholders should be the net profit or loss for the period after deducting preference dividends.*

All items of income and expense which are recognised in a period, including tax **12** expense, extraordinary items and minority interests, are included in the determination of the net profit or loss for the period (see IAS 8). The amount of net profit attributable to preference shareholders, including preference dividends for the period, is deducted from the net profit for the period (or added to the net loss for the period) in order to calculate the net profit or loss for the period attributable to ordinary shareholders.

13   The amount of preference dividends that is deducted from the net profit for the period is:

(a)   the amount of any preference dividends on non-cumulative preference shares declared in respect of the period; and

(b)   the full amount of the required preference dividends for cumulative preference shares for the period, whether or not the dividends have been declared.   The amount of preference dividends for the period does not include the amount of any preference dividends for cumulative preference shares paid or declared during the current period in respect of previous periods.

Per Share - Basic

14   *For the purpose of calculating basic earnings per share, the number of ordinary shares should be the weighted average number of ordinary shares outstanding during the period.*

15   The weighted average number of ordinary shares outstanding during the period reflects the fact that the amount of shareholders' capital may have varied during the period as a result of a larger or lesser number of shares being outstanding at any time.   It is the number of ordinary shares outstanding at the beginning of the period, adjusted by the number of ordinary shares bought back or issued during the period multiplied by a time-weighting factor.   The time-weighting factor is the number of days that the specific shares are outstanding as a proportion of the total number of days in the period; a reasonable approximation of the weighted average is adequate in many circumstances.   ...

16   In most cases, shares are included in the weighted average number of shares from the date consideration is receivable (which is generally the date of their issue), ...

17   [Not printed]

18   Where ordinary shares are issued in partly paid form, these partly paid shares are treated as a fraction of an ordinary share to the extent that they were entitled to participate in dividends relative to a fully paid ordinary share during the financial period.

19   Ordinary shares which are issuable upon the satisfaction of certain conditions (contingently issuable shares) are considered outstanding, and included in the computation of basic earnings per share from the date when all necessary conditions have been satisfied.   Outstanding ordinary shares that are contingently returnable (that is subject to recall) are treated as contingently issuable shares.

20   *The weighted average number of ordinary shares outstanding during the period and for all periods presented should be adjusted for events, other than the conversion of potential ordinary shares, that have changed the number of ordinary shares outstanding, without a corresponding change in resources.*

21   Ordinary shares may be issued, or the number of shares outstanding may be reduced, without a corresponding change in resources.   Examples include:

(a)   a capitalisation or bonus issue (known in some countries as a stock dividend);

(b)   a bonus element in any other issue, for example a bonus element in a rights issue to existing shareholders;

(c)   a share split; and

(d)   a reverse share split (consolidation of shares).

22   [Not printed]

With reference to 21 (b) above, the issue of ordinary shares at the time of exercise or **23** conversion of potential ordinary shares will not usually give rise to a bonus element, since the potential ordinary shares will usually have been issued for full value, resulting in a proportionate change in the resources available to the enterprise. In a rights issue, the exercise price is often less than the fair value of the shares. Therefore such a rights issue includes a bonus element. The number of ordinary shares to be used in calculating basic earnings per share for all periods prior to the rights issue is the number of ordinary shares outstanding prior to the issue, multiplied by the following factor:

$$\frac{\text{Fair value per share immediately prior to the exercise of rights}}{\text{Theoretical ex-rights fair value per share}}$$

The theoretical ex-rights fair value per share is calculated by adding the aggregate fair value of the shares immediately prior to the exercise of the rights to the proceeds from the exercise of the rights, and dividing by the number of shares outstanding after the exercise of the rights. Where the rights themselves are to be publicly traded separately from the shares prior to the exercise date, fair value for the purposes of this calculation is established at the close of the last day on which the shares are traded together with the rights.

...

Diluted Earnings Per Share

For the purpose of calculating diluted earnings per share, the net profit attributable **24** *to ordinary shareholders and the weighted average number of shares outstanding should be adjusted for the effects of all dilutive potential ordinary shares.*

The calculation of diluted earnings per share is consistent with the calculation of basic **25** earnings per share while giving effect to all dilutive potential ordinary shares that were outstanding during the period, that is:

(a) the net profit for the period attributable to ordinary shares is increased by the after-tax amount of dividends and interest recognised in the period in respect of the dilutive potential ordinary shares and adjusted for any other changes in income or expense that would result from the conversion of the dilutive potential ordinary shares.

(b) the weighted average number of ordinary shares outstanding is increased by the weighted average number of additional ordinary shares which would have been outstanding assuming the conversion of all dilutive potential ordinary shares.

Earnings - Diluted

For the purpose of calculating diluted earnings per share, the amount of net profit or **26** *loss for the period attributable to ordinary shareholders, as calculated in accordance with paragraph 11, should be adjusted by the after-tax effect:*

(a) any dividends on dilutive potential ordinary shares which have been deducted in arriving at the net profit attributable to ordinary shareholders as calculated in accordance with paragraph 11;

(b) interest recognised in the period for the dilutive potential ordinary shares; and

(c) any other changes in income or expense that would result from the conversion of the dilutive potential ordinary shares.

27 After the potential ordinary shares are converted into ordinary shares, the dividends, interest and other income or expense associated with those potential ordinary shares will no longer be incurred. Instead, the new ordinary shares will be entitled to participate in the net profit attributable to ordinary shareholders. Therefore, the net profit for the period attributable to ordinary shareholders calculated in accordance with paragraph 11 is increased by the amount of dividends, interest and other income or expense that will be saved on the conversion of the dilutive potential ordinary shares into ordinary shares. The expenses associated with potential ordinary shares include fees and discount or premium that are accounted for as yield adjustments (see IAS 32). The amounts of dividends, interest and other income or expense are adjusted for any taxes, borne by the enterprise, that are attributable to them.
    ...

28 [Not printed]

Per Share - Diluted

29 *For the purpose of calculating diluted earnings per share, the number of ordinary shares should be the weighted average number of ordinary shares calculated in accordance with paragraphs 14 and 20, plus the weighted average number of ordinary shares which would be issued on the conversion of all the dilutive potential ordinary shares into ordinary shares. Dilutive potential ordinary shares should be deemed to have been converted into ordinary shares at the beginning of the period or, if later, the date of the issue of the potential ordinary shares.*

30 The number of ordinary shares which would be issued on the conversion of dilutive potential ordinary shares is determined from the terms of the potential ordinary shares. The computation assumes the most advantageous conversion rate or exercise price from the standpoint of the holder of the potential ordinary shares.

31 As in the computation of basic earnings per share, ordinary shares whose issue is contingent upon the occurrence of certain events shall be considered outstanding and included in the computation of diluted earnings per share if the conditions have been met (the events occurred). Contingently issuable shares should be included as of the beginning of the period (or as of the date of the contingent share agreement, if later). If the conditions have not been met, the number of contingently issuable shares included in the diluted earnings per share computation is based on the number of shares that would be issuable if the end of the reporting period was the end of the contingency period. Restatement is not permitted if the conditions are not met when the contingency period expires. The provisions of this paragraph apply equally to potential ordinary shares that are issuable upon the satisfaction of certain conditions (contingently issuable potential ordinary shares).

32 [Not printed]

33 *For the purpose of calculating diluted earnings per share, an enterprise should assume the exercise of dilutive options and other dilutive potential ordinary shares of the enterprise. The assumed proceeds from these issues should be considered to have been received from the issue of shares at fair value. The difference between the number of shares issued and the number of shares that would have been issued at fair value should be treated as an issue of ordinary shares for no consideration.*

34 Fair value for this purpose is calculated on the basis of the average price of the ordinary shares during the period.

Options and other share purchase arrangements are dilutive when they would result in **35** the issue of ordinary shares for less than fair value. The amount of the dilution is fair value less the issue price. Therefore, in order to calculate diluted earnings per share, each such arrangement is treated as consisting of:

(a) a contract to issue a certain number of ordinary shares at their average fair value during the period. The shares so to be issued are fairly priced and are assumed to be neither dilutive nor anti-dilutive. They are ignored in the computation of diluted earnings per share; and

(b) a contract to issue the remaining ordinary shares for no consideration. Such ordinary shares generate no proceeds and have no effect on the net profit attributable to ordinary shares outstanding. Therefore such shares are dilutive and they are added to the number of ordinary shares outstanding in the computation of diluted earnings per share.

...

This method of calculating the effect of options and other share purchase arrangements **36** produces the same result as the treasury stock method which is used in some countries. This does not imply that the enterprise has entered into a transaction to purchase its own shares, which may not be practicable in certain circumstances or legal in some jurisdictions.

To the extent that partly paid shares are not entitled to participate in dividends during **37** the financial period they are considered the equivalent of warrants or options.

Dilutive Potential Ordinary Shares

Potential ordinary shares should be treated as dilutive when, and only when, their **38** *conversion to ordinary shares would decrease net profit per share from continuing ordinary operations.*

[Not printed] **39–41**

Potential ordinary shares are weighted for the period they were outstanding. Potential **42** ordinary shares that were cancelled or allowed to lapse during the reporting period are included in the computation of diluted earnings per share only for the portion of the period during which they were outstanding. Potential ordinary shares that have been converted into ordinary shares during the reporting period are included in the calculation of diluted earnings per share from the beginning of the period to the date of conversion; from the date of conversion, the resulting ordinary shares are included in both basic and diluted earnings per share.

Restatement

If the number of ordinary or potential ordinary shares outstanding increases as a **43** *result of a capitalisation or bonus issue or share split or decreases as a result of a reverse share split, the calculation of basic and diluted earnings per share for all periods presented should be adjusted retrospectively. If these changes occur after the balance sheet date but before issue of the financial statements, the per share calculations for those and any prior period financial statements presented should be based on the new number of shares. When per share calculations reflect such changes in the number of shares, that fact should be disclosed. In addition, basic and diluted earnings per share of all periods presented should be adjusted for:*

(a) *the effects of fundamental errors, and adjustments resulting from changes in accounting policies, dealt with in accordance with the benchmark treatment in IAS 8; and*

(b) *the effects of a business combination which is a uniting of interests.*

44 An enterprise does not restate diluted earnings per share of any prior period presented for changes in the assumptions used or for the conversion of potential ordinary shares into ordinary shares outstanding.

45 An enterprise is encouraged to disclose a description of ordinary share transactions or potential ordinary share transactions, other than capitalisation issues and share splits, which occur after the balance sheet date when they are of such importance that non-disclosure would affect the ability of the users of the financial statements to make proper evaluations and decisions (see IAS 10). Examples of such transactions include:
(a) the issue of shares for cash;
(b) the issue of shares when the proceeds are used to repay debt or preference shares outstanding at the balance sheet date;
(c) the redemption of ordinary shares outstanding;
(d) the conversion or exercise of potential ordinary shares, outstanding at the balance sheet date, into ordinary shares;
(e) the issue of warrants, options or convertible securities; and
(f) the achievement of conditions that would result in the issue of contingently issuable shares.

46 Earnings per share amounts are not adjusted for such transactions occurring after the balance sheet date because such transactions do not affect the amount of capital used to produce the net profit or loss for the period.

Presentation

47 *An enterprise should present basic and diluted earnings per share on the face of the income statement for each class of ordinary shares that has a different right to share in the net profit for the period. An enterprise should present basic and diluted earnings per share with equal prominence for all periods presented.*

48 *This Standard requires an enterprise to present basic and diluted earnings per share, even if the amounts disclosed are negative (a loss per share).*

Disclosure

49 *An enterprise should disclose the following:*
(a) *the amounts used as the numerators in calculating basic and diluted earnings per share, and a reconciliation of those amounts to the net profit or loss for the period; and*
(b) *the weighted average number of ordinary shares used as the denominator in calculating basic and diluted earnings per share, and a reconciliation of these denominators to each other.*

50 Financial instruments and other contracts generating potential ordinary shares may incorporate terms and conditions which affect the measurement of basic and diluted earnings per share. These terms and conditions may determine whether or not any potential ordinary shares are dilutive and, if so, the effect on the weighted average number of shares outstanding and any consequent adjustments to the net profit attributable to ordinary shareholders. Whether or not the disclosure of the terms and conditions is required by IAS 32 such disclosure is encouraged by this Standard.

If an enterprise discloses, in addition to basic and diluted earnings per share, per share amounts using a reported component of net profit other than net profit or loss for the period attributable to ordinary shareholders, such amounts should be calculated using the weighted average number of ordinary shares determined in accordance with this Standard. If a component of net profit is used which is not reported as a line item in the income statement, a reconciliation should be provided between the component used and a line item which is reported in the income statement. Basic and diluted per share amounts should be disclosed with equal prominence. 51

[Not printed] 52

Effective Date

[Not printed] 53

IAS 34: Interim Financial Reporting

IAS 34: Interim Financial Reporting		
Scope 34.1–3	Definitions 34.4	Effective Date 34.46

Content of an Interim Financial Report 34.5–25					
Minimum Components 34.8	Form and Content 34.9–14	Selected Explanatory Notes 34.15–18	Disclosure of Compliance with IAS 34.19	Reporting Period 34.20–22	Materiality 34.23–25

Disclosure in Annual Financial Statements 34.26–27

Recognition and Measurement 34.28–42				
Same Accounting Policies as Annual 34.28–36	Revenues Received Seasonally, Cyclically, or Occasionally 34.37–38	Costs Incurred Unevenly during the Financial Year 34.39	Applying the Recognition and Measurement Principles 34.40	Use of Estimates 34.41–42

Restatement of Previously Reported Interim Periods 34.43–45

Appendices [Not printed]		
Illustration of Periods Required to Be Presented	Examples of Applying the Recognition and Measurement Principles	Examples of the Use of Estimates

Scope

1 This Standard does not mandate which enterprises should be required to publish interim financial reports, how frequently, or how soon after the end of an interim period. However, governments, securities regulators, stock exchanges, and accountancy bodies often require enterprises whose debt or equity securities are publicly traded to publish interim financial reports. This Standard applies if an enterprise is required or elects to publish an interim financial report in accordance with IASs. The IASs Committee encourages publicly traded enterprises to provide interim financial reports that conform to the recognition, measurement, and disclosure principles set out in this Standard. Specifically, publicly traded enterprises are encouraged:

(a) to provide interim financial reports at least as of the end of the first half of their financial year; and

(b) to make their interim financial reports available not later than 60 days after the end of the interim period.

2 [Not printed]

If an enterprise's interim financial report is described as complying with IASs, it must **3** comply with all of the requirements of this Standard. Paragraph 19 requires certain disclosures in that regard.

Definitions

... **4**

Interim period is a financial reporting period shorter than a full financial year.
Interim financial report means a financial report containing either a complete set of financial statements (as described in IAS 1) or a set of condensed financial statements (as described in this Standard) for an interim period.

Content of an Interim Financial Report

IAS 1 defines a complete set of financial statements as including the following **5** components:
(a) balance sheet;
(b) income statement;
(c) statement showing either (i) all changes in equity or (ii) changes in equity other than those arising from capital transactions with owners and distributions to owners;
(d) cash flow statement; and
(e) accounting policies and explanatory notes.

[Not printed] **6–7**

Minimum Components of an Interim Financial Report

An interim financial report should include, at a minimum, the following components: **8**

(a) condensed balance sheet;
(b) condensed income statement;
(c) condensed statement showing either (i) all changes in equity or (ii) changes in equity other than those arising from capital transactions with owners and distributions to owners;
(d) condensed cash flow statement; and
(e) selected explanatory notes.

Form and Content of Interim Financial Statements

If an enterprise publishes a complete set of financial statements in its interim **9** *financial report, the form and content of those statements should conform to the requirements of IAS 1 for a complete set of financial statements.*

If an enterprise publishes a set of condensed financial statements in its interim **10** *financial report, those condensed statements should include, at a minimum, each of the headings and subtotals that were included in its most recent annual financial statements and the selected explanatory notes as required by this Standard. Additional line items or notes should be included if their omission would make the condensed interim financial statements misleading.*

11 *Basic and diluted earnings per share should be presented on the face of an income statement, complete or condensed, for an interim period.*

12 IAS 1 provides guidance on the structure of financial statements and includes an appendix, "Illustrative Financial Statement Structure", that provides further guidance on major headings and subtotals.

13 While IAS 1 requires that a statement showing changes in equity be presented as a separate component of an enterprise's financial statements, it permits information about changes in equity arising from capital transactions with owners and distributions to owners to be shown either on the face of the statement or, alternatively, in the notes. An enterprise follows the same format in its interim statement showing changes in equity as it did in its most recent annual statement.

14 An interim financial report is prepared on a consolidated basis if the enterprise's most recent annual financial statements were consolidated statements. The parent's separate financial statements are not consistent or comparable with the consolidated statements in the most recent annual financial report. If an enterprise's annual financial report included the parent's separate financial statements in addition to consolidated financial statements, this Standard neither requires nor prohibits the inclusion of the parent's separate statements in the enterprise's interim financial report.

Selected Explanatory Notes

15 [Not printed]

16 *An enterprise should include the following information, as a minimum, in the notes to its interim financial statements, if material and if not disclosed elsewhere in the interim financial report. The information should normally be reported on a financial year-to-date basis. However, the enterprise should also disclose any events or transactions that are material to an understanding of the current interim period:*

(a) a statement that the same accounting policies and methods of computation are followed in the interim financial statements as compared with the most recent annual financial statements or, if those policies or methods have been changed, a description of the nature and effect of the change;

(b) explanatory comments about the seasonality or cyclicality of interim operations;

(c) the nature and amount of items affecting assets, liabilities, equity, net income, or cash flows that are unusual because of their nature, size, or incidence;

(d) the nature and amount of changes in estimates of amounts reported in prior interim periods of the current financial year or changes in estimates of amounts reported in prior financial years, if those changes have a material effect in the current interim period;

(e) issuances, repurchases, and repayments of debt and equity securities;

(f) dividends paid (aggregate or per share) separately for ordinary shares and other shares;

(g) segment revenue and segment result for business segments or geographical segments, whichever is the enterprise's primary basis of segment reporting (disclosure of segment data is required in an enterprise's interim financial report only if IAS 14 requires that enterprise to disclose segment data in its annual financial statements);

(h) material events subsequent to the end of the interim period that have not been reflected in the financial statements for the interim period;

(i) the effect of changes in the composition of the enterprise during the interim period, including business combinations, acquisition or disposal of subsidiaries and long-term investments, restructurings, and discontinuing operations; and

(j) changes in contingent liabilities or contingent assets since the last annual balance sheet date.

Examples of the kinds of disclosures that are required by paragraph 16 are set out below. **17** Individual IASs provide guidance regarding disclosures for many of these items:

(a) the write-down of inventories to net realisable value and the reversal of such a write-down;

(b) recognition of a loss from the impairment of property, plant, and equipment, intangible assets, or other assets, and the reversal of such an impairment loss;

(c) the reversal of any provisions for the costs of restructuring;

(d) acquisitions and disposals of items of property, plant, and equipment;

(e) commitments for the purchase of property, plant, and equipment;

(f) litigation settlements;

(g) corrections of fundamental errors in previously reported financial data;

(h) extraordinary items;

(i) any debt default or any breach of a debt covenant that has not been corrected subsequently; and

(j) related party transactions.

[Not printed]   **18**

Disclosure of Compliance with IAS

If an enterprise's interim financial report is in compliance with this IAS, that fact **19** should be disclosed. An interim financial report should not be described as complying with IASs unless it complies with all of the requirements of each applicable Standard and each applicable Interpretation of the Standing Interpretations Committee.

Periods for which Interim Financial Statements are Required to be Presented

Interim reports should include interim financial statements (condensed or complete) **20** for periods as follows:

(a) balance sheet as of the end of the current interim period and a comparative balance sheet as of the end of the immediately preceding financial year;

(b) income statements for the current interim period and cumulatively for the current financial year to date, with comparative income statements for the comparable interim periods (current and year-to-date) of the immediately preceding financial year;

(c) statement showing changes in equity cumulatively for the current financial year to date, with a comparative statement for the comparable year-to-date period of the immediately preceding financial year; and

(d) cash flow statement cumulatively for the current financial year to date, with a comparative statement for the comparable year-to-date period of the immediately preceding financial year.

For an enterprise whose business is highly seasonal, financial information for the twelve **21** months ending on the interim reporting date and comparative information for the prior twelve-month period may be useful. Accordingly, enterprises whose business is highly seasonal are encouraged to consider reporting such information in addition to the information called for in the preceding paragraph.

22 [Not printed]

Materiality

23 *In deciding how to recognise, measure, classify, or disclose an item for interim financial reporting purposes, materiality should be assessed in relation to the interim period financial data. In making assessments of materiality, it should be recognised that interim measurements may rely on estimates to a greater extent than measurements of annual financial data.*

24 [Not printed]

25 While judgement is always required in assessing materiality for financial reporting purposes, this Standard bases the recognition and disclosure decision on data for the interim period by itself for reasons of understandability of the interim figures. ... The overriding goal is to ensure that an interim financial report includes all information that is relevant to understanding an enterprise's financial position and performance during the interim period.

Disclosure in Annual Financial Statements

26 *If an estimate of an amount reported in an interim period is changed significantly during the final interim period of the financial year but a separate financial report is not published for that final interim period, the nature and amount of that change in estimate should be disclosed in a note to the annual financial statements for that financial year.*

27 [Not printed]

Recognition and Measurement

Same Accounting Policies as Annual

28 *An enterprise should apply the same accounting policies in its interim financial statements as are applied in its annual financial statements, except for accounting policy changes made after the date of the most recent annual financial statements that are to be reflected in the next annual financial statements. However, the frequency of an enterprise's reporting (annual, half-yearly, or quarterly) should not affect the measurement of its annual results. To achieve that objective, measurements for interim reporting purposes should be made on a year-to-date basis.*

29–34 [Not printed]

35 An enterprise that reports half-yearly uses information available by mid-year or shortly thereafter in making the measurements in its financial statements for the first six-month period and information available by year-end or shortly thereafter for the twelve-month period. The twelve-month measurements will reflect possible changes in estimates of amounts reported for the first six-month period. The amounts reported in the interim financial report for the first six-month period are not retrospectively adjusted. Paragraphs 16(d) and 26 require, however, that the nature and amount of any significant changes in estimates be disclosed.

An enterprise that reports more frequently than half-yearly measures income and **36** expenses on a year-to-date basis for each interim period using information available when each set of financial statements is being prepared. Amounts of income and expenses reported in the current interim period will reflect any changes in estimates of amounts reported in prior interim periods of the financial year. The amounts reported in prior interim periods are not retrospectively adjusted. Paragraphs 16(d) and 26 require, however, that the nature and amount of any significant changes in estimates be disclosed.

Revenues Received Seasonally, Cyclically, or Occasionally

Revenues that are received seasonally, cyclically, or occasionally within a financial **37** *year should not be anticipated or deferred as of an interim date if anticipation or deferral would not be appropriate at the end of the enterprise's financial year.*

[Not printed] **38**

Costs Incurred Unevenly During the Financial Year

Costs that are incurred unevenly during an enterprise's financial year should be **39** *anticipated or deferred for interim reporting purposes if, and only if, it is also appropriate to anticipate or defer that type of cost at the end of the financial year.*

Applying the Recognition and Measurement Principles

[Not printed] **40**

Use of Estimates

The measurement procedures to be followed in an interim financial report should be **41** *designed to ensure that the resulting information is reliable and that all material financial information that is relevant to an understanding of the financial position or performance of the enterprise is appropriately disclosed. While measurements in both annual and interim financial reports are often based on reasonable estimates, the preparation of interim financial reports generally will require a greater use of estimation methods than annual financial reports.*

[Not printed] **42**

Restatement of Previously Reported Interim Periods

A change in accounting policy, other than one for which the transition is specified by **43** *a new IAS, should be reflected by:*
(a) restating the financial statements of prior interim periods of the current financial year and the comparable interim periods of prior financial years (see paragraph 20), if the enterprise follows the benchmark treatment under IAS 8; or
(b) restating the financial statements of prior interim periods of the current financial year, if the enterprise follows the allowed alternative treatment under IAS 8. In this case, comparable interim periods of prior financial years are not restated.

44–45 *[Not printed]*

Effective Date

46 *[Not printed]*

Appendix A

Illustration of Periods Required to Be Presented

[Not printed]

Appendix B

Examples of Applying the Recognition and Measurement Principles

[Not printed]

Appendix C

Examples of the Use of Estimates

[Not printed]

IAS 35: Discontinuing Operations

IAS 35: Discontinuing Operations		
Scope 35.1	Definitions 35.2–16	Effective Date 35.49–50

Recognition and Measurement 35.17–26	
Provisions 35.20–21	Impairment Losses 36.22–26

Presentation and Disclosure 35.27–48									
Initial Disclosure 35.27–30	Other Disclosures 35.31–32	Updating Disclosures 35.33–37	Separate Disclosure for Each Discontinuing Operation 35.38	Presentation of the Required Disclosures 35.39–43			Illustrative Disclosures 35.44	Restatement of Prior Periods 35.45–46	Disclosure in Interim Financial Reports 35.47–48
				Face of Financial Statements or Notes 35.39–40	Not an Extraordinary Item 35.41–42	Restricted Use of the Term 'Discontinuing Operation' 35.43			

Appendices [Not printed]	
Illustrative Disclosures	Classification of Prior Period Operations

Scope

This Standard applies to all discontinuing operations of all enterprises. **1**

Definitions

Discontinuing Operation

A *discontinuing operation* is a component of an enterprise: **2**
(a) that the enterprise, pursuant to a single plan, is:
  (i) disposing of substantially in its entirety, such as by selling the component in a single transaction, by demerger or spin-off of ownership of the component to the enterprise's shareholders;
  (ii) disposing of piecemeal, such as by selling off the component's assets and settling its liabilities individually; or
  (iii) terminating through abandonment;
(b) that represents a separate major line of business or geographical area of operations; and
(c) that can be distinguished operationally and for financial reporting purposes.

3–5 [Not printed]

6 An enterprise may terminate an operation by abandonment without substantial sales of assets. An abandoned operation would be a discontinuing operation if it satisfies the criteria in the definition. However, changing the scope of an operation or the manner in which it is conducted is not an abandonment because that operation, although changed, is continuing.

7 [Not printed]

8 Examples of activities that do not necessarily satisfy criterion (a) of paragraph 2, but that might do so in combination with other circumstances, include:
(a) gradual or evolutionary phasing out of a product line or class of service;
(b) discontinuing, even if relatively abruptly, several products within an ongoing line of business;
(c) shifting of some production or marketing activities for a particular line of business from one location to another;
(d) closing of a facility to achieve productivity improvements or other cost savings; and
(e) selling a subsidiary whose activities are similar to those of the parent or other subsidiaries.

9–10 [Not printed]

11 A component can be distinguished operationally and for financial reporting purposes – criterion (c) of the definition (paragraph 2(c)) – if:
(a) its operating assets and liabilities can be directly attributed to it;
(b) its income (gross revenue) can be directly attributed to it; and
(c) at least a majority of its operating expenses can be directly attributed to it.

12 Assets, liabilities, income, and expenses are directly attributable to a component if they would be eliminated when the component is sold, abandoned or otherwise disposed of. Interest and other financing cost is attributed to a discontinuing operation only if the related debt is similarly attributed.

13–14 [Not printed]

15 The fact that a disposal of a component of an enterprise is classified as a discontinuing operation under this Standard does not, in itself, bring into question the enterprise's ability to continue as a going concern. IAS 1 requires disclosure of uncertainties relating to an enterprise's ability to continue as a going concern and of any conclusion that an enterprise is not a going concern.

Initial Disclosure Event

16 *With respect to a discontinuing operation, the initial disclosure event is the occurrence of one of the following, whichever occurs earlier:*
(a) the enterprise has entered into a binding sale agreement for substantially all of the assets attributable to the discontinuing operation; or
(b) the enterprise's board of directors or similar governing body has both (i) approved a detailed, formal plan for the discontinuance and (ii) made an announcement of the plan.

Recognition and Measurement

An enterprise should apply the principles of recognition and measurement that are **17**
set out in other IASs for the purpose of deciding when and how to recognise and
measure the changes in assets and liabilities and the income, expenses, and cash
flows relating to a discontinuing operation.

[Not printed] **18–19**

Provisions

A discontinuing operation is a restructuring as that term is defined in IAS 37. IAS 37 **20**
provides guidance for certain of the requirements of this Standard, including:
(a) what constitutes a "detailed, formal plan for the discontinuance" as that term is
    used in paragraph 16(b) of this Standard; and
(b) what constitutes an "announcement of the plan" as that term is used in paragraph
    16(b) of this Standard.

[Not printed] **21**

Impairment Losses

The approval and announcement of a plan for discontinuance is an indication that the **22**
assets attributable to the discontinuing operation may be impaired or that an
impairment loss previously recognised for those assets should be increased or reversed.
Therefore, in accordance with IAS 36 an enterprise estimates the recoverable amount of
each asset of the discontinuing operation (the higher of the asset's net selling price and
its value in use) and recognises an impairment loss or reversal of a prior impairment
loss, if any.

In applying IAS 36 to a discontinuing operation, an enterprise determines whether the **23**
recoverable amount of an asset of a discontinuing operation is assessed for the
individual asset or for the asset's cash-generating unit (defined in IAS 36 as the smallest
identifiable group of assets that includes the asset under review and that generates cash
inflows from continuing use that are largely independent of the cash inflows from other
assets or groups of assets). For example:
(a) if the enterprise sells the discontinuing operation substantially in its entirety, none
    of the assets of the discontinuing operation generate cash inflows independently
    from other assets within the discontinuing operation. Therefore, recoverable
    amount is determined for the discontinuing operation as a whole and an
    impairment loss, if any, is allocated among the assets of the discontinuing
    operation in accordance with IAS 36;
(b) if the enterprise disposes of the discontinuing operation in other ways such as
    piecemeal sales, the recoverable amount is determined for individual assets, unless
    the assets are sold in groups; and
(c) if the enterprise abandons the discontinuing operation, the recoverable amount is
    determined for individual assets as set out in IAS 36.

After announcement of a plan, negotiations with potential purchasers of the **24**
discontinuing operation or actual binding sale agreements may indicate that the assets
of the discontinuing operation may be further impaired or that impairment losses
recognised for these assets in prior periods may have decreased. As a consequence,
when such events occur, an enterprise re-estimates the recoverable amount of the assets

of the discontinuing operation and recognises resulting impairment losses or reversals of impairment losses in accordance with IAS 36.

25 A price in a binding sale agreement is the best evidence of an asset's (cash-generating unit's) net selling price or of the estimated cash inflow from ultimate disposal in determining the asset's (cash-generating unit's) value in use.

26 The carrying amount (recoverable amount) of a discontinuing operation includes the carrying amount (recoverable amount) of any goodwill that can be allocated on a reasonable and consistent basis to that discontinuing operation.

Presentation and Disclosure

Initial Disclosure

27 *An enterprise should include the following information relating to a discontinuing operation in its financial statements beginning with the financial statements for the period in which the initial disclosure event (as defined in paragraph 16) occurs:*
    (a) *a description of the discontinuing operation;*
    (b) *the business or geographical segment(s) in which it is reported in accordance with IAS 14;*
    (c) *the date and nature of the initial disclosure event;*
    (d) *the date or period in which the discontinuance is expected to be completed if known or determinable;*
    (e) *the carrying amounts, as of the balance sheet date, of the total assets and the total liabilities to be disposed of;*
    (f) *the amounts of revenue, expenses, and pre-tax profit or loss from ordinary activities attributable to the discontinuing operation during the current financial reporting period, and the income tax expense relating thereto as required by paragraph 81(h) of IAS 12; and*
    (g) *the amounts of net cash flows attributable to the operating, investing, and financing activities of the discontinuing operation during the current financial reporting period.*

28 [Not printed]

29 *If an initial disclosure event occurs after the end of an enterprise's financial reporting period but before the financial statements for that period are authorised for issue, those financial statements should include the disclosures specified in paragraph 27 for the period covered by those financial statements.*

30 [Not printed]

Other Disclosures

31 *When an enterprise disposes of assets or settles liabilities attributable to a discontinuing operation or enters into binding agreements for the sale of such assets or the settlement of such liabilities, it should include in its financial statements the following information when the events occur:*
    (a) *for any gain or loss that is recognised on the disposal of assets or settlement of liabilities attributable to the discontinuing operation, (i) the amount of the pre-tax gain or loss and (ii) income tax expense relating to the gain or loss, as required by paragraph 81(h) of IAS 12; and*

(b) the net selling price or range of prices (which is after deducting the expected disposal costs) of those net assets for which the enterprise has entered into one or more binding sale agreements, the expected timing of receipt of those cash flows, and the carrying amount of those net assets.

[Not printed]   **32**

Updating the Disclosures

In addition to the disclosures in paragraphs 27 and 31, an enterprise should include **33**
in its financial statements for periods subsequent to the one in which the initial disclosure event occurs a description of any significant changes in the amount or timing of cash flows relating to the assets and liabilities to be disposed of or settled and the events causing those changes.

[Not printed]   **34**

The disclosures required by paragraphs 27-34 should continue in financial statements **35**
for periods up to and including the period in which the discontinuance is completed. A discontinuance is completed when the plan is substantially completed or abandoned, though payments from the buyer(s) to the seller may not yet be completed.

If an enterprise abandons or withdraws from a plan that was previously reported as **36**
a discontinuing operation, that fact and its effect should be disclosed.

For the purpose of applying the preceding paragraph, disclosure of the effect includes **37**
reversal of any prior impairment loss or provision that was recognised with respect to the discontinuing operation.

Separate Disclosure for Each Discontinuing Operation

Any disclosures required by this Standard should be presented separately for each **38**
discontinuing operation.

Presentation of the Required Disclosures

Face of Financial Statements or Notes

The disclosures required by paragraphs 27-37 may be presented either in the notes to **39**
the financial statements or on the face of the financial statements except that the disclosure of the amount of the pre-tax gain or loss recognised on the disposal of assets or settlement of liabilities attributable to the discontinuing operation (paragraph 31(a)) should be shown on the face of the income statement.

The disclosures required by paragraphs 27(f) and 27(g) are encouraged to be presented **40**
on the face of the income statement and cash flow statement, respectively.

Not an Extraordinary Item

A discontinuing operation should not be presented as an extraordinary item.   **41**

[Not printed]   **42**

Restricted Use of the Term 'Discontinuing Operation'

43 *A restructuring, transaction, or event that does not meet the definition of a discontinuing operation in this Standard should not be called a discontinuing operation.*

Illustrative Disclosures

44 [Not printed]

Restatement of Prior Periods

45 *Comparative information for prior periods that is presented in financial statements prepared after the initial disclosure event should be restated to segregate continuing and discontinuing assets, liabilities, income, expenses, and cash flows in a manner similar to that required by paragraphs 27 43.*

46 [Not printed]

Disclosure in Interim Financial Reports

47 *The notes to an interim financial report should describe any significant activities or events since the end of the most recent annual reporting period relating to a discontinuing operation and any significant changes in the amount or timing of cash flows relating to the assets and liabilities to be disposed of or settled.*

48 [Not printed]

Effective Date

49–50 [Not printed]

Appendix A

Illustrative Disclosures

[Not printed]

Appendix B

Classification of Prior Period Operations

[Not printed]

IAS 36: Impairment of Assets

IAS 36: Impairment of Assets			
Scope 36.1–4	Definitions 36.5	Transitional Provisions 36.120–121	Effective Date 36.122

Identifying an Asset that may be Impaired 36.6–14

Measurement of Recoverable Amount 36.15–56				
	Value in Use 36.26–56			
Net Selling Price 36.21–25	Basis for Estimates of Future Cash Flows 36.27–31	Composition of Estimates of Future Cash Flows 36.32–46	Foreign Currency Future Cash Flows 36.47	Discount Rate 36.48–56

Recognition and Measurement of an Impairment Loss 36.57–63

Cash-Generating Units 36.64–93		
Identification of the Cash-Generating Unit to Which an Asset Belongs 36.65–72	Recoverable Amount and Carrying Amount of a Cash-Generating Unit 36.73–87	Impairment Loss for a Cash-Generating Unit 36.88–93
	Goodwill 36.79–83 / Corporate Assets 36.84–87	

Reversal of an Impairment Loss 36.94–112		
Individual Asset 36.102–106	Cash-Generating Unit 36.107–108	Goodwill 36.109–112

Disclosure 36.113–119

Appendices [Not printed]	
Illustrative Examples	Basis for Conclusions

Scope

1   *This Standard should be applied in accounting for the impairment of all assets, other than:*

   (a) inventories (see IAS 2);

   (b) assets arising from construction contracts (see IAS 11);

   (c) deferred tax assets (see IAS 12);

   (d) assets arising from employee benefits (see IAS 19);

   (e) financial assets that are included in the scope of IAS 32;

   (f) investment property that is measured at fair value (see IAS 40); and

   (g) biological assets related to agricultural activity that are measured at fair value less estimated point-of-sale costs (see IAS 41).

2–4   [Not printed]

Definitions

5   ...

   Recoverable amount is the higher of an asset's net selling price and its value in use.

   Value in use is the present value of estimated future cash flows expected to arise from the continuing use of an asset and from its disposal at the end of its useful life.

   Net selling price is the amount obtainable from the sale of an asset in an arm's length transaction between knowledgeable, willing parties, less the costs of disposal.

   Costs of disposal are incremental costs directly attributable to the disposal of an asset, excluding finance costs and income tax expense.

   An impairment loss is the amount by which the carrying amount of an asset exceeds its recoverable amount.

   Carrying amount is the amount at which an asset is recognised in the balance sheet after deducting any accumulated depreciation (amortisation) and accumulated impairment losses thereon.

   Depreciation (Amortisation) is the systematic allocation of the depreciable amount of an asset over its useful life.

   Depreciable amount is the cost of an asset, or other amount substituted for cost in the financial statements, less its residual value.

   Useful life is either:

   (a) the period of time over which an asset is expected to be used by the enterprise; or

   (b) the number of production or similar units expected to be obtained from the asset by the enterprise.

   A cash-generating unit is the smallest identifiable group of assets that generates cash inflows from continuing use that are largely independent of the cash inflows from other assets or groups of assets.

   Corporate assets are assets other than goodwill that contribute to the future cash flows of both the cash-generating unit under review and other cash-generating units.

   An active market is a market where all the following conditions exist:

   (a) the items traded within the market are homogeneous;

   (b) willing buyers and sellers can normally be found at any time; and

   (c) prices are available to the public.

Identifying an Asset that may be Impaired

Paragraphs 7 to 14 specify when recoverable amount should be determined. These **6** requirements use the term 'an asset' but apply equally to an individual asset or a cash-generating unit.

[Not printed] **7**

An enterprise should assess at each balance sheet date whether there is any **8** *indication that an asset may be impaired. If any such indication exists, the enterprise should estimate the recoverable amount of the asset.*

In assessing whether there is any indication that an asset may be impaired, an **9** *enterprise should consider, as a minimum, the following indications:*
External sources of information
(a) during the period, an asset's market value has declined significantly more than would be expected as a result of the passage of time or normal use;
(b) significant changes with an adverse effect on the enterprise have taken place during the period, or will take place in the near future, in the technological, market, economic or legal environment in which the enterprise operates or in the market to which an asset is dedicated;
(c) market interest rates or other market rates of return on investments have increased during the period, and those increases are likely to affect the discount rate used in calculating an asset's value in use and decrease the asset's recoverable amount materially;
(d) the carrying amount of the net assets of the reporting enterprise is more than its market capitalisation;
Internal sources of information
(e) evidence is available of obsolescence or physical damage of an asset;
(f) significant changes with an adverse effect on the enterprise have taken place during the period, or are expected to take place in the near future, in the extent to which, or manner in which, an asset is used or is expected to be used. These changes include plans to discontinue or restructure the operation to which an asset belongs or to dispose of an asset before the previously expected date; and
(g) evidence is available from internal reporting that indicates that the economic performance of an asset is, or will be, worse than expected.

[Not printed] **10**

Evidence from internal reporting that indicates that an asset may be impaired includes **11** the existence of:
(a) cash flows for acquiring the asset, or subsequent cash needs for operating or maintaining it, that are significantly higher than those originally budgeted;
(b) actual net cash flows or operating profit or loss flowing from the asset that are significantly worse than those budgeted;
(c) a significant decline in budgeted net cash flows or operating profit, or a significant increase in budgeted loss, flowing from the asset; or
(d) operating losses or net cash outflows for the asset, when current period figures are aggregated with budgeted figures for the future.

The concept of materiality applies in identifying whether the recoverable amount of an **12** asset needs to be estimated. ...

[Not printed] **13**

14 If there is an indication that an asset may be impaired, this may indicate that the remaining useful life, the depreciation (amortisation) method or the residual value for the asset need to be reviewed and adjusted under the IAS applicable to the asset, even if no impairment loss is recognised for the asset.

Measurement of Recoverable Amount

15 ... Paragraphs 16 to 56 set out the requirements for measuring recoverable amount. These requirements use the term 'an asset' but apply equally to an individual asset or a cash-generating unit.

16 It is not always necessary to determine both an asset's net selling price and its value in use. For example, if either of these amounts exceeds the asset's carrying amount, the asset is not impaired and it is not necessary to estimate the other amount.

17 It may be possible to determine net selling price, even if an asset is not traded in an active market. However, sometimes it will not be possible to determine net selling price because there is no basis for making a reliable estimate of the amount obtainable from the sale of the asset in an arm's length transaction between knowledgeable and willing parties. In this case, the recoverable amount of the asset may be taken to be its value in use.

18 If there is no reason to believe that an asset's value in use materially exceeds its net selling price, the asset's recoverable amount may be taken to be its net selling price. ...

19 Recoverable amount is determined for an individual asset, unless the asset does not generate cash inflows from continuing use that are largely independent of those from other assets or groups of assets. If this is the case, recoverable amount is determined for the cash-generating unit to which the asset belongs (see paragraphs 64 to 87), unless either:
(a) the asset's net selling price is higher than its carrying amount; or
(b) the asset's value in use can be estimated to be close to its net selling price and net selling price can be determined.

20 [Not printed]

Net Selling Price

21 The best evidence of an asset's net selling price is a price in a binding sale agreement in an arm's length transaction, adjusted for incremental costs that would be directly attributable to the disposal of the asset.

22 If there is no binding sale agreement but an asset is traded in an active market, net selling price is the asset's market price less the costs of disposal. The appropriate market price is usually the current bid price. When current bid prices are unavailable, the price of the most recent transaction may provide a basis from which to estimate net selling price, provided that there has not been a significant change in economic circumstances between the transaction date and the date at which the estimate is made.

23 If there is no binding sale agreement or active market for an asset, net selling price is based on the best information available to reflect the amount that an enterprise could obtain, at the balance sheet date, for the disposal of the asset in an arm's length transaction between knowledgeable, willing parties, after deducting the costs of disposal. In determining this amount, an enterprise considers the outcome of recent

transactions for similar assets within the same industry. Net selling price does not reflect a forced sale, unless management is compelled to sell immediately.

Costs of disposal, other than those that have already been recognised as liabilities, are **24** deducted in determining net selling price. Examples of such costs are legal costs, stamp duty and similar transaction taxes, costs of removing the asset, and direct incremental costs to bring an asset into condition for its sale. However, termination benefits (as defined in IAS 19) and costs associated with reducing or reorganising a business following the disposal of an asset are not direct incremental costs to dispose of the asset.

[Not printed]   **25**

Value in Use

Estimating the value in use of an asset involves the following steps: **26**
(a) estimating the future cash inflows and outflows to be derived from continuing use of the asset and from its ultimate disposal; and
(b) applying the appropriate discount rate to these future cash flows.

Basis for Estimates of Future Cash Flows

In measuring value in use: **27**
(a) cash flow projections should be based on reasonable and supportable assumptions that represent management's best estimate of the set of economic conditions that will exist over the remaining useful life of the asset. Greater weight should be given to external evidence;
(b) cash flow projections should be based on the most recent financial budgets/ forecasts that have been approved by management. Projections based on these budgets/forecasts should cover a maximum period of five years, unless a longer period can be justified; and
(c) cash flow projections beyond the period covered by the most recent budgets/ forecasts should be estimated by extrapolating the projections based on the budgets/forecasts using a steady or declining growth rate for subsequent years, unless an increasing rate can be justified. This growth rate should not exceed the long-term average growth rate for the products, industries, or country or countries in which the enterprise operates, or for the market in which the asset is used, unless a higher rate can be justified.

[Not printed]   **28**

Cash flow projections until the end of an asset's useful life are estimated by **29** extrapolating the cash flow projections based on the financial budgets/forecasts using a growth rate for subsequent years. This rate is steady or declining, unless an increase in the rate matches objective information about patterns over a product or industry lifecycle. If appropriate, the growth rate is zero or negative.

[Not printed]   **30–31**

Composition of Estimates of Future Cash Flows

Estimates of future cash flows should include: **32**
(a) projections of cash inflows from the continuing use of the asset;
(b) projections of cash outflows that are necessarily incurred to generate the cash inflows from continuing use of the asset (including cash outflows to prepare the

asset for use) and that can be directly attributed, or allocated on a reasonable and consistent basis, to the asset; and

(c) net cash flows, if any, to be received (or paid) for the disposal of the asset at the end of its useful life.

33 [Not printed]

34 Projections of cash outflows include future overheads that can be attributed directly, or allocated on a reasonable and consistent basis, to the use of the asset.

35 [Not printed]

36 To avoid double counting, estimates of future cash flows do not include:

(a) cash inflows from assets that generate cash inflows from continuing use that are largely independent of the cash inflows from the asset under review (for example, financial assets such as receivables); and

(b) cash outflows that relate to obligations that have already been recognised as liabilities (for example, payables, pensions or provisions).

37 *Future cash flows should be estimated for the asset in its current condition. Estimates of future cash flows should not include estimated future cash inflows or outflows that are expected to arise from:*

(a) a future restructuring to which an enterprise is not yet committed; or

(b) future capital expenditure that will improve or enhance the asset in excess of its originally assessed standard of performance.

38 [Not printed]

39 A restructuring is a programme that is planned and controlled by management and that materially changes either the scope of the business undertaken by an enterprise or the manner in which the business is conducted. IAS 37 gives guidance that may clarify when an enterprise is committed to a restructuring.

40–42 [Not printed]

43 *Estimates of future cash flows should not include:*

(a) cash inflows or outflows from financing activities; or

(b) income tax receipts or payments.

44 [Not printed]

45 *The estimate of net cash flows to be received (or paid) for the disposal of an asset at the end of its useful life should be the amount that an enterprise expects to obtain from the disposal of the asset in an arm's length transaction between knowledgeable, willing parties, after deducting the estimated costs of disposal.*

46 [Not printed]

Foreign Currency Future Cash Flows

47 Future cash flows are estimated in the currency in which they will be generated and then discounted using a discount rate appropriate for that currency. An enterprise translates the present value obtained using the spot exchange rate at the balance sheet date (described in IAS 21 as the closing rate).

Discount Rate

The discount rate (or rates) should be a pre-tax rate (or rates) that reflect(s) current **48**
market assessments of the time value of money and the risks specific to the asset.
The discount rate(s) should not reflect risks for which future cash flow estimates have
been adjusted.

[Not printed] **49**

When an asset-specific rate is not directly available from the market, an enterprise uses **50**
surrogates to estimate the discount rate. The purpose is to estimate, as far as possible,
a market assessment of:
(a) the time value of money for the periods until the end of the asset's useful life; and
(b) the risks that the future cash flows will differ in amount or timing from estimates.

[Not printed] **51–56**

Recognition and Measurement of an Impairment Loss

[Not printed] **57**

If, and only if, the recoverable amount of an asset is less than its carrying amount, **58**
the carrying amount of the asset should be reduced to its recoverable amount. That
reduction is an impairment loss.

An impairment loss should be recognised as an expense in the income statement **59**
immediately, unless the asset is carried at revalued amount under another IAS (for
example, under the allowed alternative treatment in IAS 16). Any impairment loss
of a revalued asset should be treated as a revaluation decrease under that other IAS.

[Not printed] **60**

When the amount estimated for an impairment loss is greater than the carrying **61**
amount of the asset to which it relates, an enterprise should recognise a liability if,
and only if, that is required by another IAS.

After the recognition of an impairment loss, the depreciation (amortisation) charge **62**
for the asset should be adjusted in future periods to allocate the asset's revised
carrying amount, less its residual value (if any), on a systematic basis over its
remaining useful life.

[Not printed] **63**

Cash-Generating Units

[Not printed] **64**

Identification of the Cash-Generating Unit to Which an Asset Belongs

If there is any indication that an asset may be impaired, recoverable amount should **65**
be estimated for the individual asset. If it is not possible to estimate the recoverable
amount of the individual asset, an enterprise should determine the recoverable
amount of the cash-generating unit to which the asset belongs (the asset's cash-
generating unit).

[Not printed] **66–67**

68 Cash inflows from continuing use are inflows of cash and cash equivalents received from parties outside the reporting enterprise. ...

69 *If an active market exists for the output produced by an asset or a group of assets, this asset or group of assets should be identified as a cash-generating unit, even if some or all of the output is used internally. If this is the case, management's best estimate of future market prices for the output should be used:*

   (a) in determining the value in use of this cash-generating unit, when estimating the future cash inflows that relate to the internal use of the output; and

   (b) in determining the value in use of other cash-generating units of the reporting enterprise, when estimating the future cash outflows that relate to the internal use of the output.

70 [Not printed]

71 *Cash-generating units should be identified consistently from period to period for the same asset or types of assets, unless a change is justified.*

72 [Not printed]

Recoverable Amount and Carrying Amount of a Cash-Generating Unit

73 The recoverable amount of a cash-generating unit is the higher of the cash-generating unit's net selling price and value in use. For the purpose of determining the recoverable amount of a cash-generating unit, any reference in paragraphs 16 to 56 to 'an asset' is read as a reference to 'a cash-generating unit'.

74 *The carrying amount of a cash-generating unit should be determined consistently with the way the recoverable amount of the cash-generating unit is determined.*

75–78 [Not printed]

Goodwill

79 Goodwill arising on acquisition represents a payment made by an acquirer in anticipation of future economic benefits. ...

80 *In testing a cash-generating unit for impairment, an enterprise should identify whether goodwill that relates to this cash-generating unit is recognised in the financial statements. If this is the case, an enterprise should:*

   (a) perform a 'bottom-up' test, that is, the enterprise should:

   (i) identify whether the carrying amount of goodwill can be allocated on a reasonable and consistent basis to the cash-generating unit under review; and

   The enterprise should perform the second step of the 'bottom-up' test even if none of the carrying amount of goodwill can be allocated on a reasonable and consistent basis to the cash-generating unit under review; and(ii)then, compare the recoverable amount of the cash-generating unit under review to its carrying amount (including the carrying amount of allocated goodwill, if any) and recognise any impairment loss in accordance with paragraph 88.

   (b) if, in performing the 'bottom-up' test, the enterprise could not allocate the carrying amount of goodwill on a reasonable and consistent basis to the cash-generating unit under review, the enterprise should also perform a 'top-down' test, that is, the enterprise should:

   (i) identify the smallest cash-generating unit that includes the cash-generating unit under review and to which the carrying amount of goodwill can be

allocated on a reasonable and consistent basis (the 'larger' cash-generating unit); and

(ii) *then, compare the recoverable amount of the larger cash-generating unit to its carrying amount (including the carrying amount of allocated goodwill) and recognise any impairment loss in accordance with paragraph 88.*

[Not printed]   **81–83**

Corporate Assets

Corporate assets include group or divisional assets such as the building of a **84** headquarters or a division of the enterprise, EDP equipment or a research centre. ...

Because corporate assets do not generate separate cash inflows, the recoverable amount **85** of an individual corporate asset cannot be determined unless management has decided to dispose of the asset. As a consequence, if there is an indication that a corporate asset may be impaired, recoverable amount is determined for the cash-generating unit to which the corporate asset belongs, compared to the carrying amount of this cash-generating unit and any impairment loss is recognised in accordance with paragraph 88.

In testing a cash-generating unit for impairment, an enterprise should identify all the **86** *corporate assets that relate to the cash-generating unit under review. For each identified corporate asset, an enterprise should then apply paragraph 80, that is:*

(a) *if the carrying amount of the corporate asset can be allocated on a reasonable and consistent basis to the cash-generating unit under review, an enterprise should apply the 'bottom-up' test only; and*

(b) *if the carrying amount of the corporate asset cannot be allocated on a reasonable and consistent basis to the cash-generating unit under review, an enterprise should apply both the 'bottom-up' and 'top-down' tests.*

[Not printed]   **87**

Impairment Loss for a Cash-Generating Unit

An impairment loss should be recognised for a cash-generating unit if, and only if, its **88** *recoverable amount is less than its carrying amount. The impairment loss should be allocated to reduce the carrying amount of the assets of the unit in the following order:*

(a) *first, to goodwill allocated to the cash-generating unit (if any); and*

(b) *then, to the other assets of the unit on a pro-rata basis based on the carrying amount of each asset in the unit.*

These reductions in carrying amounts should be treated as impairment losses on individual assets and recognised in accordance with paragraph 59.

In allocating an impairment loss under paragraph 88, the carrying amount of an **89** *asset should not be reduced below the highest of:*

(a) *its net selling price (if determinable);*

(b) *its value in use (if determinable); and*

(c) *zero.*

The amount of the impairment loss that would otherwise have been allocated to the asset should be allocated to the other assets of the unit on a pro-rata basis.

[Not printed]   **90**

91 If there is no practical way to estimate the recoverable amount of each individual asset of a cash-generating unit, this Standard requires an arbitrary allocation of an impairment loss between the assets of that unit, other than goodwill, because all assets of a cash-generating unit work together.

92 If the recoverable amount of an individual asset cannot be determined (see paragraph 66):
   (a) an impairment loss is recognised for the asset if its carrying amount is greater than the higher of its net selling price and the results of the allocation procedures described in paragraphs 88 and 89; and
   (b) no impairment loss is recognised for the asset if the related cash-generating unit is not impaired. This applies even if the asset's net selling price is less than its carrying amount.
   ...

93 *After the requirements in paragraphs 88 and 89 have been applied, a liability should be recognised for any remaining amount of an impairment loss for a cash-generating unit if, and only if, that is required by other IASs.*

Reversal of an Impairment Loss

94 Paragraphs 95 to 101 set out the requirements for reversing an impairment loss recognised for an asset or a cash-generating unit in prior years. These requirements use the term 'an asset' but apply equally to an individual asset or a cash-generating unit. ...

95 *An enterprise should assess at each balance sheet date whether there is any indication that an impairment loss recognised for an asset in prior years may no longer exist or may have decreased. If any such indication exists, the enterprise should estimate the recoverable amount of that asset.*

96 *In assessing whether there is any indication that an impairment loss recognised for an asset in prior years may no longer exist or may have decreased, an enterprise should consider, as a minimum, the following indications:*
   External sources of information
   (a) the asset's market value has increased significantly during the period;
   (b) significant changes with a favourable effect on the enterprise have taken place during the period, or will take place in the near future, in the technological, market, economic or legal environment in which the enterprise operates or in the market to which the asset is dedicated;
   (c) market interest rates or other market rates of return on investments have decreased during the period, and those decreases are likely to affect the discount rate used in calculating the asset's value in use and increase the asset's recoverable amount materially;
   Internal sources of information
   (d) significant changes with a favourable effect on the enterprise have taken place during the period, or are expected to take place in the near future, in the extent to which, or manner in which, the asset is used or is expected to be used. These changes include capital expenditure that has been incurred during the period to improve or enhance an asset in excess of its originally assessed standard of performance or a commitment to discontinue or restructure the operation to which the asset belongs; and

(e) evidence is available from internal reporting that indicates that the economic performance of the asset is, or will be, better than expected.

[Not printed]   **97–98**

An impairment loss recognised for an asset in prior years should be reversed if, and **99** *only if, there has been a change in the estimates used to determine the asset's recoverable amount since the last impairment loss was recognised. If this is the case, the carrying amount of the asset should be increased to its recoverable amount. That increase is a reversal of an impairment loss.*

A reversal of an impairment loss reflects an increase in the estimated service potential **100** of an asset, either from use or sale, since the date when an enterprise last recognised an impairment loss for that asset. An enterprise is required to identify the change in estimates that causes the increase in estimated service potential. ...

An asset's value in use may become greater than the asset's carrying amount simply **101** because the present value of future cash inflows increases as they become closer. However, the service potential of the asset has not increased. Therefore, an impairment loss is not reversed just because of the passage of time (sometimes called the 'unwinding' of the discount), even if the recoverable amount of the asset becomes higher than its carrying amount.

Reversal of an Impairment Loss for an Individual Asset

The increased carrying amount of an asset due to a reversal of an impairment loss **102** *should not exceed the carrying amount that would have been determined (net of amortisation or depreciation) had no impairment loss been recognised for the asset in prior years.*

[Not printed]   **103**

A reversal of an impairment loss for an asset should be recognised as income **104** *immediately in the income statement, unless the asset is carried at revalued amount under another IAS (for example, under the allowed alternative treatment in IAS 16). Any reversal of an impairment loss on a revalued asset should be treated as a revaluation increase under that other IAS.*

[Not printed]   **105**

After a reversal of an impairment loss is recognised, the depreciation (amortisation) **106** *charge for the asset should be adjusted in future periods to allocate the asset's revised carrying amount, less its residual value (if any), on a systematic basis over its remaining useful life.*

Reversal of an Impairment Loss for a Cash-Generating Unit

A reversal of an impairment loss for a cash-generating unit should be allocated to **107** *increase the carrying amount of the assets of the unit in the following order:*
(a) first, assets other than goodwill on a pro-rata basis based on the carrying amount of each asset in the unit; and
(b) then, to goodwill allocated to the cash-generating unit (if any), if the requirements in paragraph 109 are met.
These increases in carrying amounts should be treated as reversals of impairment losses for individual assets and recognised in accordance with paragraph 104.

108 *In allocating a reversal of an impairment loss for a cash-generating unit under paragraph 107, the carrying amount of an asset should not be increased above the lower of:*

(a) *its recoverable amount (if determinable); and*

(b) *the carrying amount that would have been determined (net of amortisation or depreciation) had no impairment loss been recognised for the asset in prior years.*

The amount of the reversal of the impairment loss that would otherwise have been allocated to the asset should be allocated to the other assets of the unit on a pro-rata basis.

Reversal of an Impairment Loss for Goodwill

109 *As an exception to the requirement in paragraph 99, an impairment loss recognised for goodwill should not be reversed in a subsequent period unless:*

(a) *the impairment loss was caused by a specific external event of an exceptional nature that is not expected to recur; and*

(b) *subsequent external events have occurred that reverse the effect of that event.*

110–112 [Not printed]

Disclosure

113 *For each class of assets, the financial statements should disclose:*

(a) *the amount of impairment losses recognised in the income statement during the period and the line item(s) of the income statement in which those impairment losses are included;*

(b) *the amount of reversals of impairment losses recognised in the income statement during the period and the line item(s) of the income statement in which those impairment losses are reversed;*

(c) *the amount of impairment losses recognised directly in equity during the period; and*

(d) *the amount of reversals of impairment losses recognised directly in equity during the period.*

114 A class of assets is a grouping of assets of similar nature and use in an enterprise's operations.

115 [Not printed]

116 *An enterprise that applies IAS 14 should disclose the following for each reportable segment based on an enterprise's primary format (as defined in IAS 14):*

(a) *the amount of impairment losses recognised in the income statement and directly in equity during the period; and*

(b) *the amount of reversals of impairment losses recognised in the income statement and directly in equity during the period.*

117 *If an impairment loss for an individual asset or a cash-generating unit is recognised or reversed during the period and is material to the financial statements of the reporting enterprise as a whole, an enterprise should disclose:*

(a) *the events and circumstances that led to the recognition or reversal of the impairment loss;*

(b) *the amount of the impairment loss recognised or reversed;*

(c) *for an individual asset:*

    (i) *the nature of the asset; and*

    (ii) *the reportable segment to which the asset belongs, based on the enterprise's primary format (as defined in IAS 14 if the enterprise applies IAS 14);*

(d) *for a cash-generating unit:*

    (i) *a description of the cash-generating unit (such as whether it is a product line, a plant, a business operation, a geographical area, a reportable segment as defined in IAS 14 or other);*

    (ii) *the amount of the impairment loss recognised or reversed by class of assets and by reportable segment based on the enterprise's primary format (as defined in IAS 14, if the enterprise applies IAS 14); and*

    (iii)*if the aggregation of assets for identifying the cash-generating unit has changed since the previous estimate of the cash-generating unit's recoverable amount (if any), the enterprise should describe the current and former way of aggregating assets and the reasons for changing the way the cash-generating unit is identified;*

(e) *whether the recoverable amount of the asset (cash-generating unit) is its net selling price or its value in use;*

(f) *if recoverable amount is net selling price, the basis used to determine net selling price (such as whether selling price was determined by reference to an active market or in some other way); and*

(g) *if recoverable amount is value in use, the discount rate(s) used in the current estimate and previous estimate (if any) of value in use.*

If impairment losses recognised (reversed) during the period are material in aggregate to the financial statements of the reporting enterprise as a whole, an enterprise should disclose a brief description of the following: **118**

(a) *the main classes of assets affected by impairment losses (reversals of impairment losses) for which no information is disclosed under paragraph 117; and*

(b) *the main events and circumstances that led to the recognition (reversal) of these impairment losses for which no information is disclosed under paragraph 117.*

[Not printed]   **119**

Transitional Provisions

This Standard should be applied on a prospective basis only. Impairment losses (reversals of impairment losses) that result from adoption of this IAS should be recognised in accordance with this Standard (i.e., in the income statement unless an asset is carried at revalued amount. An impairment loss (reversal of impairment loss) on a revalued asset should be treated as a revaluation decrease (increase)).   **120**

[Not printed]   **121**

Effective Date

[Not printed]   **122**

Appendix A

Illustrative Examples

[Not printed]

Appendix B

Basis for Conclusions

[Not printed]

IAS 37: Provisions, Contingent Liabilities and Contingent Assets

IAS 37: Provisions, Contingent Liabilities and Contingent Assets					
	Definitions 37.10–13				
Scope 37.1–9	Definitions 37.10	Provisions and Other Liabilities 37.11	Relationship between Provisions and Contingent Liabilities 37.12–13	Transitional Provisions 37.93–94	Effective Date 37.95–96

Recognition 37.14–35					
	Provisions 37.14–26				
Present Obligation 37.15–16	Past Event 37.17–22	Probable Outflow of Resources Embodying Economic Benefits 37.23–24	Reliable Estimate of the Obligation 37.25–26	Contingent Liabilities 37.27–30	Contingent Assets 37.31–35

Measurement 37.36–52				
Best Estimate 37.36–41	Risk and Uncertainties 37.42–44	Present Value 37.45–47	Future Events 37.48–50	Expected Disposals of Assets 37.51–52

Reimbursements 37.53–58

Changes in Provisions 37.59–60

Use of Provisions 37.61–62

Application of the Recognition and Measurement Rules 37.63–83		
Future Operating Losses 37.63–65	Onerous Contracts 37.66–69	Restructuring 37.70–83

Disclosure 37.84–92

Appendices			
Tables - Provisions, Contingent Liabilities, Contingent Assets and Reimbursements	Decision Tree	Examples: Recognition	Examples: Disclosure

Scope

1 *This Standard should be applied by all enterprises in accounting for provisions, contingent liabilities and contingent assets, except:*

(a) *those resulting from financial instruments that are carried at fair value;*

(b) *those resulting from executory contracts, except where the contract is onerous;*

(c) *those arising in insurance enterprises from contracts with policyholders; and*

(d) *those covered by another IAS.*

2–9 [Not printed]

Definitions

10 ...

A *provision* is a liability of uncertain timing or amount.

A *liability* is a present obligation of the enterprise arising from past events, the settlement of which is expected to result in an outflow from the enterprise of resources embodying economic benefits.

An *obligating event* is an event that creates a legal or constructive obligation that results in an enterprise having no realistic alternative to settling that obligation.

A *legal obligation* is an obligation that derives from:

(a) *a contract (through its explicit or implicit terms);*

(b) *legislation; or*

(c) *other operation of law.*

A *constructive obligation* is an obligation that derives from an enterprise's actions where:

(a) *by an established pattern of past practice, published policies or a sufficiently specific current statement, the enterprise has indicated to other parties that it will accept certain responsibilities; and*

(b) *as a result, the enterprise has created a valid expectation on the part of those other parties that it will discharge those responsibilities.*

A *contingent liability* is:

(a) *a possible obligation that arises from past events and whose existence will be confirmed only by the occurrence or non-occurrence of one or more uncertain future events not wholly within the control of the enterprise; or*

(b) *a present obligation that arises from past events but is not recognised because:*

    (i) *it is not probable that an outflow of resources embodying economic benefits will be required to settle the obligation; or*

    (ii) *the amount of the obligation cannot be measured with sufficient reliability.*

A *contingent asset* is a possible asset that arises from past events and whose existence will be confirmed only by the occurrence or non-occurrence of one or more uncertain future events not wholly within the control of the enterprise.

An *onerous contract* is a contract in which the unavoidable costs of meeting the obligations under the contract exceed the economic benefits expected to be received under it.

A *restructuring* is a programme that is planned and controlled by management, and materially changes either:

(a) *the scope of a business undertaken by an enterprise; or*

(b) *the manner in which that business is conducted.*

Provisions and Other Liabilities

Provisions can be distinguished from other liabilities such as trade payables and accruals **11** because there is uncertainty about the timing or amount of the future expenditure required in settlement. By contrast:
(a) trade payables are liabilities to pay for goods or services that have been received or supplied and have been invoiced or formally agreed with the supplier; and
(b) accruals are liabilities to pay for goods or services that have been received or supplied but have not been paid, invoiced or formally agreed with the supplier, including amounts due to employees (for example, amounts relating to accrued vacation pay). Although it is sometimes necessary to estimate the amount or timing of accruals, the uncertainty is generally much less than for provisions.
Accruals are often reported as part of trade and other payables, whereas provisions are reported separately.

Relationship between Provisions and Contingent Liabilities

In a general sense, all provisions are contingent because they are uncertain in timing **12** or amount. However, within this Standard the term 'contingent' is used for liabilities and assets that are not recognised because their existence will be confirmed only by the occurrence or non-occurrence of one or more uncertain future events not wholly within the control of the enterprise. In addition, the term 'contingent liability' is used for liabilities that do not meet the recognition criteria.

This Standard distinguishes between: **13**
(a) provisions - which are recognised as liabilities (assuming that a reliable estimate can be made) because they are present obligations and it is probable that an outflow of resources embodying economic benefits will be required to settle the obligations; and
(b) contingent liabilities - which are not recognised as liabilities because they are either:
  (i) possible obligations, as it has yet to be confirmed whether the enterprise has a present obligation that could lead to an outflow of resources embodying economic benefits; or
  (ii) present obligations that do not meet the recognition criteria in this Standard (because either it is not probable that an outflow of resources embodying economic benefits will be required to settle the obligation, or a sufficiently reliable estimate of the amount of the obligation cannot be made).

Recognition

Provisions

A provision should be recognised when: **14**
(a) an enterprise has a present obligation (legal or constructive) as a result of a past event;
(b) it is probable that an outflow of resources embodying economic benefits will be required to settle the obligation; and
(c) a reliable estimate can be made of the amount of the obligation.
If these conditions are not met, no provision should be recognised.

Present Obligation

15 *In rare cases it is not clear whether there is a present obligation. In these cases, a past event is deemed to give rise to a present obligation if, taking account of all available evidence, it is more likely than not that a present obligation exists at the balance sheet date.*

16 In almost all cases it will be clear whether a past event has given rise to a present obligation. In rare cases, for example in a law suit, it may be disputed either whether certain events have occurred or whether those events result in a present obligation. In such a case, an enterprise determines whether a present obligation exists at the balance sheet date by taking account of all available evidence, including, for example, the opinion of experts. The evidence considered includes any additional evidence provided by events after the balance sheet date. On the basis of such evidence:
   (a) where it is more likely than not that a present obligation exists at the balance sheet date, the enterprise recognises a provision (if the recognition criteria are met); and
   (b) where it is more likely that no present obligation exists at the balance sheet date, the enterprise discloses a contingent liability, unless the possibility of an outflow of resources embodying economic benefits is remote (see paragraph 86).

Past Event

17 A past event that leads to a present obligation is called an obligating event. For an event to be an obligating event, it is necessary that the enterprise has no realistic alternative to settling the obligation created by the event. This is the case only:
   (a) where the settlement of the obligation can be enforced by law; or
   (b) in the case of a constructive obligation, where the event (which may be an action of the enterprise) creates valid expectations in other parties that the enterprise will discharge the obligation.

18 Financial statements deal with the financial position of an enterprise at the end of its reporting period and not its possible position in the future. Therefore, no provision is recognised for costs that need to be incurred to operate in the future. The only liabilities recognised in an enterprise's balance sheet are those that exist at the balance sheet date.

19 It is only those obligations arising from past events existing independently of an enterprise's future actions (i.e. the future conduct of its business) that are recognised as provisions. ...

20–22 [Not printed]

Probable Outflow of Resources Embodying Economic Benefits

23 For a liability to qualify for recognition there must be not only a present obligation but also the probability of an outflow of resources embodying economic benefits to settle that obligation. For the purpose of this Standard, an outflow of resources or other event is regarded as probable if the event is more likely than not to occur, i.e. the probability that the event will occur is greater than the probability that it will not. Where it is not probable that a present obligation exists, an enterprise discloses a contingent liability, unless the possibility of an outflow of resources embodying economic benefits is remote (see paragraph 86).

24 [Not printed]

Reliable Estimate of the Obligation

The use of estimates is an essential part of the preparation of financial statements and **25** does not undermine their reliability. This is especially true in the case of provisions, which by their nature are more uncertain than most other balance sheet items. Except in extremely rare cases, an enterprise will be able to determine a range of possible outcomes and can therefore make an estimate of the obligation that is sufficiently reliable to use in recognising a provision.

In the extremely rare case where no reliable estimate can be made, a liability exists that **26** cannot be recognised. That liability is disclosed as a contingent liability (see paragraph 86).

Contingent Liabilities

An enterprise should not recognise a contingent liability.   **27**

A contingent liability is disclosed, as required by paragraph 86, unless the possibility of **28** an outflow of resources embodying economic benefits is remote.

Where an enterprise is jointly and severally liable for an obligation, the part of the **29** obligation that is expected to be met by other parties is treated as a contingent liability. The enterprise recognises a provision for the part of the obligation for which an outflow of resources embodying economic benefits is probable, except in the extremely rare circumstances where no reliable estimate can be made.

... If it becomes probable that an outflow of future economic benefits will be required **30** for an item previously dealt with as a contingent liability, a provision is recognised in the financial statements of the period in which the change in probability occurs (except in the extremely rare circumstances where no reliable estimate can be made).

Contingent Assets

An enterprise should not recognise a contingent asset.   **31**

[Not printed]   **32–33**

A contingent asset is disclosed, as required by paragraph 89, where an inflow of **34** economic benefits is probable.

... If it has become virtually certain that an inflow of economic benefits will arise, the **35** asset and the related income are recognised in the financial statements of the period in which the change occurs. ...

Measurement

Best Estimate

The amount recognised as a provision should be the best estimate of the expenditure **36** *required to settle the present obligation at the balance sheet date.*

The best estimate of the expenditure required to settle the present obligation is the **37** amount that an enterprise would rationally pay to settle the obligation at the balance sheet date or to transfer it to a third party at that time. ...

38 [Not printed]

39 Uncertainties surrounding the amount to be recognised as a provision are dealt with by various means according to the circumstances. Where the provision being measured involves a large population of items, the obligation is estimated by weighting all possible outcomes by their associated probabilities. The name for this statistical method of estimation is 'expected value'. The provision will therefore be different depending on whether the probability of a loss of a given amount is, for example, 60 per cent or 90 per cent. Where there is a continuous range of possible outcomes, and each point in that range is as likely as any other, the mid-point of the range is used.

...

40 Where a single obligation is being measured, the individual most likely outcome may be the best estimate of the liability. However, even in such a case, the enterprise considers other possible outcomes. Where other possible outcomes are either mostly higher or mostly lower than the most likely outcome, the best estimate will be a higher or lower amount. ...

41 The provision is measured before tax, as the tax consequences of the provision, and changes in it, are dealt with under IAS 12.

Risks and Uncertainties

42 *The risks and uncertainties that inevitably surround many events and circumstances should be taken into account in reaching the best estimate of a provision.*

43 Risk describes variability of outcome. A risk adjustment may increase the amount at which a liability is measured. Caution is needed in making judgements under conditions of uncertainty, so that income or assets are not overstated and expenses or liabilities are not understated. However, uncertainty does not justify the creation of excessive provisions or a deliberate overstatement of liabilities. For example, if the projected costs of a particularly adverse outcome are estimated on a prudent basis, that outcome is not then deliberately treated as more probable than is realistically the case. Care is needed to avoid duplicating adjustments for risk and uncertainty with consequent overstatement of a provision.

44 Disclosure of the uncertainties surrounding the amount of the expenditure is made under paragraph 85(b).

Present Value

45 *Where the effect of the time value of money is material, the amount of a provision should be the present value of the expenditures expected to be required to settle the obligation.*

46 Because of the time value of money, provisions relating to cash outflows that arise soon after the balance sheet date are more onerous than those where cash outflows of the same amount arise later. Provisions are therefore discounted, where the effect is material.

47 *The discount rate (or rates) should be a pre-tax rate (or rates) that reflect(s) current market assessments of the time value of money and the risks specific to the liability. The discount rate(s) should not reflect risks for which future cash flow estimates have been adjusted.*

Future Events

Future events that may affect the amount required to settle an obligation should be **48**
reflected in the amount of a provision where there is sufficient objective evidence that
they will occur.

[Not printed]   **49**

The effect of possible new legislation is taken into consideration in measuring an **50**
existing obligation when sufficient objective evidence exists that the legislation is
virtually certain to be enacted. The variety of circumstances that arise in practice makes
it impossible to specify a single event that will provide sufficient, objective evidence in
every case. Evidence is required both of what legislation will demand and of whether
it is virtually certain to be enacted and implemented in due course. In many cases
sufficient objective evidence will not exist until the new legislation is enacted.

Expected Disposal of Assets

Gains from the expected disposal of assets should not be taken into account in **51**
measuring a provision.

[Not printed]   **52**

Reimbursements

Where some or all of the expenditure required to settle a provision is expected to be **53**
reimbursed by another party, the reimbursement should be recognised when, and only
when, it is virtually certain that reimbursement will be received if the enterprise
settles the obligation. The reimbursement should be treated as a separate asset. The
amount recognised for the reimbursement should not exceed the amount of the
provision.

In the income statement, the expense relating to a provision may be presented net of **54**
the amount recognised for a reimbursement.

[Not printed]   **55–58**

Changes in Provisions

Provisions should be reviewed at each balance sheet date and adjusted to reflect the **59**
current best estimate. If it is no longer probable that an outflow of resources
embodying economic benefits will be required to settle the obligation, the provision
should be reversed.

Where discounting is used, the carrying amount of a provision increases in each period **60**
to reflect the passage of time. This increase is recognised as borrowing cost.

Use of Provisions

A provision should be used only for expenditures for which the provision was **61**
originally recognised.

[Not printed]   **62**

Application of the Recognition and Measurement Rules

Future Operating Losses

63 *Provisions should not be recognised for future operating losses.*

64 [Not printed]

65 An expectation of future operating losses is an indication that certain assets of the operation may be impaired. An enterprise tests these assets for impairment under IAS 36.

Onerous Contracts

66 *If an enterprise has a contract that is onerous, the present obligation under the contract should be recognised and measured as a provision.*

67 [Not printed]

68 This Standard defines an onerous contract as a contract in which the unavoidable costs of meeting the obligations under the contract exceed the economic benefits expected to be received under it. The unavoidable costs under a contract reflect the least net cost of exiting from the contract, which is the lower of the cost of fulfilling it and any compensation or penalties arising from failure to fulfil it.

69 Before a separate provision for an onerous contract is established, an enterprise recognises any impairment loss that has occurred on assets dedicated to that contract (see IAS 36).

Restructuring

70 The following are examples of events that may fall under the definition of restructuring:
(a) sale or termination of a line of business;
(b) the closure of business locations in a country or region or the relocation of business activities from one country or region to another;
(c) changes in management structure, for example, eliminating a layer of management; and
(d) fundamental reorganisations that have a material effect on the nature and focus of the enterprise's operations.

71 A provision for restructuring costs is recognised only when the general recognition criteria for provisions set out in paragraph 14 are met. Paragraphs 72-83 set out how the general recognition criteria apply to restructurings.

72 *A constructive obligation to restructure arises only when an enterprise:*
(a) has a detailed formal plan for the restructuring identifying at least:
    (i) the business or part of a business concerned;
    (ii) the principal locations affected;
    (iii) the location, function, and approximate number of employees who will be compensated for terminating their services;
    (v) when the plan will be implemented; and (iv) the expenditures that will be undertaken; and

(b) has raised a valid expectation in those affected that it will carry out the restructuring by starting to implement that plan or announcing its main features to those affected by it.

[Not printed]   **73**

For a plan to be sufficient to give rise to a constructive obligation when communicated **74** to those affected by it, its implementation needs to be planned to begin as soon as possible and to be completed in a timeframe that makes significant changes to the plan unlikely. If it is expected that there will be a long delay before the restructuring begins or that the restructuring will take an unreasonably long time, it is unlikely that the plan will raise a valid expectation on the part of others that the enterprise is at present committed to restructuring, because the timeframe allows opportunities for the enterprise to change its plans.

A management or board decision to restructure taken before the balance sheet date does **75** not give rise to a constructive obligation at the balance sheet date unless the enterprise has, before the balance sheet date:
(a) started to implement the restructuring plan; or
(b) announced the main features of the restructuring plan to those affected by it in a sufficiently specific manner to raise a valid expectation in them that the enterprise will carry out the restructuring.
...

Although a constructive obligation is not created solely by a management decision, an **76** obligation may result from other earlier events together with such a decision. ...

[Not printed]   **77**

No obligation arises for the sale of an operation until the enterprise is committed to **78** *the sale, i.e. there is a binding sale agreement.*

[Not printed]   **79**

A restructuring provision should include only the direct expenditures arising from the **80** *restructuring, which are those that are both:*
(a) necessarily entailed by the restructuring; and
(b) not associated with the ongoing activities of the enterprise.

A restructuring provision does not include such costs as: **81**
(a) retraining or relocating continuing staff;
(b) marketing; or
(c) investment in new systems and distribution networks.
These expenditures relate to the future conduct of the business and are not liabilities for restructuring at the balance sheet date. Such expenditures are recognised on the same basis as if they arose independently of a restructuring.

Identifiable future operating losses up to the date of a restructuring are not included in **82** a provision, unless they relate to an onerous contract as defined in paragraph 10.

As required by paragraph 51, gains on the expected disposal of assets are not taken into **83** account in measuring a restructuring provision, even if the sale of assets is envisaged as part of the restructuring.

Disclosure

84 *For each class of provision, an enterprise should disclose:*
   (a) *the carrying amount at the beginning and end of the period;*
   (b) *additional provisions made in the period, including increases to existing provisions;*
   (c) *amounts used (i.e. incurred and charged against the provision) during the period;*
   (d) *unused amounts reversed during the period; and*
   (e) *the increase during the period in the discounted amount arising from the passage of time and the effect of any change in the discount rate.*
   ...

85 *An enterprise should disclose the following for each class of provision:*
   (a) *a brief description of the nature of the obligation and the expected timing of any resulting outflows of economic benefits;*
   (b) *an indication of the uncertainties about the amount or timing of those outflows. Where necessary to provide adequate information, an enterprise should disclose the major assumptions made concerning future events, as addressed in paragraph 48; and*
   (c) *the amount of any expected reimbursement, stating the amount of any asset that has been recognised for that expected reimbursement.*

86 *Unless the possibility of any outflow in settlement is remote, an enterprise should disclose for each class of contingent liability at the balance sheet date a brief description of the nature of the contingent liability and, where practicable:*
   (a) *an estimate of its financial effect, measured under paragraphs 36-52;*
   (b) *an indication of the uncertainties relating to the amount or timing of any outflow; and*
   (c) *the possibility of any reimbursement.*

87 [Not printed]

88 Where a provision and a contingent liability arise from the same set of circumstances, an enterprise makes the disclosures required by paragraphs 84-86 in a way that shows the link between the provision and the contingent liability.

89 *Where an inflow of economic benefits is probable, an enterprise should disclose a brief description of the nature of the contingent assets at the balance sheet date, and, where practicable, an estimate of their financial effect, measured using the principles set out for provisions in paragraphs 36-52.*

90 It is important that disclosures for contingent assets avoid giving misleading indications of the likelihood of income arising.

91 *Where any of the information required by paragraphs 86 and 89 is not disclosed because it is not practicable to do so, that fact should be stated.*

92 *In extremely rare cases, disclosure of some or all of the information required by paragraphs 84-89 can be expected to prejudice seriously the position of the enterprise in a dispute with other parties on the subject matter of the provision, contingent liability or contingent asset. In such cases, an enterprise need not disclose the information, but should disclose the general nature of the dispute, together with the fact that, and reason why, the information has not been disclosed.*

Transitional Provisions

Effective Date

Appendix A

Tables – Provisions, Contingent Liabilities, Contingent Assets and Reimbursements

[Not printed]

Appendix B

Decision Tree

The purpose of the decision tree is to summarise the main recognition requirements of the standards for provisions and contingent liabilities. The decision tree does not form part of the standards and should be read in the context of the full text of the standards.

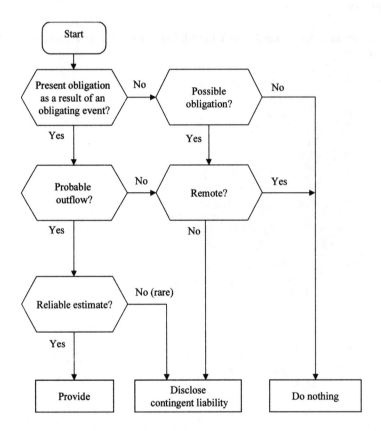

Note: in rare cases, it is not clear whether there is a present obligation. In these cases, a past event is deemed to give rise to a present obligation if, taking account of all available evidence, it is more likely than not that a present obligation exists at the balance sheet date (paragraph 15 of the Standard).

Appendix C

Examples: Recognition

[Not printed]

Appendix D

Example: Disclosures

[Not printed]

IAS 38: Intangible Assets

IAS 38: Intangible Assets			
Scope 38.1–6	Definitions 38.7–17	Transitional Provisions 38.118–121	Effective Date 38.122–123

Definitions 38.7–17		
Intangible Assests 38.8–17		
Identifiability 38.10–12	Control 38.13–16	Future Economic Benefits 38.17

Recognition and Initial Measurement of an Intangible Asset 38.18–55

Separate Acquisition 38.23–26	Acquisition as Part of a Business Combination 38.27–32	Acquisition by Way of a Government Grant 38.33	Exchanges of Assets 38.34–35	Internally Generated Goodwill 38.36–38	Internally Generated Intangible Assets 38.39–55		
					Development Phase 38.45–52	Cost of an Internally Generated Intangible Asset 38.53–55	Research Phase 38.42–44

Recognition of an Expense 38.56–59
Past Expenses not to be Recognised as an Asset 38.59

Subsequent Expenditure 38.60–62

Measurement Subsequent to Initial Recognition 38.63–78	
Benchmark Treatment 38.63	Allowed Alternative Treatment 38.64–78

IAS 38: Intangible Assets (Continued)

Amortisation 38.79–96			
Amortisation Period 38.79–87	Amortisation Method 38.88–90	Residual Value 38.91–93	Review of Amortisation Period and Amortisation Method 38.94–96

Recoverability of the Carrying Amount – Impairment Losses 38.97–102

Retirements and Disposals 38.103–106

Disclosure 38.107–117			
General 38.107–112	Intangible Assets Carried Under the Allowed Alternative Treatment 38.113–114	Research and Development Expenditure 38.115–116	Other Information 38.117

Appendix [Not printed]
Basis for Conclusions

Scope

This Standard should be applied by all enterprises in accounting for intangible assets, **1**
except:
(a) intangible assets that are covered by another IAS;
(b) financial assets, as defined in IAS 32;
(c) mineral rights and expenditure on the exploration for, or development and extraction of, minerals, oil, natural gas and similar non-regenerative resources; and
(d) intangible assets arising in insurance enterprises from contracts with policyholders.

[Not printed]   **2**

Some intangible assets may be contained in or on a physical substance such as a   **3** compact disk (in the case of computer software), legal documentation (in the case of a licence or patent) or film. In determining whether an asset that incorporates both intangible and tangible elements should be treated under IAS 16 or as an intangible asset under this Standard, judgement is required to assess which element is more significant. ...

4 This Standard applies to, among other things, expenditure on advertising, training, start-up, research and development activities. ...

5–6 [Not printed]

Definitions

7 ...

An *intangible asset is an identifiable non-monetary asset without physical substance held for use in the production or supply of goods or services, for rental to others, or for administrative purposes.*

An *asset is a resource*:

(a) controlled by an enterprise as a result of past events; and

(b) from which future economic benefits are expected to flow to the enterprise.

> *Monetary assets are money held and assets to be received in fixed or determinable amounts of money.*

Research is original and planned investigation undertaken with the prospect of gaining new scientific or technical knowledge and understanding.

Development is the application of research findings or other knowledge to a plan or design for the production of new or substantially improved materials, devices, products, processes, systems or services prior to the commencement of commercial production or use.

Amortisation is the systematic allocation of the depreciable amount of an intangible asset over its useful life.

Depreciable amount is the cost of an asset, or other amount substituted for cost in the financial statements, less its residual value.

Useful life is either:

(a) the period of time over which an asset is expected to be used by the enterprise; or

(b) the number of production or similar units expected to be obtained from the asset by the enterprise.

Cost is the amount of cash or cash equivalents paid or the fair value of the other consideration given to acquire an asset at the time of its acquisition or production.

Residual value is the net amount which an enterprise expects to obtain for an asset at the end of its useful life after deducting the expected costs of disposal.

Fair value of an asset is the amount for which that asset could be exchanged between knowledgeable, willing parties in an arm's length transaction.

An active market is a market where all the following conditions exist:

(a) the items traded within the market are homogeneous;

(b) willing buyers and sellers can normally be found at any time; and

(c) prices are available to the public.

An impairment loss is the amount by which the carrying amount of an asset exceeds its recoverable amount.

Carrying amount is the amount at which an asset is recognised in the balance sheet after deducting any accumulated amortisation and accumulated impairment losses thereon.

Intangible Assets

8 Enterprises frequently expend resources, or incur liabilities, on the acquisition, development, maintenance or enhancement of intangible resources such as scientific or technical knowledge, design and implementation of new processes or systems, licences,

intellectual property, market knowledge and trademarks (including brand names and publishing titles). Common examples of items encompassed by these broad headings are computer software, patents, copyrights, motion picture films, customer lists, mortgage servicing rights, fishing licences, import quotas, franchises, customer or supplier relationships, customer loyalty, market share and marketing rights.

... If an item covered by this Standard does not meet the definition of an intangible **9** asset, expenditure to acquire it or generate it internally is recognised as an expense when it is incurred. ...

Identifiability

The definition of an intangible asset requires that an intangible asset be identifiable to **10** distinguish it clearly from goodwill. ...

An intangible asset can be clearly distinguished from goodwill if the asset is separable. **11** An asset is separable if the enterprise could rent, sell, exchange or distribute the specific future economic benefits attributable to the asset without also disposing of future economic benefits that flow from other assets used in the same revenue earning activity.

Separability is not a necessary condition for identifiability since an enterprise may be **12** able to identify an asset in some other way. ...

Control

An enterprise controls an asset if the enterprise has the power to obtain the future **13** economic benefits flowing from the underlying resource and also can restrict the access of others to those benefits. The capacity of an enterprise to control the future economic benefits from an intangible asset would normally stem from legal rights that are enforceable in a court of law. In the absence of legal rights, it is more difficult to demonstrate control. However, legal enforceability of a right is not a necessary condition for control since an enterprise may be able to control the future economic benefits in some other way.

Market and technical knowledge may give rise to future economic benefits. An **14** enterprise controls those benefits if, for example, the knowledge is protected by legal rights such as copyrights, a restraint of trade agreement (where permitted) or by a legal duty on employees to maintain confidentiality.

An enterprise may have a team of skilled staff and may be able to identify incremental **15** staff skills leading to future economic benefits from training. The enterprise may also expect that the staff will continue to make their skills available to the enterprise. However, usually an enterprise has insufficient control over the expected future economic benefits arising from a team of skilled staff and from training to consider that these items meet the definition of an intangible asset. For a similar reason, specific management or technical talent is unlikely to meet the definition of an intangible asset, unless it is protected by legal rights to use it and to obtain the future economic benefits expected from it, and it also meets the other parts of the definition.

An enterprise may have a portfolio of customers or a market share and expect that, due **16** to its efforts in building customer relationships and loyalty, the customers will continue to trade with the enterprise. However, in the absence of legal rights to protect, or other ways to control, the relationships with customers or the loyalty of the customers to the enterprise, the enterprise usually has insufficient control over the economic benefits from customer relationships and loyalty to consider that such items (portfolio of customers, market shares, customer relationships, customer loyalty) meet the definition of intangible assets.

Future Economic Benefits

17 The future economic benefits flowing from an intangible asset may include revenue from the sale of products or services, cost savings, or other benefits resulting from the use of the asset by the enterprise. ...

Recognition and Initial Measurement of an Intangible Asset

18 The recognition of an item as an intangible asset requires an enterprise to demonstrate that the item meets the:
(a) definition of an intangible asset (see paragraphs 7-17); and
(b) recognition criteria set out in this Standard (see paragraphs 19-55).

19 *An intangible asset should be recognised if, and only if:*
   (a) it is probable that the future economic benefits that are attributable to the asset will flow to the enterprise; and
   (b) the cost of the asset can be measured reliably.

20 *An enterprise should assess the probability of future economic benefits using reasonable and supportable assumptions that represent management's best estimate of the set of economic conditions that will exist over the useful life of the asset.*

21 An enterprise uses judgement to assess the degree of certainty attached to the flow of future economic benefits that are attributable to the use of the asset on the basis of the evidence available at the time of initial recognition, giving greater weight to external evidence.

22 *An intangible asset should be measured initially at cost.*

Separate Acquisition

23 If an intangible asset is acquired separately, the cost of the intangible asset can usually be measured reliably. This is particularly so when the purchase consideration is in the form of cash or other monetary assets.

24 The cost of an intangible asset comprises its purchase price, including any import duties and non-refundable purchase taxes, and any directly attributable expenditure on preparing the asset for its intended use. Directly attributable expenditure includes, for example, professional fees for legal services. Any trade discounts and rebates are deducted in arriving at the cost.

25 If payment for an intangible asset is deferred beyond normal credit terms, its cost is the cash price equivalent; the difference between this amount and the total payments is recognised as interest expense over the period of credit unless it is capitalised under the allowed alternative treatment in IAS 23.

26 If an intangible asset is acquired in exchange for equity instruments of the reporting enterprise, the cost of the asset is the fair value of the equity instruments issued, which is equal to the fair value of the asset.

Acquisition as Part of a Business Combination

27 Under IAS 22 if an intangible asset is acquired in a business combination that is an acquisition, the cost of that intangible asset is based on its fair value at the date of acquisition.

28 Judgement is required to determine whether the cost (i.e. fair value) of an intangible asset acquired in a business combination can be measured with sufficient reliability for the purpose of separate recognition. Quoted market prices in an active market provide the most reliable measurement of fair value (see also paragraph 67). The appropriate market price is usually the current bid price. If current bid prices are unavailable, the price of the most recent similar transaction may provide a basis from which to estimate fair value, provided that there has not been a significant change in economic circumstances between the transaction date and the date at which the asset's fair value is estimated.

29 If no active market exists for an asset, its cost reflects the amount that the enterprise would have paid, at the date of the acquisition, for the asset in an arm's length transaction between knowledgeable and willing parties, based on the best information available. In determining this amount, an enterprise considers the outcome of recent transactions for similar assets.

30 Certain enterprises that are regularly involved in the purchase and sale of unique intangible assets have developed techniques for estimating their fair values indirectly. These techniques may be used for initial measurement of an intangible asset acquired in a business combination that is an acquisition if their objective is to estimate fair value as defined in this Standard and if they reflect current transactions and practices in the industry to which the asset belongs. These techniques include, where appropriate, applying multiples reflecting current market transactions to certain indicators driving the profitability of the asset (such as revenue, market shares, operating profit, etc.) or discounting estimated future net cash flows from the asset.

31 In accordance with this Standard and the requirements in IAS 22 for the recognition of identifiable assets and liabilities:
(a) an acquirer recognises an intangible asset that meets the recognition criteria in paragraphs 19 and 20, even if that intangible asset had not been recognised in the financial statements of the acquiree; and
(b) if the cost (i.e. fair value) of an intangible asset acquired as part of a business combination that is an acquisition cannot be measured reliably, that asset is not recognised as a separate intangible asset but is included in goodwill (see paragraph 56).

32 Unless there is an active market for an intangible asset acquired in a business combination that is an acquisition, IAS 22 limits the cost initially recognised for the intangible asset to an amount that does not create or increase any negative goodwill arising at the date of acquisition.

Acquisition by way of a Government Grant

33 In some cases, an intangible asset may be acquired free of charge, or for nominal consideration, by way of a government grant. This may occur when a government transfers or allocates to an enterprise intangible assets ... Under IAS 20 an enterprise may choose to recognise both the intangible asset and the grant at fair value initially.

If an enterprise chooses not to recognise the asset initially at fair value, the enterprise recognises the asset initially at a nominal amount (under the other treatment permitted by IAS 20) plus any expenditure that is directly attributable to preparing the asset for its intended use.

Exchanges of Assets

34 An intangible asset may be acquired in exchange or part exchange for a dissimilar intangible asset or other asset. The cost of such an item is measured at the fair value of the asset received, which is equivalent to the fair value of the asset given up, adjusted by the amount of any cash or cash equivalents transferred.

35 An intangible asset may be acquired in exchange for a similar asset that has a similar use in the same line of business and that has a similar fair value. An intangible asset may also be sold in exchange for an equity interest in a similar asset. In both cases, since the earnings process is incomplete, no gain or loss is recognised on the transaction. Instead, the cost of the new asset is the carrying amount of the asset given up. However, the fair value of the asset received may provide evidence of an impairment loss in the asset given up. Under these circumstances an impairment loss is recognised for the asset given up and the carrying amount after impairment is assigned to the new asset.

Internally Generated Goodwill

36 *Internally generated goodwill should not be recognised as an asset.*

37 In some cases, expenditure is incurred to generate future economic benefits, but it does not result in the creation of an intangible asset that meets the recognition criteria in this Standard. Such expenditure is often described as contributing to internally generated goodwill. Internally generated goodwill is not recognised as an asset because it is not an identifiable resource controlled by the enterprise that can be measured reliably at cost.

38 Differences between the market value of an enterprise and the carrying amount of its identifiable net assets at any point in time may capture a range of factors that affect the value of the enterprise. However, such differences cannot be considered to represent the cost of intangible assets controlled by the enterprise.

Internally Generated Intangible Assets

39 [Not printed]

40 To assess whether an internally generated intangible asset meets the criteria for recognition, an enterprise classifies the generation of the asset into:
(a) a research phase; and
(b) a development phase.
Although the terms 'research' and 'development' are defined, the terms 'research phase' and 'development phase' have a broader meaning for the purpose of this Standard.

41 If an enterprise cannot distinguish the research phase from the development phase of an internal project to create an intangible asset, the enterprise treats the expenditure on that project as if it were incurred in the research phase only.

Research Phase

No intangible asset arising from research (or from the research phase of an internal **42**
project) should be recognised. Expenditure on research (or on the research phase of
an internal project) should be recognised as an expense when it is incurred.

[Not printed] **43**

Examples of research activities are: **44**
(a) activities aimed at obtaining new knowledge;
(b) the search for, evaluation and final selection of, applications of research findings or
    other knowledge;
(c) the search for alternatives for materials, devices, products, processes, systems or
    services; and
(d) the formulation, design, evaluation and final selection of possible alternatives for
    new or improved materials, devices, products, processes, systems or services.

Development Phase

An intangible asset arising from development (or from the development phase of an **45**
internal project) should be recognised if, and only if, an enterprise can demonstrate
all of the following:
(a) the technical feasibility of completing the intangible asset so that it will be
    available for use or sale;
(b) its intention to complete the intangible asset and use or sell it;
(c) its ability to use or sell the intangible asset;
(d) how the intangible asset will generate probable future economic benefits. Among
    other things, the enterprise should demonstrate the existence of a market for the
    output of the intangible asset or the intangible asset itself or, if it is to be used
    internally, the usefulness of the intangible asset;
(e) the availability of adequate technical, financial and other resources to complete
    the development and to use or sell the intangible asset; and
(f) its ability to measure the expenditure attributable to the intangible asset during
    its development reliably.

[Not printed] **46**

Examples of development activities are: **47**
(a) the design, construction and testing of pre-production or pre-use prototypes and
    models;
(b) the design of tools, jigs, moulds and dies involving new technology;
(c) the design, construction and operation of a pilot plant that is not of a scale
    economically feasible for commercial production; and
(d) the design, construction and testing of a chosen alternative for new or improved
    materials, devices, products, processes, systems or services.

To demonstrate how an intangible asset will generate probable future economic **48**
benefits, an enterprise assesses the future economic benefits to be received from the
asset using the principles in IAS 36. If the asset will generate economic benefits only
in combination with other assets, the enterprise applies the concept of cash-generating
units as set out in IAS 36.

Availability of resources to complete, use and obtain the benefits from an intangible **49**
asset can be demonstrated by, for example, a business plan showing the technical,

financial and other resources needed and the enterprise's ability to secure those resources. In certain cases, an enterprise demonstrates the availability of external finance by obtaining a lender's indication of its willingness to fund the plan.

50 [Not printed]

51 *Internally generated brands, mastheads, publishing titles, customer lists and items similar in substance should not be recognised as intangible assets.*

52 [Not printed]

Cost of an Internally Generated Intangible Asset

53 The cost of an internally generated intangible asset for the purpose of paragraph 22 is the sum of expenditure incurred from the date when the intangible asset first meets the recognition criteria in paragraphs 19-20 and 45. Paragraph 59 prohibits reinstatement of expenditure recognised as an expense in previous annual financial statements or interim financial reports.

54 The cost of an internally generated intangible asset comprises all expenditure that can be directly attributed, or allocated on a reasonable and consistent basis, to creating, producing and preparing the asset for its intended use. The cost includes, if applicable:
   (a) expenditure on materials and services used or consumed in generating the intangible asset;
   (b) the salaries, wages and other employment related costs of personnel directly engaged in generating the asset;
   (c) any expenditure that is directly attributable to generating the asset, such as fees to register a legal right and the amortisation of patents and licences that are used to generate the asset; and
   (d) overheads that are necessary to generate the asset and that can be allocated on a reasonable and consistent basis to the asset (for example, an allocation of the depreciation of property, plant and equipment, insurance premiums and rent). Allocations of overheads are made on bases similar to those used in allocating overheads to inventories (see IAS 2). IAS 23 establishes criteria for the recognition of interest as a component of the cost of an internally generated intangible asset.

55 The following are not components of the cost of an internally generated intangible asset:
   (a) selling, administrative and other general overhead expenditure unless this expenditure can be directly attributed to preparing the asset for use;
   (b) clearly identified inefficiencies and initial operating losses incurred before an asset achieves planned performance; and
   (c) expenditure on training staff to operate the asset.
   ...

Recognition of an Expense

56 *Expenditure on an intangible item should be recognised as an expense when it is incurred unless:*
   (a) *it forms part of the cost of an intangible asset that meets the recognition criteria (see paragraphs 18-55); or*
   (b) *the item is acquired in a business combination that is an acquisition and cannot be recognised as an intangible asset. If this is the case, this expenditure (included*

in the cost of acquisition) should form part of the amount attributed to goodwill (negative goodwill) at the date of acquisition (see IAS 22).

In some cases, expenditure is incurred to provide future economic benefits to an **57** enterprise, but no intangible asset or other asset is acquired or created that can be recognised. In these cases, the expenditure is recognised as an expense when it is incurred. For example, expenditure on research is always recognised as an expense when it is incurred (see paragraph 42). Examples of other expenditure that is recognised as an expense when it is incurred include:

(a) expenditure on start-up activities (start-up costs), unless this expenditure is included in the cost of an item of property, plant and equipment under IAS 16. Start-up costs may consist of establishment costs such as legal and secretarial costs incurred in establishing a legal entity, expenditure to open a new facility or business (pre-opening costs) or expenditures for commencing new operations or launching new products or processes (pre-operating costs);

(b) expenditure on training activities;

(c) expenditure on advertising and promotional activities; and

(d) expenditure on relocating or re-organising part or all of an enterprise.

[Not printed] **58**

Past Expenses not to be Recognised as an Asset

Expenditure on an intangible item that was initially recognised as an expense by a **59** *reporting enterprise in previous annual financial statements or interim financial reports should not be recognised as part of the cost of an intangible asset at a later date.*

Subsequent Expenditure

Subsequent expenditure on an intangible asset after its purchase or its completion **60** *should be recognised as an expense when it is incurred unless:*

(a) it is probable that this expenditure will enable the asset to generate future economic benefits in excess of its originally assessed standard of performance; and

(b) If these conditions are met, the subsequent expenditure should be added to the cost of the intangible asset.

[Not printed] **61**

Consistent with paragraph 51, subsequent expenditure on brands, mastheads, **62** publishing titles, customer lists and items similar in substance (whether externally purchased or internally generated) is always recognised as an expense to avoid the recognition of internally generated goodwill.

Measurement Subsequent to Initial Recognition

Benchmark Treatment

After initial recognition, an intangible asset should be carried at its cost less any **63** *accumulated amortisation and any accumulated impairment losses.*

Allowed Alternative Treatment

64 *After initial recognition, an intangible asset should be carried at a revalued amount, being its fair value at the date of the revaluation less any subsequent accumulated amortisation and any subsequent accumulated impairment losses. For the purpose of revaluations under this Standard, fair value should be determined by reference to an active market. Revaluations should be made with sufficient regularity such that the carrying amount does not differ materially from that which would be determined using fair value at the balance sheet date.*

65 The allowed alternative treatment does not allow:
(a) the revaluation of intangible assets that have not previously been recognised as assets; or
(b) the initial recognition of intangible assets at amounts other than their cost.

66–67 [Not printed]

68 The frequency of revaluations depends on the volatility of the fair values of the intangible assets being revalued. If the fair value of a revalued asset differs materially from its carrying amount, a further revaluation is necessary. Some intangible assets may experience significant and volatile movements in fair value thus necessitating annual revaluation. Such frequent revaluations are unnecessary for intangible assets with only insignificant movements in fair value.

69 If an intangible asset is revalued, any accumulated amortisation at the date of the revaluation is either:
(a) restated proportionately with the change in the gross carrying amount of the asset so that the carrying amount of the asset after revaluation equals its revalued amount; or
(b) eliminated against the gross carrying amount of the asset and the net amount restated to the revalued amount of the asset.

70 *If an intangible asset is revalued, all the other assets in its class should also be revalued, unless there is no active market for those assets.*

71 A class of intangible assets is a grouping of assets of a similar nature and use in an enterprise's operations. The items within a class of intangible assets are revalued simultaneously in order to avoid selective revaluation of assets and the reporting of amounts in the financial statements representing a mixture of costs and values as at different dates.

72 *If an intangible asset in a class of revalued intangible assets cannot be revalued because there is no active market for this asset, the asset should be carried at its cost less any accumulated amortisation and impairment losses.*

73 *If the fair value of a revalued intangible asset can no longer be determined by reference to an active market, the carrying amount of the asset should be its revalued amount at the date of the last revaluation by reference to the active market less any subsequent accumulated amortisation and any subsequent accumulated impairment losses.*

74–75 [Not printed]

76 *If an intangible asset's carrying amount is increased as a result of a revaluation, the increase should be credited directly to equity under the heading of revaluation surplus. However, a revaluation increase should be recognised as income to the extent* *that it reverses a revaluation decrease of the same asset and that revaluation decrease was previously recognised as an expense.*

If an asset's carrying amount is decreased as a result of a revaluation, the decrease **77** *should be recognised as an expense. However, a revaluation decrease should be charged directly against any related revaluation surplus to the extent that the decrease does not exceed the amount held in the revaluation surplus in respect of that same asset.*

The cumulative revaluation surplus included in equity may be transferred directly to **78** retained earnings when the surplus is realised. The whole surplus may be realised on the retirement or disposal of the asset. However, some of the surplus may be realised as the asset is used by the enterprise; in such a case, the amount of the surplus realised is the difference between amortisation based on the revalued carrying amount of the asset and amortisation that would have been recognised based on the asset's historical cost. The transfer from revaluation surplus to retained earnings is not made through the income statement.

Amortisation

Amortisation Period

The depreciable amount of an intangible asset should be allocated on a systematic **79** *basis over the best estimate of its useful life. There is a rebuttable presumption that the useful life of an intangible asset will not exceed twenty years from the date when the asset is available for use. Amortisation should commence when the asset is available for use.*

As the future economic benefits embodied in an intangible asset are consumed over **80** time, the carrying amount of the asset is reduced to reflect that consumption. This is achieved by systematic allocation of the cost or revalued amount of the asset, less any residual value, as an expense over the asset's useful life. Amortisation is recognised whether or not there has been an increase in, for example, the asset's fair value or recoverable amount. Many factors need to be considered in determining the useful life of an intangible asset including:

(a) the expected usage of the asset by the enterprise and whether the asset could be efficiently managed by another management team;

(b) typical product life cycles for the asset and public information on estimates of useful lives of similar types of assets that are used in a similar way;

(c) technical, technological or other types of obsolescence;

(d) the stability of the industry in which the asset operates and changes in the market demand for the products or services output from the asset;

(e) expected actions by competitors or potential competitors;

(f) the level of maintenance expenditure required to obtain the expected future economic benefits from the asset and the company's ability and intent to reach such a level;

(g) the period of control over the asset and legal or similar limits on the use of the asset, such as the expiry dates of related leases; and

(h) whether the useful life of the asset is dependent on the useful life of other assets of the enterprise.

[Not printed]   **81–82**

83 In rare cases, there may be persuasive evidence that the useful life of an intangible asset will be a specific period longer than twenty years. In these cases, the presumption that the useful life generally does not exceed twenty years is rebutted and the enterprise:

(a) amortises the intangible asset over the best estimate of its useful life;

(b) estimates the recoverable amount of the intangible asset at least annually in order to identify any impairment loss (see paragraph 99); and

(c) discloses the reasons why the presumption is rebutted and the factor(s) that played a significant role in determining the useful life of the asset (see paragraph 111(a)).

...

84 [Not printed]

85 *If control over the future economic benefits from an intangible asset is achieved through legal rights that have been granted for a finite period, the useful life of the intangible asset should not exceed the period of the legal rights unless:*

(a) the legal rights are renewable; and

(b) renewal is virtually certain.

86 [Not printed]

87 The following factors, among others, indicate that renewal of a legal right is virtually certain:

(a) the fair value of the intangible asset does not reduce as the initial expiry date approaches, or does not reduce by more than the cost of renewing the underlying right;

(b) there is evidence (possibly based on past experience) that the legal rights will be renewed; and

(c) there is evidence that the conditions necessary to obtain the renewal of the legal right (if any) will be satisfied.

Amortisation Method

88 *The amortisation method used should reflect the pattern in which the asset's economic benefits are consumed by the enterprise. If that pattern cannot be determined reliably, the straight-line method should be used. The amortisation charge for each period should be recognised as an expense unless another IAS permits or requires it to be included in the carrying amount of another asset.*

89–90 [Not printed]

Residual Value

91 *The residual value of an intangible asset should be assumed to be zero unless:*

(a) there is a commitment by a third party to purchase the asset at the end of its useful life; or

(b) there is an active market for the asset and:

(i) residual value can be determined by reference to that market; and

(ii) it is probable that such a market will exist at the end of the asset's useful life.

92 [Not printed]

93 If the benchmark treatment is adopted, the residual value is estimated using prices prevailing at the date of acquisition of the asset, for the sale of a similar asset that has reached the end of its estimated useful life and that has operated under conditions

similar to those in which the asset will be used. The residual value is not subsequently increased for changes in prices or value. If the allowed alternative treatment is adopted, a new estimate of residual value is made at the date of each revaluation of the asset using prices prevailing at that date.

Review of Amortisation Period and Amortisation Method

The amortisation period and the amortisation method should be reviewed at least at **94** *each financial year end. If the expected useful life of the asset is significantly different from previous estimates, the amortisation period should be changed accordingly. If there has been a significant change in the expected pattern of economic benefits from the asset, the amortisation method should be changed to reflect the changed pattern. Such changes should be accounted for as changes in accounting estimates under IAS 8 by adjusting the amortisation charge for the current and future periods.*

[Not printed] **95-96**

Recoverability of the Carrying Amount - Impairment Losses

[Not printed] **97–98**

In addition to following the requirements included in IAS 36 an enterprise should **99** *estimate the recoverable amount of the following intangible assets at least at each financial year end, even if there is no indication that the asset is impaired:*
(a) an intangible asset that is not yet available for use; and
(b) an intangible asset that is amortised over a period exceeding twenty years from the date when the asset is available for use.
The recoverable amount should be determined under IAS 36 and impairment losses recognised accordingly.

[Not printed] **100–102**

Retirements and Disposals

An intangible asset should be derecognised (eliminated from the balance sheet) on **103** *disposal or when no future economic benefits are expected from its use and subsequent disposal.*

Gains or losses arising from the retirement or disposal of an intangible asset should **104** *be determined as the difference between the net disposal proceeds and the carrying amount of the asset and should be recognised as income or expense in the income statement.*

If an intangible asset is exchanged for a similar asset under the circumstances described **105** in paragraph 35, the cost of the acquired asset is equal to the carrying amount of the asset disposed of and no gain or loss results.

An intangible asset that is retired from active use and held for disposal is carried at its **106** carrying amount at the date when the asset is retired from active use. At least at each financial year end, an enterprise tests the asset for impairment under IAS 36 and recognises any impairment loss accordingly.

Disclosure

General

107 *The financial statements should disclose the following for each class of intangible assets, distinguishing between internally generated intangible assets and other intangible assets:*

(a) *the useful lives or the amortisation rates used;*

(b) *the amortisation methods used;*

(c) *the gross carrying amount and the accumulated amortisation (aggregated with accumulated impairment losses) at the beginning and end of the period;*

(d) *the line item(s) of the income statement in which the amortisation of intangible assets is included;*

(e) *a reconciliation of the carrying amount at the beginning and end of the period showing:*

   (i) *additions, indicating separately those from internal development and through business combinations;*

   (ii) *retirements and disposals;*

   (iii)*increases or decreases during the period resulting from revaluations under paragraphs 64, 76 and 77 and from impairment losses recognised or reversed directly in equity under IAS 36 (if any);*

   (iv) *impairment losses recognised in the income statement during the period under IAS 36 (if any);*

   (v) *impairment losses reversed in the income statement during the period under IAS 36 (if any);*

   (vi) *amortisation recognised during the period;*

   (vii)*net exchange differences arising on the translation of the financial statements of a foreign entity; and*

   (viii)*other changes in the carrying amount during the period.*

   ...

108 A class of intangible assets is a grouping of assets of a similar nature and use in an enterprise's operations. Examples of separate classes may include:

(a) brand names;

(b) mastheads and publishing titles;

(c) computer software;

(d) licences and franchises;

(e) copyrights, patents and other industrial property rights, service and operating rights;

(f) recipes, formulae, models, designs and prototypes; and

(g) intangible assets under development.

The classes mentioned above are disaggregated (aggregated) into smaller (larger) classes if this results in more relevant information for the users of the financial statements.

109 [Not printed]

110 An enterprise discloses the nature and effect of a change in an accounting estimate that has a material effect in the current period or that is expected to have a material effect in subsequent periods, under IAS 8. Such disclosure may arise from changes in:

(a) the amortisation period;

(b) the amortisation method; or

(c) residual values.

The financial statements should also disclose: **111**

(a) if an intangible asset is amortised over more than twenty years, the reasons why the presumption that the useful life of an intangible asset will not exceed twenty years from the date when the asset is available for use is rebutted. In giving these reasons, the enterprise should describe the factor(s) that played a significant role in determining the useful life of the asset;

(b) a description, the carrying amount and remaining amortisation period of any individual intangible asset that is material to the financial statements of the enterprise as a whole;

(c) for intangible assets acquired by way of a government grant and initially recognised at fair value (see paragraph 33):
  (i) the fair value initially recognised for these assets;
  (ii) their carrying amount; and
  (iii)whether they are carried under the benchmark or the allowed alternative treatment for subsequent measurement;

(d) the existence and carrying amounts of intangible assets whose title is restricted and the carrying amounts of intangible assets pledged as security for liabilities; and

(e) the amount of commitments for the acquisition of intangible assets.

[Not printed] **112**

Intangible Assets Carried Under the Allowed Alternative Treatment

If intangible assets are carried at revalued amounts, the following should be **113** *disclosed:*

(a) by class of intangible assets:
  (i) the effective date of the revaluation;
  (ii) the carrying amount of revalued intangible assets; and
  (iii)the carrying amount that would have been included in the financial statements had the revalued intangible assets been carried under the benchmark treatment in paragraph 63; and

(b) the amount of the revaluation surplus that relates to intangible assets at the beginning and end of the period, indicating the changes during the period and any restrictions on the distribution of the balance to shareholders.

It may be necessary to aggregate the classes of revalued assets into larger classes for **114** disclosure purposes. However, classes are not aggregated if this would result in the combination of a class of intangible assets that includes amounts measured under both benchmark and allowed alternative treatments for subsequent measurement.

Research and Development Expenditure

The financial statements should disclose the aggregate amount of research and **115** *development expenditure recognised as an expense during the period.*

[Not printed] **116**

Other Information

An enterprise is encouraged, but not required, to give the following information: **117**

(a) a description of any fully amortised intangible asset that is still in use; and

(b) a brief description of significant intangible assets controlled by the enterprise but not recognised as assets because they did not meet the recognition criteria in this Standard or because they were acquired or generated before this Standard was effective.

Transitional Provisions

118–121 [Not printed]

Effective Date

122–123 [Not printed]

Appendix A

Basis for Conclusions to IAS 38 and Summary of Changes to Exposure Draft E60, Intangible Assets.

[Not printed]

IAS 39: Financial Instruments: Recognition and Measurement

IAS 39: Financial Instruments: Recognition and Measurement

Scope 39.1–7

Definitions 39.8–26
- From IAS 32 39.8–9
- Additional Definitions 39.10
  - Derivative 39.10
  - Four Categories of Financial Assets 39.10
  - Recognition and Measurement 39.10
  - Hedge Accounting 39.10
  - Other 39.10
- Embedded Derivatives 39.22–26

Effective Date 39.171

Transition 39.172

Elaboration on the Definitions 39.11–21
- Equity Instrument 39.11–12
- Derivatives 39.13–16
- Transaction Costs 39.17
- Liability Held for Trading 39.18
- Loans and Receivables Originated by the Enterprise 39.19–20
- Available-for-Sale Financial Assets 39.21

Recognition 39.27–65

Initial Recognition 39.27–29

Trade Date vs. Settlement Date 39.30–34

Derecognition 39.35–65

Financial Asset 39.35–43

Part of a Financial Asset 39.47–50

Asset Derecognition Coupled with a New Financial Asset or Liability 39.51–56

Financial Liability 39.57–64

Derecognition of Part of a Financial Liability or Coupled with a New Financial Asset or Liability 39.65

Measurement 39.66–165

- Initial Measurement 39.66–67
- Subsequent Measurement 39.68–94
  - Financial Assets 39.68–92
  - Financial Liabilities 39.93–94
- Fair Value 39.95–107
  - Measurement Considerations 39.95–102
  - Gains and Losses on Remeasurement to Fair Value 39.103–107
- Gains/Losses on Financial Assets and Liabilities Not Remeasured to Fair Value 39.108
- Impairment and Uncollectability of Financial Assets 39.109–119
- Fair Value Accounting in Certain Financial Services industries 39.120

Hedging 39.121–165

- Hedging Instruments 39.122–126
- Hedged Items 39.127–135
- Hedge Accounting 39.136–145
- Assessing Hedge Effectiveness 39.146–152
- Fair Value Hedges 39.153–157
- Cash Flow Hedges 39.158–163
- Hedges of a Net Investment in a Foreign Entity 39.164
- Hedges that Do Not Qualify for Special Hedge Accounting 39.165

Disclosure 39.166–170

Scope

This Standard should be applied by all enterprises to all financial instruments except: **1**
(a) *those interests in subsidiaries, associates, and joint ventures that are accounted for under IAS 27, IAS 28, and IAS 31. However, an enterprise applies this Standard in its consolidated financial statements to account for an interest in a subsidiary, associate, or joint venture that (a) is acquired and held exclusively with a view to its subsequent disposal in the near future; or (b) operates under severe long-term restrictions that significantly impair its ability to transfer funds to the enterprise. In these cases, the disclosure requirements in IAS 27, IAS 28, and IAS 31 apply in addition to those in this Standard;*
(b) *rights and obligations under leases, to which IAS 17 applies; however, (i) lease receivables recognised on a lessor's balance sheet are subject to the derecognition provisions of this Standard (paragraphs 35-65 and 170(d)) and (ii) this Standard does apply to derivatives that are embedded in leases (see paragraphs 22-26);*
(c) *employers' assets and liabilities under employee benefit plans, to which IAS 19 applies;*
(d) *rights and obligations under insurance contracts as defined in paragraph 3 of IAS 32: Disclosure and Presentation, but this Standard does apply to derivatives that are embedded in insurance contracts (see paragraphs 22-26);*
(e) *equity instruments issued by the reporting enterprise including options, warrants, and other financial instruments that are classified as shareholders' equity of the reporting enterprise (however, the holder of such instruments is required to apply this Standard to those instruments);*
(f) *financial guarantee contracts, including letters of credit, that provide for payments to be made if the debtor fails to make payment when due (IAS 37 provides guidance for recognising and measuring financial guarantees, warranty obligations, and other similar instruments). In contrast, financial guarantee contracts are subject to this Standard if they provide for payments to be made in response to changes in a specified interest rate, security price, commodity price, credit rating, foreign exchange rate, index of prices or rates, or other variable (sometimes called the 'underlying'). Also, this Standard does require recognition of financial guarantees incurred or retained as a result of the derecognition standards set out in paragraphs 35-65;*
(g) *contracts for contingent consideration in a business combination (see paragraphs 65-76 of IAS 22);*
(h) *contracts that require a payment based on climatic, geological, or other physical variables (see paragraph 2), but this Standard does apply to other types of derivatives that are embedded in such contracts (see paragraphs 22-26).*

Contracts that require a payment based on climatic, geological, or other physical **2** variables are commonly used as insurance policies. (Those based on climatic variables are sometimes referred to as weather derivatives.) In such cases, the payment made is based on an amount of loss to the enterprise. Rights and obligations under insurance contracts are excluded from the scope of this Standard by paragraph 1(d). ...

[Not printed]   **3–5**

This Standard should be applied to commodity-based contracts that give either party **6** *the right to settle in cash or some other financial instrument, with the exception of commodity contracts that (a) were entered into and continue to meet the enterprise's*

343

expected purchase, sale, or usage requirements, (b) were designated for that purpose at their inception, and (c) are expected to be settled by delivery.

7   If an enterprise follows a pattern of entering into offsetting contracts that effectively accomplish settlement on a net basis, those contracts are not entered into to meet the enterprise's expected purchase, sale, or usage requirements.

Definitions

From IAS 32

8   ...

A *financial instrument* is any contract that gives rise to both a financial asset of one enterprise and a financial liability or equity instrument of another enterprise.

A *financial asset* is any asset that is:

(a) *cash;*

(b) *a contractual right to receive cash or another financial asset from another enterprise;*

(c) *a contractual right to exchange financial instruments with another enterprise under conditions that are potentially favourable; or*

(d) *an equity instrument of another enterprise.*

A *financial liability* is any liability that is a contractual obligation:

(a) *to deliver cash or another financial asset to another enterprise; or*

(b) *to exchange financial instruments with another enterprise under conditions that are potentially unfavourable.*

An *equity instrument* is any contract that evidences a residual interest in the assets of an enterprise after deducting all of its liabilities (see paragraph 11).

Fair value is the amount for which an asset could be exchanged, or a liability settled, between knowledgeable, willing parties in an arm's length transaction.

9   For purposes of the foregoing definitions, IAS 32 states that the term 'enterprise' includes individuals, partnerships, incorporated bodies, and government agencies.

Additional Definitions

10   *The following terms are used in this Standard with the meanings specified:*

Definition of a Derivative

A *derivative* is a financial instrument:

(a) *whose value changes in response to the change in a specified interest rate, security price, commodity price, foreign exchange rate, index of prices or rates, a credit rating or credit index, or similar variable (sometimes called the 'underlying');*

(b) *that requires no initial net investment or little initial net investment relative to other types of contracts that have a similar response to changes in market conditions; and*

(c) *that is settled at a future date.*

Definitions of Four Categories of Financial Assets

A *financial asset or liability held for trading is one that was acquired or incurred principally for the purpose of generating a profit from short-term fluctuations in price or dealer's margin. A financial asset should be classified as held for trading if, regardless of why it was acquired, it is part of a portfolio for which there is evidence of a recent actual pattern of short-term profit-taking (see paragraph 21). Derivative financial assets and derivative financial liabilities are always deemed held for trading unless they are designated and effective hedging instruments. (See paragraph 18 for an example of a liability held for trading.)*

Held-to-maturity investments are financial assets with fixed or determinable payments and fixed maturity that an enterprise has the positive intent and ability to hold to maturity (see paragraphs 80-92) other than loans and receivables originated by the enterprise.

Loans and receivables originated by the enterprise are financial assets that are created by the enterprise by providing money, goods, or services directly to a debtor, other than those that are originated with the intent to be sold immediately or in the short term, which should be classified as held for trading. Loans and receivables originated by the enterprise are not included in held-to-maturity investments but, rather, are classified separately under this Standard (see paragraphs 19-20).

Available-for-sale financial assets are those financial assets that are not (a) loans and receivables originated by the enterprise, (b) held-to-maturity investments, or (c) financial assets held for trading (see paragraph 21).

Definitions Relating to Recognition and Measurement

Amortised cost of a financial asset or financial liability is the amount at which the financial asset or liability was measured at initial recognition minus principal repayments, plus or minus the cumulative amortisation of any difference between that initial amount and the maturity amount, and minus any write-down (directly or through the use of an allowance account) for impairment or uncollectability.

The effective interest method is a method of calculating amortisation using the effective interest rate of a financial asset or financial liability. The effective interest rate is the rate that exactly discounts the expected stream of future cash payments through maturity or the next market-based repricing date to the current net carrying amount of the financial asset or financial liability. That computation should include all fees and points paid or received between parties to the contract. The effective interest rate is sometimes termed the level yield to maturity or to the next repricing date, and is the internal rate of return of the financial asset or financial liability for that period. (See IAS 18 paragraph 31, and IAS 32, paragraph 61.)

Transaction costs are incremental costs that are directly attributable to the acquisition or disposal of a financial asset or liability (see paragraph 17).

A firm commitment is a binding agreement for the exchange of a specified quantity of resources at a specified price on a specified future date or dates.

Control of an asset is the power to obtain the future economic benefits that flow from the asset.

Derecognise means remove a financial asset or liability, or a portion of a financial asset or liability, from an enterprise's balance sheet.

Definitions Relating to Hedge Accounting

Hedging, for accounting purposes, means designating one or more hedging instruments so that their change in fair value is an offset, in whole or in part, to the change in fair value or cash flows of a hedged item.

A hedged item is an asset, liability, firm commitment, or forecasted future transaction that (a) exposes the enterprise to risk of changes in fair value or changes in future cash flows and that (b) for hedge accounting purposes, is designated as being hedged (paragraphs 127-135 elaborate on the definition of hedged items).

A <u>hedging instrument</u>, for hedge accounting purposes, is a designated derivative or (in limited circumstances) another financial asset or liability whose fair value or cash flows are expected to offset changes in the fair value or cash flows of a designated hedged item (paragraphs 122-126 elaborate on the definition of a hedging instrument). Under this Standard, a non-derivative financial asset or liability may be designated as a hedging instrument for hedge accounting purposes only if it hedges the risk of changes in foreign currency exchange rates.

<u>Hedge effectiveness</u> is the degree to which offsetting changes in fair value or cash flows attributable to a hedged risk are achieved by the hedging instrument (see paragraphs 146-152).

Other Definitions

<u>Securitisation</u> is the process by which financial assets are transformed into securities. A <u>repurchase agreement</u> is an agreement to transfer a financial asset to another party in exchange for cash or other consideration and a concurrent obligation to reacquire the financial asset at a future date for an amount equal to the cash or other consideration exchanged plus interest.

Elaboration on the Definitions

Equity Instrument

11 *An enterprise may have a contractual obligation that it can settle either by payment of financial assets or by payment in the form of its own equity securities. In such a case, if the number of equity securities required to settle the obligation varies with changes in their fair value so that the total fair value of the equity securities paid always equals the amount of the contractual obligation, the holder of the obligation is not exposed to gain or loss from fluctuations in the price of the equity securities. Such an obligation should be accounted for as a financial liability of the enterprise and, therefore, is not excluded from the scope of this Standard by paragraph 1(e).*

12 An enterprise may have a forward, option, or other derivative instrument whose value changes in response to something other than the market price of the enterprise's own equity securities but that the enterprise can choose to settle or is required to settle in its own equity securities. In such case, the enterprise accounts for the instrument as a derivative instrument, not as an equity instrument, because the value of such an instrument is unrelated to the changes in the equity of the enterprise.

Derivatives

13 Typical examples of derivatives are futures and forward, swap, and option contracts. A derivative usually has a notional amount, which is an amount of currency, a number of shares, a number of units of weight or volume, or other units specified in the contract. However, a derivative instrument does not require the holder or writer to invest or receive the notional amount at the inception of the contract. Alternatively, a derivative could require a fixed payment as a result of some future event that is unrelated to a notional amount. ...

14 Commitments to buy or sell non-financial assets and liabilities that are intended to be settled by the reporting enterprise by making or taking delivery in the normal course

of business, and for which there is no practice of settling net (either with the counterparty or by entering into offsetting contracts), are not accounted for as derivatives but rather as executory contracts. Settling net means making a cash payment based on the change in fair value.

[Not printed]   15–16

Transaction Costs

Transaction costs include fees and commissions paid to agents, advisers, brokers, and   17
dealers; levies by regulatory agencies and securities exchanges; and transfer taxes and duties. Transaction costs do not include debt premium or discount, financing costs, or allocations of internal administrative or holding costs.

Liability Held for Trading

Liabilities held for trading include (a) derivative liabilities that are not hedging   18
instruments and (b) the obligation to deliver securities borrowed by a short seller (an enterprise that sells securities that it does not yet own). The fact that a liability is used to fund trading activities does not make that liability one held for trading.

Loans and Receivables Originated by the Enterprise

A loan acquired by an enterprise as a participation in a loan from another lender is   19
considered to be originated by the enterprise provided it is funded by the enterprise on the date that the loan is originated by the other lender. However, the acquisition of an interest in a pool of loans or receivables, for example in connection with a securitisation, is a purchase, not an origination, because the enterprise did not provide money, goods, or services directly to the underlying debtors nor acquire its interest through a participation with another lender on the date the underlying loans or receivables were originated. Also, a transaction that is, in substance, a purchase of a loan that was previously originated – for example, a loan to an unconsolidated special purpose entity that is made to provide funding for its purchases of loans originated by others – is not a loan originated by the enterprise. A loan acquired by an enterprise in a business combination is considered to be originated by the acquiring enterprise provided that it was similarly classified by the acquired enterprise. The loan is measured at acquisition under IAS 22. A loan acquired through a syndication is an originated loan because each lender shares in the origination of the loan and provides money directly to the debtor.

Loans or receivables that are purchased by an enterprise, rather than originated, are   20
classified as held to maturity, available for sale, or held for trading, as appropriate.

Available-for-Sale Financial Assets

A financial asset is classified as available for sale if it does not properly belong in one   21
of the three other categories of financial assets – held for trading, held to maturity, and loans and receivables originated by the enterprise. A financial asset is classified as held for trading, rather than available for sale, if it is part of a portfolio of similar assets for which there is a pattern of trading for the purpose of generating a profit from short-term fluctuations in price or dealer's margin.

Embedded Derivatives

22 Sometimes, a derivative may be a component of a hybrid (combined) financial instrument that includes both the derivative and a host contract – with the effect that some of the cash flows of the combined instrument vary in a similar way to a stand-alone derivative. Such derivatives are sometimes known as 'embedded derivatives'. An embedded derivative causes some or all of the cash flows that otherwise would be required by the contract to be modified based on a specified interest rate, security price, commodity price, foreign exchange rate, index of prices or rates, or other variable.

23 *An embedded derivative should be separated from the host contract and accounted for as a derivative under this Standard if all of the following conditions are met:*
    (a) the economic characteristics and risks of the embedded derivative are not closely related to the economic characteristics and risks of the host contract;
    (b) a separate instrument with the same terms as the embedded derivative would meet the definition of a derivative; and
    (c) the hybrid (combined) instrument is not measured at fair value with changes in fair value reported in net profit or loss.
    If an embedded derivative is separated, the host contract itself should be accounted for (a) under this Standard if it is, itself, a financial instrument and (b) in accordance with other appropriate IASs if it is not a financial instrument.

24 The economic characteristics and risks of an embedded derivative are not considered to be closely related to the host contract (paragraph 23(a)) in the following examples. In these circumstances, assuming the conditions in paragraphs 23(b) and 23(c) are also met, an enterprise accounts for the embedded derivative separately from the host contract under this Standard:
    (a) a put option on an equity instrument held by an enterprise is not closely related to the host equity instrument;
    (b) a call option embedded in an equity instrument held by an enterprise is not closely related to the host equity instrument from the perspective of the holder (from the issuer's perspective, the call option is an equity instrument of the issuer if the issuer is required to or has the right to require settlement in shares, in which case it is excluded from the scope of this Standard);
    (c) an option or automatic provision to extend the term (maturity date) of debt is not closely related to the host debt contract held by an enterprise unless there is a concurrent adjustment to the market rate of interest at the time of the extension;
    (d) equity-indexed interest or principal payments – by which the amount of interest or principal is indexed to the value of equity shares – are not closely related to the host debt instrument or insurance contract because the risks inherent in the host and the embedded derivative are dissimilar;
    (e) commodity-indexed interest or principal payments – by which the amount of interest or principal is indexed to the price of a commodity – are not closely related to the host debt instrument or insurance contract because the risks inherent in the host and the embedded derivative are dissimilar;
    (f) an equity conversion feature embedded in a debt instrument is not closely related to the host debt instrument;
    (g) a call or put option on debt that is issued at a significant discount or premium is not closely related to the debt except for debt (such as a zero coupon bond) that is callable or puttable at its accreted amount; and

(h) arrangements known as credit derivatives that are embedded in a host debt instrument and that allow one party (the 'beneficiary') to transfer the credit risk of an asset, which it may or may not actually own, to another party (the 'guarantor') are not closely related to the host debt instrument. Such credit derivatives allow the guarantor to assume the credit risk associated with a reference asset without directly purchasing it.

On the other hand, the economic characteristics and risks of an embedded derivative **25** are considered to be closely related to the economic characteristics and risks of the host contract in the following examples. In these circumstances, an enterprise does not account for the embedded derivative separately from the host contract under this Standard:

(a) the embedded derivative is linked to an interest rate or interest rate index that can change the amount of interest that would otherwise be paid or received on the host debt contract (that is, this Standard does not permit floating rate debt to be treated as fixed rate debt with an embedded derivative);

(b) an embedded floor or cap on interest rates is considered to be closely related to the interest rate on a debt instrument if the cap is at or above the market rate of interest or if the floor is at or below the market rate of interest when the instrument is issued, and the cap or floor is not leveraged in relation to the host instrument;

(c) the embedded derivative is a stream of principal or interest payments that are denominated in a foreign currency. Such a derivative is not separated from the host contract because IAS 21 requires that foreign currency translation gains and losses on the entire host monetary item be recognised in net profit or loss;

(d) the host contract is not a financial instrument and it requires payments denominated in (i) the currency of the primary economic environment in which any substantial party to that contract operates or (ii) the currency in which the price of the related good or service that is acquired or delivered is routinely denominated in international commerce (for example, the U.S. dollar for crude oil transactions). That is, such contract is not regarded as a host contract with an embedded foreign currency derivative;

(e) the embedded derivative is a prepayment option with an exercise price that would not result in a significant gain or loss;

(f) the embedded derivative is a prepayment option that is embedded in an interest-only or principal-only strip that (i) initially resulted from separating the right to receive contractual cash flows of a financial instrument that, in and of itself, did not contain an embedded derivative and that (ii) does not contain any terms not present in the original host debt contract;

(g) with regard to a host contract that is a lease, the embedded derivative is (i) an inflation-related index such as an index of lease payments to a consumer price index (provided that the lease is not leveraged and the index relates to inflation in the enterprise's own economic environment), (ii) contingent rentals based on related sales, and (iii) contingent rentals based on variable interest rates; or

(h) the embedded derivative is an interest rate or interest rate index that does not alter the net interest payments that otherwise would be paid on the host contract in such a way that the holder would not recover substantially all of its recorded investment or (in the case of a derivative that is a liability) the issuer would pay a rate more than twice the market rate at inception.

If an enterprise is required by this Standard to separate an embedded derivative from **26** *its host contract but is unable to separately measure the embedded derivative either* *at acquisition or at a subsequent financial reporting date, it should treat the entire combined contract as a financial instrument held for trading.*

Recognition

Initial Recognition

27 *An enterprise should recognise a financial asset or financial liability on its balance sheet when, and only when, it becomes a party to the contractual provisions of the instrument. (See paragraph 30 with respect to 'regular way' purchases of financial assets.)*

28 As a consequence of the principle in the preceding paragraph, an enterprise recognises all of its contractual rights or obligations under derivatives in its balance sheet as assets or liabilities.

29 The following are some examples of applying the principle in paragraph 27:
   (a) unconditional receivables and payables are recognised as assets or liabilities when the enterprise becomes a party to the contract and, as a consequence, has a legal right to receive, or a legal obligation to pay, cash;
   (b) assets to be acquired and liabilities to be incurred as a result of a firm commitment to purchase or sell goods or services are not recognised under present accounting practice until at least one of the parties has performed under the agreement such that it either is entitled to receive an asset or is obligated to disburse an asset. For example, an enterprise that receives a firm order does not recognise an asset (and the enterprise that places the order does not recognise a liability) at the time of the commitment but, rather, delays recognition until the ordered goods or services have been shipped, delivered, or rendered;
   (c) in contrast to (b) above, however, a forward contract – a commitment to purchase or sell a specified financial instrument or commodity subject to this Standard on a future date at a specified price – is recognised as an asset or a liability on the commitment date, rather than waiting until the closing date on which the exchange actually takes place. When an enterprise becomes a party to a forward contract, the fair values of the right and obligation are often equal, so that the net fair value of the forward is zero, and only any net fair value of the right and obligation is recognised as an asset or liability. However, each party is exposed to the price risk that is the subject of the contract from that date. Such a forward contract satisfies the recognition principle of paragraph 27, from the perspectives of both the buyer and the seller, at the time the enterprises become parties to the contract, even though it may have a zero net value at that date. The fair value of the contract may become a net asset or liability in the future depending on, among other things, the time value of money and the value of the underlying instrument or commodity that is the subject of the forward;
   (d) financial options are recognised as assets or liabilities when the holder or writer becomes a party to the contract; and
   (e) planned future transactions, no matter how likely, are not assets and liabilities of an enterprise since the enterprise, as of the financial reporting date, has not become a party to a contract requiring future receipt or delivery of assets arising out of the future transactions.

Trade Date vs. Settlement Date

A 'regular way' purchase or sale of financial assets should be recognised using either **30** *trade date accounting or settlement date accounting as described in paragraphs 32 and 33. The method used should be applied consistently for all purchases and sales of financial assets that belong to the same category of financial assets defined in paragraph 10.*

A contract for the purchase or sale of financial assets that requires delivery of the assets **31** within the time frame generally established by regulation or convention in the market place concerned (sometimes called a 'regular way' contract) is a financial instrument as described in this Standard. The fixed price commitment between trade date and settlement date meets the definition of a derivative – it is a forward contract. However, because of the short duration of the commitment, such a contract is not recognised as a derivative financial instrument under this Standard.

The trade date is the date that an enterprise commits to purchase or sell an asset. Trade **32** date accounting refers to (a) the recognition of an asset to be received and the liability to pay for it on the trade date and (b) the derecognition of an asset that is sold and the recognition of a receivable from the buyer for payment on the trade date. Generally, interest does not start to accrue on the asset and corresponding liability until the settlement date when title passes.

The settlement date is the date that an asset is delivered to or by an enterprise. **33** Settlement date accounting refers to (a) the recognition of an asset on the day it is transferred to an enterprise and (b) the derecognition of an asset on the day that it is transferred by the enterprise. When settlement date accounting is applied, under paragraph 106 an enterprise will account for any change in the fair value of the asset to be received during the period between the trade date and the settlement date in the same way as it will account for the acquired asset under this Standard. That is, the value change is not recognised for assets carried at cost or amortised cost; it is recognised in net profit or loss for assets classified as trading; and it is recognised in net profit or loss or in equity (as appropriate under paragraph 103) for assets classified as available for sale.

[Not printed] **34**

Derecognition

Derecognition of a Financial Asset

An enterprise should derecognise a financial asset or a portion of a financial asset **35** *when, and only when, the enterprise loses control of the contractual rights that comprise the financial asset (or a portion of the financial asset). An enterprise loses such control if it realises the rights to benefits specified in the contract, the rights expire, or the enterprise surrenders those rights.*

If a financial asset is transferred to another enterprise but the transfer does not satisfy **36** the conditions for derecognition in paragraph 35, the transferor accounts for the transaction as a collateralised borrowing. In that case, the transferor's right to reacquire the asset is not a derivative.

Determining whether an enterprise has lost control of a financial asset depends both **37** *on the enterprise's position and that of the transferee. Consequently, if the position* *of either enterprise indicates that the transferor has retained control, the transferor should not remove the asset from its balance sheet.*

38 A transferor has not lost control of a transferred financial asset and, therefore, the asset is not derecognised if, for example:

(a) the transferor has the right to reacquire the transferred asset unless either (i) the asset is readily obtainable in the market or (ii) the reacquisition price is fair value at the time of reacquisition;

(b) the transferor is both entitled and obligated to repurchase or redeem the transferred asset on terms that effectively provide the transferee with a lender's return on the assets received in exchange for the transferred asset. A lender's return is one that is not materially different from that which could be obtained on a loan to the transferor that is fully secured by the transferred asset; or

(c) the asset transferred is not readily obtainable in the market and the transferor has retained substantially all of the risks and returns of ownership through a total return swap with the transferee or has retained substantially all of the risks of ownership through an unconditional put option on the transferred asset held by the transferee (a total return swap provides the market returns and credit risks to one of the parties in return for an interest index to the other party, such as a LIBOR payment).

39-40 [Not printed]

41 A transferor generally has lost control of a transferred financial asset only if the transferee has the ability to obtain the benefits of the transferred asset. That ability is demonstrated, for example, if the transferee:

(a) is free either to sell or to pledge approximately the full fair value of the transferred asset; or

(b) is a special-purpose entity whose permissible activities are limited, and either the special purpose entity itself or the holders of beneficial interests in that entity have the ability to obtain substantially all of the benefits of the transferred asset.

That ability may be demonstrated in other ways.

42 [Not printed]

43 *On derecognition, the difference between (a) the carrying amount of an asset (or portion of an asset) transferred to another party and (b) the sum of (i) the proceeds received or receivable and (ii) any prior adjustment to reflect the fair value of that asset that had been reported in equity should be included in net profit or loss for the period.*

44-46 [Deleted]

Derecognition of Part of a Financial Asset

47 *If an enterprise transfers a part of a financial asset to others while retaining a part, the carrying amount of the financial asset should be allocated between the part retained and the part sold based on their relative fair values on the date of sale. A gain or loss should be recognised based on the proceeds for the portion sold. In the rare circumstance that the fair value of the part of the asset that is retained cannot be measured reliably, then that asset should be recorded at zero. The entire carrying amount of the financial asset should be attributed to the portion sold, and a gain or loss should be recognised equal to the difference between (a) the proceeds and (b) the previous carrying amount of the financial asset plus or minus any prior adjustment*

that had been reported in equity to reflect the fair value of that asset (a 'cost recovery' approach).

[Not printed]   **48–50**

Asset Derecognition Coupled with a New Financial Asset or Liability

If an enterprise transfers control of an entire financial asset but, in doing so, creates **51**
a new financial asset or assumes a new financial liability, the enterprise should recognise the new financial asset or financial liability at fair value and should recognise a gain or loss on the transaction based on the difference between:
(a) the proceeds; and
(b) the carrying amount of the financial asset sold plus the fair value of any new financial liability assumed, minus the fair value of any new financial asset acquired, and plus or minus any adjustment that had previously been reported in equity to reflect the fair value of that asset.

[Not printed]   **52–53**

In the rare circumstance that the fair value of the new financial asset or new **54**
financial liability cannot be measured reliably, then:
(a) if a new financial asset is created but cannot be measured reliably, its initial carrying amount should be zero, and a gain or loss should be recognised equal to the difference between (i) the proceeds and (ii) the previous carrying amount of the derecognised financial asset plus or minus any prior adjustment that had been reported in equity to reflect the fair value of that asset; and
(b) if a new financial liability is assumed but cannot be measured reliably, its initial carrying amount should be such that no gain is recognised on the transaction and, if IAS 37 requires recognition of a provision, a loss should be recognised.
...

To illustrate paragraph 54(b), the excess of the proceeds over the carrying amount is not **55**
recognised in net profit or loss. Instead it is recorded as a liability in the balance sheet.

If a guarantee is recognised as a liability under this Standard, it continues to be **56**
recognised as a liability of the guarantor, measured at its fair value (or at the greater of its original recorded amount and any provision required by IAS 37, if fair value cannot be reliably measured), until it expires. If the guarantee involves a large population of items, the guarantee should be measured by weighting all possible outcomes by their associated probabilities.

Derecognition of a Financial Liability

An enterprise should remove a financial liability (or a part of a financial liability) **57**
from its balance sheet when, and only when, it is extinguished – that is, when the obligation specified in the contract is discharged, cancelled, or expires.

The condition in paragraph 57 is met when either: **58**
(a) the debtor discharges the liability by paying the creditor, normally with cash, other financial assets, goods, or services; or
(b) the debtor is legally released from primary responsibility for the liability (or part thereof) either by process of law or by the creditor (the fact that the debtor may have given a guarantee does not necessarily mean that this condition is not met).

59 Payment to a third party including a trust (sometimes called 'in-substance defeasance') does not by itself relieve the debtor of its primary obligation to the creditor, in the absence of legal release.

60 While legal release, whether judicially or by the creditor, will result in derecognition of a liability, the enterprise may have to recognise a new liability if the derecognition criteria in paragraphs 35-57 are not met for the non-cash financial assets that were transferred. If those criteria are not met, the transferred assets are not removed from the transferor's balance sheet, and the transferor recognises a new liability relating to the transferred assets that may be equal to the derecognised liability.

61 *An exchange between an existing borrower and lender of debt instruments with substantially different terms is an extinguishment of the old debt that should result in derecognition of that debt and recognition of a new debt instrument. Similarly, a substantial modification of the terms of an existing debt instrument (whether or not due to the financial difficulty of the debtor) should be accounted for as an extinguishment of the old debt.*

62 For the purpose of paragraph 61, the terms are substantially different if the discounted present value of the cash flows under the new terms, including any fees paid net of any fees received, is at least 10 per cent different from the discounted present value of the remaining cash flows of the original debt instrument. If an exchange of debt instruments or modification of terms is accounted for as an extinguishment, any costs or fees incurred are recognised as part of the gain or loss on the extinguishment. If the exchange or modification is not accounted for as an extinguishment, any costs or fees incurred are an adjustment to the carrying amount of the liability and are amortised over the remaining term of the modified loan.

63 *The difference between the carrying amount of a liability (or part of a liability) extinguished or transferred to another party, including related unamortised costs, and the amount paid for it should be included in net profit or loss for the period.*

64 In some cases, a creditor releases a debtor from its present obligation to make payments, but the debtor assumes an obligation to pay if the party assuming primary responsibility defaults. In this circumstance the debtor:
   (a) recognises a new financial liability based on the fair value of its obligation for the guarantee; and
   (b) recognises a gain or loss based on the difference between (i) any proceeds and (ii) the carrying amount of the original financial liability (including any related unamortised costs) minus the fair value of the new financial liability.

Derecognition of Part of a Financial Liability or Coupled with a New Financial Asset or Liability

65 *If an enterprise transfers a part of a financial liability to others while retaining a part, or if an enterprise transfers an entire financial liability and in so doing creates a new financial asset or assumes a new financial liability, the enterprise should account for the transaction in the manner set out in paragraphs 47-56.*

Measurement

Initial Measurement of Financial Assets and Financial Liabilities

When a financial asset or financial liability is recognised initially, an enterprise **66** *should measure it at its cost, which is the fair value of the consideration given (in the case of an asset) or received (in the case of a liability) for it. Transaction costs are included in the initial measurement of all financial assets and liabilities.*

The fair value of the consideration given or received normally is determinable by **67** reference to the transaction price or other market prices. If such market prices are not reliably determinable, the fair value of the consideration is estimated as the sum of all future cash payments or receipts, discounted, if the effect of doing so would be material, using the prevailing market rate(s) of interest for a similar instrument (similar as to currency, term, type of interest rate, and other factors) of an issuer with a similar credit rating (see IAS 18 paragraph 11). As an exception to paragraph 66, paragraph 160 requires that certain hedging gains and losses be included as part of the initial measurement of the cost of the related hedged asset.

Subsequent Measurement of Financial Assets

For the purpose of measuring a financial asset subsequent to initial recognition, this **68** Standard classifies financial assets into four categories:
(a) loans and receivables originated by the enterprise and not held for trading;
(b) held-to-maturity investments;
(c) available-for-sale financial assets; and
(d) financial assets held for trading.

After initial recognition, an enterprise should measure financial assets, including **69** *derivatives that are assets, at their fair values, without any deduction for transaction costs that it may incur on sale or other disposal, except for the following categories of financial assets, which should be measured under paragraph 73:*
(a) loans and receivables originated by the enterprise and not held for trading;
(b) held-to-maturity investments; and
(c) any financial asset that does not have a quoted market price in an active market and whose fair value cannot be reliably measured (see paragraph 70).
Financial assets that are designated as hedged items are subject to measurement under the hedge accounting provisions in paragraphs 121-165 of this Standard.

There is a presumption that fair value can be reliably determined for most financial **70** *assets classified as available for sale or held for trading. However, that presumption can be overcome for an investment in an equity instrument (including an investment that is in substance an equity instrument – see paragraph 71) that does not have a quoted market price in an active market and for which other methods of reasonably estimating fair value are clearly inappropriate or unworkable. The presumption can also be overcome for a derivative that is linked to and that must be settled by delivery of such an unquoted equity instrument. See paragraphs 95-102 for guidance on estimating fair value.*

[Not printed] **71**

If a financial asset is required to be measured at fair value and its fair value is below **72** zero, it is accounted for as a financial liability as set out in paragraph 93.

73 *Those financial assets that are excluded from fair valuation under paragraph 69 and that have a fixed maturity should be measured at amortised cost using the effective interest rate method. Those that do not have a fixed maturity should be measured at cost. All financial assets are subject to review for impairment as set out in paragraphs 109-119.*

74 Short-duration receivables with no stated interest rate are normally measured at original invoice amount unless the effect of imputing interest would be significant.

75 Loans and receivables originated by an enterprise and not held for trading are measured at amortised cost without regard to the enterprise's intent to hold them to maturity.

76 For floating rate financial instruments, periodic re-estimation of determinable cash flows to reflect movements in market rates of interest changes the effective yield on a monetary financial asset. Such changes in cash flows are recognised over the remaining term of the asset, or the next repricing date if the asset reprices at market. In the case of a floating rate financial asset recognised initially at an amount equal to the principal repayable on maturity, re-estimating the future interest payments normally has no significant effect on the carrying amount of the asset.

77 [Not printed]

78 An enterprise applies IAS 21 to financial assets that are monetary items under IAS 21 and that are denominated in a foreign currency. Under IAS 21, any foreign exchange gains and losses on monetary assets are reported in net profit or loss. An exception is a monetary item that is designated as a hedging instrument in a cash flow hedge (see paragraphs 121-165). Any recognised change in the fair value of such a monetary item apart from foreign exchange gains and losses is accounted for under paragraph 103. With respect to financial assets that are not monetary items under IAS 21 (...), any recognised change in fair value, including any component of that change that may relate to changes in foreign exchange rates, is accounted for under paragraph 103. Under the hedge accounting provisions of this Standard (paragraphs 121-165), if there is a hedging relationship between a non-derivative monetary asset and a non-derivative monetary liability, changes in the fair values of those financial instruments are reported in net profit or loss.

Held-to-Maturity Investments

79 *An enterprise does not have the positive intent to hold to maturity an investment in a financial asset with a fixed maturity if any one of the following conditions is met:*
 (a) the enterprise has the intent to hold the financial asset for only an undefined period;
 (b) the enterprise stands ready to sell the financial asset (other than if a situation arises that is non-recurring and could not have been reasonably anticipated by the enterprise) in response to changes in market interest rates or risks, liquidity needs, changes in the availability of and the yield on alternative investments, changes in financing sources and terms, or changes in foreign currency risk; or
 (c) the issuer has a right to settle the financial asset at an amount significantly below its amortised cost.

80 A debt security with a variable interest rate can satisfy the criteria for a held-to-maturity investment. Most equity securities cannot be held-to-maturity investments either because they have an indefinite life (such as ordinary shares) or because the amounts the holder may receive can vary in a manner that is not predetermined (...). With respect to held-to-maturity investments, fixed or determinable payments and fixed maturity means a contractual arrangement that defines the amounts and dates of payments to the holder, such as interest and principal payments on debt.

A financial asset that is callable by the issuer satisfies the criteria for a held-to-maturity **81** investment if the holder intends and is able to hold it until it is called or until maturity and if the holder would recover substantially all of its carrying amount. The call option, if exercised, simply accelerates the asset's maturity. However, if the financial asset is callable in a manner such that the holder would not recover substantially all of its carrying amount, the financial asset is not classified as held-to-maturity. The enterprise considers any premium paid and capitalised transaction costs in determining whether the carrying amount would be substantially recovered.

A financial asset that is puttable (the holder has the right to require that the issuer repay **82** or redeem the financial asset before maturity) is classified as a held-to-maturity investment only if the holder has the positive intent and ability to hold it until maturity and not to exercise the put feature.

An enterprise should not classify any financial assets as held-to-maturity if the **83** *enterprise has, during the current financial year or during the two preceding financial years, sold, transferred, or exercised a put option on more than an insignificant amount of held-to-maturity investments before maturity (more than insignificant in relation to the total held-to-maturity portfolio) other than by:*

(a) sales close enough to maturity or exercised call date so that changes in the market rate of interest did not have a significant effect on the financial asset's fair value;

(b) sales after the enterprise has already collected substantially all of the financial asset's original principal through scheduled payments or prepayments; or

(c) sales due to an isolated event that is beyond the enterprise's control and that is non-recurring and could not have been reasonably anticipated by the enterprise.

...

Under this Standard, fair value is a more appropriate measure for most financial assets **84** than amortised cost. ...

[Not printed] **85**

Sales before maturity could satisfy the condition in paragraph 83 – and therefore not **86** raise a question about the enterprise's intent to hold other investments to maturity – if they are due to:

(a) a significant deterioration in the issuer's creditworthiness;

(b) a change in tax law that eliminates or significantly reduces the tax-exempt status of interest on the held-to-maturity investment (but not a change in tax law that revises the marginal tax rates applicable to interest income);

(c) a major business combination or major disposition (such as sale of a segment) that necessitates the sale or transfer of held-to-maturity investments to maintain the enterprise's existing interest rate risk position or credit risk policy (although the business combination itself is an event within the enterprise's control, the changes to its investment portfolio to maintain interest rate risk position or credit risk policy may be consequential rather than anticipated);

(d) a change in statutory or regulatory requirements significantly modifying either what constitutes a permissible investment or the maximum level of certain kinds of investments, thereby causing an enterprise to dispose of a held-to-maturity investment;

(e) a significant increase by the regulator in the industry's capital requirements that causes the enterprise to downsize by selling held-to-maturity investments; or

(f) a significant increase in the risk weights of held-to-maturity investments used for regulatory risk-based capital purposes.

87 *An enterprise does not have a demonstrated ability to hold to maturity an investment in a financial asset with a fixed maturity if either one of the following conditions is met:*

(a) it does not have the financial resources available to continue to finance the investment until maturity; or

(b) it is subject to an existing legal or other constraint that could frustrate its intention to hold the financial asset to maturity (however, an issuer's call option does not necessarily frustrate an enterprise's intent to hold a financial asset to maturity – see paragraph 81).

88 [Not printed]

89 An enterprise assesses its intent and ability to hold its held-to-maturity investments to maturity not only when those financial assets are initially acquired but also at each balance sheet date.

90 *If, due to a change of intent or ability, it is no longer appropriate to carry a held-to-maturity investment at amortised cost, it should be remeasured at fair value, and the difference between its carrying amount and fair value should be accounted for in accordance with paragraph 103.*

91 *Similarly, if a reliable measure becomes available for a financial asset for which such a measure previously was not available, the asset should be remeasured at fair value, and the difference between its carrying amount and fair value should be accounted for in accordance with paragraph 103.*

92 *If, due to a change of intent or ability or in the rare circumstance that a reliable measure of fair value is no longer available or because the 'two preceding financial years' referred to in paragraph 83 have now passed, it becomes appropriate to carry a financial asset at amortised cost rather than at fair value, the fair value carrying amount of the financial asset on that date becomes its new amortised cost. Any previous gain or loss on that asset that has been recognised directly in equity in accordance with paragraph 103 should be accounted for as follows:*

(a) in the case of a financial asset with a fixed maturity, a previous gain or loss on that asset that has been recognised directly in equity should be amortised over the remaining life of the held-to-maturity investment. Any difference between the new amortised cost and maturity amount should be amortised over the remaining life of the financial asset as an adjustment of yield, similar to amortisation of premium and discount; and

(b) in the case of a financial asset that does not have a fixed maturity, a previous gain or loss on that asset that has been recognised directly in equity should be left in equity until the financial asset has been sold or otherwise disposed of, at which time it should enter into the determination of net profit or loss.

Subsequent Measurement of Financial Liabilities

93 *After initial recognition, an enterprise should measure all financial liabilities, other than liabilities held for trading and derivatives that are liabilities, at amortised cost.*

After initial recognition, an enterprise should measure liabilities held for trading and derivatives that are liabilities at fair value, except for a derivative liability that is linked to and that must be settled by delivery of an unquoted equity instrument whose fair value cannot be reliably measured, which should be measured at cost. Financial liabilities that are designated as hedged items are subject to measurement under the hedge accounting provisions in paragraphs 121-165 of this Standard.

An enterprise applies IAS 21 to financial liabilities that are monetary items under IAS 21 and that are denominated in a foreign currency. Under IAS 21, any foreign exchange gains and losses on monetary liabilities are reported in net profit or loss. An exception is a monetary item that is designated as a hedging instrument in a cash flow hedge (see paragraphs 121-165). Any recognised change in the fair value of such a monetary item apart from foreign exchange gains and losses is accounted for under paragraph 103. With respect to financial liabilities that are not monetary items under IAS 21 (such as some mandatorily redeemable preferred stock issued by the enterprise), any recognised change in fair value, including any component of that change that may relate to changes in foreign exchange rates, is accounted for under paragraph 103. ... **94**

Fair Value Measurement Considerations

The fair value of a financial instrument is reliably measurable if (a) the variability in the range of reasonable fair value estimates is not significant for that instrument or (b) if the probabilities of the various estimates within the range can be reasonably assessed and used in estimating fair value. ... **95**

Situations in which fair value is reliably measurable include (a) a financial instrument for which there is a published price quotation in an active public securities market for that instrument, (b) a debt instrument that has been rated by an independent rating agency and whose cash flows can be reasonably estimated, and (c) a financial instrument for which there is an appropriate valuation model and for which the data inputs to that model can be measured reliably because the data come from active markets. **96**

The fair value of a financial asset or financial liability may be determined by one of several generally accepted methods. Valuation techniques should incorporate the assumptions that market participants would use in their estimates of fair values, including assumptions about prepayment rates, rates of estimated credit losses, and interest or discount rates. Paragraph 167(a) requires disclosure of the methods and significant assumptions applied in estimating fair values. **97**

[Not printed] **98**

The existence of published price quotations in an active market is normally the best evidence of fair value. The appropriate quoted market price for an asset held or liability to be issued is usually the current bid price and, for an asset to be acquired or liability held, the current offer or asking price. When current bid and offer prices are unavailable, the price of the most recent transaction may provide evidence of the current fair value provided that there has not been a significant change in economic circumstances between the transaction date and the reporting date. When an enterprise has matching asset and liability positions, it may appropriately use mid-market prices as a basis for establishing fair values. **99**

100 If the market for a financial instrument is not an active market, published price quotations may have to be adjusted to arrive at a reliable measure of fair value. If there is infrequent activity in a market, the market is not well established (...) or small volumes are traded relative to the number of trading units of a financial instrument to be valued, quoted market prices may not be indicative of the fair value of the instrument. In some cases where the volume traded is relatively small, a price quotation for a larger block may be available from the market maker in that instrument. In other circumstances, as well as when a quoted market price is not available, estimation techniques may be used to determine fair value with sufficient reliability to satisfy the requirements of this Standard. Techniques that are well established in financial markets include reference to the current market value of another instrument that is substantially the same, discounted cash flow analysis, and option pricing models. In applying discounted cash flow analysis, an enterprise uses the discount rate(s) equal to the prevailing rate of return for financial instruments having substantially the same terms and characteristics, including the creditworthiness of the debtor, the remaining term over which the contractual interest rate is fixed, the remaining term to repayment of the principal, and the currency in which payments are to be made.

101 If a market price does not exist for a financial instrument in its entirety but markets exist for its component parts, fair value is constructed on the basis of the relevant market prices. If a market does not exist for a financial instrument but a market exists for a similar financial instrument, fair value is constructed on the basis of the market price of the similar financial instrument.

102 [Not printed]

Gains and Losses on Remeasurement to Fair Value

103 *A recognised gain or loss arising from a change in the fair value of a financial asset or financial liability that is not part of a hedging relationship (see paragraphs 121-165) should be reported as follows:*
(a) a gain or loss on a financial asset or liability held for trading should be included in net profit or loss for the period in which it arises (in this regard, a derivative should always be considered to be held for trading unless it is a designated hedging instrument – see paragraph 122);
(b) a gain or loss on an available-for-sale financial asset should be either:
(i) included in net profit or loss for the period in which it arises; or
(ii) recognised directly in equity, through the statement of changes in equity (see IAS 1 paragraphs 86-88), until the financial asset is sold, collected, or otherwise disposed of, or until the financial asset is determined to be impaired (see paragraphs 117-119), at which time the cumulative gain or loss previously recognised in equity should be included in net profit or loss for the period.

104 *An enterprise should choose either paragraph 103(b)(i) or paragraph 103(b)(ii) as its accounting policy and should apply that policy to all of its available-for-sale financial assets (except for hedges – see paragraph 121).*

105 [Not printed]

106 *If an enterprise recognises purchases of financial assets using settlement date accounting (see paragraph 30), any change in the fair value of the asset to be received during the period between the trade date and the settlement date is not recognised* *for assets carried at cost or amortised cost (other than impairment losses). For assets remeasured to fair value, however, the change in fair value should be recognised in net profit or loss or in equity, as appropriate under paragraph 103.*

Because the designation of a financial asset as held for trading is based on the **107** *objective for initially acquiring it, an enterprise should not reclassify its financial assets that are being remeasured to fair value out of the trading category while they are held. An enterprise should reclassify a financial asset into the trading category only if there is evidence of a recent actual pattern of short-term profit taking that justifies such reclassification (see paragraph 21).*

Gains and Losses on Financial Assets and Liabilities Not Remeasured to Fair Value

For those financial assets and financial liabilities carried at amortised cost **108** *(paragraphs 73 and 93), a gain or loss is recognised in net profit or loss when the financial asset or liability is derecognised or impaired, as well as through the amortisation process. However, if there is a hedging relationship between those financial assets or liabilities (the items being hedged) and a hedging instrument as described in paragraphs 121-152, accounting for the gain or loss should follow paragraphs 153-164.*

Impairment and Uncollectability of Financial Assets

A financial asset is impaired if its carrying amount is greater than its estimated **109** *recoverable amount. An enterprise should assess at each balance sheet date whether there is any objective evidence that a financial asset or group of assets may be impaired. If any such evidence exists, the enterprise should estimate the recoverable amount of that asset or group of assets and recognise any impairment loss in accordance with paragraph 111 (for financial assets carried at amortised cost) or paragraph 117 (for financial assets remeasured to fair value).*

Objective evidence that a financial asset or group of assets is impaired or uncollectable **110** includes information that comes to the attention of the holder of the asset about:
(a) significant financial difficulty of the issuer;
(b) an actual breach of contract, such as a default or delinquency in interest or principal payments;
(c) granting by the lender to the borrower, for economic or legal reasons relating to the borrower's financial difficulty, of a concession that the lender would not otherwise consider;
(d) a high probability of bankruptcy or other financial reorganisation of the issuer;
(e) recognition of an impairment loss on that asset in a prior financial reporting period;
(f) the disappearance of an active market for that financial asset due to financial difficulties; or
(g) a historical pattern of collections of accounts receivable that indicates that the entire face amount of a portfolio of accounts receivable will not be collected.

The disappearance of an active market because an enterprise's securities are no longer publicly traded is not evidence of impairment. A downgrade of an enterprise's credit rating is not, of itself, evidence of impairment, though it may be evidence of impairment when considered with other available information.

Financial Assets Carried at Amortised Cost

111 *If it is probable that an enterprise will not be able to collect all amounts due (principal and interest) according to the contractual terms of loans, receivables, or held-to-maturity investments carried at amortised cost, an impairment or bad debt loss has occurred. The amount of the loss is the difference between the asset's carrying amount and the present value of expected future cash flows discounted at the financial instrument's original effective interest rate (recoverable amount). Cash flows relating to short-term receivables generally are not discounted (see paragraph 74). The carrying amount of the asset should be reduced to its estimated recoverable amount either directly or through use of an allowance account. The amount of the loss should be included in net profit or loss for the period.*

112 Impairment and uncollectability are measured and recognised individually for financial assets that are individually significant. Impairment and uncollectability may be measured and recognised on a portfolio basis for a group of similar financial assets that are not individually identified as impaired.

113 Impairment of a financial asset carried at amortised cost is measured using the financial instrument's original effective interest rate because discounting at the current market rate of interest would, in effect, impose fair-value measurement on financial assets that this Standard would otherwise measure at amortised cost. If a loan, receivable, or held-to-maturity investment has a variable interest rate, the discount rate for measuring recoverable amount pursuant to paragraph 111 is the current effective interest rate(s) determined under the contract. As a surrogate for such a fair value calculation, a creditor may measure impairment based on an instrument's fair value using an observable market price. If an asset is collateralised and foreclosure is probable, then the holder measures impairment based on the fair value of the collateral.

114 *If, in a subsequent period, the amount of the impairment or bad debt loss decreases and the decrease can be objectively related to an event occurring after the write-down (such as an improvement in the debtor's credit rating), the write-down of the financial asset should be reversed either directly or by adjusting an allowance account. The reversal should not result in a carrying amount of the financial asset that exceeds what amortised cost would have been, had the impairment not been recognised, at the date the write-down of the financial asset is reversed. The amount of the reversal should be included in net profit or loss for the period.*

115 *The carrying amount of any financial asset that is not carried at fair value because its fair value cannot be reliably measured (paragraph 69(c)) should be reviewed for an indication of impairment at each balance sheet date based on an analysis of expected net cash inflows. If there is an indication of impairment, the amount of the impairment loss of such a financial asset is the difference between its carrying amount and the present value of expected future cash flows discounted at the current market rate of interest for a similar financial asset (recoverable amount).*

Interest Income After Impairment Recognition

116 Once a financial asset has been written down to its estimated recoverable amount, interest income is thereafter recognised based on the rate of interest that was used to discount the future cash flows for the purpose of measuring the recoverable amount. Additionally, after initially recognising an impairment loss, the enterprise will review this asset for further impairment at subsequent financial reporting dates (see paragraph

110(e)). IAS 18 paragraph 30 provides guidance for recognising interest income on unimpaired financial assets.

Financial Assets Remeasured to Fair Value

If a loss on a financial asset carried at fair value (recoverable amount is below **117** *original acquisition cost) has been recognised directly in equity in accordance with paragraph 103(b)(ii) and there is objective evidence (see paragraph 110) that the asset is impaired, the cumulative net loss that had been recognised directly in equity should be removed from equity and recognised in net profit or loss for the period even though the financial asset has not been derecognised.*

The amount of the loss that should be removed from equity and reported in net profit **118** *or loss is the difference between its acquisition cost (net of any principal repayment and amortisation) and current fair value (for equity instruments) or recoverable amount (for debt instruments), less any impairment loss on that asset previously recognised in net profit or loss. The recoverable amount of a debt instrument remeasured to fair value is the present value of expected future cash flows discounted at the current market rate of interest for a similar financial asset.*

If, in a subsequent period, the fair value or recoverable amount of the financial asset **119** *carried at fair value increases and the increase can be objectively related to an event occurring after the loss was recognised in net profit or loss, the loss should be reversed, with the amount of the reversal included in net profit or loss for the period.*

Fair Value Accounting in Certain Financial Services Industries

In some countries, either based on national law or accepted industry practice, **120** enterprises in certain financial services industries measure substantially all financial assets at fair value. ... Under this Standard, such an enterprise will be able to continue to measure its financial assets at fair value if its financial assets are classified under this Standard as either available for sale or held for trading.

Hedging

If there is a hedging relationship between a hedging instrument and a related item **121** *being hedged as described in paragraphs 122-152, accounting for the gain or loss should follow paragraphs 153-164.*

Hedging Instruments

This Standard does not restrict the circumstances in which a derivative may be **122** designated as a hedging instrument, for hedge accounting purposes, if the conditions in paragraph 142 are met, except for certain written options (see paragraph 124). However, a non-derivative financial asset or liability may be designated as a hedging instrument, for hedge accounting purposes, only for a hedge of a foreign currency risk. The reason for this limitation is the different bases for measuring derivatives and non-derivatives. Under this Standard derivatives are always regarded as held for trading or hedging and, therefore, are (unless they are linked to and must be settled by delivery of an unquoted equity instrument whose fair value is not reliably measurable) remeasured to fair value, with changes in fair value included in net profit or loss, or in equity if the instrument is a cash flow hedge. Non-derivatives, on the other hand, are sometimes measured at fair value with changes in fair value included in net profit or loss, sometimes measured at fair value with changes in fair value reported in equity, and sometimes measured at amortised cost. To allow non-derivatives to be designated as hedging instruments in more than limited circumstances creates measurement inconsistencies.

123 [Not printed]

124 Hedging involves a proportionate income offset between changes in fair value of, or cash flows attributable to, the hedging instrument and the hedged item. The potential loss on an option that an enterprise writes could be significantly greater than the potential gain in value of a related hedged item. That is, a written option is not effective in reducing the exposure on net profit or loss. Therefore, a written option is not a hedging instrument unless it is designated as an offset to a purchased option, including one that is embedded in another financial instrument, for example, a written option used to hedge callable debt. In contrast, a purchased option has potential gains equal to or greater than losses and, therefore, has the potential to reduce profit or loss exposure from changes in fair values or cash flows. Accordingly, it can qualify as a hedging instrument.

125 [Not printed]

126 A financial asset or financial liability whose fair value cannot be reliably measured cannot be a hedging instrument except in the case of a nonderivative instrument (a) that is denominated in a foreign currency, (b) that is designated as a hedge of foreign currency risk, and (c) whose foreign currency component is reliably measurable.

Hedged Items

127 A hedged item can be a recognised asset or liability, an unrecognised firm commitment, or an uncommitted but highly probable anticipated future transaction ('forecasted transaction'). The hedged item can be (a) a single asset, liability, firm commitment, or forecasted transaction or (b) a group of assets, liabilities, firm commitments, or forecasted transactions with similar risk characteristics. Unlike originated loans and receivables, a held-to-maturity investment cannot be a hedged item with respect to interest-rate risk because designation of an investment as held-to-maturity involves not accounting for associated changes in interest rates. However, a held-to-maturity investment can be a hedged item with respect to risks from changes in foreign currency exchange rates and credit risk.

128 If the hedged item is a financial asset or liability, it may be a hedged item with respect to the risks associated with only a portion of its cash flows or fair value, if effectiveness can be measured.

129 *If the hedged item is a non-financial asset or liability, it should be designated as a hedged item either (a) for foreign currency risks or (b) in its entirety for all risks, because of the difficulty of isolating and measuring the appropriate portion of the cash flows or fair value changes attributable to specific risks other than foreign currency risks.*

130 [Not printed]

131 A single hedging instrument may be designated as a hedge of more than one type of risk provided that: (a) the risks hedged can be clearly identified, (b) the effectiveness of the hedge can be demonstrated, and (c) it is possible to ensure that there is a specific designation of the hedging instrument and the different risk positions.

If similar assets or similar liabilities are aggregated and hedged as a group, the individual **132** assets or individual liabilities in the group will share the risk exposure for which they are designated as being hedged. Further, the change in fair value attributable to the hedged risk for each individual item in the group will be expected to be approximately proportional to the overall change in fair value attributable to the hedged risk of the group.

Because hedge effectiveness must be assessed by comparing the change in value or cash **133** flow of a hedging instrument (or group of similar hedging instruments) and a hedged item (or group of similar hedged items), comparing a hedging instrument to an overall net position rather than to a specific hedged item (...), does not qualify for hedge accounting. However, approximately the same effect on net profit or loss of hedge accounting for this kind of hedging relationship can be achieved by designating part of the underlying items as the hedged position. ...

For hedge accounting purposes, only derivatives that involve a party external to the **134** enterprise can be designated as hedging instruments. Although individual companies within a consolidated group or divisions within a company may enter into hedging transactions with other companies within the group or divisions within the company, any gains and losses on such transactions are eliminated on consolidation. Therefore, such intra-group or intra-company hedging transactions do not qualify for hedge accounting treatment in consolidation.

A firm commitment to acquire a business in a business combination cannot be a hedged **135** item except with respect to foreign exchange risk because the other risks being hedged cannot be specifically identified and measured. It is a hedge of a general business risk.

Hedge Accounting

Hedge accounting recognises symmetrically the offsetting effects on net profit or loss of **136** changes in the fair values of the hedging instrument and the related item being hedged.

Hedging relationships are of three types: **137**
(a) *fair value hedge: a hedge of the exposure to changes in the fair value of a recognised asset or liability, or an identified portion of such an asset or liability, that is attributable to a particular risk and that will affect reported net income;*
(b) *cash flow hedge: a hedge of the exposure to variability in cash flows that (i) is attributable to a particular risk associated with a recognised asset or liability (such as all or some future interest payments on variable rate debt) or a forecasted transaction (such as an anticipated purchase or sale) and that (ii) will affect reported net profit or loss. A hedge of an unrecognised firm commitment to buy or sell an asset at a fixed price in the enterprise's reporting currency is accounted for as a cash flow hedge even though it has a fair value exposure; and*
(c) *hedge of a net investment in a foreign entity as defined in IAS 21.*

An example of a fair value hedge is a hedge of exposure to changes in the fair value of **138** fixed rate debt as a result of changes in interest rates. Such a hedge could be entered into either by the issuer or by the holder.

Examples of cash flow hedges are: **139**
(a) a hedge of the future foreign currency risk in an unrecognised contractual commitment by an airline to purchase an aircraft for a fixed amount of a foreign currency;

(b) a hedge of the change in fuel price relating to an unrecognised contractual commitment by an electric utility to purchase fuel at a fixed price, with payment in its domestic currency; and

(c) use of a swap to, in effect, change floating rate debt to fixed rate debt (this is a hedge of a future transaction; the future cash flows being hedged are the future interest payments).

140 A hedge of a firm commitment in an enterprise's own reporting currency is not a hedge of a cash flow exposure but rather of an exposure to a change in fair value. Nonetheless, such a hedge is accounted for as a cash flow hedge under this Standard, rather than as a fair value hedge, to avoid recognising as an asset or a liability a commitment that otherwise would not be recognised as an asset or liability under current accounting practice.

141 As defined in IAS 21, a foreign entity is a foreign operation, the activities of which are not an integral part of the reporting enterprise. Under IAS 21, all foreign exchange differences that result from translating the financial statements of the foreign entity into the parent's reporting currency are classified as equity until disposal of the net investment.

142 *Under this Standard, a hedging relationship qualifies for special hedge accounting as set out in paragraphs 153-164 if, and only if, all of the following conditions are met:*

(a) at the inception of the hedge there is formal documentation of the hedging relationship and the enterprise's risk management objective and strategy for undertaking the hedge. That documentation should include identification of the hedging instrument, the related hedged item or transaction, the nature of the risk being hedged, and how the enterprise will assess the hedging instrument's effectiveness in offsetting the exposure to changes in the hedged item's fair value or the hedged transaction's cash flows that is attributable to the hedged risk;

(b) the hedge is expected to be highly effective (see paragraph 146) in achieving offsetting changes in fair value or cash flows attributable to the hedged risk, consistent with the originally documented risk management strategy for that particular hedging relationship;

(c) for cash flow hedges, a forecasted transaction that is the subject of the hedge must be highly probable and must present an exposure to variations in cash flows that could ultimately affect reported net profit or loss;

(d) the effectiveness of the hedge can be reliably measured, that is, the fair value or cash flows of the hedged item and the fair value of the hedging instrument can be reliably measured (see paragraph 95 for guidance on fair value); and

(e) the hedge was assessed on an ongoing basis and determined actually to have been highly effective throughout the financial reporting period.

143 [Not printed]

144 There is normally a single fair value measure for a hedging instrument in its entirety, and the factors that cause changes in fair value are co-dependent. Thus a hedging relationship is designated by an enterprise for a hedging instrument in its entirety. The only exceptions permitted are (a) splitting the intrinsic value and the time value of an option and designating only the change in the intrinsic value of an option as the hedging instrument, while the remaining component of the option (its time value) is excluded and (b) splitting the interest element and the spot price on a forward. Those exceptions recognise that the intrinsic value of the option and the premium on the forward generally can be measured separately. ...

A proportion of the entire hedging instrument, such as 50 per cent of the notional **145** amount, may be designated in a hedging relationship. However, a hedging relationship may not be designated for only a portion of the time period in which a hedging instrument is outstanding.

Assessing Hedge Effectiveness

A hedge is normally regarded as highly effective if, at inception and throughout the life **146** of the hedge, the enterprise can expect changes in the fair value or cash flows of the hedged item to be almost fully offset by the changes in the fair value or cash flows of the hedging instrument, and actual results are within a range of 80 per cent to 125 per cent. ...

The method an enterprise adopts for assessing hedge effectiveness will depend on its **147** risk management strategy. ...

[Not printed] **148**

To qualify for special hedge accounting, the hedge must relate to a specific identified **149** and designated risk, and not merely to overall enterprise business risks, and must ultimately affect the enterprise's net profit or loss. A hedge of the risk of obsolescence of a physical asset or the risk of expropriation of property by a government would not be eligible for hedge accounting; effectiveness cannot be measured since those risks are not measurable reliably.

An equity method investment cannot be a hedged item in a fair value hedge because **150** the equity method recognises the investor's share of the associate's accrued net profit or loss, rather than fair value changes, in net profit or loss. If it were a hedged item, it would be adjusted for both fair value changes and profit and loss accruals – which would result in double counting because the fair value changes include the profit and loss accruals. For a similar reason, an investment in a consolidated subsidiary cannot be a hedged item in a fair value hedge because consolidation recognises the parent's share of the subsidiary's accrued net profit or loss, rather than fair value changes, in net profit or loss. A hedge of a net investment in a foreign subsidiary is different. There is no double counting because it is a hedge of the foreign currency exposure, not a fair value hedge of the change in the value of the investment.

This Standard does not specify a single method for assessing hedge effectiveness. An **151** enterprise's documentation of its hedging strategy will include its procedures for assessing effectiveness. Those procedures will state whether the assessment will include all of the gain or loss on a hedging instrument or whether the instrument's time value will be excluded. Effectiveness is assessed, at a minimum, at the time an enterprise prepares its annual or interim financial report. If the critical terms of the hedging instrument and the entire hedged asset or liability (as opposed to selected cash flows) or hedged forecasted transaction are the same, an enterprise could conclude that changes in fair value or cash flows attributable to the risk being hedged are expected to completely offset at inception and on an ongoing basis. For example, an entity may assume that a hedge of a forecasted purchase of a commodity with a forward contract will be highly effective and that there will be no ineffectiveness to be recognised in net profit or loss if:

(a) the forward contract is for purchase of the same quantity of the same commodity at the same time and location as the hedged forecasted purchase;

(b) the fair value of the forward contract at inception is zero; and

(c) either the change in the discount or premium on the forward contract is excluded from the assessment of effectiveness and included directly in net profit or loss or the change in expected cash flows on the forecasted transaction is based on the forward price for the commodity.

152 In assessing the effectiveness of a hedge, an enterprise will generally need to consider the time value of money. ...

Fair Value Hedges

153 *If a fair value hedge meets the conditions in paragraph 142 during the financial reporting period, it should be accounted for as follows:*
   (a) *the gain or loss from remeasuring the hedging instrument at fair value should be recognised immediately in net profit or loss; and*
   (b) *the gain or loss on the hedged item attributable to the hedged risk should adjust the carrying amount of the hedged item and be recognised immediately in net profit or loss. This applies even if a hedged item is otherwise measured at fair value with changes in fair value recognised directly in equity under paragraph 103(b). It also applies if the hedged item is otherwise measured at cost.*

154–155 [Not printed]

156 *An enterprise should discontinue prospectively the hedge accounting specified in paragraph 153 if any one of the following occurs:*
   (a) *the hedging instrument expires or is sold, terminated, or exercised (for this purpose, the replacement or a rollover of a hedging instrument into another hedging instrument is not considered an expiration or termination if such replacement or rollover is part of the enterprise's documented hedging strategy); or*
   (b) *the hedge no longer meets the criteria for qualification for hedge accounting in paragraph 142.*

157 *An adjustment to the carrying amount of a hedged interest-bearing financial instrument should be amortised to net profit or loss. Amortisation should begin no later than when the hedged item ceases to be adjusted for changes in its fair value attributable to the risk being hedged. The adjustment should be fully amortised by maturity.*

Cash Flow Hedges

158 *If a cash flow hedge meets the conditions in paragraph 142 during the financial reporting period, it should be accounted for as follows:*
   (a) *the portion of the gain or loss on the hedging instrument that is determined to be an effective hedge (see paragraph 142) should be recognised directly in equity through the statement of changes in equity (see IAS 1, paragraphs 86-88); and*
   (b) *the ineffective portion should be reported:*
       (i) *immediately in net profit or loss if the hedging instrument is a derivative; or*
       (ii) *in accordance with paragraph 103 in the limited circumstances in which the hedging instrument is not a derivative.*

159 [Not printed]

160 *If the hedged firm commitment or forecasted transaction results in the recognition of an asset or a liability, then at the time the asset or liability is recognised the associated gains or losses that were recognised directly in equity in accordance with*

paragraph 158 should be removed from equity and should enter into the initial measurement of the acquisition cost or other carrying amount of the asset or liability.

The gain or loss on the hedging instrument that was included in the initial **161** measurement of the acquisition cost or other carrying amount of the asset or liability is subsequently included in net profit or loss when the asset or liability affects net profit or loss (such as in the periods that depreciation expense, interest income or expense, or cost of sales is recognised). ...

For all cash flow hedges other than those covered by paragraph 160, amounts that **162** *had been recognised directly in equity should be included in net profit or loss in the same period or periods during which the hedged firm commitment or forecasted transaction affects net profit or loss (for example, when a forecasted sale actually occurs).*

An enterprise should discontinue prospectively the hedge accounting specified in **163** *paragraphs 158-162 if any one of the following occurs:*
(a) the hedging instrument expires or is sold, terminated, or exercised (for this purpose, the replacement or a rollover of a hedging instrument into another hedging instrument is not considered an expiration or termination if such replacement or rollover is part of the enterprise's documented hedging strategy). In this case, the cumulative gain or loss on the hedging instrument that initially had been reported directly in equity when the hedge was effective (see paragraph 158(a)) should remain separately in equity until the forecasted transaction occurs. When the transaction occurs, paragraphs 160 and 162 apply;
(b) the hedge no longer meets the criteria for qualification for hedge accounting in paragraph 142. In this case, the cumulative gain or loss on the hedging instrument that initially had been reported directly in equity when the hedge was effective (see paragraph 158(a)) should remain separately in equity until the committed or forecasted transaction occurs. When the transaction occurs, paragraphs 160 and 162 apply; or
(c) the committed or forecasted transaction is no longer expected to occur, in which case any related net cumulative gain or loss that has been reported directly in equity should be reported in net profit or loss for the period.

Hedges of a Net Investment in a Foreign Entity

Hedges of a net investment in a foreign entity (see IAS 21) should be accounted for **164** *similarly to cash flow hedges:*
(a) the portion of the gain or loss on the hedging instrument that is determined to be an effective hedge (see paragraph 142) should be recognised directly in equity through the statement of changes in equity (see IAS 1, paragraphs 86-88); and
(b) the ineffective portion should be reported:
(i) immediately in net profit or loss if the hedging instrument is a derivative; or
(ii) in accordance with paragraph 19 of IAS 21, in the limited circumstances in which the hedging instrument is not a derivative.
The gain or loss on the hedging instrument relating to the effective portion of the hedge should be classified in the same manner as the foreign currency translation gain or loss.

If a Hedge Does Not Qualify for Special Hedge Accounting

165 If a hedge does not qualify for special hedge accounting because it fails to meet the criteria in paragraph 142, gains and losses arising from changes in the fair value of a hedged item that is measured at fair value subsequent to initial recognition are reported in one of the two ways set out in paragraph 103. Fair value adjustments of a hedging instrument that is a derivative would be reported in net profit or loss.

Disclosure

166 *Financial statements should include all of the disclosures required by IAS 32, except that the requirements in IAS 32 for supplementary disclosure of fair values (paragraphs 77 and 88) are not applicable to those financial assets and financial liabilities carried at fair value.*

167 *The following should be included in the disclosures of the enterprise's accounting policies as part of the disclosure required by IAS 32 paragraph 47(b):*
   (a) the methods and significant assumptions applied in estimating fair values of financial assets and financial liabilities that are carried at fair value, separately for significant classes of financial assets (paragraph 46 of IAS 32 provides guidance for determining classes of financial assets);
   (b) whether gains and losses arising from changes in the fair value of those available-for-sale financial assets that are measured at fair value subsequent to initial recognition are included in net profit or loss for the period or are recognised directly in equity until the financial asset is disposed of; and
   (c) for each category of financial assets defined in paragraph 10, whether 'regular way' purchases and sales of financial assets are accounted for at trade date or settlement date (see paragraph 30).

168 In applying paragraph 167(a), an enterprise will disclose prepayment rates, rates of estimated credit losses, and interest or discount rates.

169 *Financial statements should include all of the following additional disclosures relating to hedging:*
   (a) describe the enterprise's financial risk management objectives and policies, including its policy for hedging each major type of forecasted transaction (see paragraph 142(a));
   ...
   (b) disclose the following separately for designated fair value hedges, cash flow hedges, and hedges of a net investment in a foreign entity:
   (i) a description of the hedge;
   (ii) a description of the financial instruments designated as hedging instruments for the hedge and their fair values at the balance sheet date;
   (iii) the nature of the risks being hedged; and
   (iv) for hedges of forecasted transactions, the periods in which the forecasted transactions are expected to occur, when they are expected to enter into the determination of net profit or loss, and a description of any forecasted transaction for which hedge accounting had previously been used but that is no longer expected to occur; and

(c) if a gain or loss on derivative and non-derivative financial assets and liabilities designated as hedging instruments in cash flow hedges has been recognised directly in equity, through the statement of changes in equity, disclose:

  (i) the amount that was so recognised in equity during the current period;

  (ii) the amount that was removed from equity and reported in net profit or loss for the period; and

  (iii) the amount that was removed from equity and added to the initial measurement of the acquisition cost or other carrying amount of the asset or liability in a hedged forecasted transaction during the current period (see paragraph 160).

Financial statements should include all of the following additional disclosures relating to financial instruments: **170**

(a) if a gain or loss from remeasuring available-for-sale financial assets to fair value (other than assets relating to hedges) has been recognised directly in equity, through the statement of changes in equity, disclose:

  (i) the amount that was so recognised in equity during the current period; and

  (ii) the amount that was removed from equity and reported in net profit or loss for the period;

(b) if the presumption that fair value can be reliably measured for all financial assets that are available for sale or held for trading has been overcome (see paragraph 70) and the enterprise is, therefore, measuring any such financial assets at amortised cost, disclose that fact together with a description of the financial assets, their carrying amount, an explanation of why fair value cannot be reliably measured, and, if possible, the range of estimates within which fair value is highly likely to lie. Further, if financial assets whose fair value previously could not be measured reliably are sold, that fact, the carrying amount of such financial assets at the time of sale, and the amount of gain or loss recognised should be disclosed;

(c) disclose significant items of income, expense, and gains and losses resulting from financial assets and financial liabilities, whether included in net profit or loss or as a separate component of equity. For this purpose:

  (i) total interest income and total interest expense (both on a historical cost basis) should be disclosed separately;

  (ii) with respect to available-for-sale financial assets that are adjusted to fair value after initial acquisition, total gains and losses from derecognition of such financial assets included in net profit or loss for the period should be reported separately from total gains and losses from fair value adjustments of recognised assets and liabilities included in net profit or loss for the period (a similar split of 'realised' versus 'unrealised' gains and losses with respect to financial assets and liabilities held for trading is not required);

  (iii) the enterprise should disclose the amount of interest income that has been accrued on impaired loans pursuant to paragraph 116 and that has not yet been received in cash;

(d) if the enterprise has entered into a securitisation or repurchase agreement, disclose, separately for such transactions occurring in the current financial reporting period and for remaining retained interests from transactions occurring in prior financial reporting periods:

(i) the nature and extent of such transactions, including a description of any collateral and quantitative information about the key assumptions used in calculating the fair values of new and retained interests;

(ii) whether the financial assets have been derecognised;

(e) if the enterprise has reclassified a financial asset as one required to be reported at amortised cost rather than at fair value (see paragraph 92), disclose the reason for that reclassification;

(f) disclose the nature and amount of any impairment loss or reversal of an impairment loss recognised for a financial asset, separately for each significant class of financial asset (...);

(g) a borrower should disclose the carrying amount of financial assets pledged as collateral for liabilities and (consistent with IAS 32.47(a) and IAS 32.49(g)) any significant terms and conditions relating to pledged assets; and

(h) a lender should disclose:

(i) the fair value of collateral (both financial and non-financial assets) that it has accepted and that it is permitted to sell or repledge in the absence of default;

(ii) the fair value of collateral that it has sold or repledged; and

(iii) (consistent with IAS 32.47(a) and IAS 32.49(g)) any significant terms and conditions associated with its use of collateral.

Effective Date and Transition

171–172   [Not printed]

IAS 40: Investment Property

IAS 40: Investment Property			
Scope 40.1–3	Definitions 40.4–14	Transitional Provisions 40.70–73	Effective Date 40.74–75

Recognition 40.15–16

Measurement 40.17–50			
Initial Measurement 40.17–21	Subsequent Expenditure 40.22–23	Measurement Subsequent to Initial Recognition 40.24–50	
		Fair Value Model 40.27–49	Cost Model 40.50
		Determination Fair Value 40.27–49	Inability to Measure Fair Value Reliably 40.47–49	

Transfers 40.51–59

Disposals 40.60–64

Disclosure 40.65–69		
Fair Value Model and Cost Model 40.65–66	Additional Disclosures: Fair Value Model 40.67–68	Additional Disclosures: Cost Model 40.69

Appendix A - Decision Tree [Not printed] Appendix B - Basis for Conclusions [Not printed]

Scope

This Standard should be applied in the recognition, measurement and disclosure of **1** *investment property.*

Among other things, this Standard deals with the measurement in a lessee's financial **2** statements of investment property held under a finance lease and with the measurement in a lessor's financial statements of investment property leased out under an operating lease. This Standard does not deal with matters covered in IAS 17 including:

(a) classification of leases as finance leases or operating leases;

(b) recognition of lease income earned on investment property (see also IAS 18);

(c) measurement in a lessee's financial statements of property held under an operating lease;

(d) measurement in a lessor's financial statements of property leased out under a finance lease;

(e) accounting for sale and leaseback transactions; and

(f) disclosure about finance leases and operating leases.

3 [Not printed]

Definitions

4 ...

Investment property *is property (land or a building - or part of a building - or both) held (by the owner or by the lessee under a finance lease) to earn rentals or for capital appreciation or both, rather than for:*

(a) use in the production or supply of goods or services or for administrative purposes; or

(b) sale in the ordinary course of business.

Owner-occupied property *is property held (by the owner or by the lessee under a finance lease) for use in the production or supply of goods or services or for administrative purposes.*

Fair value *is the amount for which an asset could be exchanged between knowledgeable, willing parties in an arm's length transaction.*

Cost *is the amount of cash or cash equivalents paid or the fair value of other consideration given to acquire an asset at the time of its acquisition or construction. Carrying amount is the amount at which an asset is recognised in the balance sheet.*

5–7 [Not printed]

8 Certain properties include a portion that is held to earn rentals or for capital appreciation and another portion that is held for use in the production or supply of goods or services or for administrative purposes. If these portions could be sold separately (or leased out separately under a finance lease), an enterprise accounts for the portions separately. If the portions could not be sold separately, the property is investment property only if an insignificant portion is held for use in the production or supply of goods or services or for administrative purposes.

9–11 [Not printed]

12 Judgement is needed to determine whether a property qualifies as investment property. An enterprise develops criteria so that it can exercise that judgement consistently in accordance with the definition of investment property and with the related guidance in paragraphs 5 to 11. Paragraph 66(a) requires an enterprise to disclose these criteria when classification is difficult.

13 [Not printed]

14 In some cases, an enterprise owns property that is leased to, and occupied by, its parent or another subsidiary. The property does not qualify as investment property in consolidated financial statements that include both enterprises, because the property is owner-occupied from the perspective of the group as a whole. However, from the perspective of the individual enterprise that owns it, the property is investment property if it meets the definition in paragraph 4. Therefore, the lessor treats the property as investment property in its individual financial statements.

Recognition

Investment property should be recognised as an asset when, and only when: **15**
(a) it is probable that the future economic benefits that are associated with the investment property will flow to the enterprise; and
(b) the cost of the investment property can be measured reliably.

[Not printed] **16**

Initial Measurement

An investment property should be measured initially at its cost. Transaction costs **17**
should be included in the initial measurement.

The cost of a purchased investment property comprises its purchase price, and any **18**
directly attributable expenditure. Directly attributable expenditure includes, for example, professional fees for legal services, property transfer taxes and other transaction costs.

The cost of a self-constructed investment property is its cost at the date when the **19**
construction or development is complete. Until that date, an enterprise applies IAS 16. At that date, the property becomes investment property and this Standard applies (see paragraphs 51(e) and 59 below).

The cost of an investment property is not increased by start-up costs (unless they are **20**
necessary to bring the property to its working condition), initial operating losses incurred before the investment property achieves the planned level of occupancy or abnormal amounts of wasted material, labour or other resources incurred in constructing or developing the property.

If payment for an investment property is deferred, its cost is the cash price equivalent. **21**
The difference between this amount and the total payments is recognised as interest expense over the period of credit.

Subsequent Expenditure

Subsequent expenditure relating to an investment property that has already been **22**
recognised should be added to the carrying amount of the investment property when it is probable that future economic benefits, in excess of the originally assessed standard of performance of the existing investment property, will flow to the enterprise. All other subsequent expenditure should be recognised as an expense in the period in which it is incurred.

The appropriate accounting treatment for expenditure incurred subsequently to the **23**
acquisition of an investment property depends on the circumstances which were taken into account on the initial measurement and recognition of the related investment. For instance, when the carrying amount of an investment property already takes into account a loss in future economic benefits, subsequent expenditure to restore the future economic benefits expected from the asset is capitalised. This is also the case when the purchase price of an asset reflects the enterprise's obligation to incur expenditure that is necessary in the future to bring the asset to its working condition. An example of this might be the acquisition of a building requiring renovation. In such circumstances, the subsequent expenditure is added to the carrying amount.

Measurement Subsequent to Initial Recognition

24 *An enterprise should choose either the fair value model in paragraphs 27 to 49 or the cost model in paragraph 50 as its accounting policy and should apply that policy to all of its investment property.*

25-26 [Not printed]

Fair Value Model

27 *After initial recognition, an enterprise that chooses the fair value model should measure all of its investment property at its fair value, except in the exceptional cases described in paragraph 47.*

28 *A gain or loss arising from a change in the fair value of investment property should be included in net profit or loss for the period in which it arises.*

29 The fair value of investment property is usually its market value. Fair value is measured as the most probable price reasonably obtainable in the market at the balance sheet date in keeping with the fair value definition. It is the best price reasonably obtainable by the seller and the most advantageous price reasonably obtainable by the buyer. This estimate specifically excludes an estimated price inflated or deflated by special terms or circumstances such as atypical financing, sale and leaseback arrangements, special considerations or concessions granted by anyone associated with the sale.

30 An enterprise determines fair value without any deduction for transaction costs that the enterprise may incur on sale or other disposal.

31 *The fair value of investment property should reflect the actual market state and circumstances as of the balance sheet date, not as of either a past or future date.*

32-33 [Not printed]

34 The definition of fair value refers to "knowledgeable, willing parties". In this context, "knowledgeable" means that both the willing buyer and the willing seller are reasonably informed about the nature and characteristics of the investment property, its actual and potential uses, and the state of the market as of the balance sheet date.

35 A willing buyer is motivated, but not compelled to buy. This buyer is neither over-eager nor determined to buy at any price. This buyer is also one who purchases in accordance with the realities of the current market, and with the current market expectations, rather than an imaginary or hypothetical market that cannot be demonstrated or anticipated to exist. The assumed buyer would not pay a higher price than the market requires. The present owner of an investment property is included among those who constitute the market.

36 A willing seller is neither an over-eager nor a forced seller, prepared to sell at any price, nor one prepared to hold out for a price not considered reasonable in the current market. The willing seller is motivated to sell the investment property at market terms for the best price obtainable in the open market after proper marketing, whatever that price may be. The factual circumstances of the actual investment property owner are not a part of this consideration because the willing seller is a hypothetical owner.

37 The expression "after proper marketing" means that the investment property would be exposed to the market in the most appropriate manner to effect its disposal at the best price reasonably obtainable. The length of exposure time may vary with market conditions, but must be sufficient to allow the investment property to be brought to the attention of an adequate number of potential purchasers. The exposure period is assumed to occur prior to the balance sheet date.

The definition of fair value refers to an arm's length transaction. An arm's length **38** transaction is one between parties who do not have a particular or special relationship that makes prices of transactions uncharacteristic of the market. The transaction is presumed to be between unrelated parties, each acting independently.

The best evidence of fair value is normally given by current prices on an active market **39** for similar property in the same location and condition and subject to similar lease and other contracts. An enterprise takes care to identify any differences in the nature, location or condition of the property, or in the contractual terms of the leases and other contracts relating to the property.

In the absence of current prices on an active market of the kind described in **40** paragraph 39, an enterprise considers information from a variety of sources, including:
(a) current prices on an active market for properties of different nature, condition or location (or subject to different lease or other contracts), adjusted to reflect those differences;
(b) recent prices on less active markets, with adjustments to reflect any changes in economic conditions since the date of the transactions that occurred at those prices; and
(c) discounted cash flow projections based on reliable estimates of future cash flows, supported by the terms of any existing lease and other contracts and (where possible) by external evidence such as current market rents for similar properties in the same location and condition, and using discount rates that reflect current market assessments of the uncertainty in the amount and timing of the cash flows.

[Not printed] **41–42**

Fair value differs from value in use, as defined in IAS 36. Fair value reflects knowledge **43** and estimates of participants in the market, as well as factors that are relevant to market participants in general. In contrast, value in use reflects the enterprise's knowledge and estimates, as well as entity-specific factors that may be specific to the enterprise and that are not applicable to enterprises in general. For example, fair value does not reflect any:
(a) additional value derived from the creation of a portfolio of properties in different locations;
(b) synergies between investment property and other assets;
(c) legal rights or legal restrictions that are specific only to the current owner; and
(d) tax benefits or tax burdens that are specific to the current owner.

In determining the fair value of investment property, an enterprise avoids double **44** counting of assets or liabilities that are recognised in the balance sheet as separate assets or liabilities. ...

The fair value of investment property does not reflect future capital expenditure that **45** will improve or enhance the property and does not reflect the related future benefits from this future expenditure.

[Not printed] **46**

Inability to Measure Fair Value Reliably

47 *There is a rebuttable presumption that an enterprise will be able to determine the fair value of an investment property reliably on a continuing basis. However, in exceptional cases, there is clear evidence when an enterprise first acquires an investment property (or when an existing property first becomes investment property following the completion of construction or development, or after a change in use) that the enterprise will not be able to determine the fair value of the investment property reliably on a continuing basis. This arises when, and only when, comparable market transactions are infrequent and alternative estimates of fair value (for example, based on discounted cash flow projections) are not available. In such cases, an enterprise should measure that investment property using the benchmark treatment in IAS 16. The residual value of the investment property should be assumed to be zero. The enterprise should continue to apply IAS 16 until the disposal of the investment property.*

48 [Not printed]

49 *If an enterprise has previously measured an investment property at fair value, the enterprise should continue to measure the property at fair value until disposal (or until the property becomes owner-occupied property or the enterprise begins to develop the property for subsequent sale in the ordinary course of business) even if comparable market transactions become less frequent or market prices become less readily available.*

Cost Model

50 *After initial recognition, an enterprise that chooses the cost model should measure all of its investment property using the benchmark treatment in IAS 16 that is, at cost less any accumulated depreciation and any accumulated impairment losses.*

Transfers

51 *Transfers to, or from, investment property should be made when, and only when, there is a change in use, evidenced by:*
   (a) commencement of owner-occupation, for a transfer from investment property to owner-occupied property;
   (b) commencement of development with a view to sale, for a transfer from investment property to inventories;
   (c) end of owner-occupation, for a transfer from owner-occupied property to investment property;
   (d) commencement of an operating lease to another party, for a transfer from inventories to investment property; or
   (e) end of construction or development, for a transfer from property in the course of construction or development (covered by IAS 16) to investment property.

52 [Not printed]

53 Paragraphs 54 to 59 deal with recognition and measurement issues that apply when an enterprise uses the fair value model for investment property. When an enterprise uses the cost model, transfers between investment property, owner-occupied property and

inventories do not change the carrying amount of the property transferred and they do not change the cost of that property for measurement or disclosure purposes.

For a transfer from investment property carried at fair value to owner-occupied **54** *property or inventories, the property's cost for subsequent accounting under IAS 16 or IAS 2 should be its fair value at the date of change in use.*

If an owner-occupied property becomes an investment property that will be carried at **55** *fair value, an enterprise should apply IAS 16 up to the date of change in use. The enterprise should treat any difference at that date between the carrying amount of the property under IAS 16 and its fair value in the same way as a revaluation under IAS 16.*

Up to the date when an owner-occupied property becomes an investment property **56** carried at fair value, an enterprise continues to depreciate the property and to recognise any impairment losses that have occurred. The enterprise treats any difference at that date between the carrying amount of the property under IAS 16 and its fair value in the same way as a revaluation under IAS 16. In other words:

(a) any resulting decrease in the carrying amount of the property is recognised in net profit or loss for the period. However, to the extent that an amount is included in revaluation surplus for that property, the decrease is charged against that revaluation surplus; and

(b) any resulting increase in the carrying amount is treated as follows:

(i) to the extent that the increase reverses a previous impairment loss for that property, the increase is recognised in net profit or loss for the period. The amount recognised in net profit or loss for the period does not exceed the amount needed to restore the carrying amount to the carrying amount that would have been determined (net of depreciation) had no impairment loss been recognised; and

(ii) any remaining part of the increase is credited directly to equity under the heading of revaluation surplus. On subsequent disposal of the investment property, the revaluation surplus included in equity may be transferred to retained earnings. The transfer from revaluation surplus to retained earnings is not made through the income statement.

For a transfer from inventories to investment property that will be carried at fair **57** *value, any difference between the fair value of the property at that date and its previous carrying amount should be recognised in net profit or loss for the period.*

The treatment of transfers from inventories to investment property that will be carried **58** at fair value is consistent with the treatment of sales of inventories.

When an enterprise completes the construction or development of a self-constructed **59** *investment property that will be carried at fair value, any difference between the fair value of the property at that date and its previous carrying amount should be recognised in net profit or loss for the period.*

Disposals

An investment property should be derecognised (eliminated from the balance sheet) **60** *on disposal or when the investment property is permanently withdrawn from use and no future economic benefits are expected from its disposal.*

[Not printed] **61**

62 *Gains or losses arising from the retirement or disposal of investment property should be determined as the difference between the net disposal proceeds and the carrying amount of the asset and should be recognised as income or expense in the income statement (unless IAS 17 requires otherwise on a sale and leaseback).*

63 The consideration receivable on disposal of an investment property is recognised initially at fair value. In particular, if payment for an investment property is deferred, the consideration received is recognised initially at the cash price equivalent. The difference between the nominal amount of the consideration and the cash price equivalent is recognised as interest revenue under IAS 18 on a time proportion basis that takes into account the effective yield on the receivable.

64 An enterprise applies IAS 37 or other IASs, as appropriate, to any liabilities that the enterprise retains after disposal of an investment property.

Disclosure

Fair Value Model and Cost Model

65 [Not printed]

66 *An enterprise should disclose:*
   (a) when classification is difficult (see paragraph 12), the criteria developed by the enterprise to distinguish investment property from owner-occupied property and from property held for sale in the ordinary course of business;
   (b) the methods and significant assumptions applied in determining the fair value of investment property, including a statement whether the determination of fair value was supported by market evidence or was more heavily based on other factors (which the enterprise should disclose) because of the nature of the property and lack of comparable market data;
   (c) the extent to which the fair value of investment property (as measured or disclosed in the financial statements) is based on a valuation by an independent valuer who holds a recognised and relevant professional qualification and who has recent experience in the location and category of the investment property being valued. If there has been no such valuation, that fact should be disclosed;
   (d) the amounts included in the income statement for:
      (i) rental income from investment property;
      (ii) direct operating expenses (including repairs and maintenance) arising from investment property that generated rental income during the period; and
      (iii) direct operating expenses (including repairs and maintenance) arising from investment property that did not generate rental income during the period;
   (e) the existence and amounts of restrictions on the realisability of investment property or the remittance of income and proceeds of disposal; and
   (f) material contractual obligations to purchase, construct or develop investment property or for repairs, maintenance or enhancements.

Fair Value Model

67 *In addition to the disclosure required by paragraph 66, an enterprise that applies the fair value model in paragraphs 27-49 should also disclose a reconciliation of the carrying amount of investment property at the beginning and end of the period showing the following (comparative information is not required):*

(a) additions, disclosing separately those additions resulting from acquisitions and those resulting from capitalised subsequent expenditure;

(b) additions resulting from acquisitions through business combinations;

(c) disposals;

(d) net gains or losses from fair value adjustments;

(e) the net exchange differences arising on the translation of the financial statements of a foreign entity;

(f) transfers to and from inventories and owner-occupied property; and

(g) other movements.

In the exceptional cases when an enterprise measures investment property using the **68** benchmark treatment in IAS 16 (because of the lack of a reliable fair value, see paragraph 47 above), the reconciliation required by the previous paragraph should disclose amounts relating to that investment property separately from amounts relating to other investment property. In addition, an enterprise should disclose

(a) a description of the investment property;

(b) an explanation of why fair value cannot be reliably measured;

(c) if possible, the range of estimates within which fair value is highly likely to lie; and

(d) on disposal of investment property not carried at fair value:

(i) the fact that the enterprise has disposed of investment property not carried at fair value;

(ii) the carrying amount of that investment property at the time of sale; and

(iii) the amount of gain or loss recognised.

Cost Model

In addition to the disclosure required by paragraph 66, an enterprise that applies the **69** cost model in paragraph 50 should also disclose:

(a) the depreciation methods used;

(b) the useful lives or the depreciation rates used;

(c) the gross carrying amount and the accumulated depreciation (aggregated with accumulated impairment losses) at the beginning and end of the period;

(d) a reconciliation of the carrying amount of investment property at the beginning and end of the period showing the following (comparative information is not required):

(i) additions, disclosing separately those additions resulting from acquisitions and those resulting from capitalised subsequent expenditure;

(ii) additions resulting from acquisitions through business combinations;

(iii) disposals;

(iv) depreciation;

(v) the amount of impairment losses recognised, and the amount of impairment losses reversed, during the period under IAS 36;

(vi) the net exchange differences arising on the translation of the financial statements of a foreign entity;

(vii) transfers to and from inventories and owner-occupied property; and

(viii) other movements; and

(e) the fair value of investment property. In the exceptional cases described in paragraph 47, when an enterprise cannot determine the fair value of the investment property reliably, the enterprise should disclose:

(i) a description of the investment property;

(ii) an explanation of why fair value cannot be determined reliably; and
(iii) if possible, the range of estimates within which fair value is highly likely to lie.

Transitional Provisions

Fair Value Model

70–72 [Not printed]

Cost Model

73 [Not printed]

Effective Date

74–75 [Not printed]

Withdrawal of IAS 25, Accounting for Investments

[Not printed]

Appendix A

Decision Tree

[Not printed]

Appendix B

Basis for Conclusions

[Not printed]

IAS 41: Agriculture

IAS 41: Agriculture			
Scope 41.1–4	Definitions 41.5–9		Effective Date and Transition 41.58–59
	Agriculture-Related 41.5–7	General 41.8–9	

Recognition and Measurement 41.10–33			
Recognition 41.10–11	Measurement 41.12–33		
	Fair Value Less Estimated Point-of-Sale Costs 41.12–25	Gains and Losses 41.26–29	Inability to Measure Fair Value Reliably 41.30–33

Government Grants 41.34–38

Presentation and Disclosure 41.39–57			
Presentation 41.39	Disclosure 41.40–57		
	General 41.40–53	Additional Disclosures for Biological Assets Where Fair Value Cannot Be Measured Reliably 41.54–56	Government Grants 41.57

Appendix A - Illustrative Examples [Not printed] Appendix B - Basis for Conclusions [Not printed]

Scope

This Standard should be applied to account for the following when they relate to **1**
agricultural activity:
(a) biological assets;
(b) agricultural produce at the point of harvest; and
(c) government grants covered by paragraphs 34-35.

This Standard does not apply to: **2**
(a) land related to agricultural activity (see IAS 16 and IAS 40); and
(b) intangible assets related to agricultural activity (see IAS 38).

This Standard is applied to agricultural produce, which is the harvested product of the **3**
enterprise's biological assets, only at the point of harvest. Thereafter, IAS 2 or another
applicable IAS is applied. ...

4 The table below provides examples of biological assets, agricultural produce, and products that are the result of processing after harvest:

Biological assets	Agricultural produce	Products that are the result of processing after harvest
Sheep	Wool	Yarn, carpet
Trees in a plantation forest	Logs	Lumber
Plants	Cotton	Thread, clothing
	Harvested cane	Sugar
Dairy cattle	Milk	Cheese
Pigs	Carcass	Sausages, cured hams
Bushes	Leaf	Tea, cured tobacco
Vines	Grapes	Wine
Fruit trees	Picked fruit	Processed fruit

Definitions

Agriculture-Related Definitions

5 ...

Agricultural activity is the management by an enterprise of the biological transformation of biological assets for sale, into agricultural produce, or into additional biological assets.

Agricultural produce is the harvested product of the enterprise's biological assets.

A biological asset is a living animal or plant.

Biological transformation comprises the processes of growth, degeneration, production, and procreation that cause qualitative or quantitative changes in a biological asset.

A group of biological assets is an aggregation of similar living animals or plants.

Harvest is the detachment of produce from a biological asset or the cessation of a biological asset's life processes.

6–7 [Not printed]

General Definitions

8 ...

An active market is a market where all the following conditions exist:
(a) the items traded within the market are homogeneous;
(b) willing buyers and sellers can normally be found at any time; and
(c) prices are available to the public.

Carrying amount is the amount at which an asset is recognised in the balance sheet.

Fair value is the amount for which an asset could be exchanged, or a liability settled, between knowledgeable, willing parties in an arm's length transaction.

Government grants are as defined in IAS 20.

9 [Not printed]

Recognition and Measurement

An enterprise should recognise a biological asset or agricultural produce when, and **10**
only when:
(a) the enterprise controls the asset as a result of past events;
(b) it is probable that future economic benefits associated with the asset will flow to
the enterprise; and
(c) the fair value or cost of the asset can be measured reliably.

[Not printed] **11**

A biological asset should be measured on initial recognition and at each balance sheet **12**
date at its fair value less estimated point-of-sale costs, except for the case described
in paragraph 30 where the fair value cannot be measured reliably.

Agricultural produce harvested from an enterprise's biological assets should be **13**
measured at its fair value less estimated point-of-sale costs at the point of harvest.
Such measurement is the cost at that date when applying IAS 2 or another applicable
IAS.

Point-of-sale costs include commissions to brokers and dealers, levies by regulatory **14**
agencies and commodity exchanges, and transfer taxes and duties. Point-of-sale costs
exclude transport and other costs necessary to get assets to a market.

The determination of fair value for a biological asset or agricultural produce may be **15**
facilitated by grouping biological assets or agricultural produce according to significant
attributes; for example, by age or quality. An enterprise selects the attributes
corresponding to the attributes used in the market as a basis for pricing.

[Not printed] **16**

If an active market exists for a biological asset or agricultural produce, the quoted price **17**
in that market is the appropriate basis for determining the fair value of that asset. If
an enterprise has access to different active markets, the enterprise uses the most relevant
one. ...

If an active market does not exist, an enterprise uses one or more of the following, when **18**
available, in determining fair value:
(a) the most recent market transaction price, provided that there has not been a
significant change in economic circumstances between the date of that transaction
and the balance sheet date;
(b) market prices for similar assets with adjustment to reflect differences; and
(c) sector benchmarks ...

[Not printed] **19**

In some circumstances, market-determined prices or values may not be available for a **20**
biological asset in its present condition. In these circumstances, an enterprise uses the
present value of expected net cash flows from the asset discounted at a current market-
determined pre-tax rate in determining fair value.

The objective of a calculation of the present value of expected net cash flows is to **21**
determine the fair value of a biological asset in its present location and condition. An
enterprise considers this in determining an appropriate discount rate to be used and in
estimating expected net cash flows. The present condition of a biological asset excludes
any increases in value from additional biological transformation and future activities of

the enterprise, such as those related to enhancing the future biological transformation, harvesting, and selling.

22 An enterprise does not include any cash flows for financing the assets, taxation, or re-establishing biological assets after harvest (...).

23 In agreeing an arm's length transaction price, knowledgeable, willing buyers and sellers consider the possibility of variations in cash flows. It follows that fair value reflects the possibility of such variations. Accordingly, an enterprise incorporates expectations about possible variations in cash flows into either the expected cash flows, or the discount rate, or some combination of the two. In determining a discount rate, an enterprise uses assumptions consistent with those used in estimating the expected cash flows, to avoid the effect of some assumptions being double-counted or ignored.

24 Cost may sometimes approximate fair value, particularly when:
(a) little biological transformation has taken place since initial cost incurrence (...); or
(b) the impact of the biological transformation on price is not expected to be material (...).

25 Biological assets are often physically attached to land (...). There may be no separate market for biological assets that are attached to the land but an active market may exist for the combined assets, that is, for the biological assets, raw land, and land improvements, as a package. An enterprise may use information regarding the combined assets to determine fair value for the biological assets. ...

Gains and Losses

26 *A gain or loss arising on initial recognition of a biological asset at fair value less estimated point-of-sale costs and from a change in fair value less estimated point-of-sale costs of a biological asset should be included in net profit or loss for the period in which it arises.*

27 A loss may arise on initial recognition of a biological asset, because estimated point-of-sale costs are deducted in determining fair value less estimated point-of-sale costs of a biological asset. A gain may arise on initial recognition of a biological asset, such as when a calf is born.

28 *A gain or loss arising on initial recognition of agricultural produce at fair value less estimated point-of-sale costs should be included in net profit or loss for the period in which it arises.*

29 [Not printed]

Inability to Measure Fair Value Reliably

30 *There is a presumption that fair value can be measured reliably for a biological asset. However, that presumption can be rebutted only on initial recognition for a biological asset for which market-determined prices or values are not available and for which alternative estimates of fair value are determined to be clearly unreliable. In such a case, that biological asset should be measured at its cost less any accumulated depreciation and any accumulated impairment losses. Once the fair value of such a biological asset becomes reliably measurable, an enterprise should measure it at its fair value less estimated point-of-sale costs.*

31 [Not printed]

In all cases, an enterprise measures agricultural produce at the point of harvest at its fair **32** value less estimated point-of-sale costs. ...

In determining cost, accumulated depreciation and accumulated impairment losses, an **33** enterprise considers IAS 2, IAS 16 and IAS 36.

Government Grants

An unconditional government grant related to a biological asset measured at its fair **34** *value less estimated point-of-sale costs should be recognised as income when, and only when, the government grant becomes receivable.*

If a government grant related to a biological asset measured at its fair value less **35** *estimated point-of-sale costs is conditional, including where a government grant requires an enterprise not to engage in specified agricultural activity, an enterprise should recognise the government grant as income when, and only when, the conditions attaching to the government grant are met.*

[Not printed] **36**

If a government grant relates to a biological asset measured at its cost less any **37** accumulated depreciation and any accumulated impairment losses (see paragraph 30), IAS 20 is applied.

[Not printed] **38**

Presentation and Disclosure

Presentation

An enterprise should present the carrying amount of its biological assets separately **39** *on the face of its balance sheet.*

Disclosure

General

An enterprise should disclose the aggregate gain or loss arising during the current **40** *period on initial recognition of biological assets and agricultural produce and from the change in fair value less estimated point-of-sale costs of biological assets.*

An enterprise should provide a description of each group of biological assets. **41**

[Not printed] **42–45**

If not disclosed elsewhere in information published with the financial statements, an **46** *enterprise should describe:*
(a) the nature of its activities involving each group of biological assets; and
(b) non-financial measures or estimates of the physical quantities of:
    (i) each group of the enterprise's biological assets at the end of the period; and
    (ii) output of agricultural produce during the period.

An enterprise should disclose the methods and significant assumptions applied in **47** *determining the fair value of each group of agricultural produce at the point of harvest and each group of biological assets.*

48 *An enterprise should disclose the fair value less estimated point-of-sale costs of agricultural produce harvested during the period, determined at the point of harvest.*

49 *An enterprise should disclose:*
(a) *the existence and carrying amounts of biological assets whose title is restricted, and the carrying amounts of biological assets pledged as security for liabilities;*
(b) *the amount of commitments for the development or acquisition of biological assets; and*
(c) *financial risk management strategies related to agricultural activity.*

50 *An enterprise should present a reconciliation of changes in the carrying amount of biological assets between the beginning and the end of the current period. Comparative information is not required. The reconciliation should include:*
(a) *the gain or loss arising from changes in fair value less estimated point-of-sale costs;*
(b) *increases due to purchases;*
(c) *decreases due to sales;*
(d) *decreases due to harvest;*
(e) *increases resulting from business combinations;*
(f) *net exchange differences arising on the translation of financial statements of a foreign entity; and*
(g) *other changes.*

51–52 [Not printed]

53 Agricultural activity is often exposed to climatic, disease, and other natural risks. If an event occurs that because of its size, nature, or incidence is relevant to understanding the enterprise's performance for the period, the nature and amount of related items of income and expense are disclosed under IAS 8. ...

Additional Disclosures for Biological Assets Where Fair Value Cannot Be Measured Reliably

54 *If an enterprise measures biological assets at their cost less any accumulated depreciation and any accumulated impairment losses (see paragraph 30) at the end of the period, the enterprise should disclose for such biological assets:*
(a) *a description of the biological assets;*
(b) *an explanation of why fair value cannot be measured reliably;*
(c) *if possible, the range of estimates within which fair value is highly likely to lie;*
(d) *the depreciation method used;*
(e) *the useful lives or the depreciation rates used; and*
(f) *the gross carrying amount and the accumulated depreciation (aggregated with accumulated impairment losses) at the beginning and end of the period.*

55 *If, during the current period, an enterprise measures biological assets at their cost less any accumulated depreciation and any accumulated impairment losses (see paragraph 30), an enterprise should disclose any gain or loss recognised on disposal of such biological assets and the reconciliation required by paragraph 50 should disclose amounts related to such biological assets separately. In addition, the reconciliation should include the following amounts included in net profit or loss related to those biological assets:*
(a) *impairment losses;*

(b) reversals of impairment losses; and
(c) depreciation.

If the fair value of biological assets previously measured at their cost less any **56**
accumulated depreciation and any accumulated impairment losses becomes reliably
measurable during the current period, an enterprise should disclose for those
biological assets:
a description of the biological assets;
an explanation of why fair value has become reliably measurable; and
(c) the effect of the change.

Government Grants

An enterprise should disclose the following related to agricultural activity covered by **57**
this Standard:
(a) the nature and extent of government grants recognised in the financial
statements;
(b) unfulfilled conditions and other contingencies attaching to government grants;
and
(c) significant decreases expected in the level of government grants.

Effective Date and Transition

[Not printed]   **58–59**

Appendix A

Illustrative Examples

[Not printed]

Appendix B

Basis for Conclusions

[Not printed]

Interpretations of International Financial Reporting Standards
[Not printed]

Index

References are to standards and paragraphs. Thus, '8.26' refers to IAS 8 paragraph 26. 'FW' refers to the *Framework for the Preparation and Presentation of Financial Statements*.

Printed and bound in Great Britain by William Clowes Limited, Beccles and London